AMERICAN EDUCATION

Its Men,

Ideas,

and

Institutions

Advisory Editor

Lawrence A. Cremin
Frederick A. P. Barnard Professor of Education
Teachers College, Columbia University

AMERICAN EDUCATION: *Its Men, Ideas, and Institutions* presents selected works of thought and scholarship that have long been out of print or otherwise unavailable. Inevitably, such works will include particular ideas and doctrines that have been outmoded or superseded by more recent research. Nevertheless, all retain their place in the literature, having influenced educational thought and practice in their own time and having provided the basis for subsequent scholarship.

EDUCATIONAL LEGISLATION AND ADMINISTRATION

OF THE

COLONIAL GOVERNMENTS

ELSIE W. CLEWS [PARSONS]

NYT

ARNO PRESS & THE NEW YORK TIMES
*New York * 1971*

Reprint Edition 1971 by Arno Press Inc.

Reprinted from a copy in
  The University of Illinois Library

American Education:
  Its Men, Ideas, and Institutions - Series II
ISBN for complete set: 0-405-03600-0
See last pages of this volume for titles.

Manufactured in the United States of America

Library of Congress Cataloging in Publication Data

Parsons, Elsie Worthington (Clews) 1875-1941.
    Educational legislation and administration of
the colonial governments.
    (Columbia University contributions to philos-
ophy, psychology, and education, v. 6, no. 1-4)
(American education: its men, ideas, and
institutions. Series II)
    Originally presented as the author's thesis,
Columbia, 1899.
    Reprint of the 1899 ed.
    Bibliography: p.
    1. Educational law and legislation--U. S.
--History. I. Title. II. Series: Columbia
University. Columbia University contributions
to philosophy and psychology, v. 6, no. 1-4.
III. Series: American education: its men, ideas,
and institutions. Series II.
KF4119.P36 1971   344'.73'07   79-165741
ISBN 0-405-03612-4

1-4

EDUCATIONAL LEGISLATION AND ADMINISTRATION

OF THE

COLONIAL GOVERNMENTS

COLUMBIA UNIVERSITY CONTRIBUTIONS

TO

PHILOSOPHY, PSYCHOLOGY AND EDUCATION

VOL. 6   NOS. 1-4

EDUCATIONAL LEGISLATION AND ADMINISTRATION

OF THE

COLONIAL GOVERNMENTS

BY

ELSIE W. CLEWS Ph. D.,

MAY, 1899

THE MACMILLAN CO., 66 FIFTH AVENUE, NEW YORK
MAYER AND MÜLLER, MARKGRAFENSTRASSE, BERLIN

PREFACE

In spite of the emphasis that in recent years has fallen upon the significance of educational history, the history of American education is as yet unwritten. On closer thought, however, this delay is not at all surprising. The very realization of the weight of educational theory and practice as factors in social evolution must occasion hesitation in the undertaking of any educational history. Moreover, since a people's educational system is so intricately woven into its whole social system and is so entirely the expression and outcome of the whole social life, it would seem as if the historian of our national education were driven to make great requisitions upon the work of our national historians. Is it impertinent, at this point, to suggest that from the sociological point of view at any rate, and that is the necessary point of view of educational thought, the story of American civilization, as well as that of its educational phase, remains untold?[1]

In a country of representative government one of the most fruitful and available means of historical study for the sociologist lies in the tracing out of the development of important social principles through a continuous process of legislation. Single acts of legislation indicate little; but the history of successful and *unsuccessful* legislation on any given subject cannot fail to point out the course of a society's thought and activity in relation to such subject. In this view I have endeavored, in the following account of the educational legislation of the

---

[1] In effect, the new conception of social growth which the science of sociology is giving us will before long necessitate the rewriting of universal history.

central governments of the American colonies, to put into available shape the records of that legislative interest in education which was at times the formulation of, and at times the stimulus to, the colonists' educational efforts.

But this endeavor has taken the form of a compilation, not a history. A history of the educational legislation of the colonial governments would demand a far greater knowledge of the general legislative history of the colonies than I possess. It would demand a profound insight into the highly complex relations of legislation to popular thought and habit. And such an insight would in turn depend upon a closer and fuller analysis of the characteristics of the American colonists than the historian has hitherto made. Moreover, as all colonial institutions are in major part imitative,[1] and as the character of the colonist is the result of inheritance as well as of adopted environment, the social histories of England, Scotland, Holland, Sweden, France, Germany must lie open to the student of American colonial education. But, in fact, the social history of those parent countries, or that part at least of their social history which may properly be called their educational history,[2] is still unburied treasure; and yet, until we appreciate, for example, the social aims and standards which were em-

---

[1] Social imitation may be both conscious and unconscious. The college and school of the theocratic New England commonwealth were the outcome of conscious, critical imitation; the college and school of the aristocratic crown colony of Virginia, of unconscious, uncritical imitation. In the educational activities of the colonies many varieties of both types are to be found. To the student of social imitation American colonization is the richest of all fields of observation.

[2] Obviously, by educational history I do not mean merely the account of the development of a scholastic system. Educational history may be in making without the founding of a single school. The most primitive of societies soon learn that the training of their young is one of the readiest means to the satisfaction of their wants. Therefore the educational history of a society begins as soon as the process of social selection, the adoption of social means of satisfying social and individual wants, begins to encroach upon the process of natural selection, the unconscious and instinctive satisfaction of individual wants. In this sense, the history of education is the history of social selection.

bodied in the grammar schools and endowed foundations of old England, shall we be able to understand the development of the town school of New England or of the charity school of the Southern colony? How can we comprehend the relations of the College of William and Mary, of Harvard and Yale Colleges to the people of Virginia, of Massachusetts and Connecticut, until we have given careful and detailed study to the growth of the college foundations of the Universities of Oxford and Cambridge? Can we understand the meaning of the early attempts at industrial education in the colonies without a knowledge of the economic conditions of the parent countries, or without close inquiry into the bearing of the poor laws and apprenticeship laws of those countries upon their industrial systems? Finally, can we obtain any realization whatsoever of the educational aim and purpose of the American colonists without a deep insight into the profound influences of the Reformation in England and Holland? Queries such as these, and such as are suggested by the relation of the governing agencies of the parent countries, of the sovereign, the legislature and the local administrative board or officer, towards education, demand solution as the indispensable introduction to a study of educational legislation in America.

In emphasizing colonial tradition, I do not wish to belittle the great part played by environment in colonial education. The reader of the following records can not fail to question how it happened that the colonists of New Hampshire and Rhode Island, although of the same Puritan stock as the zealous settlers in the Bay, were so backward in educational legislation, or why it was that the charity idea continued to attach to the schools of the South long after it had disappeared from the educational thought of the Northern colonies, or how it came about that in spite of the liberal and enlightened educational views of the early rulers of Pennsylvania, the greater part of the eighteenth century saw the arrest of all attempt to establish public education in that colony. For the answering of such questions and of a hundred others of more or less scope and detail, a wide knowledge of colonial environment will alone suffice.

From such considerations it becomes readily apparent what a profound knowledge of colonial circumstance and tradition will be needed by the future historians of early American education. Their labor can not fail to be enormous. And yet their reward will prove commensurate. It will be stamped with a twofold significance. Through the history of the education of our forefathers, we may obtain a deeper insight into the complex American character and civilization of our own day, an insight essential to all those who would be influential in the development of our national character and civilization; and through the forceful realization of the chief end and aim of *all* colonial education as that of *public usefulness and service,* a realization which is borne in upon us at every turn of our early educational history, we may be enabled to add new meaning and vigor to our thought and effort in behalf of the ethical needs of the American people.

———

In glancing over the table of contents of this volume, the reader will at once observe that it contains no reference to the educational legislation of the colony of Georgia. Georgia was not settled until 1733, and with the exception of a rejection by the Crown of a petition for the establishment of a collegiate institution,[1] I have been unable to find in the brief records of this colony any reference whatsoever to a relation between its government and the education of its people.

In the following compilation reference has been made

---

[1] This petition was submitted in 1765 in behalf of a charter for the Bethesda Orphan House. (Education in Georgia, p. 14, Charles Edgeworth Jones. Bureau of Education, Circular IV., 1888.)

whenever possible to the primary sources, but as the printed records of the colonies are very incomplete, and as I have been unable to consult the manuscript records, I have been forced to rely in a few instances upon the most accurate of the secondary sources of authority.

I am greatly indebted to Dr. Nicholas Murray Butler and to Dr. Herbert L. Osgood for their kind encouragement and helpful suggestions.

TABLE OF CONTENTS

(xi)

MASSACHUSETTS

HARVARD COLLEGE

THE permanent colonization of Massachusetts began in 1620 with the settlement of a company of English Puritans at Plymouth.[1] Eight years later settlements were made at Salem and Charleston under a grant made by the Council of New England to divers English merchants of London and Devon. In 1629 this company was incorporated by the King as the Governor and Company of Massachusetts Bay in New England. In 1630 the corporation removed to the home of the colonists. To the share-holders were allotted larger land-holdings, but all the freemen had a voice in the government of the colony, at first directly and then through representation. Two deputies from each town were elected by the freemen. At a yearly court of election the governor, deputy governor, and 18 magistrates were elected by the General Court, i. e., deputies, magistrates, governor and deputy governor. In 1644 deputies and magistrates were divided into two distinct bodies.[2] The General Court was authorized by the charter of the company to enact laws and ordinances for the general welfare of the colony.

At a session held at Boston, October 28, 1636, the Court

---

[1] Plymouth colony was united to the province of Massachusetts in 1691. Although there were 12 towns and a population of 5000 under the Plymouth jurisdiction in 1665, it was not until 1673 that the central government made any provision for education. In that year, the court voted for the setting up of a public school in the town of Plymouth to be supported by the revenue from the Cape Fishery. (*History of New England*, III, 35, 36, 99. John G. Palfrey, Boston, 1892, and *Plymouth Colony Records*, XI, 233, 237.)

[2] Palfrey's History, I, 287–88, 290, 291, 312, 354.

(7)

"agreed to give £400 toward a school or college, whereo £200 to be paid the next year, and £200 when the work is finished, and the next Court to appoint where and what building."[1]

At a General Court met on November 15, 1637, "the college is ordered to be at Newtown."[2]   The following year the Court changes the name of Newtown to Cambridge.[3]

On November 20, 1637, Governor Winthrop, Deputy-Governor Dudley, Treasurer Bellingham, Mr. Humphrey, Mr. Herlakenden, Mr. Stoughton, Mr. Colton, Mr. Wilson, Mr. Davenport, Mr. Wells, Mr. Shepherd, Mr. Peters, "or the greater part of them whereof Mr. Winthrop, Mr. Dudley or Mr. Bellingham to be always one," are appointed a committee "to take order for a college at Newtown."[4]

In 1638, "the Rev. Mr. John Harvard, sometime minister of God's word at Charlestown, by his last will and testament, gave towards the erecting the abovesaid school or college the one moiety or half part of his estate, the said moiety amounting to the sum of £729 19s. 2d."[5]

As a result of this gift it is ordered in General Court March 13, 1639, "that the college agreed upon formerly to be built at Cambridge shall be called Harvard College."[6]

[1] *Records of the Governor and Company of the Massachusetts Bay in New England*, I, 183.   Edited by Nathaniel B. Shurtleff, M. D., Boston, 1853.

According to the colony treasurer's accounts in 1644, only £41 15d. of this sum had been paid into the college treasury.   (Given by President Quincy in App. I, vol. I, p. 455 of his History of Harvard University from College Book no. I, p. 9.)   See *Rec.*, II, 28.   On November 13, 1644, the Court ordered the colony treasurer to pay over to President Dunster £150 " out of the money due for the children sent out of England, to be expended for a house to be built for the said president, in part of the £400 promised unto him for his use to belong to the college." (*Ibid.*, II, 84.)

[2] *Ibid.*, I, 208.   [3] *Ibid.*, I, 228.   [4] *Ibid.*, I, 217.

[5] Quoted by President Quincy in App. I. of his History of Harvard University, I, 451, from College Book, no. III, p. 1.   John Harvard also bequeathed his entire library of 260 volumes to the College.

[6] *Rec.*, I, 253.

At this time Mr. Nathaniel Eaton was in charge of the college, and on June 6, 1639, the Court granted 500 acres to him and his heirs on condition that he would continue his employment for life.[1] Only three months later, however, on September 9th, " Mr. Nathaniel Eaton being accused for cruel and barbarous beating of Mr. Naza. Briscoe [usher to Mr. Eaton] and for other neglecting and misusing of his scholars, it was ordered that Mr. Eaton should be discharged from keeping of school with us without license; and Mr. Eaton is fined to the country £66 13s. 4d, which fine is respited till the next Court, unless he remove the mean while. The Court agreed Mr. Eaton should give Mr. Naza. Briscoe £30 for satisfaction for the wrong done him and to be paid presently." [2]

The Court proceeded to appoint a committee to " call Mr. Nathaniel Eaton to account the beginning of the next week," and a committee for this purpose was continued by the Court on November 5th of this year,[3] and on October 7th of the year following.[4]

Mr. Samuel Shephard was appointed by the General Court[5] to fill Mr. Eaton's place until the autumn of 1640, when the Rev. Henry Dunster accepted the call to be president of Harvard College.[6]

On October 7, 1640, " the ferry between Boston and Charlestown is granted to the College." [7] Two years later, on Septem-

---

[1] *Ibid.*, I, 262. In 1637 Mr. Eaton was freed from assessment, it having been left to his discretion " what he will freely give." (*Ibid.*, I, 210.)

[2] *Ibid.*, I, 275.   [3] *Ibid.*, I, 277.   [4] *Ibid.*, I, 302.

[5] Quincy, I, 14.

[6] A History of Harvard University, App., 79. Benjamin Pierce, A. M , Cambridge, 1833.

[7] *Rec.*, I, 304. Mr. Samuel Shephard stated in his accounts for the year 1639 [?] that he had received £50 from the Ferry. (Quincy's History, I, App. I, 453.) The management of the Ferry seems to have been very troublesome to the college people. In answer to President Dunster's petition in 1647, the Court appointed a committee " to examine the ferrymen of Charlestown, therefore they make such complaints to the President as tends [sic] to the loss and damage of the Col-

ber 27, 1642, the General Court, considering the fact that of the six magistrates and six elders who had been appointed in 1637 to order the college at Cambridge, some had removed out of the jurisdiction, ordered " that the Governor and Deputy for the time being, and all the magistrates of this jurisdiction, together with the teaching elders of the six next adjoining towns, that is, Cambridge, Watertown, Charlestown, Boston, Roxbury and Dorchester, and the president of the College for the time being, shall have from time to time full power and authority to make and establish all such orders, statutes and constitutions as they shall see necessary for the instituting, guiding and furthering of the said college and the several members thereof from time to time in piety, morality and learning; as also that they shall have full power to dispose, order and manage, to the use and behoof of the said college and members thereof, all gifts, legacies, bequeathals, revenues, lands and donations, as either have been, are, or shall be conferred, bestowed, or any ways shall fall to the said college; and whereas it may come to pass that many of the said magistrates and elders may be absent, or otherwise empiled in weighty affairs, when the said college need their present help, council and authority, therefore it is ordered, that the greater number of the said magistrates, elders and president shall have the power of the whole; provided, also, that if any constitution, order, or orders shall be made, that is found hurtful to the said college, or the members thereof, or to the weal public, that then, upon the appeal of the party or parties aggrieved to the said overseers, that they shall appeal the said order or orders at their next meeting, or stand accountable thereof to the next General Court." [1]

lege." (*Rec.*, II, 200.) In May, 1650, the court told President Dunster that they were unable to alter the agreements with the ferrymen, as he had desired (*Ibid.*, IV, Pt. I, 12); but in the following October they empowered Mr. Dunster to dispose of the ferry " by lease or otherwise," at the expiration of the existing lease. (*Ibid.*, IV, Pt. I, 30.)

[1] *Ibid.*, II, 30.

Through Mr. Shephard, pastor of the church in Cambridge, President Dunster appealed to the Commissioners of the United Colonies to use their influence in behalf of the College.[1] The following order made by the General Court on November 13, 1644, was one of the results of this appeal:

" Upon advice from the Commissioners of the United Colonies for general care to be taken for the encouragement of learning and maintenance of poor scholars in the college at Cambridge,

" It is ordered, that the deputies shall commend it to the several towns (and the elders are to be desired to give their furtherance hereto) with declaration of the course which was propounded by the said Commissioners, and hath been put in practice already by some of the other colonies, viz.: of every family allowing one peck of corn, twelve pence in money, or other commodity, to be sent in to the Treasurer, for the college at Cambridge, or where else he shall appoint, in Boston, or Charlestown."[2]

During his administration President Dunster repeatedly petitioned the government of Massachusetts, as well as the Commissioners of the United Colonies, for aid for the College.

In 1647, the General Court stated, in answer to a petition that had been presented by Mr. Dunster, that the colony was in debt to the College to the extent of £379 16s, £133 having been entrusted to the colony treasurer for the College by " several donors in England," £190 16s. being arrears of the colony's annual subscription to the College, and £56 " in relation to the President having fallen short so much of that which he should have received annually from the country." In view of these facts, the Court ordered that according to Mr. Dunster's request, £50 should be paid to Mr. Davison, and that the remaining sum should be paid to the College directly,

[1] *State Papers of the United States of America*, II, 17, 84. Ebenezer Hazard, A. M., Philadelphia, 1794.

[2] *Rec.*, II, 86.

or if it remained in the colony treasury, it should pay interest to the College at the rate of 8 per cent.[1] At the same time the Court opines that "we conceive it very necessary that such as studies physics or chirurgery, may have liberty to read anatomy, and to anatomize once in four years some malefactor, in case there be such as the Court shall allow of."[2]

Three years later, on May 30, 1650, the Court granted President Dunster's petition (1) in directing Mr. Danforth, the surveyor of Cambridge, to serve on a committee to lay out a piece of land which Mr. Stoughton had bequeathed to Harvard College; (2) in exempting the College from certain customs; (3) in ordering the annual appropriation of £100 to be paid over to the College;[3] (4) in incorporating the institution in the following terms:

"Whereas, through the good hand of God, many well-devoted persons have been, and daily are, moved and stirred up to give and bestow sundry gifts, legacies, lands and revenues for the advancement of all good literature, arts and sciences in Harvard College, in Cambridge, in the county of Middlesex, and to the maintenance of the president and fellows, and for all accommodations and all other necessary provisions that may conduce to the education of the English and Indian youth of the country in knowledge and godliness, it is there-

[1] In 1713, the legislature ordered £426 10s. 4d. to be paid out of the public treasury to Treasurer Brattle of Harvard College:—" £160 16s. 4d. thereof being the whole principal remaining due of money borrowed by the late colony of the Massachusetts Bay of the said college, both that which was the Lady Moulson's gift and all others—£263 14s. being interest in full for the said sum at six pound per cent. per annum from the year 1685 to this time. To which year the interest seems to have been paid by the treasury book of the said college." (*Court Records* (MSS.), IX, 231.)

[2] *Rec.*, II, 200–1.

[3] This order does not seem to have been enforced, for in the following October President Dunster again petitions for the payment of the appropriation and the Court again directs the stated £100 to be paid over by the treasurer to the College "with two years forbearance." (*Ibid.*, IV, Pt. I, 30.)

fore ordered and enacted by this Court and the authority thereof, that for the furthering of so good a work, and for the purposes aforesaid, from henceforth that the said college in Cambridge, in Middlesex, in New England, shall be a corporation consisting of seven persons, viz., a president, five fellows, and a treasurer or bursar; and that Henry Dunster shall be the first president, Samuel Mather, Samuel Danford, Masters of Art, Jonathan Michell, Comfort Starr and Samuel Eaton, Bachelors of Art, shall be the five fellows, and Thomas Danford to be present treasurer, all of them being inhabitants in the Bay, and shall be the first seven persons of which the said corporation shall consist; and that the said seven persons, or the greater number of them, procuring the presence of the overseers of the college, and by their counsel and consent, shall have power, and are hereby authorized, at any time or times, to elect a new president, fellows, or treasurer, so oft and from time to time as any of the said persons shall die or be removed, which said president and fellows for the time being shall for ever hereafter, in name and fact, be one body politic and corporate, in law, to all intents and purposes and shall have perpetual succession, and shall be called by the name of President and Fellows of Harvard College, and shall from time to time be eligible as aforesaid, and by that name they and their successors shall and may purchase and acquire to themselves, or take and receive, upon free gift and donation, any lands, tenements, or hereditaments, within the jurisdiction of Massachusetts, not exceeding five hundred pounds per annum, and any goods and sums of money what so ever, to the use and behoof of the said president, fellows and scholars of the said college, and also may sue and plead, or be sued and impleaded, by the name aforesaid, in all courts and places of judicature within the jurisdiction aforesaid; and that the said president, with any three of the fellows, shall have power and are hereby authorized, when they shall think fit, to make and appoint a common seal for the use of the said corporation;

and the president and fellows, or major part of them, from time to time, may meet and choose such officers and servants for the College and make such allowance to them, and them also to remove, and after death or removal, to choose such others, and to make from time to time such orders and by-laws for the better ordering and carrying on the work of the College, as they shall think fit, provided the said orders be allowed by the overseers; and, also, that the president and fellows, or major part of them, with the treasurer, shall have power to make conclusive bargains for lands and tenements, to be purchased by the said corporation for valuable consideration. And for the better ordering of the government of the said college and corporation, be it enacted by the authority aforesaid, that the president and three more of the fellows shall and may, from time to time, upon due warning or notice, given by the president to the rest, hold a meeting for the debating and concluding of affairs concerning the profits and revenues of any lands, and disposing of their goods; provided, that all the said disposings be according to the will of the donors,[1] and for direction in all emergent occasions, execution of all orders and by laws, and for the procuring of a general meeting of all the overseers and society in great and difficult cases, and in case of non-agreement, in all which cases aforesaid the conclusion shall be made by the major part; the said president having a casting voice, the overseers consenting thereunto; and that all the aforesaid transactions shall tend to and for the use and behoof of the president, fellows, scholars and officers of the said college, and for all accommodations of buildings, books, and all other necessary provisions and furnitures as may be for the advancement and education of youth in all manner of good

---

[1] In 1671 a special order was passed by the Court providing that "all gifts and legacies given and bequeathed to the College, schools of learning, or any other public use" should be disposed of according to the declared intent of the donors. And all trustees of such gifts were required to account concerning these trusts to their respective county courts. (*Ibid.*, IV, Pt. II, 488.)

literature, arts and sciences. And further, be it ordered by this Court and the authority thereof, that all the lands, tenements, hereditaments, houses or revenues within this jurisdiction, to the aforesaid president or college appertaining, not exceeding the value of £500 per annum, shall from henceforth be freed from all civil impositions, taxes and rates; all goods to the said corporation, or to any scholars thereof appertaining, shall be exempt from all manner of toll, customs, excise whatsoever; and that the president, fellows, and scholars, together with the servants and other necessary officers to the said president or college appertaining, not exceeding ten, viz.: three to the president, and seven to the college belonging, shall be exempted from all personal, civil offices, military exercise, or services, watchings, and wardings;[1] and such of their estates, not exceeding one hundred pounds a man, shall be freed from all country taxes and rates whatsoever, and no other."[2]

On May 27, 1652, the president and fellows of Harvard College petition " for the removal of sundry difficulties and obstructions in payments assigned unto them by the country, and that such course may be taken as the ruinous and straightened buildings of the College may be enlarged and repaired." Whereupon the Court, " considering the care the Commissioners of the United Colonies took at their last meeting for the advancement of learning, etc., sending into England, that if it might be, some help might be procured for the corporation out of such money as it collected there,[3] judge it meet to

---

[1] See *Ibid.*, IV, Pt. II, 61. In November, 1675, at the outbreak of King Philip's War, the Court ordered that the officers and servants of the College (the corporation excepted), should be liable to war taxes and military services. (*Ibid.*, V, 65.)

[2] *Ibid.*, IV, Pt. I, 12–14.

[3] President Dunster suggested, in a petition to the United Colonies' Commissioners in 1651, that the funds of the missionary Society for the Propagation of Knowledge might be drawn upon for Harvard College ; but the commissioners answered that although they themselves conceived that the advancement of learning in the College

respite the answer to this petition until we hear from England; in the meantime, the overseers, president and fellows of the College are desired to write to the elders of the several churches, that they may, with all convenient speed, commend it to the consideration of the towns where they dwell for a voluntary contribution, that so there may be a speedy reparation of that which present necessity calls for tò be done."[1]

The answer from England was apparently unfavorable,[2] for on October 19, 1652, the Court makes a more positive recommendation for a general contribution throughout the colony.

" *A declaration concerning the advancement of learning in New England by the General Court.*

If it should be granted that learning, namely, skill in the tongues and liberal arts, is not absolutely necessary for the being of a commonwealth and churches, yet we conceive that the judgment of the godly wise it is beyond all question, not only laudable, but necessary for the being of the same. And although New England (blessed be God), is competently furnished (for this present age) with men in place, and, upon occasion of death or otherwise, to make supply of magistrates, associates in courts, physicians and officers in the commonwealth and of teaching elders in the churches, yet for the better discharge of our trust for the next generation, and so to posterity, being the first founders do wear away apace, and that it grows more and more difficult to fill

---

would also promote " the work of Christ among the Indians," yet before contributing out of the Society's fund it would be necessary to send to England for permission. They also stated that in case this was not granted, they would further recommend to the colonies the wonted contribution " by pecks, half bushels and bushels of wheat," suggesting that " herein, if the Massachusetts please to give a leading example, the rest may probably the more readily follow." (Hazard's *State Papers,* II, 197.)

[1] *Rec.,* IV, Pt. I, 91.

[2] The next year the Society for the Propagation of Knowledge made a special donation to Harvard College for Indian education. See p. 70.

places of most eminence as they are empty or wanting, and this Court, finding by manifest experience, that though the number of scholars at our college doth increase, yet as soon as they are grown up, ready for public use, they leave the country and seek for and accept of employment elsewhere,[1] so that if timely provision be not made, it will tend much to the disparagement, if not to the ruin of this commonwealth, it is, therefore, ordered and hereby enacted by this Court that a voluntary collection be commended to the inhabitants of this jurisdiction for the raising of such a sum as may be employed for the maintenance of the president and certain fellows and poor scholars of Harvard College, and for that purpose do further order that every town of this jurisdiction do choose one meet person to take the voluntary subscriptions of all such as shall underwrite any sum or sums of money for that purpose, and to make return thereof to the next Court. And, forasmuch as all the colonies are concerned therein, this Court doth order the secretary to signify to the governors of the several colonies our endeavors herein, and to commend the same to them for their help and furtherance in so good a work."[2]

Later in this same month, " in answer to the petition of the president and fellows of Harvard College, the Court doth grant them eight hundred acres of land, and liberty to employ such as they please, to find out such a place or places as may be most commodious and convenient for them, and to return to this Court what they have done therein to the end it may be laid out and confirmed unto them."[3]

The following year, May 18, 1653, in a similar provision

In 1646, the United Colonies' Commissioners recommended the General Court of Massachusetts to take some course with the parents of the scholars at the College "that these, when furnished with learning, remove not into other countries, but improve their parts and abilities in the service of the colonies." (Hazard's *State Papers*, II, 17.)

[2] *Rec.*, IV, Pt. I, 100–1.   [3] *Ibid.*, IV, Pt. I, 114.

the Court granted 2,000 acres "for the encouragement of Harvard College . . . and for the more comfortable maintenance and provision for the president, fellows, and students thereof in time to come."[1]

Both these grants failed. And so in 1658, the Court made another grant of 2,100 acres of land in the Pequod country to the College. To this land, however, the colony of Connecticut laid a successful claim.[2]

On September 10, 1653, the Court "being informed that the present condition of the college at Cambridge calls for supply, do order, that the Cambridge rate for this year, now to be collected, be paid into the steward of the college, for the discharge of any debt due from the country to the said college; and if there be any overplus, to be and remain as the college stock; and for further clearing and setting all matters in the college in reference to the yearly maintenance of the president, fellows and necessary officers thereof, and repairing the houses, that so yearly complaints may be prevented, and a certain way for the due encouragement of all persons concerned in that work, do hereby appoint Mr. Increase Nowell, Captain Daniel Gookin, Captain John Leveret, Captain Edward Johnson and Mr. Edward Jackson, or any three of them, to be a committee to examine the state of the College in all respects, as hereafter is expressed, Mr. Nowell to give notice of the time and place of meeting.

1. First, to take account of all the incomes of the college profits arising due to the officers thereof, either by gifts, revenues, studies, rents, tuitions, commencements, or any other profits arising due from time to time, as near as may be, since the president undertook the work.

2. To examine what hath been paid and disbursed, either for buildings, repairings, or otherwise, paid and received annually for the maintenance of the president, fellows and other officers thereof.

[1] *Rec.*, IV, Pt. I, 136.   [2] Quincy, I, 40.

3. To consider what hath been yearly received by the president out of any of the incomes and profits for his own use and maintenance (as near as conveniently may be), ever since he came to the place of president; also what allowances yearly have been made to the fellows and other officers.

4. To weigh and consider what may be fit for an honorable and comfortable allowance annually for the president heretofore and for the future, and how it may be paid hereafter.

5. To consider what number of fellows may be necessary for carrying on the work in the said college, and what yearly allowance they shall have and how to be paid.

6. To direct some way how the necessary officers, as stewards, butler and cook, may be provided for, that so the scholars' commons may not be so short as they now are occasioned thereby.

7. To take cognizance of all and every matter or thing concerning the said college, in reference to the welfare thereof in outward things, and to present a way how to regulate and rectify any thing that is out of order.

8. To examine what sums have been, and of late are promised by several towns and persons for the use of the College, and to give order for the collection thereof and propose a way how such monies may be improved for the best benefit of that society for the future; and this committee are hereby authorized with full power to act in all the premises, and to make return of what they do to the next Court of Election to be confirmed, if they shall judge meet." [1]

On May 3, 1654, the committee appointed in the foregoing order make their report to the Court. Accordingly the Court "do judge that the ten pounds brought in upon account by the president of the College for his care and pains for these twelve years last past, in looking after the affairs of the College, in respect of building, repairing or otherwise, be respited till this Court take further order therein; and that the contributions

---

[1] *Rec.*, IV, Pt. I, 178-80.

and subscriptions lately given in, or which shall hereafter be given in by several towns or persons, together with all other stock appertaining to the College, shall be committed to the care and trust of the overseers of the said college, who have hereby power to give order to the treasurer of the College to collect the several subscriptions and contributions which are or shall be hereafter due from time to time; and in case of non-payment thereof, that it be secured by the several towns and persons, so long as it shall remain unpaid, and the produce of it to be paid to the said treasurer, and to be for the maintenance of the president and fellows and other necessary charges of the College, and the several yearly allowance of the said president and fellows to be proportioned as the said overseers shall determine concerning the same." [1]

In 1653 worthy President Dunster fell into "the briers of anti-paedobaptism," and was indicted by the grand jury for disturbing the ordinances of infant baptism in the church at Cambridge. Subsequently he was sentenced to a public admonition on lecture day, laid under bond for good behavior, and in the spring of 1654 he was compelled to resign from the presidency of the College. [2]

On June 12, the Court directed the board of overseers "to make provision, in case he [President Dunster] persist in his resolution more than one month,[3] . . . for some meet person

---

[1] *Rec.*, IV, Pt. I, 186-7.

[2] Quincy's *History of Harvard University*, I, 18.

[3] After further conference with the overseers, Mr. Dunster "in submissive willingness reassumed his place," and kept it until October 24th, when he again resigned. He then petitioned the Court to consider of some allowance to be made to him "for his extraordinary labors in, about and concerning the weal of the college over and beside his daily employment in the education of youth." Mr. Dunster furthermore petitioned that he might continue to enjoy the house which he had erected "with singular industry through great difficulties," until the corporation had paid him all that was due to him. (Pierce's History, Notes, 151-2.) The governor and magistrates refused to grant these requests. (Quincy's History, I, App. III, 465-6.) Mr. Dunster then presented certain "considerations" to

to carry an end that work for the present, and also to act in whatever necessity shall call for," until the next session of the Court.[1]

Mr. Dunster based his resignation, in the formal letter which he addressed to the General Court on June 10, upon the invalidity of his original appointment to office;[2] but a measure that was passed by the Court on the third of the preceding month points to the real reason of his resignation.

"For as much as it greatly concerns the welfare of this country that the youth thereof be educated, not only in good literature, but sound doctrine, this Court doth therefore commend it to the serious consideration and special care of the overseers of the College and the selectmen in the towns, not to admit or suffer any such to be continued in the office or place of teaching, educating or instructing of youth or child in the college or schools that have manifested themselves unsound in the faith or scandalous in their lives, and not giving due satisfaction according to the rules of Christ."[3]

In October, 1654, the Court, in view of the fact that some of the overseers of the College had died and others had gone abroad, appoint to the board Mr. John Allin, pastor of Dedham, Mr. John Norton, teacher at Boston, Mr. Samuel Whiting and Mr. Thomas Cobbett, pastor and teacher at Lynn.[4]

the Court, setting forth the hardships that would fall upon him and his family upon his removal at that time of the year, and so the Court consented to its postponement to the following March. (*Ibid.*, I, 18–20.) At that time the corporation report to the Court that they are still £40 in debt to Mr. Dunster and are unable to pay him. They suggest that the Court pay this debt and £100 in addition in consideration of Mr. Dunster's "extraordinary pains in raising up and carrying on the College for so many years past." (*Ibid.*, I, App. II, 462.) To this plea a committee of the Deputies retorted : "What extraordinary labor in, about and concerning the weal of the College . . . we know of none, except what was the president's duty." And so the petition of the corporation was rejected. (*Ibid.*, I, 21.)

[1] *Rec.*, IV, Pt. I, 197.

[2] Pierce's History, Appendix XV., 79–80.

[3] *Rec.*, IV, Pt. I, 182–3. [4] *Ibid.*, IV, Pt. I, 204.

At this time the government makes its first annual appropriation to the College.

" Whereas we cannot but acknowledge the great goodness of God towards his people in this wilderness in raising up schools of learning and especially the College, from whence there hath sprung many useful instruments both in church and commonwealth, both to this and other places, and whereas at present the work of the College hath been several ways obstructed, and seems yet at present, for want of comfortable maintenance for the encouragement of a president, this Court taking the same into their serious consideration, and finding that though many propositions have been made for a voluntary contribution, yet nothing have been hitherto obtained from several persons and towns, although some have done very liberally and freely, and fearing lest we should show ourselves ungrateful to God, or unfaithful to posterity, if so good a seminary of knowledge and virtue should fall to the ground through any neglect of ours, it is therefore ordered by this Court and the authority thereof, that, besides the profit of the ferry formerly granted to the College, which shall be continued, that there shall be yearly levied, by addition to the country rate, one hundred pounds, to be paid by the treasurer of the country to the college treasurer, for the behoof and maintenance of the president and fellows, to be distributed between the president and fellows according to the determination of the overseers of the College, and this to continue during the pleasure of the country; and it is hereby ordered, that no man stand engaged to pay his voluntary contribution that he hath underwrit by virtue of this proposition, and that such persons as have already done voluntarily for the same in the country rate such a proportion as this addition of one hundred pounds do add to the rate, to be allowed by the constable to each person, and by the Treasurer to the constable." [1]

The Court was urged on to making this appropriation by a

---

[1] *Rec.*, IV, Pt. I, 205.

desire to secure Mr. Charles Chauncy, pastor at Scituate, as president of the College.

On November 1st, the Court took into consideration a motion that had been made "in behalf of Mr. Chauncy for the providing of a house and other accommodations for his settlement at Cambridge," and decided to refer the matter to the overseers "to whom it most properly belongs."[1]

Mr. Chauncy accepted the call, and in May, 1655, the Legislature granted him 500 acres of land at Billerica, "so as he continue in that place three years."[2] At the same time, in answer to a petition on his part, Mr. Chauncy was advanced £30 out of the rents of the ferry "to furnish his necessary occasions."[3]

During the next two years the Court proceeded to enlarge the powers of the president and fellows in relation both to the students and to the overseers of the College.

On October 14, 1656, it is ordered "that the president and fellows of Harvard College, for the time being, or the major part of them, are hereby empowered, according to their best discretion, to punish all misdemeanors of the youth in their society, either by fine or whipping in the hall openly, as the nature of the offense shall require, not exceeding ten shillings or ten stripes for one offense; and this law to continue in force until this Court, or the overseers of the College, provide some other order to punish such offenses."[4]

On October 23, 1657, "in answer to certain proposals presented to this Court by the overseers of Harvard College, as an appendix to the college charter, it is ordered, the corporation shall have power from time to time to make such orders and by-laws for the better ordering and carrying on of the work of the College as they shall see cause, without dependence upon the consent of the overseers foregoing; provided always that the corporation shall be responsible unto, and those orders and by-laws shall be alterable by the overseers according to their

---

[1] *Rec.*, IV, Pt. I, 216. [2] *Ibid.*, IV, Pt. I, 237.
[3] *Ibid.* [4] *Ibid.*, IV, Pt. I, 278-9.

discretion. And when the corporation shall hold a meeting, and agreeing with college servants, for making of orders and by-laws, for debating and concluding of affairs concerning the profits and revenues of any land or gifts, and the disposing, thereof, (provided that all the said disposals be according to the will of the donors), for managing of all emergent occasions, for the procuring of a general meeting of the overseers and society in great and difficult cases, and in cases of non-agreement, and for all other college affairs to them pertaining, in all these cases the conclusion shall be valid, being made by the major part of the corporation, the president having a casting vote; provided always, that in these things also they be responsible to the overseers as aforesaid. And in case the corporation shall see cause to call a meeting of the overseers, or the overseers shall think good to meet of themselves, it shall be sufficient unto the validity of college acts that notice be given to the overseers in the six towns mentioned in the printed law, anno 1642, when the rest of the overseers, by reason of the remoteness of their habitations, cannot conveniently be acquainted therewith." [1]

On May 27, 1663, President Chauncy petitioned the General Court for a more liberal allowance, on the ground that "his family being great,[2] the stipend allowed him by the honored Court has been insufficient for his comfortable subsistence, and the maintenance of his family with necessary supplies of food and raiment, for want whereof he hath been forced both to expend his own estate that he brought with him, and is

---

[1] *Rec.*, IV, Pt. I, 315.

[2] Consisting of ten persons, according to Mr. Chauncy's statement in a former unsuccessful application which he made to the legislature on October 25, 1655. At this time he also stated that his salary, plus £100 of his personal estate, had been expended on the fittings of his office ; that the country pay of Indian corn did not pass for food or clothing ; that "if any part thereof by entreaties be put off, 12d. or 8d. in the bushel must be lost; that the returns which he was supposed to receive from commencement, were hardly sufficient to defray its charges." Quincy's History, I, App. IV, 468.

besides by this means run far into debt."[1] Mr. Chauncy then set forth in support of his plea, the fact "that there are no colleges in our English universities (wherein the petitioner hath continued long) but that the presidents thereof, besides their yearly stipend, are allowed their diet, with other necessary provisions, according to their wants."[2]

A committee of the Magistrates reported on this petition, June 9, 1663:

"We conceive the country have done honorably towards the recompense and encouragement of the petitions both for annual allowance and grant of land, and that his parity with English colleges is not pertinent, and as for other things respecting his removal, that it properly belongs to the feoffees of the College, and that it be referred unto them."[3]

The Deputies refused to concur with this report, but "in regard to the urgent necessities of the petitioner, do judge meet that there be allowed: £5 a quarter out of the country treasury to supply his wants, and this to be continued during the country's pleasure, with reference to the consent of the honorable Magistrates thereto."[4] The honorable Magistrates, however, refused their consent.[5]

In the following October, Mr. Thomas Danforth, the college treasurer, recalls the affairs of the College to the attention of the Court, which proceeds to appoint "a committee to repair to the College and enquire concerning the state thereof in all respects, and to take the treasurer's accounts, and give him direction for the disposing of the college estate for the future, and what they shall do herein they are to make return to the next General Court, together with such proposals as they may conceive a meet expedient for the redress of any inconveniency that at present doth obstruct the prosperity of the said college."[6]

---

[1] *Ibid.*, I, App. IV, 469.   [2] *Ibid.*   [3] *Ibid.*, I, App. IV, 470.
[4] *Ibid.*   [5] *Ibid.*   [6] *Ibid.*, IV, Pt. II, 92.

On September 11, 1666, "the Court, having been informed that the president of the College is in some necessity, by reason of the afflicting hand of God upon him in his son,[1] and other things concurring thereto, judge meet to order the treasurer of the country forthwith to pay unto the said president the sum of twenty pounds, as a gratuity from the Court for a supply of his present wants."[2]

President Chauncy died in 1672, and Dr. Hoar was called to the presidency by the corporation and board of overseers. Dr. Hoare was highly acceptable to the legislature, having been recommended to Governor Leverett by the colonial agent in England and by many friends of the colony.[3] In October, the Court increased its allowance to the college president to £150, "provided Dr. Hoar be the man for a supply of that place." This salary was moreover to be paid quarterly and in money.[4]

Following upon the above provision, a new charter for Harvard College is entered in the General Court records. This charter was probably procured through the influence of Dr. Hoar; but its authority was never accepted by the corporation of the College. It enlarged the powers and privileges of the president and corporation in several particulars. The corporation, henceforward to be known as "the President, Fellows and Treasurer of Harvard College," are expressly empowered to appoint and remove all inferior officers of the College. In suits at

---

[1] This son was "so far distempered as to render him wholly unable to do any thing towards his own maintenance," so states Elnathan Chauncy, another son of the President, in his address to the legislature, after his father's death in 1672. He petitioned for payment in money of the arrears in his father's salary and for support for his afflicted brother. Both requests were granted by the legislature, the Deputies having moved that ten pounds should be paid annually to the deacons of Cambridge for the support of the petitioner's brother. (Quincy's History, I, 27–28.) See also *Rec.*, IV, Pt. II, 540.

[2] *Ibid.*, IV, Pt. II, 314.

[3] Quincy's History, I, 31.

[4] *Rec.*, IV, Pt. II, 535. Quincy's History, I, 32–33.

law, the personal property of members of the corporation is not to be liable to attachment. The personal property, to the value of £100, of all members of the corporation and their officers, is to be exempted from taxation. Any three members of the corporation, the president being one, are empowered to " sconse," fine and " otherwise correct " all inferior officers and members of the college in all crimes which were punishable by one magistrate, and to this end the corporation is privileged to enter with the constable " into any houses licensed for public entertainment, where they shall be informed or may be suspicious of any enormities to be plotting or acting by any members" of the society. Moreover, all persons who have been legally expelled from the College are forbidden to remain over ten days in Cambridge, providing their parents do not reside in that town.[1]

Soon after Dr. Hoar's installment in office, he obtained permission from the Court to devote £300 of the funds which had of late been contributed at home and abroad to the rebuilding of the college house,[2] and which the Court had entrusted to the college overseers,[3] to " the better repair necessary to be done to his lodging, by addition of a kitchen, etc., and making of fences for orchards and gardens, meet for such a place and society." [4]

During the first year of President Hoar's administration trouble seems to have arisen within the corporation. In the autumn of 1673, four of the fellows resigned from that body, and the overseers, finding that they were determined to persist in their resignation, reported the affair to the legislature.[5]

" This Court, having by some of the honored overseers of

---

[1] *Rec.*, IV, Pt. II, 535-7.

[2] In 1669 the towns of Massachusetts and New Hampshire subscribed £2,697 to this purpose; and from 1669 to 1672, £152 were contributed from England. (Quincy's History, I, App. XXIII, 508-9.)

[3] *Rec.*, IV, Pt. II, 516.   [4] *Ibia.*, IV, Pt. II, 537.

[5] Quincy's History, I, 34-35, and I, App. VI, 471.

Harvard College, received a narrative of the uncomfortable debates and motions of the said college lately happening, yet judge not meet at present to take the same into their cognizance, but, considering of what great moment it is that the work be not obstructed, which, by divine blessing, hath been of so great advantage, do declare that they highly approve of the pious and diligent endeavors and actings of the honored and reverend overseers therein, and do further commend it to their care and prudence (to whom it properly belongs) to promote a resettlement and encouragement of that society, and that it be, from time to time, so inspected that it may, by the blessing of God, answer the cost and expectation of such whose hearts the Lord hath or shall move to bring up their children in those studies; likewise declaring, if this means shall be ineffectual, they shall, upon all occasions, be ready to manifest their due resentment as to the obstructors hereof." [1]

During the following year the " resettlement" of the society failed to take place, and it seemed to the Court that a manifestation of its resentment was called for.

" This Court, by good information, understanding that, notwithstanding all former endeavors, the College yet remains in a languishing and decaying condition, do therefore order, that on Wednesday next, at one of the clock, all persons concerned be required to appear, and, accordingly, the Secretary to issue out his warrant to require the president and former and present fellows, graduate and student, that were then in the College, whether resident or non-resident, to make appearance before the Court, and in like manner that the overseers be desired to attend the Court to give information in that case, that so a full hearing being obtained, and the grounds of the present decay discerned, this Court may, if possible, take further effectual course for the revival of that great work, and its future flourishing and establishment amongst us.

After the Court had a full hearing of the doctor, the presi-

[1] *Rec.*, IV, Pt. II, 567.

dent, fellows and several students, for the settlement of the College, the president, upon his own voluntary motion, in consideration of the paucity of scholars, doth freely lay down fifty pounds of his salary, and rests satisfied in one hundred pounds money per annum. Upon the same consideration of fewness of scholars, this Court doth judge meet to dismiss all the officers of salary, until Court and overseers take further order; that the president continue his place until next Election Court; in the meantime, the reverend overseers are entreated to use utmost endeavors for removing of all obstructions therein against the said Court's session, when, if the College be found in the same languishing condition, the president is concluded to be dismissed without further hearing of the case."[1]

In May, 1675, the Court is informed by Deacon John Cooper and Mr. Wm. Manning, who were in charge of the new college building, that several towns that had subscribed to that object in 1669 had not yet sent in their subscriptions. Whereupon the Court directs that "the Secretary do forthwith signify to the towns respectively the pleasure of this Court, which is, that the selectmen in each of the towns (who are behind in their payments according to their subscriptions) do forthwith make such effectual provision, that the one-half thereof, at least, may be speedily brought into the said committee, and the remaining part as soon as may be;[2] as likewise that letters[3] may be sent

[1] *Rec.*, V, 20–21. On March 15, 1675, Dr. Hoar resigned from the presidency of the College. Quincy's History, I, 35.

[2] In the letter written by the colony secretary in accordance with this order, the delinquent towns are entreated to send in the promised sums within two months, so that the building may be finished and the court "prevented further trouble of taking the same by distress." (*Rec.*, V, 143.)

[3] "*Gentlemen:* The necessity of the case presseth us to write these lines to excite and stir up the godly and well disposed minds of yourselves, brethren and neighbors, the inhabitants of Ipswich, &c., to join your helping hands in a free contribution for finishing the new brick college at Cambridge, which being begun about two years since, and advanced in a good measure, but during the war hath

to the secretary to those towns that yet have not subscribed, requiring the elders or minister in the said towns to stir up the inhabitants to so pious and necessary a work." [1]

This matter of getting in the subscriptions to the new college building dragged on for several years. In October, 1678, the Court recommended the selectmen of the towns to appoint special committees in their respective towns to aid them in the work. [2]

In May, 1680, the Court is informed through a committee that had been appointed to receive the returns of the towns in the preceding month, that the selectmen had neglected the order of Court, and consequently the Court orders that unless these officers bring in the underwritten sums in the following September they shall be liable to a fine of £20 for each town. [3]

In May, 1684, the Court adds Mr. Samuel Gookin to the committee on subscriptions, and directs that £35 shall be

stood at a stay for want of money to finish it; but now the old college being fallen down, a part of it, and thereby rendered not habitable, and the new college is like to suffer much damage if it be not speedily finished, these considerations urge us to desire you will follow the example of your brethren and neighbors in other parts of the country, and speedily collect what the Lord doth encline the hearts of the good people of your town to contribute for this good and public work. Touching the way and manner to effect this matter, we leave it to your prudence, only desire your dispatch in this affair within a month or two at the furthest, and that you will endeavor to procure what you can in money, or that which is equivalent, because the work will need such specie; and what you shall do herein, either by way of subscription, or receive in money or other pay, we desire that you will transmit it to Mr. Manning and Deacon Cooper of Cambridge, stewards for that affair, whose receipt shall be sufficient. We hope there is no need of arguments to excite you hereunto; we shall only desire you to consider that scripture, 1 Chron. 29, especially from verse 10 to 17, wherein David and the people of Israel gave liberally unto a good work, praising God that He had given them hearts to offer so willingly, acknowledging that all their substance came from God, and that of His own they had given Him, verse 13. But we shall add no more, but commit you to God, and remain,

Your loving friends, the General Court of the Massachusetts.

Signed by their order,   EDWARD RAWSON, *Secretary.*

BOSTON, 23 May, 1677." (*Rec.*, V, 143-4.)

[1] *Ibid.*, V, 32.   [2] *Ibid.*, V, 195.   [3] *Ibid.*, V, 268.

given to Mr. Manning and £15 to Mr. Cooper out of the subscriptions which they may have collected.[1]

In 1679, Mr. Urian Oakes, Fellow of Harvard, and pastor of the Church at Cambridge, was chosen by the corporation and approved by the overseers as president of the College. He had practically been serving in that capacity since Dr. Hoar's dismissal, but up to this time had refused to accept the nominal appointment.[2] In February, 1679, the General Court voted, for " the better encouragement " of Mr. Oakes and ' 'of the Church for providing help for carrying on that work," that £50 per annum in country pay, over and above the hundred pounds already settled, should be allowed to the reverend doctor, provided he accepted the presidentship.[3] On commencement day, in August, 1680, Mr. Oakes was installed as President of Harvard College by Governor Bradstreet.[4]

The following year President Oakes died. His office was offered in turn to the Rev. Mr. Increase Mather, and to Mr. Samuel Torrey, and declined by both these gentlemen. In each case the General Court agreed to continue the same allowance as had been voted to President Oakes.[5] Finally, the Rev. Mr. John Rogers accepted the President's chair, and was granted £100 in money, and £50 " in other pay" during his continuance in that place and employ.[6] At the same time, the Court voted £50 to Mr. Samuel Andrews and Mr. John Cotton, two of the fellows who had taken " much pains and used much diligence in carrying on the president's work since Mr. Oakes' death." [7]

---

[1] *Ibia.,* V, 445.

[2] Quincy's History, I, 35 and App. VI, 472.

[3] *Rec.,* V, 263.　　　　[4] Quincy, I, App. VI, 472.

[5] *Rec.,* V, 324, 345.

[6] On President Rogers' petition the colony treasurer was ordered in May, 1684, to pay out this salary quarterly. (*Ibid.,* V, 445.)

[7] *Ibid.,* V, 352.

In March, 1683, the legislature granted to the College Merrykoneag neck of land, in Casco Bay in the Province of Maine, with one thousand acres of land adjacent, and ordered the President to lay out the land " as may be most behoofful for the College." [1]

President Rogers died within a year of his inauguration, and consequently in May, 1685, " in answer to a motion made by the overseers of the College," the Court orders "that the hundred pounds, part of the annual salary due to the president, be paid to the corporation for the encouragement of such as have done the work that appertains to the president, and discharge of some other accounts that have been made for the College benefit." [2]

In June, 1685, Mr. Increase Mather agreed, at the request of the overseers, to superintend the affairs of the College until a further settlement could be made. [3]

On July 23, 1686, President Dudley, who after the abrogation of the Massachusetts charter in 1684, was appointed president of the colony, met the Council at Cambridge, and appointed Mr. Mather, rector, and John Leverett and Thomas Brattle, tutors of the college.   President and Council charged the rector to make his usual visitations to the College and vested the government in the fellows. [4]

In 1688 Increase Mather was sent to England to obtain a new charter for the colony. During his absence Governor Andros appointed William Hubbard to the vacant rectorship. [5]

Mr. Mather returned to Massachusetts in 1692 with the desired charter. He now occupied a position of great influence

---

[1] *Ibid.*, V, 397. In 1731 the corporation petitioned the General Court for liberty to survey this grant. *Court Rec.* (MSS.), XV, 13. The corporation then became involved in a law suit and the property was eventually lost to the college. Quincy, I, 399–400.

[2] *Rec.*, V, 479.   [3] Quincy, I, 57.   [4] *Ibid.*, I, 58.

[5] Collections of the Massachusetts Historical Society. Third Series, I, 83. Boston, 1825.

in the colony, for he had been given by the Crown the right to nominate all the colonial officers who were to be appointed under the new charter, and the first provincial governor, lieutenant-governor and councilmen were consequently Mr. Mather's personal supporters.[1] Through the influence of Mr. Mather the first Provincial Assembly re-incorporated Harvard College on June 27, 1692.

The new charter created a corporation consisting of ten persons, to whom the entire control of the College was entrusted. There was no provision for a board of overseers or for any kind of visitorial authority. All the real and personal property of the College and of the resident college officers was exempted from taxation. The corporation could hold land to the value of £4,000 per annum, and personal property to any amount whatsoever. The president, fellows, scholars and 15 of the college servants were freed from all public imposition. The corporation was given a common seal and empowered to confer academical degrees similar to those conferred in English universities.[2]

In February, 1693, the legislature voted £100 salary to President Mather for the past year. At the same time the Lower House, which now began to show opposition to Mr. Mather and other ecclesiastical leaders, resolved that " it is desired that for the future that the President be resident at the College." [3] This order was read in Council on February 16, but no further action was taken by that body.[4] On November 29, the Lower House again voted that " the President of Harvard College for the time being shall reside there as hath been accustomed in times past." [5] Again the Council refused to concur with this order.[6] On October 31, 1694, the Lower

---

[1] Quincy, I, 59–60.

[2] *The Acts and Resolves of the Province of Massachusetts Bay*, I, 38–39. Boston, 1869.

[3] *Ibid.*, VII, 452.   [4] *Ibid.*   [5] *Ibid.*

[6] *Ibid.*, but see Quincy's History, I, 74.

House "voted the Rev. Mr. Increase Mather be thanked for his pains and labor he hath taken at the College in the absence of a settled President there, and that fifty pounds in money be paid to him. . . . . and that he be requested to settle there, or else be serviceable as formerly until the corporation or this Court shall agree with some person that they shall call to settle there who will attend said work." The Upper House merely "voted a concurrence in £50 to be paid unto Mr. Mather for his pains and labor at the College the last year." [1]

The wishes of the Lower House were completely ignored by President Mather, and so on June 15, 1695, that body, in voting him £50 for his past services, again desire him to go and settle at the College. On this condition he is to be allowed £150; otherwise the corporation is to "propose some other meet person to the General Court, who may be treated with to settle there, that the College may no longer be destitute of a settled president." As usual, this resolve was non-concurred by the Upper House. [2] Mr. Mather now gave notice to the corporation of his intention to resign from the presidency; but the corporation refused with much heat to accept his resignation, and so he continued in office and persisted in non-residence at the College. [3] For the next two years he was allowed the usual salary of £50, but the usual request was omitted. [4]

In 1696 the college charter of 1692 was negatived by the Crown, ostensibly because the visitatorial power had not been been exclusively reserved to the King or his immediate appointee. [5]

In view of the state of disorganization to which Harvard College was now reduced, Lieutenant Governor Stoughton came to Cambridge in October, 1696, and "desired and ap-

---

[1] *Acts and Resolves*, VII, 452, 60.

[2] *Ibid.*, VII, 467, 78.　　　　　　　[3] Quincy, I, 75-6.

[4] *Acts and Resolves*, VII, 115, 504, 156.　　[5] *Ibid.*, 608.

pointed" the former president, fellows and treasurer " to continue and proceed in the institution and government of the
house, and in the management of the estate of the College
according to the late rules of said college until his Majesty's
further pleasure shall be known, or a legal settlement of said
college shall be obtained."[1]

On November 9, the corporation voted that " the obtaining
a charter of incorporation for the College would be of singular
advantage to the churches of New England, both in present
and after times."[2]   In accordance with this vote a bill for a
charter was introduced into the Upper House on November
27, and passed by that body on December 27.

As soon as this bill passed the Council, President Mather
and three members of the corporation protested against it, on
the score that it provided for no president, except one in residence, before the confirmation of the act, that it reduced the
corporation estate to £2000, that it diminished the number of
college servants, and that it required an inconveniently large
quorum for corporation meetings.[3]   President Mather then
proceeded to draft a more satisfactory bill, with the consent of
the Lieut.-Governor.   His draft was presented to the legislature and passed by that body on June 4, 1697.

According to this charter, the corporation was to consist of
seventeen persons, a president, vice-president, treasurer and
fourteen fellows.   As in former charters, the corporation was
empowered to fill the vacancies which occurred in its body
through death or removal.   The vice-president was to be elected
annually, and any member was liable to dismissal by the corporation for disability or misdemeanor, " saving to the party
grieved his appeal to the visitors."   His Majesty's Governor
and the Council for the time being were constituted " visitors"
and given a power of visitation at need.   The corporation was

---

[1] Quincy, I, 82.   [2] *Ibid*, I, 82.

[3] *Ibid*, I, 86, and App. XI, 488–9, foot note.

allowed to hold property to the value of £3000, and ten college servants were privileged to the usual exemptions. The president and all salaried fellows were to reside at the college. No fellow was to hold a salaried fellowship for more than seven years without re-election.[1]

Three days after the passage of this act, the corporation unanimously petitioned the legislature to promote the sending of President Mather to England to recommend the charter to the King or to procure from the King another charter, which would be satisfactory to all concerned.[2]

On June 15th, the Lower House voted against complying with this petition. On this same day a second petition was read in the House, in which the members of the corporation threaten to resign from office unless their petition be granted. In support of their position, they urge that "the time has been, when the College has accommodated this colony with a considerable sum of money, not repaid unto this hour, and we would persuade ourselves that this province will, in point of gratitude, not refuse to be helpful unto the good settlement of that society, on which the welfare of the public so much depends."[3] This petition was read, but not acted upon by the House.

On June 14, 1698, another "unanimous" petition from the corporation for the sending of the President to England was read in Council and rejected.[4] Later in this year the corporation urged the appointment of a vice-president upon the legislature;[5] but the plan was ignored, and on December 7th the

---

[1] *Acts and Resolves*, I, 288–290.

[2] Quincy, I, 90, and App. XII, 495–6.

[3] *Ibid.*, I, App. XIII, 496–7. President Quincy calls attention to the fact that neither of these petitions which were signed by only one member of the corporation, although stated to be by unanimous consent, appears to have been acted upon by the corporation. "There is no record of any meeting on either of the days mentioned in them." (Quincy, I, 91.)

[4] *Ibid.*, I, App. XIV, 497–8.　　　　　[5] *Acts and Resolves*, VII, 609.

legislature passed an act allowing a salary of £200 per annum "for an encouragement unto the Rev. Mr. Increase Mather, President, to remove and take up his residence " at the college. It was also ordered that this allowance was to begin " from the time of his removal."[1] The original bill which passed the Council fixed the salary at £250. This was negatived by the House; then after a conference with the Council, the above compromise measure resulted.[2] A joint committee was at once appointed to wait upon President Mather. He promised this committee to communicate his decision to the Lieut.-Governor, and so on December 16th, he writes to Stoughton, declining the proposition of the General Court, both on account of his health and his unwillingness to desert his Boston congregation; and he again offers to resign from the presidency.[3]

This offer was not accepted, and at a meeting of the Council and corporation on February 23, 1699, President Mather promised to remove to Cambridge upon the consent of his wife and his church.[4]

In June, 1699, Governor Bellamont in his opening speech to the Assembly, observed that " he would gladly promote a charter of incorporation for the college at Cambridge [the charter of 1697 had been negatived by the Crown], and would heartily join in an address to his Majesty for his royal grant of such privileges and franchises as his majesty, in his goodness, shall think fit."[5] On the 8th of July following, a bill for a charter was introduced into the Lower House, which with two exceptions, was similar to the charter of 1697. The visitatorial power was reserved exclusively to the governor of the province. On the other hand five members of the Council were appointed members of the corporation. On the strength

---

[1] *Ibid.*, VII, 202.   [2] *Ibid.*, VII, 608.
[3] *Ibid.*, VII, 609-610., and Quincy's History, I, 95-6.
[4] *Ibid.*, I, 97.
[5] *Ibid.*, I, 97-8.

of a petition signed by eight leading clergymen,[1] a religious qualification was also incorporated in the bill:

"Provided that no person shall be chosen and continued president, vice-president, or fellow of said corporation but such as shall declare and continue their adherence unto the principles of reformation, which were espoused and intended by those who first settled this country and founded the College, and have hitherto been the profession and practice of the generality of the churches of Christ in New England."[2]

On July 13th, the Governor refused to sign this bill as it had passed both Houses; and as the Lower House would not agree to the omission of the above clause, the bill was not enacted.[3]

On July 25th, the Council, on a motion of the Lower House, advised that the Governor should "continue the government and direction of the College with the gentlemen of the said late corporation [of 1697], to have and exercise the same until further order."[4] The following year the legislature passed a similar resolve.[5] In his opening speech at this session the Governor expressed his regret that "what he had proposed last May session for the advantage of the College, in relation to the settlement of the College, had been so coldly received."[6] He then suggested that the legislature should petition the King for a royal act of incorporation.

Consequently, on June 14th, the legislature voted to petition the King for the settlement of the College;[7] and on July 12th, both Houses sent in "an humble address" on the subject to Governor Bellomont.

"Right Honorable. It having pleased your Excellency to consent and join with us in an humble address to his Majesty referring to the encroachments of the French in our neighbor-

---

[1] *Acts and Resolves*, I, 99, foot note.   [2] *Ibid.*, I, 100.   [3] *Ibia.*
[4] *Ibid.*, VII, 228.   [5] *Ibia.*, VII, 230.
[6] Quincy's History, I, 104.   [7] *Acts and Resolves*, VII, 245.

hood . . . also for a settlement of the college at Cambridge within this province, agreeable to the ends and intent of the first founders. And several articles as the heads of a charter[1] for incorporating of the said college having been agreed to,[2] we are bold to present the same herewith unto your Lordship. And withal humbly to pray that your Lordship would be pleased to improve your interest in his Majesty and the ministers of state on behalf of this province, for the obtainment of his Majesty's grace and favor in those matters of so momentous and important concern contained in our said address.

We repose an entire confidence in your Lordship's good inclinations and favorable disposition to his people, and are very much encouraged to hope that by your Excellency's mediation, we may find the desired success of our said humble supplications to our gracious sovereign. And we pray your Lordship's advice what further steps are fit to be taken by us in order thereto." . . .[3]

The legislature likewise voted £500 to be paid over to the Governor " to be improved in managing " their address to the King.[4]

On July 9th, the Lower House voted a salary of £220 per annum to the President of Harvard College, " already chosen, or that shall be chosen by this Court;" also, "that the person chosen President of Harvard College shall reside at Cambridge." A committee was then appointed "to wait on the Rev. Mr. Increase Mather and acquaint him that this Court

---

[1] Herein the obnoxious religious qualification clause was omitted ; but the visitatorial power was conferred upon the Council as well as upon the Governor—an equally objectionable arrangement to the King and his representative. (Quincy's History, I, 107.)

[2] The motion to submit a drafted charter to the king had proceeded from the Lower House. After a certain amount of controversy between the Houses, the appointments to the corporation were also made by the Lower Branch of Assembly. (*Ibid.*, I, 105–6. Also, *Court Records* (MSS.), VII, 124.)

[3] *Acts and Resolves*, VII, 252–3.

[4] *Ibid.*, VII, 250.

hath chosen him President of Harvard College and desires him to accept of said office, and so expects that he repair to and reside at Cambridge as soon as may be."[1] The following day the Council concurred with this order and added Mr. Samuel Sewall to the above committee.[2]

On July 11th, the committee reported that Mr. Mather could not remove to Cambridge without acquainting his church. A message was immediately sent by the court to Mr. Mather bidding him to call a meeting of his church that very evening. Now, at last, his congregation consented to his removal to Cambridge, and consequently on July 13th the Lower House appointed a committee "to take care that a suitable place at Cambridge be provided for the reception and entertainment of the President of Harvard College, and to see and consider what is meet to be done with respect to the house already built for a president's house."[3] At the same time the legislature vested the care of the College in the corporation named in the charter of 1699 "until his Majesty's pleasure shall be known referring to the settlement of said college, or that this Court take further order therein."[4]

President Mather resided at the College from July until October. On the 17th of that month he returned to Boston and addressed a letter to Lieut.-Governor Stoughton giving the reasons of his return, and offering to resign.[5] This letter was communicated to the legislature on February 26, 1701, and on March 14th the Court confirmed the corporation which had been nominated in the preceding July, and stated that " in case of Mr. Mather's refusal, absence, sickness or death, that Mr. Samuel Willard, nominated to be vice-president, with the other gentlemen before named," should be intrusted with the entire charge of the College.[6] On the following day, the

---

[1] *Acts and Resolves*, VII, 255.   [2] *Ibid.*

[3] *Ibid.*, VII, 262.   [4] *Ibid.*, VII, 265.

[5] Quincy, I, 111.   [6] *Acts and Resolves*, VII, 271-2.

Court ordered that the president's house should be repaired and fitted up for use, and a committee was appointed for that purpose and directed to bring in their accounts to the Governor and Council.[1]

President Mather returned after this to Cambridge, and continued there until June 30th.[2]

On August 1st, the General Court took into consideration the letter to Lieutenant Governor Stoughton, in which Mr. Mather announced his return for a second time to Boston, and a committee was appointed " to signify to President Mather that the Court desired to speak with him at 3 o'clock, post meridian, relating to the affairs of the College." Thereupon the Representatives were summoned to the Council Chamber, and " Mr. Mather acquainted the Court that he was removed from Cambridge to Boston, and as the College remained unsettled, he did not think fit to continue his residence there, and looked at it as a hardship to expect his removing his family thither; but, if the Court thought fit he should continue his care of the College as formerly, he would do so."

This suggestion was not, however, acceptable to the Court, and a committee was appointed to offer the Presidency to the Rev. Samuel Willard.[3]   On August 5th, the Council appointed a special committee to intercede with Mr. Willard's congregation in favor of his removal to Cambridge.[4]   On August 9th, the Lower House resolved to leave the settlement of college affairs to the care of the Council until the next meeting of the Court, providing " that, if it may be, the person who shall have the chief government of the College reside there."[5]   Mr. Willard proved to be reluctant to promise to reside at the College, and so on September 5th, the Lower House passed a resolve to again invite Mr. Mather " to take care of and reside

[1] *Acts and Resolves*, VII, 275.

[2] Quincy, I, 112, and App. XVII, 501–2.

[3] *Ibid.*, I, 112–13.   [4] *Ibid.*, I, 114.

[5] *Rec.*, VII, 308.

at the College."[1]   This resolve was sent up to the Council,
where it was negatived on the following day.   Meanwhile the
Council sent again to Mr. Willard, and on the return of their
committee, a resolve was passed by the Council and concurred
in by the House of Representatives that Mr. Willard should
be accepted as vice-president on his own terms, *i. e.*, "to reside
there [Cambridge] for one or two days and nights in a week,
and to perform prayers and expositions in the Hall, and to
bring forward the exercise of analyzing."[2]

Mr. Willard continued to serve as vice-president until his
death, in 1707, and he was annually allowed £60 by the General
Court.[3]

On August 17, 1707, Mr. Willard sent in his resignation on
account of illness, and humbly thanked the Governor and legislature
"for their support and acceptance of his service."
The Council thereupon appointed a committee to join with a
committee of the House "to visit the Rev. Mr. Willard and
give him the thanks of this Court for his good service in the
care and government of the College for six years past."[4]

On November 11, 1707, the Council,

"Upon reading an humble address by the Fellows of Harvard
College in Cambridge, representing their choice of Mr.
John Leverett[5] to be the present president of the said college,
and recommending him to his Excellency's favorable acceptation,
withal praying that he would please to present him to the
General Assembly and move for his honorable subsistence;

---

[1] Quincey's History, I, 115–16.

[2] *Rec.*, VII, 312.

[3] *Court Rec.* (MSS), VIII, 12, 97, 185, 286, 360.

[4] *Court Rec.* (MSS), VIII, 327.

[5] Mr. John Leverett had been appointed fellow of the corporation in 1685.   He
became obnoxious to President Mather on account of his liberal religious views,
and in the President's draft of a charter in 1697, his name was excluded from the
corporation.   It was reinserted, however, by the Lower House.   In the drafts of
1699 and 1701 Leverett was again excluded.   In 1701, Mr. Leverett was speaker
of the House.   (Quincy's History, I, 87, 101, 106.)

the above said address being also accompanied with addresses from thirty-nine ministers, voted that the said election be accepted, and that Mr. Leverett be desired and impowered to take the care and government of the College as president accordingly."[1]

The Lower House refused to concur in this vote; and on November 29th, they sent up to the Council a message in writing for " the choice of a suitable person to take care of the College until the session of the Court in May next."[2] On December 3d, the Council refused to act with the House in this matter. On December 4th, the House passed a measure rescinding their vote of July, 1700, for establishing the President's salary at £220 per annum.[3] The Council then proposed that the House should grant a suitable salary to Mr. John Leverett while " residing at Cambridge and discharging the proper duties to a president belonging :—and entirely devote himself to that service." At the same time, the Council resolve :

"And inasmuch, as the first foundation and establishment of that house [Harvard College], and the government thereof, had its original from an act of the General Court, made and passed in the year, 1650 which has not been repealed or nulled, the president and fellows of the said college are directed, from time to time, to regulate themselves according to the rules of the constitution by the said act prescribed; and to exercise the powers and authorities thereby granted for the government of that house and the support thereof."[4]

---

[1] *Court Rec.* (MSS.), VIII, 340.

[2] *Ibid.*, I, 157. [3] *Acts and Resolves*, VIII, 255.

[4] *Ibid.*, VIII, 257. Governor Dudley, shortly after his arrival in Massachusetts in 1703, assured the General Court of his willingness to appeal to Queen Anne in behalf of Harvard College. Again, in 1705, Dudley intimated to the Council that in case of proper application there was reason to hope for the granting of a royal charter to the College. But no application had been made. (Quincy's History, I, 149, 153-4.)

The House concurred with this resolve on December 6th, and appropriated £150 for a president's salary.

In November, 1708, the Lower House appointed a committee " to take care for the repairs of the house built for the use of the President of Harvard College at Cambridge."[1]   In August, the House orders £12 to be paid to this committee for the purchase of necessary materials.[2]   In February, 1709, this account, together with a further account of £11 1s. 2d., was approved by the committee on repairs, "excepting a pump of three pounds," and reported to the House. The House voted that £8 1s. 2d. should be paid over to President Leverett, to defray the cost of the articles approved of by the committee.[3]   In all the above particulars the Council concurred.

In November, 1711, the Lower House resolved on a memorial of President Leverett to increase his allowance for the coming year by £30.   The Council concurred.[4]   This additional grant was probably continued to President Leverett during his presidency.[5]

On February 6, 1717, Governor Shute, who had succeeded Governor Dudley in 1715, opened a special legislative session with the following words :

"Gentlemen : I had not given you or myself the trouble of a winter session, but that through the providence of God in the late sickness we were obliged to break up the last session before some affairs of importance were finished, and among others a proposal that was then made for some additional building to your college at Cambridge. I doubt not but it was very acceptable to hear the sons of the prophets say the place where we dwell is too straight for us. You are very much in the right to have the interests of learning much at heart, and therefore, if any further building for that purpose

---

[1] *Court Rec.* (MSS.), VIII, 420.   [2] *Ibid.*, VIII, 478–9.   [3] *Ibid.*, IX, 7–8.
[4] *Ibid.*, IX, 147.   [5] Quincy, II, 227.

be intended the next summer, you must make the proper provision for it this session." [1]

On the same day the committee of both Houses that had been appointed to consider a memorial that had been addressed to the legislature in the preceding October, reported that " having met at the college in Cambridge, December 27, 1717, and enquired into the accommodations that are there at present for the students (graduates and undergraduates)," they " find it necessary that some further building be erected for the making provision of 40 or 50 studies more, that all the students may be entertained within the College." [2] On February 7, this committee was instructed by both Houses to draw up a plan for the needed building, with an estimate of its cost. [3] On February 14th, it is moved in the Lower House and concurred in by the Council that thanks should be returned to the Governor " for his care to promote good literature, without which religion will not be upheld amongst us ; but in as much as the charge of the said building is like to be very considerable, and a great part of this House is absent," it is further voted that consideration of the affair be postponed to the next May session of the legislature. [4]

On July 4th, the Lower House appointed a committee to take charge of the new building and voted £1500 to that object. [5] On May 29, 1719, petitions from the corporation of Harvard College and the committee on building were presented in the House, [6] and it was accordingly voted that the new building should extend 100 instead of 50 feet, and that an additional appropriation of £2,000 [7] should be made. It is

---

[1] *Court Rec.* (MSS.), X, 228–9.   [2] *Ibid.*, X, 229–30.

[3] *Ibid.*, X, 233   [4] *Ibid.*, X, 245.   [5] *Ibid.*, X, 315.

[6] By a committee which had been appointed at a special meeting of the Governor and Council and the overseers of the College called to discuss the affair. Quincy, I, 222–3.

[7] Only £3339 19s. 11d. of the total appropriation were expended by the committee. The remaining £160 1d. were given by the Court to the committee for their good services. (*Court Rec.* (MSS.), XI, 45.)

also resolved " that the rent paid by the students . . . in the said building shall not exceed 20s. per man per annum. And that the said rents from time to time shall be improved for no other use than the repairs of the said building unless by the direction of this Court.[1]

On June 20, 1718, the Lower House ordered " that an additional building of brick be made to Harvard College to begin about 6 foot to the southwest of Stoughton House, and to extend in length westward 47 and an half foot or thereabouts not exceeding 50, of the same breadth of Harvard College and of a suitable height not exceeding the height of Harvard College; with three upright stories and a convenient roof of a suitable pitch."[2] The Council concurred in this order.

In the year 1722 there was much activity in the legislature concerning the administration of the College. In June the Lower House voted, " Whereas, by reason of the small pox being in the town of Boston and several other towns the summer past, several of the students of Harvard College were absent a great part of the year past. And upon its approach into the town of Cambridge in November last, that society was broken up for some time, and being not long since got together, and the commencement near at hand . . . that the gentlemen of the corporation be advised that the vacation usually allowed and given to the students after the commencement, which was four or five weeks, do not exceed one week, but that the students may in some measure regain their lost time by reason of their long absence occasioned as aforesaid, that the fellows, tutors and students be not allowed to be absent more than a week from the commencement; and then put into commons again, and so follow their usual studies and recitations.

[June 21] In Council read and concurred. Consented to.
                                        SAMUEL SHUTE."[3]

---

[1] *Court Rec.* (MSS.), X, 397.   [2] *Ibid.*, X, 297.   [3] *Ibid.*, XI, 323.

On June 28th the committee of both Houses, which had been appointed to consider a petition of the overseers for the enlargement of the corporation,[1] reported:

" First, that it was the interest of the said college that the tutors of the said college, or such as have the instruction and government of the students there, should be fellows and members of the corporation of the said college, provided they exceed not five in number.

" Secondly, that none of the said fellows be overseers.

" Thirdly, that the president and fellows of the said college, or the major part of them, are not warranted to fix or establish any salary or allowance for their service without the approbation and consent of the overseers."

The Council sent this report to the House with a message " that the Council, being overseers of the College, it is thought proper that the House pass first on the report." The report was accepted by the House of Representatives, and it was resolved " that the corporation for the future practice accordingly." [2]

The object of these provisions on the part of the legislature was the exclusion from the corporation of three non-resident fellows who had become obnoxious to the majority of the overseers on account of their ecclesiastical liberality. In view of this fact Governor Shute signed the measures on condition that " the Rev. Mr. Benjamin Wadsworth and the Rev. Mr. Benjamin Colman and the Rev. Mr. Appleton are not removed by said orders, but still remain fellows of the corporation." [3]

---

[1] This petition, which was presented to the legislature on June 13, urged that " for as much as by the good hand of God . . . the number of students . . . is greatly increased, and the affairs and business of the college also much enlarged, it is apprehended that the corporation should be enlarged, which cannot be without the aid of the General Assembly; . . . and that if in their wisdom they shall think it beneficial, they will please . . . to make a convenient addition to the corporation, and therein to have regard to the President, Fellows and Tutors that they may be of that number." (*Ibid.*, XI, 311.)

[2] *Ibid.*, XI, 333-4.   [3] Quincy's History, I, 303.

On July 5th, the Lower House acquaint the Governor that, inasmuch as this proviso "has a tendency entirely to defeat the design and purpose of those votes," they, therefore, "desire his Excellency to pass absolutely thereupon, according to the constant usage and practice ever since the present happy constitution."

To this the governor answered: "Gentleman, I received your message relating to the affairs of the College, and altho' I am not obliged to give my reasons for my manner of signing or my refusing to sign any vote, yet I think it proper so to do upon this occasion, and therefore I do now inform you, that the limitations with which I signed the Resolve were agreeable to the explanation made to me by the Council at the time of my signing, and also agreeable to the intention of the Overseers in their address to the General Court; wherefore I can not consent unto those votes upon any other terms than what I have already done, until I have appointed an overseers' meeting for their further opinion in this matter."

It was thereupon voted in the House of Representatives "that the explanation made by the Council to his Excellency seems inconsistent with their own vote upon the Resolve; and therefore this House insist upon their desire that his Excellency would pass upon it absolutely without any proviso or limitation."[1]

The struggle between the corporation and the overseers continued. The Lower House sided with the overseers, and on November 22d, they warned the corporation to keep more strictly within the limits of the charter "lest they endanger the early privileges of the institution."[2] The corporation formally protested against this charge and petitioned for a hearing, "the corporation not having as yet been heard thereupon."[3] On December 12th the Lower House voted that the petition be dismissed "as altogether groundless and no ways to be justified."[4]

[1] *Court Rec.* (MSS.), XI, 352.
[2] Quincy's History, I, 306.
[3] *Ibid.*, I, 306-7.
[4] *Ibid.*, I, 307.

On January 18, 1723, the House revived those measures to which the Governor had refused his unqualified consent in the preceding summer. The Council referred this action of the Lower Branch to the following session.[1] Then, on August 24th, after a hearing had been given to the president of the corporation on the one hand and to tutors Sever and Welsted, who represented the opposition party, the January vote of the Lower House was re-read and non-concurred.[2]

The Council likewise non-concurred in an attack which the House made upon the College in the preceding month of June. "The theses of the bachelors to be graduated at the Commencement, to be held at Cambridge the first Wednesday of July next, being produced at the House, and the House observing the dedication thereof not to be properly addressed,[3] voted that it is derogatory to the honor of the Lieut. Governor, who is now Commander-in-Chief of this province[4] and the head of the overseers of the College to have the impression of those theses go out as they now are; and therefore ordered that the printer, Mr. Bartholomew Green, be and hereby is directed not to deliver any of those theses till they shall be properly addressed."[5]

In May, 1724, President Leverett died.[6] On June 12th, the Corporation represent to the Council that it will be necessary to provide a residence for the incoming president, and they suggest that as Mr. Leverett's house is about to be sold by his heirs,[7] it would be well for the Court to appoint a com-

---

[1] *Court Rec.* (MSS.), XI, 465-6.   [2] *Ibid.*, XII, 23.

[3] The objection of the House cannot be ascertained from the records. Quincy's History, I, 311.

[4] Governor Shute went to England on January 1, 1723.

[5] *Court Rec.* (MSS.), XI, 525.

[6] Quincy, I, 323.

[7] President Leverett's estate was in debt to the extent of £2,000. In 1726 Mr. Leverett's daughters stated to the General Court that their father had been obliged to pile up a debt of £100 every year during his presidency. They also stated that the President's house had been pulled down to make way for the new college

mittee to negotiate its purchase in view of the fact that the college revenues are appropriated elsewhere. This memorial "was sent down recommended" to the Lower House;[1] but the only attention it received by that body resulted in the appointment of a committee "to make enquiry into the state of the college treasury, and how the income and profits thereof are appropriated, and how the rents of the new college have been disposed of and what are the necessary charges of the colleges."[2] This vote was non-concurred by the Council.

On December 11th, a committee of the overseers informed the Court of the election of the Rev. Mr. Colman[3] to the presidency of the College, and petitioned the Court to allow him a larger salary than had been usually allowed. The opposition of the Lower House to Mr. Colman is evident from the procrastinating nature of their vote on this subject. "For as much as at present it is uncertain whether the church, of which the Rev. Mr. Colman is pastor, can be persuaded to part from him, or whether Mr. Colman is inclinable to leave his church and undertake the office of President of Harvard College, and this being a matter of great weight and importance, especially to the establishment of the churches in this province, as well as to the said college ; therefore, voted that the further consideration of this memorial be referred until the

building, and that for four years they had been put to the expense of £20 annual rent; moreover, that two months' rent was due for their house while it was occupied by their father's successor. The Lower House refused to grant more than £30 to the petitioners, £20 for arrears of salary antecedent to President Leverett's death and £10 for the two months' rent of his house by President Wadsworth. The House refused to reconsider this vote, although "earnestly recommended to do so by the Council, who stated that in their opinion "the justice and power of this Court is much concerned in making compensation to the heirs of the said president for the loss accruing to his estate through the insufficiency of his allowance." (*Court Rec.* (MSS.), XIII, 237.)

[1] *Ibid.*, XII, 177–8.   [2] *Ibid.*, XII, 200.

[3] Mr. Colman had been pastor of the reform Brattle Street church since its foundation in 1698.

said Mr. Colman's mind, as well as of the church of which he is pastor, be communicated to this Court." [1]

This vote was non-concurred in by the Council. Mr. Colman having refused to accept the presidency until the question of salary was settled, the overseers again petitioned the General Court on the subject. [2] Accordingly, on December 18th, the question was put in the House of Representatives "Whether the Court will establish a salary or allowance on the President of Harvard College for the time being before the person chosen to that office had accepted the duty and trust thereof." [3] It passed in the negative *nemine contradicente.* This vote was non-concurred in by the Council.

On June 17, 1725, the Rev. Mr. Benjamin Wadsworth was elected President of the College, and on the following day the Lower House appointed a committee to enquire into the financial condition of the College and "to look out a suitable house for the reception of the president, that so an honorable settlement and support may be allowed for the Reverend the President of Harvard College, which is the full intention of this Court." At the same time the Court voted a salary of £150 to Mr. Wadsworth.

These measures were concurred in by the Council and consented to by Governor Dummer. [4]

On June 23d, this Committee was further empowered by the General Court to procure a temporary residence for President Wadsworth and his family until the next legislative session. [5] On January 1, 1726, the Lower House

" Resolved, That the sum of £70 be allowed and paid out of the public treasury to the Rev. Mr. Benjamin Wadsworth, President of Harvard College, which, with the sum of £150 granted to the said Mr. President Wadsworth the last session of this Court, and the sum of £139, so much remaining in the

[1] Quincy, I, 333. [2] *Ibid.*, I, 337.
[3] *Court Rec.* (MSS.), XII, 296.
[4] *Ibid.*, XII, 371-2. [5] *Ibid.*, XII, 390.

hands of the corporation of the College, being for the rents of Massachusetts Hall for the first five years, exclusive of all charges and repairs thereon, together with the sum of £41 for the rent of the said Massachusetts Hall for the year current, which this Court do hereby appropriate and order to be paid to the said Mr. President Wadsworth, making in the whole the sum of £400, the Court are of opinion is a sufficient and honorable support and maintenance for him, the said president, for one year.

"And that the said Mr. President Wadsworth may be further encouraged cheerfully to go through the momentous affairs of his office, it is further resolved, and this Court do freely give, grant and appropriate the future annual rents and incomes of Massachusetts Hall to him, the said Mr. President Wadsworth.

"And, whereas, there is not at present any convenient house provided for the reception and entertainment of the president of the said college for the future, and the Court being willing and desirous to repeat their intentions and inclinations in all things for the prosperity of that society, and that the same may flourish under the divine influence, it is resolved that the sum of £1000 be allowed and paid out of the public treasury to the corporation of Harvard College, and by them to be forthwith used and disposed of for the building and finishing a handsome wooden dwelling house, barn, housing, etc., on some part of the land adjacent and belonging to the said college, which is for the reception and accommodation of the Rev. the President of Harvard College for the time being." [1]

"And it appearing by the accounts rendered by the college treasurer, that there has been occasion to disburse very considerable sums of money the year past out of the incomes and revenues of the said colleges' estate, partly to the resident

---

[1] The President's house eventually cost £1800. The corporation twice petitioned the legislature to appropriate an additional £800 to the building, but both times they were unsuccessful. (Quincy, I, 381, 382.)

fellows before the election of Mr. President Wadsworth, and other charges occasioned for repairing the ways at Charlestown for the better accommodation of travellers passing over the Ferry at Charles River, which it is to be hoped there will not be the like occasion of for the future, the corporation will be able to grant such allowances out of their unappropriated incomes and revenues which will in a great measure support and maintain the Rev. Mr. President, and this Court will not have occasion to make such drafts on the public treasury as they have done for the present year for his support and maintenance. . . .

" In Council read and concurred. Consented to.

" WM. DUMMER." [1]

In June, 1727, Dr. Timothy Cutler [2] and Mr. Samuel Myles, ministers of the Episcopal church in Boston, petitioned the general court to be assigned a place on the Board of Overseers as " teaching elders " of Boston. This petition was accompanied by a memorial signed by seventy representative members of the Episcopal church in and near Boston, who urged that the College was " the common nursery of piety and learning to New England in general, as well to those that are of the order of the Church of England as to them that are of the order of the churches of New England." [3]

In August, the Court sent copies of these memorials to the board of overseers and postponed the discussion of the question to the following session.[4] On December 28th, these memorials, the overseers' replies and the counter replies of the petitioners were taken into consideration by the House, and " the question was put whether it is within the intent and

---

[1] *Court Rec.* (MSS.), XIII, 98–9.

[2] Having been converted to episcopacy Dr. Cutler was forced to resign from the rectorship of Yale College in 1722. He then went to England, was ordained in the established church and in 1724 was sent as missionary to Boston. (Quincy's History, I, 365.)

[3] *Ibid.*, I, 369–70.   [4] *Ibid.*, I, 371.

meaning of the charter granted to the said college that the
reverend memorialists, the said Dr. Timothy Cutler and Mr·
Samuel Myles, ought to be deemed members of the Board of
overseers." The resulting negative vote in the House was
concurred in by the Council and consented to by the Governor.[1]

On January 11, 1728, this question was again discussed by
the Court with the same result.

In 1737 President Wadsworth died and the Rev. Mr. Holyoke was elected president. The legislature appropriated £200
to President Holyoke for one year over and above the rents of
Massachusetts Hall, and for the encouragement of his separa-
tion from the society at Marblehead where he had been officiating as minister, £140 were voted to be granted to the society
upon the ordination of his successor.[2] About this time the
legislature began to make annual grants to the members of the
faculty, £100 to the Hollisian professor of divinity " as a gratuity in consideration of his faithful discharge of the great and
important trust reposed in him and for his further encouragement therein;" £90 to the Hollisian professor of mathematics
and natural philosophy, and later in the century, from £20 to
£40 to the instructor in Hebrew. The grant to the president
continued to be from £200 to £250.[3]

During President Holyoke's administration the corporation
became involved in a dispute with the tax assessors of Boston
and Chelsea. The action of the General Court was favorable
to the corporation,[4] and on January 5, 1753, upon the report
of the joint committee which had been appointed to consider
the question of Harvard's liability to taxation, the legislature
took occasion to resolve " that the real and personal estate belonging to the corporation and the president, . . . not exceeding the sum of £500 per annum ought to be, and the same is

[1] *Court Rec.* (MSS.), XIII, 501.　　　　[2] Quincy, II, 10.

Ibid., II, 227-8, and *Court Rec.* (MSS.), XXII, 497-8; XXIII, 244-6;
XXV, 136-7, 378-380; XXVI, 166, 383.

[4] *Court Rec.* (MSS.), XIX, 186-7.

hereby exempted from all civil impositions whatsoever, and that for the future a clause be inserted in the several tax acts to exempt the same accordingly, and that as soon as the revenue of the college amounts to £500 per annum, the college treasurer do give an account thereof into the secretary's office." [1]

In 1754 the legistature passed an act empowering the corporation to sell all real-estate which might accrue to the College by virtue of a judgment recovered on any mortgage or by virtue of an execution for the satisfaction of a judgment in any personal action.[2] At the same time the corporation was also empowered to dispose of a farm which belonged to the College and was situated in that part of the town of Billerica called Shawshin." [3]

On January 29, 1762, the inhabitants of the county of Hampshire petitioned the legislature for a charter for a college in the western part of Massachusetts. The Council rejected the petition by a large majority. But the House voted in its favor by a small majority. An appeal was then made to Governor Bernard, and he agreed to sign a charter for the petitioners. The overseers of Harvard College at once remonstrated, on the ground that the establishment of a second collegiate institution would be most prejudicial to Harvard College. Governor Bernard was influenced by the stand of the Harvard overseers, and so the scheme for a western seminary was defeated.[4]

In 1762 the board of overseers appointed a committee, presided over by Lieutenant Governor Hutchinson, to petition the

---

[1] *Court Rec.* (MSS.), XIX, 537.

[2] The charter of 1650 gave no power to the corporation to alienate land. To this end an act of legislature was necessary; as, for example, in 1733, when the legislature granted a petition of the corporation to sell certain small tracts of land in the town of Rowly—a bequest of one Mr. Ezekiel Rogers—and to invest the proceeds in land more advantageously situated. (*Court Rec.* (MSS.), XV, 429, 464.)

[3] *Acts and Resolves*, III, 749. See also *Court Rec.* (MSS.), XX, 230.

[4] Quincy, II, 105–111.

legislature for aid in the erection of a new college building.[1]
Accordingly, on June 12th, the Lower House appropriated
£2000 to this purpose. It was provided that the new building
should be of the same dimensions as Massachusetts Hall, and
that its cost should be limited to the estimate which had been
presented to the Court the preceding year. A joint committee
of the two Houses was appointed to carry out the work.[2]

Two days later, the Court voted a further sum of £500 sterling to Royal Tyler " toward purchasing from England nails,
glass and other materials for the building the new college in
Cambridge, which materials the said Royal Tyler, Esq., has
generously offered to procure for the province free from any
advance or profit."[3]

In February, 1763, an additional sum of £1000 was appropriated to the use of the committee.[4]

On December 30th, the committee delivered the keys of the
completed structure into the custody of the General Court.
The committee also stated that the new hall had cost £530
7s. and 2d. more than had been estimated, *i. e.*, £4283. After
a debate in the House the extra sum was voted in full payment of the building. A committee was then appointed by
both Houses to consider to what use the rents of the new
building should be applied."[5]

On January 13, 1764, both branches of the legislature met
in the college chapel, and Governor Bernard, at the request of
the President, christened the new building Hollis Hall.[6] Three
days after this dedication the members of the legislature took
refuge in Cambridge from the small pox, which had broken
out in Boston. They assembled in Harvard Hall. On the
night of January 24th this building was burned to the ground.[7]

[1] *Ibid.*, II, 100.   [2] *Court Rec.* (MSS.), XXIV, 436.

[3] *Ibid.*, XXIV, 439.

[4] *Ibid.*, XXIV, 617.   [5] *Ibid.*, XXV, 110–1.

[6] Quincy, II, 102.   [7] *Ibid.*, II, 112.

On January 26th, Governor Bernard sent the following message to the House of Representatives:

" I heartily condole with you on the unfortunate accident which has happened to the College, and we have been the melancholy spectators of. As your bounty has just now been largely extended to that society, I should not so soon ask you to repeat it upon any common occasion. But as this extraordinary event occurred whilst the building was in your immediate occupation, there seems to be an obligation that you should replace it. However it is considered, as a duty or a fresh call for your benevolence, I shall be glad to join with you and the Council in proper measures to retrieve this loss." [1]

Both branches of the legislature at once voted unanimously that " the college be rebuilt at the charge of the province." A joint committee [2] was appointed, and £2000 were appropriated for that purpose. This committee was directed " to procure a water engine for the use of the College, not exceeding £100." [3] During the following year the General Court ordered £379 4s. 18d. to be paid over to those students who had lost property in the fire. [4]

On November 3d, the legislature voted an additional £2000 to the committee on rebuilding. [5]

In March, 1765, the legislature voted that the cellars and rooms of Hollis Hall should be rented, so as to produce £100 of annual rental, £10 to be reserved as a repair fund, and £90 to be applied for the support of the college tutors, and the purchase of books for the library [6]

---

[1] *Court Rec.* (MSS), XXV, 152.

[2] On January 31 President Holyoke was added to this committee.

[3] *Ibid.*, XXV, 153.   [4] *Ibid.*, XXV, 192, 321.   [5] *Ibid.*, XXV, 321.

[6] Quincy, II, 102. The old library had been entirely destroyed in the burning of Harvard Hall. (*Ibid.*, II, 113.) In the winter of '65–'66 the laws of the province and the journals of the Lower House were presented to the library by the legislature. (*Court Rec.* (MSS.), XXVI, 108.)

On June 20th, the legislature voted £1000 to the committee on rebuilding "to enable them to proceed in that affair." [1]

On June 13th, 1766, the sum of £1112 18s. 7d. was ordered to be paid to the committee as payment in full for the rebuilding of Harvard Hall. [2]

In this same month a lottery act was passed by the legislature to provide funds for the building of a new college hall.

The preamble reads as follows :

"Whereas, the buildings belonging to Harvard College are greatly insufficient for lodging the students of the said college, and will become much more so when Stoughton Hall shall be pulled down, as, by its present ruinous state, it appears it soon must be ; and, whereas, there is no fund for erecting such buildings, and considering the great expense which the General Court has lately been at in building Hollis Hall, and also in rebuilding Harvard College, it cannot be expected that any further provision for the College should be made out of the public treasury, so that no other resort is left but private benefactions, which it is conceived, will be best excited by means of a lottery. . . . Be it enacted," etc. [3]

ELEMENTARY AND SECONDARY EDUCATION

Six years after the General Court had made provision for collegiate education, it turned its attention to the general educational conditions [4] of the colony. At a General Court of Elections held at Boston on June 14, 1642, the Court,   taking into consideration the great neglect in many parents and masters in training up their children in learning and labor and other employments which may be profitable to the Commonwealth, do hereupon order and decree that in every town the chosen men appointed for managing the prudential affairs of the same shall

---

[1] *Court Rec.* (MSS.), XXVI, 49.   [2] *Ibid.*, XXVI, 254–5.

[3] *Acts and Resolves*, iv, 834, and v, 212–13.

[4] As early as June 2, 1641, the Court desired the elders to make out "a catechism for the instruction of youth in the grounds of reiigion." Mass. Col. Rec. I, 328.

henceforth stand charged with the care of the redress of this evil, so as they shall be liable to be punished or fined for the neglect thereof upon any presentment of the grand jurors or other information or complaint in any plantations in this jurisdiction ; and for this end they, or the greater part of them, shall have power to take account from time to time of their parents and masters and of their children, concerning their calling and employment of their children, especially of their ability to read and understand the principles of religion and the capital laws of the country, and to impose fines upon all those who refuse to render such accounts to them when required; and they shall have power, with consent of any court or magistrate, to put forth apprentices the children of such as shall not be able and fit to employ and bring them up, nor shall take course to dispose of them, of such as they shall find not to be able and fit to employ and bring them up, nor shall take course to dispose of them themselves; and they are to take care that such as are set to keep cattle be set to some other employment withal, as spinning up on the rock, knitting, weaving tape, etc.;[1] and that boys and girls be not suffered to converse together, so as may occasion any wanton, dishonest or immodest behavior. And for their better performance of this trust committed to them, they may divide the town amongst them, appointing to every of the said townsmen a certain number of families to have special oversight of. They are also to provide that a sufficient quantity of materials, as hemp, flax, etc., may be raised in their several towns, and tools and implements provided for working out the same. And for their assistance in this so needful and beneficial employment, if they meet with any difficulty or opposition which they cannot well master by their own power,

---

[1] All subsequent poor and apprenticeship laws provided for the instruction of apprentices to read and write "as they may be capable." (*Acts and Resolves*, I, 538, 654.) In 1741 poor children who were bound out were ordered to be taught, "males to read, write and cypher; females to read, as they respectively may be capable." (*Temporary Acts and Laws of His Majesty's Province of the Massachusetts Bay in New England*, p. 30. Boston, 1742.)

they may have recourse to some of the magistrates, who shall take such course for their help and encouragement as the occasion shall require, according to justice. And the said townsmen, at the next court in those limits, after the end of their year, shall give a brief account in writing of their proceedings herein; provided, that they have been so required by some court or magistrate a month at least before. And this order to continue for two years, and till the Court shall take further order." [1]

On May 14, 1645, the General Court passed an order for the military training of youth, an outcome probably of the recently formed defensive league of the United Colonies.

" Whereas, it is conceived that the training up of youth to the art and practice of arms will be of great use to this country in divers respects, and amongst the rest, that the use of bows and arrows may be of great concernment, in defect of powder upon any occasion, it is therefore ordered that all youth within this jurisdiction from ten years old to the age of sixteen years, shall be instructed by some one of the officers of the band." [2]

Two years later, on November 11, 1647, the General Court laid the foundation of all subsequent school legislation in the colony.

" It being one chief point of that old deluder, Satan, to keep men from the knowledge of the Scriptures, as in former times, by keeping them in an unknown tongue, so in these latter times, by persuading from the use of tongues, that so at last the true sense and meaning of the original might be clouded by false glosses of saint-seeming deceivers, that learning might not be buried in the grave of our fathers in church and commonwealth, the Lord assisting our endeavors,— It is therefore ordered that every township in this jurisdiction, after the Lord hath increased them to the number of fifty householders, shall then forthwith appoint one within their

[1] *Mass. Col. Rec.*, II, 8–9.   [2] *Ibid.*, III, 12.

town to teach all such children as shall resort to him to write and read, whose wages shall be paid either by the parents or masters of such children, or by the inhabitants in general, by way of supply, as the major part of those that order the prudentials of the town shall appoint ;[1] providing, those that send

[1] Many of the towns within the colony had already set to keeping schools or schoolmasters.

In 1635 the town of Boston, "at a general meeting upon public notice," agreed " that our brother Philemon Pormort shall be entreated to become schoolmaster for the teaching and nurturing children with us." (*Second Report of the Record Commissioners of the city of Boston*, p. 5, Boston, 1881.) The next year " at a general meeting of the richer inhabitants, there was given towards the maintenance of a free school master for the youth with us, Mr. Daniel Maud being now also chosen thereunto." (*Ibid.*, p. 160, note.) In 1641 a general townsmeeting ordered that Deare Island should be improved for the maintenance of a free school for the town. (*Ibid.*, p. 65.) In 1644 the island was let for three years, paying £7 a year for the use of the school. (*Ibid.*, p. 82.)

In a general meeting of the town of Dedham in 1643, and by " unanimous consent . . . 40 acres at the least or 60 acres at the most," were " set apart for public use, viz.: for the town, the church and a free school." (*Dedham Town Records*, III, 92.) In 1644, " the inhabitants taking into serious consideration the great necessity for providing some means for the education of the youth . . . did with unanimous consent declare by vote their willingness to promote that work, promising to provide maintenance for a free school . . . and farther did resolve and consent . . . to raise the sum of £20 per annum towards the maintaining of a schoolmaster. . . . *Ibid.*, III, 105.

In August, 1645, the inhabitants of Roxbury " in consideration of their religious care of posterity " having taken thought " how necessary the education of their children in literature will be to fit them for public service both in church and commonwealth," unanimously agree to erect a free school and to allow £20 per annum to the schoolmaster to be raised out of properties given by certain of the inhabitants of the town. These donors also elect seven trustees to attend to the whole business of the school. (*A History of the Grammar School*, pp. 7–9. C. K. Dillaway, Boston, 1860.)

In Charlestown, the school was supported in 1647 by the rent of some islands, the income from the Mystic weir and a rate. (*The Evolution of the Massachusetts Public School System*, p. 49. George H. Martin, A. M., New York, 1894.) Prior to 1647 the school at Cambridge was supported wholly by tuition fees. (*Ibid.*) In Dorchester the school was supported by private donations and leased town lands. (*Ibid.*, pp. 49–50.) In Ipswich, income from rents, lands, annuities and tuition fees constituted the school fund. (*Ibid.*, p. 50.) In Salem, parents subscribed to the school and poor children depended on a town rate. (*Ibid.*)

their children be not oppressed by paying much more than they can have them taught for in other towns ; and it is forthwith ordered that where any town shall increase to the number of 100 families or householders, they shall set up a grammar school, the master thereof being able to instruct youth so far as they may be fitted for the university, provided, that if any town neglect that performance hereof above one year, that every such town shall pay £5 to the next school till they shall perform this order." [1]

In November, 1659, the General Court granted, on petition, one thousand acres of land to Charlestown and Cambridge "upon condition that they forever appropriate it to that use [grammar school], and within three years, at farthest, lay out the same, and put it on improvement; and in case that they fail of maintaining a grammar school during the said time, they shall so do, the next grammar school of what town so ever, shall have the sole benefit thereof." [2]   The next year the Court grants 500 acres of land to Roxbury [3] and 1000 acres to Boston [4] (to the latter in answer to a petition) for the maintenance of their free sehools.

The feoffees of the Roxbury school petitioned the General Court on May 20, 1669, to confirm the agreement which had been made by the first inhabitants of the town for a "foundation of a grammar school for the glory of God, the future good and service of the country and of the church of Christ.'   This action was occasioned by some opposition in the town to the school corporation, and by the loss of the school records in a recent fire. [5]   Accordingly on June 2, "for the due encouragement of the school at Roxbury," the Court appoints "Major General Leveret, Mr. Edward Tyng, Mr. Stoughton and Mr. Thomas Shepheard, or any three of them, to be a committee to enquire into the state of this affair, to hear

[1] *Rec.* II, 203.   [2] *Ibid.*, IV, Pt. I, 400.
[3] *Ibid.*, IV, Pt. I, 438.   [4] *Ibid.*, IV, Pt. I, 444.
[5] Dillaway's *Grammar School*, pp. 15-17.

what may be said *pro et con*, endeavoring what in them lies an amicable agreement and full settlement of that affair amongst themselves, and if that cannot be obtained, to make their report where the obstruction lies, and what it is, to the next sessions of this Court, that so the obstructions may be removed, and so good and pious a work may be confirmed and determined according to the mind of the donors of so charitable a work."[1] This committee reported on May 19, 1670, in favor of the petitioners, stating that the opponents of the endowed school had admitted that, but for it there would be no school in Roxbury at all.[2] The Court then ratified the school trusteeship and empowered the feoffees "for the ordering of all things for the settlement and reparation of the school house, choice of master, and order of scholars, to improve all donations, either past or future, for the behoof and benefit of the said school, without any personal or private respects, as also the ordering of 20 acres of arable land, lying in the great lots, which hath been in occupation for the said school about 20 years ; as also, that if, for the necessary and convenient future being of a schoolmaster, there be necessary the future levying of any further sums of money, that the said donors be absolutely and wholly free from any such levy or imposition. . . . And the said feoffees to be always responsible to the court of assistants and donors for their faithful discharge of their trust, provided there be constant provision of an able grammar schoolmaster, and the school house be settled where it was first intended, and may be accommodable to those whose home stalls are engaged towards the maintenance thereof; and in case there be need of further contribution, that the levy be equally made on all the inhabitants, excepting only those that do, by virtue of their subscription, pay their full proportion of the annual charges."[3]

In 1671 the General Court judged meet "upon weighty reasons," to increase the fine upon towns failing to keep a gram-

---

[1] *Rec.*, IV, Pt. II, 434–5.   [2] *Ibid.*, IV, Pt. II, 455–6.
[3] *Ibid.*, IV, Pt. II, 457–8.

mar school according to law from £8 to £10.[1]   In 1683 the school law was again amended. It was provided that every town of more than 500 families or householders should set up and maintain two grammar schools and two writing schools, and in towns of 200 families, where the school law was not observed, the fine was increased from £10 to £20.[2]

King William's charter of 1691 to the Massachusetts Bay confirmed all lawful grants which had previously been made, to all persons and corporate bodies, towns, villages, colleges and schools.[3]

Chapter 26 of the laws passed by the first Provincial Assembly was " an act for the settlement and support of ministers and schoolmasters."   It reënacted that every town of the number of fifty householders or upwards should " be constantly provided of a schoolmaster to teach children and youth to read and write;" and that every town of one hundred families should set up a grammar school and procure for it a " discreet person of good conversation, well instructed in the tongues." The selectmen[4] and inhabitants of every town were directed to " take effectual care and make due provision for the settlement and maintenance of such schoolmasters and masters," all contracts made with them to continue valid for the time agreed upon.   Failure to observe this act involved a fine of ten pounds upon complaint made to the justices in quarter sessions, to be paid towards the support of the school or schools, within the

---

[1] *Rec.*, IV, Pt. II, 486.   [2] *Ibid.*, V, 414–5.

[3] *Acts and Resolves*, I, 9–10. " In 1694 the General Assembly passed an act which gave school trustees and others full control over their property, under the title of " an act to enable towns, villages and proprietors in common and divided lands, etc., to sue and be sued." (*Ibid.*, I, 182–3.)

[4] By Section 6 of Chapter 28, "an act for regulating of townships, choice of town officers, and setting forth their power," selectmen were empowered to assess the inhabitants of the towns for the charges of the ministry, the schools and the poor according to the agreement of the major part of the inhabitants in town meeting, and the constables of the towns were empowered to levy and collect such assessments, and to make distress upon all those refusing payment. (*Ibid*, I, 66.)

same county as the defective town, at the discretion of the magistrate. This fine was to be levied by warrant from the court of sessions upon the inhabitants of the defective towns "as other public charges," and to be paid into the county treasurer."[1]

At this same session grammar school masters were exempted from poll taxes.[2] The following year "professed schoolmasters" were freed from military service.[3] In 1699, grammar schoolmasters were also exempted from watch and ward and from taxes on their personal estate.[4]

In the general excise law that was passed in May, 1700, it was provided that of the fine of £4 for breaking the law, one-half was to go to the informer, and the other half to the support of the grammar or writing school or schools of the town in which the offence should be committed, or in the absence of a school in such town, then to the school in the adjacent town.[5] This act was renewed in 1701, and again in 1703.[6]

On June 28, 1701, the legislature passed an act in addition to an act for the settlement and support of schools and schoolmasters. The additional act is necessary, according to the preamble, because the observance of the former, " wholesome and necessary law is shamefully neglected by divers towns, and the penalty therefore not required, tending greatly to the nourishing of ignorance and irreligion, whereof grievous complaint is made." Therefore it is " enacted and declared by the Lieutenant-Governor, Council and Representatives in General Court assembled, and by the authority of the same, that the penalty or forfeiture for non-observance of the said law shall henceforth be twenty pounds per annum, and so proportionably for a lesser time that any town shall be without such settled schoolmaster respectively, to be recovered, paid and employed in manner and to the use as by the law is directed; any law, usage or custom to the contrary notwithstanding. Every grammar

---

[1] *Ibid.*, I, 62–3. [2] *Ibid.*, I, 29. [3] *Ibid.*, I, 130.

[4] *Ibid.*, I, 382, 416. [5] *Ibid.*, I, 435. [6] *Ibid.*, I, 477, 478, 528–9.

schoolmaster to be approved by the minister of the town, and the ministers of the two next adjacent towns, or any two of them by certificate under their hands. And be it further enacted, that no minister of any town shall be deemed, held or accepted to be the schoolmaster of such town within the intent of the law. And the justices of the peace in each respective county are hereby directed to take effectual care that the laws respecting schools and schoolmasters be duely observed and put in execution ; and all grand jurors, within their respective counties, shall diligently inquire and make presentment of all breaches and neglect of the said laws, that so due proscution may be made against the offenders."[1]

In 1703, fines of 40 s. incurred by failure of tax assessors to enforce the law were ordered to be paid over one-half to the informer, and one-half to the support of the schoolmaster of the town. In case there was no schoolmaster in the town, then the money was to go to the next grammar schoolmaster in the county.[1]

Towards the close of Queen Anne's war strenuous efforts were made in the colony towards checking the demoralization natural to a prolonged period of warfare. Chapter 6 of the laws passed at the spring session of 1712, was "An Act against intemperance, immorality and prophaneness, and for reformation of manners." Sections 16, 17 and 18 bear upon education.

[Section XVI.] " And for as much as the well educating and instructing of children and youth in families and schools are a necessary means to propagate religion and good manners ; and the conversation and example of heads of families and schools having great influence on those under their care and government to an imitation thereof:"

[Section XVII.] " Be it enacted by the authority aforesaid, that no person or persons shall or may presume to set up or keep a school for the teaching and instructing of children or youth in reading, writing, or any other science, but such as are of sober and good conversation, and have the allowance and approbation of the selectmen of the town in which any such school is to be kept; grammar schoolmasters to have approbation as the law in such case already provides."

[Section XVIII.] " And if any person or persons, after publication of this act, shall be so hardy as to set up or continue to keep any such school, without allowance and approbation as aforesaid, the person or persons so offending shall forfeit and pay the sum of forty shillings to the use of the poor of the town where such school shall be set up or continued to be kept, contrary to this act; and so, *toties quoties*, as often as they shall be convicted, any law, usage or custom to the contrary notwithstanding."[1]

Six years later the school law itself was made more stringent by " An Act in addition to the several acts for settlement and support of schoolmasters.

" Whereas, notwithstanding the many good and wholesome laws of this province for the encouraging of schools, and the penalty, first of ten pounds, and afterwards increased to twenty pounds, on such towns as are obliged to have a grammar schoolmaster, and neglect the same; yet by sad experience it is found that many towns that not only are obliged by law, but are very able to support a grammar school, yet chose rather to incur and pay the fine or penalty than maintain a grammar school,

" Be it enacted by his excellency the Governor, Council and Representatives in General Court assembled, and by the authority of the same, that the penalty or forfeiture for non-observance of the said law henceforth shall be thirty pounds on every town that shall have the number of one hundred and fifty families, and forty pounds on every town that shall have the numbumber of two hundred families, and so, *pro rata*, in case the town consist of two hundred and fifty or three hundred fami-

---

[1] *Ibid.*, I, 681-2.

lies, to be recovered, paid and employed in manner and to the use as by the law is directed; any law, usage or custom to the contrary notwithstanding."[1]

Laxness of school regulations does not seem to have been checked by increasing severity in the school law. Sections 5 and 6 of an act passed in 1735 for employing and providing for the poor of the town of Boston are proof of this condition.

[Section V.] "And forasmuch as there is great negligence in sundry persons as to the instructing and educating their children, to the great scandal of the Christian name, and of dangerous consequence to the rising generation:

[Section VI.] "Be it further enacted that where persons bring up their children in such gross ignorance that they do not know or are not able to distinguish the alphabet or twenty-four letters, at the age of six years, in such case, the overseers of the poor are hereby empowered and directed to put or bind out into good families such children, for a decent and Christian education, as when parents are indigent and rated nothing to the public taxes, unless the children are judged incapable, through some inevitable infirmity."[2]

In 1759 the legislature granted a petition of the inhabitants of the West Wing of Rutland, in the county of Worcester, to be incorporated into a precinct, and the inhabitants were empowered, among other privileges, to "appoint and pay" a schoolmaster for the instruction of their children.[3] Nine years later a general law was passed for precinct schools.

"An Act in further addition to the several Acts for the settlement and support of schools and schoolmasters.

"Whereas, it may happen that where towns or districts consist of several precincts, some such precincts may be disposed to expend more for the instruction of children and youth, in useful learning, within their own bounds, than, as parts of such towns or districts, they are, by law, held to do, and no provision has hitherto been made to enable precincts to raise money

---

[1] *Ibid.*, II, 100.   [2] *Ibid.*, II, 757-8.   [3] *Ibid.*, IV, 174.

for that purpose; and whereas, the encouragement of learning tends to the promotion of religion and good morals, and the establishment of liberty, civil and religious:

" Be it therefore enacted by the Governor, Council and House of Representatives, that when and so often as the major part of the inhabitants of any precinct, at their annual meeting legallly warned, shall agree on the building, finishing or repairing of any school house, or the defraying any other charge for the support of schools and schoolmasters, and shall also agree on any sum or sums of money for such purpose or purposes, the assessors of such precinct are hereby empowered and required to assess the same on the polls and estates within the said precinct; and all such rates or assessments shall be paid to the constable or collector to whom the same shall be committed, with a warrant from said assessors in form as by law is prescribed for collecting of town assessments ; and every constable or collector to whom any such rates or assessments shall be committed, with a warrant as aforesaid, shall levy, gather and receive the same, according to the direction in the warrant to him given, and shall account for all such sums as he shall so receive, and make payment of the same to the treasurer of such precinct or other receiver, as, by his warrant, he shall be required ; and be subject to the pains and penalties, in case of neglect, as is by law provided in the several acts of this province, respecting the levying and collecting of other precinct assessments.

This act to continue and be in force until July, one thousand seven hundred and seventy, and no longer.

Passed February 26 ; published March 5, 1768."[1]

INDIAN EDUCATION.

In a letter written on February 16, 1629, by Mr. Matthew Craddock, Governor of the Massachusetts Company in England, to Mr. John Endicott in New England, the colonists are

---

[1] *Ibid.*, IV, 988.

urged not to be "unmindful of the main end" of their plantation, "by endeavoring to bring the Indians to a knowledge of
the gospel." They are further instructed to "get some of
their children to train up to reading, and consequently to
religion, while they are young."[1]   In this earnest purpose to
educate and convert the natives, the Company remained stead-
fast; but the General Court appears to have delegated the work
to the commissioners of the United Colonies, to the corporation of Harvard College, and to individual effort.   Through
the influence of the agent of the United Colonies in England,
the "Society for Propagating the Gospel in New England"
was incorporated by act of Parliament in 1649.   The society
contributed to the education of Indian youths at Harvard.[2]   It
may have been noted that the college charter of 1650 provided
for the training of Indian as well as English youth.   The report made by the colony secretary in answer to the enquiries
of the royal commissioners in 1665, is suggestive of the general
relation of the government to the education of their Indian
neighbors.

"Concerning the civilizing and instructing the Indians in
the knowledge of God and humane learning, there is a small
college or fabric of brick erected in Cambridge, peculiarly appropriated to the Indians, which was built on the account and
by order of the corporation.   There are eight Indian youths,
one whereof is in the College and ready to commence bachelor
of art, . . . and at other schools, some ready to come into
the College, all of which have been and are maintained on the
state's account and charge.   There are six towns of Indians
within this jurisdiction who profess the Christian religion, who
have lands and townships set forth and appropriated to them
by this Court; there are also persons appointed to govern and

---

[1] *Mass. Col. Rec.*, I, 384.

[2] *English Institutions and the American Indian*, pp. 53-4.   James A. James,
Ph. D.   Johns Hopkin's University Studies, Baltimore, 1894.

instruct them in civility and religion.[1] . . . They have schools to teach their youth to read and write in several of their towns, and many of their youth and elder persons can read and write."[2]

In 1727 we find the general Court directly promoting a special case of Indian education. The title to a certain tract of land which a body of settlers had bought from the Indians of Hassanico was confirmed by the Court upon condition that within three years a meeting house and school house should be built in the settlement, the latter to be for the use of Indian as well as English children, and that a minister and schoolmaster should be always maintained in the place for the benefit of the Indians and their children.[3]

In 1762 the legislature passed an act " to incorporate certain persons by the name of the society for propagating Christian knowledge among the Indians of North America." The act was disallowed by the Privy Council in the following year on the grounds that although the corporation consisted only of inhabitants of Massachusetts, its power extended beyond the province, and that this extensive control might interfere with the King's management of Indian affairs in America.[4]

---

[1] In 1646 the Court ordered two ministers to be chosen yearly by the elders of the churches to " gospelize " the Indians. (*Rec.*, III, 100.) The following year the establishment of a court for Indians was ordered. Fines imposed at this court were to go to the "building of some meeting-house, or education of their poorer children in learning or other public use." At this time a gratuity of £10 was given by the Court to Mr. Eliott in recognition of his work among "the praying Indians." (*Ibid.*, III, 106.)

[2] *Ibid.*, IV, Pt. II, 198–9.

[3] *Acts and Resolves*, II, 466.   [4] *Ibid.*, IV, 520–3.

CONNECTICUT

CONNECTICUT was settled between 1634 and 1638 by immigrants from Massachusetts and from England. Two groups of settlements were made, the one on the Connecticut River, the other along the sea coast. It will be well to consider separately the educational histories of these two groups of towns.

In 1634 and 1635, colonists from Newtown, Watertown and Dorchester moved westwards and founded the towns of Hartford, Wethersfield and Windsor.[1] Four years later the freemen of these towns met together at Hartford and adopted a general constitution of government. It was provided that the admitted inhabitants of each town were to choose annually four deputies to the General Court. Each spring there was to be a Court of Election, at which a governor and six magistrates were to be chosen by the whole body of freemen. The deputies were to attend this Court, and after the elections, other public business could be transacted. In September of every year the General Court, consisting of governor, magistrates and deputies, was to meet to make and repeal laws, to grant levies, to admit freemen, to dispose of unappropriated lands to towns or persons, to try magistrates and private persons and to deal with any matters concerning the good of the Commonwealth.[2]

The first educational project which this Court conceived of as affecting the good of the Commonwealth, resulted from the

[1] Saybrook was also settled at this time, but was not united with the other river towns until 1644.

[2] *The Public Records of the Colony of Connecticut*, I, 20–25. Compiled by J. Hammond Trumbull, Hartford, 1850.

recommendation of the Commissioners of the United Colonies in September, 1644, that a general contribution in kind should be made throughout the colonies for the benefit of Harvard College in Cambridge.[1]

At a General Court, held at Hartford, October 25, 1644,

" The propositions concerning the maintenance of scholars at Cambridge, made by the said Commissioners is confirmed, and it is ordered that two men shall be appointed in every town with in this jurisdiction, who shall demand what every family will give, and the same to be gathered and brought into some room, in March ; and this to continue yearly as it shall be considered by the Commissioners. The persons to demand what will be given are,

" For Hartford, Nathaniell Waird and Ed. Stebbing.

(to gather it, Rich. Fellowes, Tho. Woodford.)

" For Windsor, Will. Gaylard, Henry Clarke.

" For Wethersfield, Mr. Trott, Mr. Wells.

" For Stratford, Will. Judson, Jo. Hurd.

" For Uncowaue, Jehue Burre, Ephraim Wheeler.

" For Southampton, Mr. More and Robert Band."[2]

Eighteen months later, the Court " recommended to the several towns seasonably to attend the collection for the College, and send it thither in convenient time."[3]

This provision concerning " college corn " was incorporated in the code of laws[4] which was adopted by the colony in 1650.[5] The code of 1650 contained two other educational enactments.

---

[1] *Acts of the Commissioners of the United Colonies of New England,* vol. I, pp. 20-21. In *Plymouth Col. Rec.,* vol. IV. Edited by David Pulsifer. Boston, 1859.

[2] *Conn. Col. Rec.,* I, 112.

[3] *Ibid.,* I, 139.

[4] This code was drawn up by Roger Ludlow, who had served at different times as magistrate, deputy governor and United Colonies' commissioner.

[5] *Ibid.,* I, 555.

" CHILDREN

" Forasmuch as the good education of children is of singular behalf and benefit to any commonwealth, and whereas many parents and masters are too indulgent and negligent of their duty in that kind; it is therefore ordered by this Court and authority thereof, that the selectmen of every town,[1] in the several precincts and quarters where they dwell, shall have a vigilant eye over their brethren and neighbors, to see first, that none of them shall suffer so much barbarism in any of their families as not to endeavor to teach by themselves or others their children and apprentices so much learning as may enable them perfectly to read the English tongue and knowledge of the capital laws, upon penalty of twenty shillings for each neglect therein;[2] also, that all masters of families do once a week at least, catechise their children and servants in the grounds and principles of religion; and if any be unable to do so much, that then, at the least, they procure such children or apprentices to learn some short orthodox catechism, without book, that they may be able to answer to the questions that shall be propounded to them out of such catechisms by their parents or masters or any of the selectmen, when they shall call them to a trial of what they have learned in this kind.[3] And further, that all parents and masters do breed

---

[1] On October 10, 1639, the General Court had incorporated the several towns in the colony, giving them power " to dispose of their own lands undisposed of . . . to choose their own officers, and make such orders as may be for the well ordering of their own towns, being not repugnant to any law " established by the General Court; and " to choose but 3, 5 or 7 of their chief inhabitants " to meet together once every two months as a court of judicature. (*Ibid.*, I, 36–37.)

[2] In the revision of the laws in 1702, the law entitled " An Act for educating of children " provides that the grand jurymen in each town, as well as the selectmen, should be " very careful in seeing the education of children duly performed ;" and grand jurymen and selectmen, as well as parents and masters, were to be fined 20s. for neglecting this law by any one assistant or justice of the peace. The fines were to go to the town poor. (*Acts and Laws of Connecticut*, p. 16. New London, 1715. This revision is a copy of the revision of 1702.)

[3] In May, 1676, the Court " solemnly recommend " the ministry to look into the

and bring up their children and apprentices in some honest lawful labor or employment, either in husbandry, or some other trade profitable for themselves and the commonwealth, if they will not nor cannot train them up in learning to fit them for higher employments. And if any of the selectmen, after admonition by them given to such masters of families, shall find them still negligent of their duty in the particulars aforementioned, whereby children and servants become rude, stubborn and unruly, the said selectmen with the help of two magistrates shall take such children or apprentices from them, and place them with some masters for years, boys till they come to twenty-one and girls to eighteen years of age complete, which will more strictly look unto, and force them to submit unto government, according to the rules of this order, if by fair means and former instructions they will not be drawn unto it." [1]

" SCHOOLS

" It being one chief project of that old deluder Satan, to keep men from the knowledge of the Scriptures, as in former times keeping them in an unknown tongue, so in these later times by persuading them from the use of tongues, so that at least the true sense and meaning of the original might be clouded with false glosses of saint-seeming deceivers ; and that learning may not be buried in the grave of our forefathers, in Church and commonwealth, the Lord assisting our endeavors, —It is therefore ordered by this Court and authority thereof, that every township within this jurisdiction, after the Lord hath

state of religious instruction in families and " the townsmen are to . . . assist the ministry for the reformation and education of the children in good literature and the knowledge of the Scripture," according to law. (*Conn. Col. Rec.*, II, 281.) In May, 1680, the Court urges the ministers to catechise young people under twenty in some orthodox catechism on the Sabbath days. (*Rec.*, III, 65. See also *Ibid.*, III, 148.)

[1] *Ibid.*, I, 520–1.

increased them to the number of fifty house holders, shall then forthwith appoint one within their town to teach all such children as shall resort to him, to write and read, whose wages shall be paid either by the parents or masters of such children, or by the inhabitants in general by way of supply, as the major part of those who order the prudentials of the town shall appoint; provided that those who send their children, be not oppressed by more than they can have them taught for in other towns. And it is further ordered, that where any town shall increase to the number of one hundred families or house holders, they shall set up a grammar school, the masters thereof being able to instruct youths so far as they may be fitted for the University. And if any town neglect the performance hereof above one year, then every such town shall pay five pounds per annum, to the next such school, till they shall perform this order." [1]

---

[1] *Ibid.*, I, 554–5. In 1642, Hartford appropriated £30 a year for a town school. In this school tuition fees were 20s. a year or 6d. per week, and those not able to pay were supported at town charge. In 1648, provision for a school house was made. (*The History of Education in Connecticut*, pp. 16–17, and foot-note 9, p. 16. Bernard C. Steiner, A. M. Bureau of Education, Circular of Information, No. 2, 1893.)

The records of the town of Windsor previous to the year 1650 are not extant. In February, 1656–7, the town voted that one Branker should have £5 paid to him out of the next town rate toward his maintenance of a school. In 1666–7 the first school house was built. (*The History and Genealogies of Ancient Windsor*, I, 398. Henry R. Stiles, A. M., M. D., Hartford, 1891.)

There is no record of school provision in Wethersfield previous to the year 1658. In that year a schoolmaster's salary was set at £25 per annum, each child to pay 8s. for tuition and the town to pay the balance. (*The River Towns of Connecticut*, p. 115. Charles M. Andrews. Published in Johns Hopkins University Studies, Baltimore, 1889.)

In 1650, the town of Stratford agreed "to give £36 by the year to a schoolmaster, the town to bear one-half and the parents of the children the other half." (*Town Rec.*, quoted in *History of the old town of Stratford and the city of Bridgeport, Connecticut*, I, 159. Rev. Samuel Orcutt. Published 1886.)

The town of Farmington was not incorporated until 1645, and there seems to be no record of an established school or schoolmaster prior to 1650. (See *History*

In 1647 President Dunster of Harvard College laid before the commissioners of the United Colonies a plan for a more regular contribution from the colonies that had hitherto been managed. He suggested the founding of scholarships of £8 per annum and fellowships of £16 per annum. The commissioners refused to make any special requisitions upon the respective colonies, but promised " to promote the contributions according to the former propositions."[1] President Dunster's suggestion, however, seems to have been acted upon in part by Connecticut, for on November 23, 1653, the Court " agrees and concludes that the £20 formerly[2] granted to a fellowship in Harvard College, shall be paid next spring."[3]

In 1637 a number of colonists from Yorkshire, Hertford-shire and Kent arrived in Boston Harbor and from there set forth during the two following years to plant settlements in Connecticut. They founded the towns of New Haven, Milford and Guilford. In 1643 these towns agreed upon a constitution for a general jurisdiction. It was agreed that all the free burgesses of the towns, i. e. church members, should, in person or by proxy, elect the Governor, Deputy Governor, Magistrates, Treasurer, Secretary and Marshall of the jurisdiction; and that two courts of Magistrates and two general courts consisting of Governor, Deputy Governor, Magistrates and Deputies—two Deputies from each town—should be held

---

of New Britain, with sketches of Farmington and Berlin, Connecticut, pp. 212–214. David N. Camp, A. M., New Britain, 1889.)

In 1654, the number of rateable persons in these towns was distributed as follows: (Conn. Col. Rec., I, 265.)

Towns.	Persons.	Towns.	Persons.
Hartford	177	Saybrook	53
Windsor	165	Stratford	74
Wethersfield	113	Farmington	46
Fairfield	94		

[1] Acts of Commissioners, I, 94–95, 96.

[2] There is no record of this former grant.

[3] Conn. Col. Rec., I, 250.

every year at New Haven. The General Court was to " with all care and diligence provide for the maintenance of the purity of religion and * * * suppress the contrary, according to their best light from the word of God, and all wholesome and sound advice which shall be given by the Elders and churches in the jurisdiction, so far as may concern their civil power to deal therein." [1]   The Court was also to make and repeal laws and to require their execution, " to settle and levy rates and contributions upon all the several plantations, for the public service of the jurisdiction," [2] and to act as a final court of appeals.

In addition to this constitution of government, certain general laws were adopted by the jurisdiction during the next few years, which were collected and digested about 1648 or 1649, revised in 1655 and published in 1656. [3]   In this code occurs the following provision:

" CHILDREN[S'] EDUCATION

" Whereas too many parents and masters, either through an over-tender respect to their own occasions and business, or not duly considering the good of their children and apprentices, have too much neglected duty in their education while they are young and capable of learning, it is ordered that the deputies for the particular court, in each plantation within this jurisdiction for the time being, or where there are no such deputies, the constable or other officer or officers in public

---

[1] *Records of the Colony and Plantation of New Haven*, p. 115. Edited by Charles J. Hoadley, M. A. Hartford, 1857.

[2] *Ibid.*

[3] *Records of the Colony or Jurisdiction of New Haven*. Preface, p. IV. Edited by Charles J. Hoadley, M. A. Hartford, 1858.

[4] Governor Eaton had been requested by the Court to make this compilation. In 1655, the Court " further desired the Governor to send for one of the new book of laws in the Massachusetts colony, and to view over a small book of laws newly come from New England which is said to be Mr. Cotton's, and to add to what is already done as he shall think fit." (*Ibid.*, pp. 146-7.)

trust, shall from time to time, have a vigilant eye over their brethren and neighbors within the limit of the said plantation, that all parents and masters do duly endeavor, either by their own ability and labor, or by improving such school masters or other helps and means as the plantation doth afford, or the family may conveniently provide, that all their children and apprentices, as they grow capable, may, through God's blessing, attain at least so much as to be able duly to read the Scriptures and other good and profitable printed books in the English tongue, being their native language, and in some competent measure to understand the main grounds and principles of Christian religion necessary to salvation, and to give a due answer to such plain and ordinary questions as may by the said deputies, officers or others, be propounded concerning the same. And where such deputies or officers, whether by information or examination, shall find any parent or master, one or more, negligent, he or they shall first give warning, and if thereupon due reformation follow, if the said parents or masters shall thenceforth seriously and constantly apply themselves to their duty in manner before expressed, the former neglect may be passed by; but if not, then the said deputies or other officer or officers, shall three months after such warning, present each such negligent person or persons to the next plantation court, where every such delinquent, upon proof, shall be fined ten shillings to the plantation, to be levied as other fines. And if in any plantation there be no such court kept for the present, in such case the constable or other officer or officers warning such person or persons before the freemen, or so many of them as upon notice shall meet together, and proving the neglect after warning, shall have power to levy the fines as aforesaid. But if, in three months after, there be no due care taken and continued for the education of such children or apprentices as aforesaid, the delinquent (without any further private warning) shall be be proceeded against as before, but the fine doubled. And lastly, if after the said warning, and fines paid or levied, the said deputies, officer or officers shall still find a continuance of the former negligence, if it be not obstinacy, so that such children or servants may be in danger to grow barbarous, rude and stubborn, through ignorance, they shall give due and reasonable notice.   That every such parent or master be summoned to the next court of magistrates, who are to proceed as they find cause, either to a greater fine, taking security for due conformity to the scope and intent of this law, or may take such children or apprentices from such parents or masters, and place them for years, boys till they come to the age of one and twenty, and girls till they come to the age of eighteen years, with such others who shall better educate and govern them, both for public conveniency, and for the particular good of the said children or apprentices."[1]

The first reference to the subject of higher education, which is recorded in the proceedings of the jurisdiction court[2] oc-

---

[1] *Ibid.*, pp. 583–4.

[2] The records of this General Court for the Jurisdiction between the years 1644 and 1653 are lost.   From the records of the town court of New Haven for this period it may be inferred, however, that the Jurisdiction Court took similar measures concerning the "college corn" as were taken by the General Court of Connecticut.   In 1645, at a Court in New Haven, "a proposition made to the commissioners at Hartford, August, 1644, by Mr. Sheppard, pastor of the church at Cambridge in the Bay, for a free contribution out of these parts of a peck of wheat or the value of it of every person whose part is willing for an increase of maintenance to the college there begun, that children (to what colony soever they belong), being fit for learning, but their parents not able to bear the whole charge, might the better be trained up for public service, was considered and fully approved, and Mr. Atwater and Goodman Davis were intreated for that first year to receive and collect it that it may be sent accordingly."   (*Rec. of Col. and Plantation*, p. 210.) Accordingly the following year, the Treasurer reported that he had sent 40 bushels of wheat to the College by Goodman Codman, "although he had not received so much."   (*Ibid.*, p. 225.)   At the same Court " it was propounded that the free gift of corn to the College might be continued as it was the last year, and it was granted."   (*Ibid.*)   And Brother Abraham Bell and Brother Matthew Camfield were chosen collectors for the current year.   Wampum was allowed to be paid by those that had not corn to pay in, and 2 or 3 months time was allowed for men to

curred in the year 1655. On May 30 of that year, Governor Eaton " remembered the Court of some purposes which have formerly been to set up a college at New Haven, and informed them that now again the motion is revived,[1] and that the deputies might be prepared to speak to it, letters were sent to the

bring it in to the collectors. (*Ibid.*, pp. 225-6.) In 1647, " the Governor propounded that the college corn might be forthwith paid, and that considering the work is a service to Christ, to bring up young plants for his service, and besides it will be a reproach that it shall be said New Haven is fallen off from this service." (*Ibid.*, pp. 311-312.)

[1] On March 23, 1647, the town court of New Haven appointed a committee to dispose of certain town lots and " to consider and reserve what lot they shall see meet and most commodious for a college, which they desire may be set up so soon as their ability will reach thereunto." (*Rec. of Col. and Plantation*, p. 376.)

In the records of the town of Guilford for 1652, it is noted that "the matter about a college at New Haven was thought to be too great a charge for us of this Jurisdiction to undergo alone, especially considering the unsettled state of New Haven town, being publicly declared from the deliberate judgment of the most understanding men to be a place of no comfortable subsistence for the present inhabitants there. But if Connecticut do join, the planters are generally willing to bear their just proportion for erecting and maintaining a college there, however they desire thanks to Mr. Goodyear [Deputy Governor] for his kind proffer to the setting forward of such work." (Given in Steiner's History of Education in Connecticut, p. 19.)

On May 22, 1654, the town of New Haven " was informed that there is some motion again on foot concerning the setting up of a college here at New Haven, which, if attained, will in all likelihood prove very beneficial to this place, but now it is only propounded to know the town's mind and whether they are willing to further the work by bearing a meet proportion of charge, if the Jurisdiction, upon the proposal thereof, shall see cause to carry it on. No man objected, but all seemed willing, provided that the pay which they can raise here will do it. (*Town Rec.*, II, 151, given in *Rec. of Col. or Jurisdiction*, p. 141, foot-note.)

The next year, on May 21st, 1655, the subject is revived in town meeting, and because " in some respects this seems to be a season, some disturbances being at present at the college in the Bay, and it is now intended to be propounded to the General Court, therefore this town may declare what they will do by way of encouragement for the same, and it would be well if they herein give a good example to the other towns in the jurisdiction, being free in so good a work. Mr. Davenport and Mr. Hooke [assistants to Mr. Davenport] were both present upon this occasion, and spake much to encourage the work." (*Town Rec.*, II, 169, given in *Ibid.*)

plantations to inform them that it would now be propounded. He acquainted them also that New Haven have, in a free way of contribution, raised above three hundred pound to encourage the work, and now desired to know what the other towns will do. The magistrate and deputies from Milford declared that if the work might comfortably be carried on, their town would give one hundred pounds; but those from the other towns seemed not prepared, as not having taken a right course, and therefore desired further time to speak with their towns again and take the same course New Haven have done, and they will then return answer. And for a committee to receive these accounts and upon receipt of them to consider whether it be meet to carry on the work, and how, and whatever considerations and conclusions may be meet for the furtherance of it, they agree that each town choose some whom they will intrust therein and send them to New Haven upon Tuesday come fortnight, which will be the nineteenth of June, to meet in the afternoon, by whom also they promise to send the account, what their several towns will raise for the work; the major part of which committee meeting and the major part of them that meet agreeing, shall conclude what shall be done in this business."[1]

The following July, Governor Eaton[2] reported in a town meeting at New Haven, that about £240 had been promised for the college outside of New Haven. The town thereupon agreed to pay £60 a year for the president's salary and incidental expenses.[3]

[1] *Rec. of Col. or Jurisdiction*, pp. 141–2.

[2] Theophilus Eaton was the son of a minister at Stony Stratford, Oxfordshire. He became deputy governor of the East India Company. In 1637 he came out to New England with his pastor, the Rev. Mr. Davenport. He officiated for a short time as magistrate in Massachusetts, and from 1639 to 1657, the year of his death, he was governor of New Haven Colony. (*History of Connecticut*, I, 240. Benjamin Trumbull, D. D., Hartford, 1797.)

[3] The Founding of Yale College, p. 2. Franklin B. Dexter. *New Haven Historical Society Papers*, Vol. III. New Haven, 1882.

Here the project for a college came to a standstill. Two years later, however, the General Court renewed its activity in behalf of education, and on May 27, 1657, " it was propounded that the Court should think of some way to further the setting up of schools for the education of youth in each plantation, for though some do take care that way, yet some others neglect it, which the Court took into consideration, and seeing that New Haven [1] hath provided that a school master be maintained at the town's charge, and Milford hath made provision in a comfortable way, they desire the other towns [2] should follow their example, and therefore did now order, that in every plantation where a school is not already set up and maintained, forthwith endeavors shall be used that a schoolmaster be procured they may attend that work, and what salary shall be allowed unto such school master for his pains, one-third shall be paid by the town in general as other rates, the good education of children being of public concernment, and the other two-thirds by them who have the benefit thereof by the teaching of their children." [3]

In 1659 provision for a colony school was undertaken by the General Court. " The Court looking upon it as their great

[1] On February 25, 1642, New Haven orders " that a free school shall be set up in this town, and our pastor, Mr. Davenport, together with the magistrates shall consider what yearly allowance is meet to be given to it out of the common stock of the town, and also what rules and orders are meet to be observed in and about the same." (*Rec. of Col. and Plantation*, p. 62.) Four years later in a revision of certain orders of the town court, which was made in February, 1645, the following statement occurs: " For the better training up of youth in this town, that through God's blessing they may be fitted for public service hereafter, either in church or commonwealth, it is ordered, that a free school be set up. Ac cording to which order, twenty pounds a year was paid to Mr. Ezekiell Cheevers, the present schoolmaster, for two or three years at first, but that not proving a competent maintenance, in August, 1644, it was enlarged to thirty pounds a year and so continued." (*Ibid.*, p. 210. See also *The Republic of New Haven*, p. 68, and foot notes. Charles H. Levermore, Ph. D. Baltimore, 1886.)

[2] Guilford, Stamford, Branford.

[3] *Rec. of Col. or Jurisdiction*, pp. 219–220.

duty to establish some course that (through the blessing of God) learning may be promoted in the jurisdiction as a means for the fitting of instruments for public service in church and commonwealth, did order that £40 a year shall be paid by the treasurer for the furtherance of a grammar school for the use of the inhabitants of this jurisdiction, and that £8 more shall be disbursed by him for the procuring of books of Mr. Blinman [some time pastor of the church at New London] such as shall be approved by Mr. Davenport and Mr. Peirson [pastor of the church at Branford], as suitable for this work. The appointing of the place where this school shall be settled, the person or persons to be employed, the time of beginning, etc., is referred to the Governor, Deputy Governor, the magistrates and ministers settled in the jurisdiction, or so many of them as upon due notice shall meet to consider of this matter."[1]

At this meeting the Deputy Governor[2] and deputies of Guilford offered the house which formerly belonged to their minister " for the furtherance of this work," and declared " that they judged it reasonable that if the said school should be settled in any other place by those which are appointed to determine this question, that the like allowance should be made by that plantation where it falls, answerable to what by Guilford is now propounded."[3]

The next year the subject of a colony school was revived through the activity of the Rev. Mr. Davenport in procuring an endowment from Edward Hopkins[4] " for the furtherance of the work of Christ " in the colony.[5]

---

[1] *Rec. of Col. or Jurisdiction*, p. 301.

[2] William Leete of Guilford, Governor of Connecticut, 1676–1683.

[3] *Ibid.*, pp. 301–2.

[4] About 1655, Mr. Davenport had written to Edward Hopkins in England for aid for the projected college. Hopkins was a son-in-law of Governor Eaton, and was among the first settlers of New Haven. He was alternately Governor and Deputy Governor of Connecticut between 1643 and 1654. He died in England in 1657, and bequeathed all his American estate, about 1000 lbs., with the exception of certain legacies, to the interests of education. (Trumbull's History, I, 241–2; *Rec. of Col. or Jurisdiction*, pp. 370–372.)

[5] *Ibid.*, p. 370.

On May 30, 1660, Mr. Davenport delivered over to the court of magistrates his part in the trusteeship which had been confided to him, together with the late Governor Eaton and Captain Cullick and Mr. Goodwin,[1] of Hartford, for the advancement of learning in the colony. The charge was "thankfully accepted" by the magistrates,[2] and on June 4th Mr. Davenport presented the matter in General Court. He attached certain conditions to the government's acceptance of the bequest. The town of New Haven was to appropriate a town lot and the rent of the oyster shell field, "formerly separated and reserved for the use and benefit of a college," to the erection and yearly support of the college.[3]

The colony school was to open before the beginning of winter, and a schoolmaster was to be provided to teach Latin, Greek and Hebrew, "so far as shall be necessary to prepare them [the scholars] for the college." Moreover, if the Court settled this school in New Haven and contributed £100, over and above the £40 already promised, to the building of a school-house and library, the town was to appropriate to this common school part of the amount that it had formerly granted to the town school.

The governor, magistrates, elders and deputies were to "solemnly and together visit the grammar school once every year,—to examine the scholars' proficiency in learning," and a committee of church members, presided over by the governor, were to consult together in "emergent difficult cases" concerning the school and college.

The teaching elders were to make orders for the school and college, to be approved by the magistrates and ratified by the General Court,—Mr. Davenport himself to be consulted in emergencies and given a negative vote.

[1] The ruling elder of the church at Hartford.

[2] *Ibid.*, p. 356.

[3] Compare the donation of the town of Cambridge of 2 acres and 2/3 of an acre to Harvard College. Pierce's *Hist. of Harvard University*, p. 5, foot-note 3.

It is moreover stipulated "that parents will keep such of their sons constantly to learning in the schools, whom they intend to train up for public serviceableness, and that all their sons may learn, at the least to write and cast up accounts competently, and may make some entrance into the Latin tongue."

To the above propositions the Court responded as follows:

" The Court being deeply sensible of the small progress or efficiency in learning that hath yet been accomplished, in the way of more particular town schools, of later years in this colony, and of the great difficulty and charge to make pay, etc., for the maintaining children at the schools or colleges in the Bay, and that notwithstanding what this Court did order last year or formerly, nothing hath yet been done to attain the ends desired, upon which considerations and other like, this Court, for further encouragement of this work, doth now order, that over and above the £40 per annum, granted the last year for the end then declared, that £100 stock shall be duly paid in from the jurisdiction treasury, according to the manner and times agreed and expressed in the court records, giving and granting that special respect to our brethren at New Haven, to be first in embracing or refusing the Court's encouragement or provision for a school, whether to be settled at New Haven town or not; but if they shall refuse, Milford is to have the next choice, then Guilford, and so in order every other town on the main within the jurisdiction have their liberty to accept or refuse the Court's tender, yet it is most desired of all that New Haven would accept the business, as being a place most to advantage the well carrying on of the school, for the ends sought after and endeavored after thereby; but the college (after spoken of) is affixed to New Haven (if the Lord shall succeed that undertaking.) It is further agreed that all and every plantation who have any mind to accept the propositions about the school, shall prepare and send in their answer unto the

1 *Rec. of Col. or Jurisdiction*, pp. 372-4.

committee chosen (of all the magistrates and settled elders of this jurisdiction, to order, regulate and dispose all matters concerning the school, as the providing instruments and well carrying on of the business, from time to time as they shall judge best), before the 24 of June instant, that so if any plantation do accept, the committee may put forth their endeavors to settle the business; but if all refuse, then it must be suspended until another meeting of this General Court.

And for further encouragement of learning, and the good of posterity in that way, Mr. John Davenport, pastor of the church of Christ at New Haven, delivered up all his power and interest, as a trustee by Mr. Hopkins, for recovering and beetowing all that legacy given by him, for the end of furtherance to the settlement of a college at New Haven; . . . The General Court . . . accepted the trust and shall endeavor by God's help to get in the said estate and improve it to the end it was given for.[1] By way of further answer to what was propounded by Mr. Davenport in his writing presented, the Court declared that it was their desire that the colony school may begin at the time propounded, and to that end desire that endeavors may be put forth by the committee of magistrates and settled elders formerly appointed for the providing a schoolmaster, etc. and to whom also they leave it to appoint a steward or receiver, which steward or receiver they empower as is propounded, and to settle a committee from among themselves to issue emergent cases, and to take order that a chest be provided wherein the writings may be laid up that concern this business. The Court further declared that they do invest Mr. Davenport with the power of a negative vote, for the reason and in the cases according to the terms in his writing specified, and that they shall be ready to confirm such orders as shall be presented which in the judgement of the Court shall be conducible to the main end intended.

[1] The General Court of Connecticut laid a restraint upon Mr. Hopkins' estate which was not removed until March, 1664. (*Conn. Col. Rec.*, I, 578, foot note.)

It is ordered for the encouragement of such as shall diligently and constantly (to the satisfaction of the civil authority in each plantation) apply themselues to due use of means for the attainment of learning which may fit them for public service, that they shall be freed from payment of rates with respect to their persons; provided that if any such shall leave off or not constantly attend those studies, they shall then be liable to pay rates in all respects as other men are.

It is ordered that if the colony school shall begin at any time within the first half year from this court of election, that £40 shall be paid by the treasurer for this year, and if it shall begin at any time before the election next, that £20 shall be paid by the treasurer upon that account.

To the printed law concerning the education of children, it is now added, that the sons of all the inhabitants within this jurisdiction, shall (under the same penalty) be learned to write a legible hand so soon as they are capable of it." [1]

In accordance with the above orders, the school committee, consisting of the Governor, the Deputy Governor, Mr. Treat, Mr. Davenport and Mr. Street, successor to Mr. Hooke, magistrates and settled elders, met together on June 28, and "agreed that Mr. Peck, now at Guilford, should be schoolmaster, and that it should begin in October next, when his half year expires there; he is to keep the school, to teach the scholars Latin, Greek and Hebrew, and fit them for the college; and for the salary, he knows the allowance from the colony is £40 a year; and for further treaties, they must leave it to New Haven, where the school is; and for further orders concerning the school and well carrying it on, the elders will consider of some against the court of magistrates in October next, when things as there is cause, may be further considered." [2]

At a General Court in May, 1661, " sundry propositions" were presented by Mr. Peck, school-master: " 1. That the

[1] *Rec. of Col. or Jurisdiction*, pp. 374–6.
[2] *Ibid.*, p. 377.

master shall be assisted with the power and counsel of any of the honored magistrates or reverend elders, as he finds need or the case may require. 2. That Rectores scholæ be now appointed and established. 3. What is it the jurisdiction expects from the master, whether anything besides instruction in the languages and oratory? 4. That two indifferent men be appointed to prove and send to the master such scholars as be fitted for his tuition. 5. That two men be appointed to take care of the school, to repair and supply necessaries as the case may require. 6. Whether the master shall have the liberty to be at neighbors' meetings once every week. 7. Whether it may not be be permitted that the school may begin but at eight of the clock all the winter half year. 8. That the master shall have the liberty to use any books that do or shall belong to the school. 9. That the master shall have liberty to receive into and instruct in the school scholars sent from other places out of this jurisdiction, and that he shall receive the benefit of them, over and above what the jurisdiction doth pay him. 10. That the master may have a settled habitation not at his own charge. 11. That he shall have a week's vacation in the year to improve as the case may require. 12. That his person and estate shall be rate-free in every plantation of this jurisdiction. 13. That half the year's payment shall be made to, and accounts cleared with the master, within the compass of every half year. 14. That 40 li, alias forty pounds, per annum, be paid to the schoolmaster by the jurisdiction treasurer and that 10 li, alias ten pounds, per annum, be paid to him by New Haven treasurer. 15. That the major part of the aforesaid payments shall be made to the schoolmaster in these particulars as followeth, viz.: thirty bus. of wheat, two bbls. of pork, and two bbls. of beef, forty bus. of Indian corn, thirty bus. of pease, two firkins of butter, one hundred pounds of flax, thirty bus. of oats. Lastly, that the honored Court would be pleased to consider of, and settle these things, this court times, and to confirm the consequent of them, the want of which things, especially some of them, doth hold the master under discouragement and settlement; yet these things being suitably considered and confirmed, if it please the honored Court further to improve him who at present is schoolmaster, although unworthy of any such respect, and weak for such a work, yet his real intention is to give up himself to the work of a grammar school, as it shall please God to give opportunity and assistance.[1]

The Court considering of these things, did grant as followeth, viz.: to the second, they did desire and appoint Mr. J. Davenport, senior, Mr. Street and Mr. Pearson to take that care and trust upon them; to the third, they declared that besides that which he expressed, they expected he should teach them to write so far as was necessary to his work; to the fourth, they declared, that they left it to those before mentioned; to the eight, they declared that he should have the use of those books, provided a list of them be taken; and the ninth, they left to the committee for the school; and the rest they granted in general, except the pork and butter, and for that, they did order that he should have one barrel of pork and one firkin of butter provided by the jurisdiction treasurer, though it be with some loss to the jurisdiction, and that he should have wheat for the other barrel of pork. This being done Mr. Peck seemed to be very well satisfied."[2]

But Mr. Peck's school did not prosper in any high degree, for at a meeting of the committee for the colony school, on June 18, 1662, "the committee considering of the business left to them about the laying down or continuing of the colony school, after serious debate of the business, did this conclude, that finding not sufficient grounds of discouragement at present so as to lay it down, did leave it to go on for further trial, until the General Court should again meet, desiring that those who have any children fit to send, that they would send them

---

[1] *Ibid*, pp. 407–8.   [2] *Ibid.*, p, 408.

to it for the encouragement of the school."[1]   By the following
November the school committee decided to close the school
at the end of the month, "considering the distraction of the
time, that the end is not attained for which it was settled no
way proportionable to the charges expended, and that the
colony is in expectation of unavoidable necessary charges to
be expended."[2]   After hearing this report, the General Court
proposed that New Haven should pay back 40 lbs. of the 100
lbs. that had been granted out of the jurisdiction treasury to
the colony school, "but the deputies for New Haven told them
that the colony school had occasioned a considerable charge
to them about the school house and other ways more than else
they need have expended in that way, and that they was ready
still, if they would continue the school, to perform their condition to provide schoolhouse and house for school master, if
need require." ' Then "Mr. Peck propounded about some
difference between the treasurer and himself in making up their
accounts, but the Court left it to them to issue it between
themselves."   "It was also propounded about four lb. abated
of Mr. Peck's salary, for some time that he left the school,
whether it should not return to the jurisdiction. It being
debated, it was by vote concluded that so much of it as is
proper to them should, and the rest to New Haven."[3]

"The distraction of the time" referred to in the report of
the school committee was mainly the outcome of the controversy which the colony of New Haven had entered into with
the neighboring colony of Connecticut.   In 1661, Connecticut
petitioned Charles II. for a royal charter.   The charter which
the King granted to the colony on April 23, 1662, incorporated

----

[1] *Ibid.*, p. 458.   Two months later we find Mr. Davenport upbraiding the town
of New Haven because "the committee for the school made it a great objection
against the keeping of it up, that this town did not send scholars only five or six."
Steiner's Hist., p. 22.

[2] *Ibid.*, p. 471.

[3] *Ibid.*, p. 472.

all the freemen of Connecticut colony as a body politic by the name of the Governor and Company of the English colony of Connecticut in New England in America; it provided for two general assemblies in May and in October, to consist of a governor, deputy governor, 12 assistants and 2 deputies from every town or city; it authorized the company to elect officers, establish laws, impose fines and unite in military defence; and it granted the company all the territory between Narragansett Bay and the South Sea, *i. e.*, the Pacific Ocean.[1] As the settlement of New Haven was obviously included within this patent, measures were promptly taken by Connecticut to extend her control over that colony. Supported at first by the Commissioners of the United Colonies and stiffened by the intense opposition of the ecclesiastical party, under the leadership of Mr. Davenport, to conciliation with Connecticut, New Haven held out against the union for almost three years; but finally in December, 1664, on account of disaffection from within and pressure from without through the general alarm over Charles the Second's arbitrary treatment of New England, New Haven submitted to the authority of Connecticut, and in the following spring sent representatives to the General Court of that colony.

After the receipt of the royal charter, the General Court of Connecticut enacted that all previous laws and orders should continue in full force except those that might be " cross to the tenor " of the charter.[2]

In 1666 the enlarged jurisdiction of Connecticut was divided into 4 counties, and county courts were ordered to be held in the towns of Hartford, New London, New Haven and Fairfield.[3] In 1672, at a court of elections held at Hartford, 600 acres of land was granted by the Court to each of these county towns, " to be taken up where it may not prejudice any former

---

[1] *Connecticut Acts and Charter.* New London, 1718.
[2] *Conn. Col. Rec.*, I, 387.
[3] *Ibid..* II, 34–35.

grant; which said land shall be and belong to the said county towns forever,[1] to be improved in the best manner that may be for the benefit of a grammar school in the said county towns, and to no other use or end whatsoever."[2]   In this year a revision of the laws was made " out of the records of the General Court," " with some emendations and additions . . by the authority of the General Court."[3]   In this code under the title " Schools," the preamble and the provisions for elementary education are almost identical with those of the Connecticut code of 1650.[4]   The provision for secondary education reads as follows : " That in every county town there shall be set up and kept a grammar school, for the use of the county, the master thereof being able to instruct youths so far as they may be fitted for the college."[5]   The code of 1672 furthermore provides for the exemption of schoolmasters from poll taxes[6] and military service.[7]   They were also freed from highway summons.[8]   Five years later the school law was again amended.

" As an addition to the law title Schools, it is ordained that every town by the said law ordered to keep a school that shall neglect the same above three months in the year, shall forfeit

---

[1] In 1722, upon petition of the town of New London, the legislature granted permission for the sale of its school lands. (*Ibid.*, VI, 316.)

[2] *Ibid.*, II, 176. These land grants were not surveyed until 1702, when the General Court appointed committees for that purpose composed of residents of the respective towns. (*Ibid.*, IV, 402.) A committee was *appointed* as early as 1679 to survey the New London grant. (*Ibid.*, III, 29.)

[3] See title page of the Laws of 1672. Printed at Cambridge, 1673. Reprint Hartford, 1865.

[4] Under a sub-title " rebellious children and servants," this law furthermore provides that " whatsoever child or servant within this colony, upon complaint, shall be convicted of any stubborn or rebellious carriage against their parents or governors, the Governor or any two Assistants have liberty and power from this court to commit such person or persons to the House of Correction, there to remain under hard labor and severe punishment, so long as the Court or Assistants shall judge meet." (*Ibid.*, p. 14.)

[5] *Ibid.*, p. 63.   [6] *Ibid.*, p. 59.   [7] *Ibid.*, p. 49.   [8] *Ibid.*, p. 28.

five pounds for every defect, which said fine shall be paid towards the maintenance of the Latin school in their county. All breaches of this order to be taken notice of, and presented by the grand jury at every county court." [1]

" Whereas in the law title Schools it is ordered that every county town shall keep and maintain a Latin school in the said town, which is not fully attended in some places, to move, excite and stir up to the attendance of so wholesome an order, it is ordered by this Court that if any county town shall neglect to keep a Latin school according to order, there shall be paid a fine of ten pounds by the said county town to the next town in their county that will engage and keep a Latin school in it, and so ten pounds annually till they shall come up to the attendance of this order. The grand jury to make presentment of the breach of this order to the county court, of all such breaches as they shall find after September next. It is also ordered by this Court where schools are to be kept in any town, whether it be county town or other, what shall be necessary to the maintaining the charge of such schools, it shall be raised upon the inhabitants by way of rate, except any town shall agree upon some other way to raise the maintenance of him they shall employ in the aforesaid work, any order to the contrary notwithstanding." [2]

In 1678, towns of 30 families were required to keep a school " to teach children to read and write." [3] In this year the inhabitants of the village of Poquanock, on the outskirts of Fairfield, stated to the General Court that as they lived four miles distant from the centre of that town they had found it extremely difficult to send their children to the town school, and so had employed a schoolmaster for themselves. They petitioned to be free from the taxes for the Fairfield school, a request that had been refused to them by the town of Fairfield. The General Court recommended the request of

[1] *Conn. Col. Rec.*, II, 307–308.

[2] *Ibid.*, II, 312.　　　　　　　[3] *Ibid.*, III, 9.

Poquanock to the county court of Fairfield, and suggested furthermore that some of the county revenues might be spared towards the encouragement of the grammar school at Poquanock.[1] In October, 1684, the Court orders "for the encouragement of learning and promoting of public concernments . . . that for the future all such houses and lands as are or shall by any charitable persons be given or purchased for, or to help on the maintenance of the ministry, or schools, or poor, in any part of this colony, they shall remain to the use or uses for which they were given forever, and shall be exempted out of the list of estates, and be rate free, any former law or order notwithstanding."[2] In January, 1687, the Court orders a contingent surplus in the colonial treasury to be distributed among the county towns for the improvement of their grammar schools.[3]

In 1686 Sir Edmund Andros came to Boston as royal governor of New England, and at a General Court held at Hartford, October 31, 1687, he " took into his hands the government of this colony of Connecticut, it being by his Majesty annexed to the Massachusetts and other colonies under his excellency's government."[4] Two years later, after the accession of William and Mary to the English throne, the charter government of Connecticut was resumed and legislative activity speedily returned to its wonted channels. In 1690, at a court of election held at Hartford, the Court " observing that notwithstanding the former orders made for the erudition of children and servants, there are many persons unable to read the English tongue, and thereby uncapable to read the holy word of God, or the good laws of the colony, which evil, that it grow no farther upon their majesties' subjects here, it is hereby ordered that all parents and masters shall cause their respective children and servants, as they are capable, to be taught to read distinctly the English tongue, and that the grand jurymen in

---

[1] *Ibid.*, III, 8, foot-note.   [2] *Ibid.*, III, 158.
[3] *Ibid.*, III, 224-5.   [4] *Ibid.*, III, 248.

each town do once in the year at least, visit each family they suspect to neglect this order, and satisfy themselves whether all children under age and servants in such suspect families can read well the English tongue, or be in a good procedure to learn the same or not, and if they find any such children and servants not taught as their years are capable of, they shall return the names of the parents or masters of the said children so untaught, to the next county court, where the said parents or masters shall be fined twenty shillings for each child or servant whose teaching is or shall be neglected, contrary to this order, unless it shall appear to the satisfaction of the court, that the said neglect is not voluntary, but necessitated by the incapacity of the parent or master or their neighbors, to cause them to be taught as aforesaid, or the incapacity of the said children or servants to learn. This Court, considering the necessity and great advantage of good literature, do order and appoint that there shall be two free schools kept and maintained in this colony, for the teaching of all such children as shall come there, after they can first read the psalter, to teach such, reading, writing, arithmetic, the Latin and Greek tongues; —the one at Hartford, the other at New Haven, the masters whereof shall be chosen by the magistrates and ministers of the said county, and shall be inspected and again displaced by them if they see cause, and that each of the said masters shall have annually for the same the sum of sixty pounds in county pay, thirty pounds of it to be paid out [of the] country treasury, the other thirty to be paid in the school revenue given by particular persons,[1] or to be given to that use, so as it will ex-

---

[1] William Gibbons of Hartford died in 1655, and bequeathed about 30 acres of land in Wethersfield for a Latin school in Hartford. In 1660 John Talcott made a small bequest for the same purpose. (*Ibid.*, IV, 31 foot-note.) In 1664 Hartford received 350 lbs. of the Edward Hopkins bequest. Mr. Davenport paid over 10 lbs. per annum out of this estate to the so-called Hopkins Grammar School at New Haven, and in 1668 settled the capital, 412 lbs., in the hands of a self-perpetuating board of trustees. (*The Republic of New Haven*, pp. 162–3. Charles H. Levermore, Ph. D. Baltimore, 1886.)

tend, and the rest to be paid by the respective towns of Hartford and New Haven. This Court considering the necessity many parents or masters may be under to improve their children and servants in labor for a great part of the year, do order that if the town schools in the several towns, as distinct from the free school, be, according to law already established, kept up six months in each year to teach to read and write the English tongue, the said towns so keeping their respective schools six months in every year, shall not be presentable or fineable by law, for not having a school according to law, notwithstanding any former law or order to the contrary."[1] In 1691, Jehu Burr, deputy from Fairfield, introduced a bill providing that " for the increase and encouragement of good literature in the education of youth for public service and usefulness, . . there shall be two other grammar schools besides them already appointed, viz: one at Fairfield, and another at New London, for the ease and better advantage of the said two counties: and that for the future, the 60 lbs. payable out of the public treasury shall be paid as followeth, viz: 15 lbs. per annum to each of the said county towns that doth maintain a grammar school according to the true intent of this act, and the said 15 lbs. to be made 50 lbs. per annum to each of the said schools."[2] This bill was read twice in Court, but the Court at this time " did not see reason to make any alteration " in the established law.[3] Two years later, however, the Court did grant 20 lbs. apiece to the county schools of New London and Fairfield.[4]

In 1700, the legislature took further measures to insure the maintenance of the county and town schools. " Ordered, etc., That there shall be four grammar schools constantly kept at the four county towns of this colony, viz.: at Hartford, New Haven, New London, and Fairfield, and all other towns consisting of seventy families and upwards shall constantly keep up from year to year, a public and sufficient school for the

[1] *Ibid.*, IV, 30–31. [2] *Ibid.*, IV, 50, foot-note.
[3] *Ibid.*, IV, 50. [4] *Ibid.*, IV, 97.

teaching children to write and read. And that all towns within this colony of any number of families under seventy shall keep up yearly a public school, for the teaching to read and write for one-half of the year, these schools to be furnished with able and sufficient schoolmasters, according to law. And towards the maintenance of the schools respectively, it is ordered, that from the colony rates, as the country rates are paid by the treasurer, shall be yearly paid forty shillings upon every thousand pounds of the public list of persons and estates unto the several towns of this colony, and proportionably for lesser sums, for the use of their schools as aforesaid. And if any town shall be wanting of a sufficient and able school-master as aforesaid, then for the fine they shall not have the allowance as aforesaid, but the sum of the forty shillings upon the thousand pounds shall be paid to the public treasury; provided that one month's want shall not be any bar to them. And it is further ordered, that the forementioned sums for the use of the scoools, shall by the treasurer be added to the assessments of each town respectively in his order to the constables, and by the treasurer's order paid by the constables to the several schoolmasters; and when the above said allowance shall not be sufficient for the maintenance of the school there, a sufficient maintenance shall be made up of such estate as hath been bequeathed by any for that use, and for want thereof the one-half to be paid by the town, and the other by the children that go to school, unless any town agree otherwise. And all former orders respecting schools are hereby repealed.[1]

In 1702, the General Court enacted that the town constables should deliver the school tax, as provided for in the above law, "to the committees for the school in such towns where committees are, or in defect of such officers, to the selectmen of the town or their order."[2]

[1] *Ibid.,* IV, 331-2.

[2] *Ibid.,* IV, 375. In 1711, the Court, "upon consideration of the great back-

In 1712, the legislature passed an "act for encouragement of learning," which provided that the parishes, the new town divisions which were arising from growth in population and from congregational church quarrels, should have "to the bringing up of their children, and maintenance of a school in some fixed place within the bounds of their parish, the 40s. in every £1,000 arising on the list of estates within their said parish, any other law notwithstanding."[1]

In 1713, the General Court appointed five inhabitants of New London trustees of the estate which one Robert Bartlet had bequeathed to the town in 1673 for the use and encouragement of a school, and thereby relinquished all claim that the government might have against the land as escheated property. The trustees were ordered to improve the property for the use of a public Latin school according to the directions of the school committee or selectmen of the town, and, as the land lay in small parcels, the trustees were empowered to sell it with the consent of the town.[2]

In October, 1714, an act was passed "for the encouragement and better improvement of town schools." "Forasmuch as the upholding and good ordering of the schools erected in towns by order of this Assembly, and partly maintained out of the public treasury, is of great importance to the public weal, and the neglect thereof will be the occasion of much

wardness and neglect " . . . in paying this tax, ordered that for the preceding year and until it should be ordered otherwise, the school revenue should be paid directly by the Colony Treasurer to the school committees of the respective towns. (*Ibid.*, V, 213-14.) In 1723, a return was made to the prior method of payment by the town constables to the town committees (*Ibid.*, VI, 400); but in 1726, the Court having observed that this provision occasioned some difficulty in the audit, and that some money was or might be taken when no school was legally kept, the law of 1723 was repealed (*Ibid.*, VII, 40), and in 1728, payment by the Colony Treasurer to the school committees was again ordered. (*Ibid.*, VII, 178.)

[1] *Ibid.*, V, 353.

[2] *Ibid.*, V, 377-8. The following year the Court appointed a committee to survey Bartlet's land. (*Ibid.*, V, 454, also 498.)

ignorance, disorder and profaneness. Be it therefore ordered
and enacted by the Governor, Council and Representatives, in
General Court assembled, and by the authority of the same,
that the civil authority, together with the select men in every
town, or major part of them, shall inspect, and they are hereby
empowered, as visitors to inspect the state of all such schools
as are appointed in the said town from time to time, and particularly once in each quarter of the year, at such time as they
shall think proper to visit such schools, and inquire into the
qualifications of the masters of such schools, and their diligence in attending to the service of the said school, together
with the proficiency of the children under their care. And
they are hereby further required to give such directions as
they shall find needful to render such schools most serviceable
to the increase of that knowledge, civility and religion, which
is designed in the erecting of them. And it is further enacted,
that if, in this inspection of the said schools, the said inspectors
observe any such disorder, or misapplication of the public
money allowed to the support of such schools, as render the
said schools not so likely to attain the good ends proposed,
they shall lay the same before this Assembly, that the proper
orders in such cases necessary may be given." [1]

The above act was undoubtedly the outcome of the general
solicitude which was shown by the government about this time
concerning the state of religion and morality in the colony.
At the close of Queen Anne's war, in May, 1714, the legislature directed the colonial ministry to enquire whether there
was a "suitable" number of bibles in the families of the different parishes, and particularly whether catechising was duly
attended. [2] The report that was made by the general association of churches in October, 1715, was so discouraging that
the General Court opined that they were "fearful that there
hath been too great a neglect of a due execution of those good
laws already enacted . . . for the prevention of such decays

[1] *Ibid.*, V, 462.   [2] *Ibid.*, V, 436.

in religion." [1] It was then enacted " that the constables and grand jurymen in the respective towns in this colony shall make diligent search after, and presentment, of all breaches of the following laws of this colony :

First. An act entitled, Children to be educated." [2]

Two years later the school law was made more stringent by the following measures ;

" An Act in addition to the Law Concerning Schools.

Resolved by this Assembly, That every society or parish within the colony shall be obliged to keep a school ; where there are seventy families in any parish, the school shall be there kept at least eleven months in a year ; and where there is a less number of families, not less than half the year ; and the major part of the householders in any parish or society shall have full power to grant rates for the support of any such school, and choose a collector to gather said rates ; and what the major part of the householders in any parish shall enact and agree to, respecting the encouragement and support of the school amongst themselves, shall be obliging to the whole parish." [3]

" An Act for the Better Ordering and Regulating Parishes or Societies, and for their Supporting the Ministry and Schools there.

It is ordered by the Governor, Council and Representatives, in General Court assembled, and by the authority of the same, That the settled and approved inhabitants in each respective parish or society within this colony, shall annually meet together in December. And the said inhabitants thus met and convened together are hereby fully empowered by their major vote, to choose a clerk for their society and three or more discreet, able inhabitants to be a committee to order the affairs of the society for the year ensuing. And also the said inhabitants assembled as above, or the major part of them,

---

[1] *Ibid.*, V, 530.   [2] *Ibid.*, V, 531. See *Acts and Laws*, 1715, p. 16.
[3] *Conn. Col. Rec.*, V, 10.

shall have power to grant and levy such rates and taxes on the inhabitants for the advancing of such sum or sums of money for the support of the ministry and school there as the law directs, and to appoint a collector or collectors for gathering thereof, who are hereby ordered and empowered to proceed in collecting the same, according to the direction of the law to collectors chosen for gathering the town and minister's rates. And in case the collector or collectors shall not perform the trust hereby committed to him or them, he or they shall be accountable for such arrearages by him or them neglected to be gathered, to the committee of such society, who are empowered to demand or distrain for the same, according to the direction of said law."[1]

The following year, the General Court summarily proceeds to the enforcement of the foregoing law for the good of a society in Wethersfield. " Whereas, upon the petition of the inhabitants of the south part of Weathersfield, this Assembly did in May last appoint John Hamlin and Joseph Talcott, Esq,, and Mr. Izahiah Whetmore, a committee to inquire what limits might be most convenient for the bounds of a school precinct, and what place might be most proper to set up a school house there, for the accommodating that precinct, and to report the same to this Assembly, which they having done: This Assembly, for divers good causes, do now appoint the foresaid committee to go once more to said place, at the charge of said inhabitants, and do hereby fully empower said committee fully to determine both the bounds and limits of the precinct, and the place or places for erecting a school house or school houses there, according to their best discretion ; which said inhabitants shall be obliged to abide by, and to bear their rateable part of their charge of erecting such house or houses, and of maintaining a school master there, according to law, and according to the determination of said committee."[2]

In 1733, a committee which the legislature had appointed to

1 *Ibid.*, V, 33-34.   2 *Ibid.*, V, 83.

draw up a plan for the disposal of seven new townships [1] which had been laid out in the western part of the colony, suggested that the money raised by the sale of this land should be divided among the already settled towns " according to the list of their polls and rateable estate in the year last past, and to be secured and forever improved for the use of the schools kept in said towns according to law." The committee also advised that each of the seven towns should be divided into 53 shares, 50 shares to be offered for sale, and 3 shares to be set apart, one for the first settled minister, " one to be sequestered for the use of the present established ministry for ever, and one for the use of the school or schools in such towns forever." [2] This latter suggestion was acted upon by the legislature in an act passed in 1737 " for the ordering and directing the sale and settlement of all the townships in the western lands." [3] The first part of the report was embodied in " an act for the encouragement and better supporting the schools that by law ought to be kept in the several towns and parishes in this colony." This law furthermore provides that the appropriation shall be divided among the parishes of each town and that " the committee of each parish, or town (where there is but one parish), shall receive the proportion of money arising as aforesaid, and give a receipt (which receipts shall be delivered to the Secretary and kept in his office), that they have received such a sum of money to be let out and improved for the support of a school in such town or parish where they are a committee as aforesaid. And that if at any time the said money, or interest thereof, shall be, by order of such town or parish, or the committee chosen by them, put to, or employed for any other use than for the support of a school there, that then such sum of money shall be returned into the treasury of the colony, and the treasurer of the colony shall, upon refusal thereof, recover the same sum of such town or parish for the

---

[1] Norfolk, Goshen, Canaan, Cornwall, Kent, Salisbury, Sharon.

[2] *Ibid.*, VII, 457–8. [3] *Ibid.*, VIII, 134–5.

use of the colony; and such town or parish that have misimproved such money shall forever lose the benefit thereof." [1]

In this same year, the deputies of the town of New London represented to the legislature that the members of the major part of the committees which had been appointed in 1713 and in 1723 to attend respectively to the management of the Bartlet School estate and to the sale of the government grant of 600 acres for a grammar school had died, and the deputies therefore petitioned the legislature to fill the vacancies in the committees. Accordingly, the General Court appointed three New Londoners to join with the two surviving committee men in the management of both the affairs, and the town of New London was empowered to fill any future vacancies in the committee. The committee was also ordered to make its reports to the town. [2] The following year the school committee of Middletown reported to the General Court " that sundry well-disposed persons had granted several tracts of land for the benefit of a school in said Middletown," and prayed the Court " to appoint a committee to take care of all such lands, and improve the same, for the benefit of the school in said town." Whereupon the General Court appointed " Capt. Giles Hart, Capt. George Phillips and Mr. Jabez Hamlin, to be a committee to take care of and lease all such lands given as aforesaid, and to receive the rents thereof, and improve the same to and for the use and support of the said school, with full power to sue for, answer and defend, in all cases relating to the said land and premises." This committee was furthermore empowered to fill its own vacancies. [3]

---

[1] *Ibid.*, VII, 459. In 1737, an act was passed by the legislature which empowered the towns or parishes to divert this appropriation to the support of the established ministry. (*Ibid.*, VIII, 122–3.) In 1740, this act was repealed, on the ground that the original act of 1733 and its amendment of 1737 were "differently understood and . . . like so to be practised upon to the dissatisfaction of many." (*Ibid.*, VIII, 334);—a strong hint of the Separatist controversy of the time.

[2] *Ibid.*, VII, 468–9.   [3] *Ibid.*, VII, 509.

In 1737 all lands "sequestered to or improved for schools and other pious uses" were exempted from taxation.[1]

In May, 1741, a considerable estate and interest had been sequestered from the sale of the western lands, and the legislature consequently ordered the proceeds to be handed over to the selectmen or society committees or school committees of the different towns. These school bodies were given full powers of trustees over all the school property belonging to their towns, with the exception of those special school trusts which had already been created by particular persons, or by the General Court. They were, however, to be accountable for the western lands school fund to their respective towns or societies, which were in turn to be accountable to the General Court.[2]

In October, 1741, the Neck and Nahantick societies of New London, petitioned to be divided into two societies with school privileges. The legislature granted the petition and ordered that each society should have the same powers and privileges for the management of their school affairs, as were granted by law to the other societies of the colony for their ecclesiastical affairs.[3]

The religious agitation which harried New England during the middle of the 18th century did not fail to impress the school legislation of Connecticut. An act " relating to, and for the better regulating schools of learning," that was passed in 1742, was directed against the educational work of the " New Lights" in general, and particularly against a training school for preachers and teachers which had been set up in

---

[1] *Ibid.*, VIII, 133.

[2] *Ibid.*, VIII, 387–9. At this same legislative session a committee was appointed to carry out the above order. (*Ibid.*, VIII, 392–3.) In 1761, a committee was appointed to dispose in a similar way of the bonds which had only then come in from the sale of Norfolk township. (*Ibid.*, XI, 504–5; see also XII, 79–80.)

[3] *Ibid.*, VIII, 428.

New London, and was known as the Shepherd's Tent.[1] "Whereas, by sundry acts and laws of this Assembly, they have founded, erected, endowed and provided for the maintenance of a college at New Haven, and inferior schools of learning in every town or parish, for the education and instruction of the youth of this colony, which have (by the blessing of God) been very serviceable to promote useful learning and Christian knowledge, and, more especially, to train up a learned and orthodox ministry for the supply of our churches: And inasmuch as the well ordering of such public schools is of great importance to the public weal, this Assembly, by one act entitled An Act for the encouragement and better improvement of town schools, did order and provide, that the civil authority and selectmen in every town should be visitors, to inspect the state of such schools, and to inquire into the qualifications of the masters of them and the proficiency of the children, to give such directions as they shall think needful to render such schools most serviceable to increase that knowledge, civility and religion, which is designed in the erecting of them ; and in case those visitors shall apprehend that any such schools are so ordered as not to be likely to attain to those good ends proposed, they shall lay the state thereof before the Assembly, who shall give such orders thereupon as they shall think proper; as by the said act may more fully appear : And whereas the erecting of any other schools, which are not under the establishment and inspection aforesaid, may tend to train up youth in ill principles and practices, and introduce such disorders as may be of fatal consequence to the public peace and weal of this Colony: Which to prevent,

Be it enacted by the Governor, Council and Representatives, in General Court assembled, and by the authority of the same, that no particular persons whatsoever shall presume of themselves to erect, establish, set up, keep or maintain any college, seminary of learning, or any public school whatsoever, for the

[1] *Ibid.*, VIII, 500, foot-note.

instruction of young persons, other than such as are erected and established or allowed by the laws of this colony, without special license or liberty first had and obtained of this Assembly.

And be it enacted by the authority aforesaid, that if any person shall presume to act as a master, tutor, teacher or instructor, in any unlawful school or seminary of learning erected as aforesaid, he shall suffer the penalty of five pounds lawful money per month for every month he shall continue to act as aforesaid. And every grand jury, within any county where such school or seminary of learning is erected, shall make presentment of all breaches of this act to the next assistant, justice of the peace, or county court.

And be it further enacted by the authority aforesaid, that the civil authority and selectmen in each town, or the major part of them, shall inspect and visit all such unlawful schools or seminaries of learning, erected as aforesaid, and shall proceed with all such scholars, students or residents in such school, and all such as harbor, board or entertain them, according to the laws of this colony respecting transient persons or inmates residing in any town without the approbation of the selectmen.

And be it further enacted by the authority aforesaid, that if any student or resident in such school shall pretend that he is bound as by indenture an apprentice to learn any manual art or trade, and the said civil authority or selectmen shall suspect that such indenture was given only as a color to reside in said town contrary to law, that then it shall be in the power of the said civil authority to examine all the parties to such indentures under oath, in all such questions which they shall think proper, relating to the true intention of such indenture and their practice thereupon; and if it shall appear to the said authority or selectmen, or the major part of them, that such indenture was given upon a fraudulent design, as aforesaid, that then such authority shall proceed as if no such indenture had been made. . . .

And be it further enacted by the authority aforesaid, that no person that has not been educated or graduated in Yale College or Harvard College in Cambridge, or some other allowed foreign protestant college or university, shall take the benefit of the laws of this government respecting the settlement and support of ministers.

Always provided, nothing in this act be construed to forbid or prevent any society, allowed by law in this colony to keep a school, by a major vote in such society to order more parish schools than one to be kept therein, and appoint the school or schools to be kept in more places than one in each society.

This act to continue in force for the space of four years from the rising of this Assembly and no longer." [1]

In May, 1743, on petition, the legislature divided the West School Society of New London into two distinct school societies.[2]

In October, the General Court granted on petition 25 acres of land which had escheated to the colony on the death of one Edward Pierce intestate, for the use of the school in the parish of Wintonbury.[3]

In 1752, the General Court, empowered, on petition, the grammar school committee of New London to sell the common and undivided land of the town which had been donated by its proprietors[4] to the grammar school.[5]

In 1754, as a result of the pressure of war expenditures, an act was passed cutting down the colony allowance to town

---

[1] *Ibid.*, VIII, 500–502.　　　　[2] *Ibid*, VIII, 532.

[3] *Ibid.*, VIII, 575-6. This parish came into existence in 1736. It was formed by the inhabitants of Windsor, Farmington and Symsbury. The twenty-five acres of land referred to lay in the town of Symsbury, near the limits of Wintonbury parish. (*Ibid.*, VIII, 76, 575.)

[4] Town proprietors formed a land community distinct from the political community of the town. "In origin, they were a body of men who collectively purchased lands of the natives through grant of the General Court or otherwise." (*The River Towns of Connecticut*, pp. 48, 90.)

[5] *Conn. Col. Rec.*, X, 129–30.

schools for the year preceding and for the future from 40 to
10 shillings on every 1000 lbs.[1] In October, 1766, this allowance was raised to 20 s., it having been found that the former
provision was "insufficient to answer the important design of
educating and instructing children."[2] And in May, 1767, the
school allowance was again raised to 40 s.[3]

In May, 1766, all arrears of excise duties in the towns were
ordered to be paid by the selectmen of the towns to the school
committees, and the interest of the excise money at that date
in the colony treasury was ordered to be paid at the rate of 5
per cent. to the several towns in proportion to the sums paid
in by them, for the benefit of the school or schools in said
towns.[4]

In October, power was given to every town and society
" to divide themselves into proper and necessary districts for
keeping their schools, and to alter and regulate the same from
time to time." And it was provided that such districts were
to draw upon the school money appropriated to the town, in
proportion to their lists of taxables.[5]

In 1774, the legislature chartered a private academy in New
London. "Upon the memorial of Richard Law, Jeremiah
Miller, Thomas Mumford, Duncan Steward, Esqrs. and the rest
of the proprietors of a school-house in New London, showing
to this Assembly that they have at great cost erected a school-
house for the advancement of learning, hired and paid school
masters &c. and that difficulties attend their prosecuting their
designs from their not being incorporated &c.; praying that
they may be made a body corporate &c. as per memorial on
file: Resolved by this Assembly, that the proprietors of said

---

[1] *Ibid.*, X, 317.   [2] *Ibid.*, XII, 497.   [3] *Ibid.*, XII, 561.

[4] *Ibid.*, XII, 463-4. In October, 1774, the treasurer of the colony was ordered
to " pay out to the several towns the principal sums paid in by them as excise
money, together with the interest due at the time of payment." And at the same
time the second provision in the act of 1766 was repealed. (*Ibid.*, XIV, 330.)

[5] *Ibid.*, XII, 497-8.

school-house be and they are hereby made and constituted a body politic and corporate, and shall be called and known by the name of the Union School in New London, and they and their successors, proprietors of said school-house, have, and they have hereby granted unto them, to have perpetual succession, and shall and may be persons able and capable in law to sue and to be sued, to plead and implead, to answer and be answered unto, to defend and be defended, in all and singular suits, causes, matters, actions and things whatsoever, and also to have, take, possess, acquire and purchase lands and estates, real, personal and mixed, not exceeding the sum of three thousand pounds, lawful money, and the same to sell and dispose of as any other corporation may lawfully do. And said proprietors of said Union School and their successors shall and may have a common seal, to serve and use for all causes, matters and things and affairs whatsoever, of them and their successors, and the same to alter at their will and pleasure. And for the better ordering the affairs of said school-house and school, the proprietors and their successors have granted to them full power and authority to choose a committee, to consist of such number of persons as to them shall seem fit and meet, to order and direct the prudentials of said school from time to time, who shall have full power to make such rules and orders as they judge necessary for the management and ordering the affairs of said school, which rules and orders shall be binding on all concerned therein unless the same are revoked and disannulled by the proprietors of said school, which they are hereby empowered at any of their legal meetings to do. And said proprietors of said school and their successors are hereby enabled and empowered to choose a clerk and any other officer they judge necessary to advance the best interest of said school, and such officers so chosen shall continue in their respective offices until by said proprietors or their committee they shall be removed. And all the votes of the voters present at any meeting of said proprietors shall be determined by a majority of the interest of the members present. Provided, that nothing herein shall be construed to exempt any of the proprietors of said school from any duties or taxes which by law they are subjected to, nor shall they by this act be entitled to any donations, grants or public moneys already made, or which may hereafter be made, for the purposes of advancing schooling, unless the same be given expressly to said Union School." [1]

CONCERNING INDIAN EDUCATION

The Connecticut code of 1650, provided that one of the teaching elders " with the help of Thomas Stanton, should be desired, twice at least in every year, to go among the neighboring Indians and endeavor to make known to them the counsels of the Lord," and the Governor, Deputy Governor and Magistrates were desired " to see to the accomplishment of this end." [2]

Four years later the government adopted another plan for the "gospelizing " of the neighboring Indians.

"Whereas, notwithstanding former provision made for the conveyance of the knowledge of God to the natives amongst us, little hath hitherto been attended through want of an able interpreter, this Court being earnestly desirous to promote and further what lies in them a work of that nature, wherein the glory of God and the everlasting welfare of those poor, lost, naked sons of Adam is so deeply concerned, do order that Thomas Mynor, of Pequot, shall be wrote unto from this Court and desired that he would forthwith send his son, John Mynor, to Hartford, where this Court will provide for his maintenance and schooling, to the end he may be for the present assistant to such elder, elders or others, as this Court shall appoint to interpret the things of God to them as he shall be directed, and in the meantime to fit himself to be instrumental that way as God shall fit and incline him thereunto for the future. [3]

[1] *Ibid.*, XIII, 382-384.   [2] *Conn. Col. Rec.*, I, 531.

[3] *Ibid.*, I, 265. At a meeting of the Commissioners of the United Colonies, on

During the remainder of the century, as a result of in-
cessant Indian warfare, no systematic effort seems to have
been made in the colony for the conversion and education of
the Indians; although the subject was brought several times
to the attention of the legislature.[1]

In 1706, at the request of the Society for Propogating
Christian Knowledge, the General Court advised the ministry
to draw up a plan for the conversion of Indians;[2] and again,
in 1717, the Court requested the Governor and Council to
consider concerning " the business of gospelizing the Indians,"
and present the matter at the next session of the legislature.[3]
But nothing seems to have come of either recommendation.

In 1727, however, a general measure was passed, providing for the conversion and education of Indian children.
" Whereas this Assembly is informed that many of the Indians
in this government put out their children to the English, to be
brought up by them, and yet sundry of the persons having
such children, do neglect to learn them to read and to instruct
them in the principles of the Christian faith, so that such

September 23, Magistrate Cullick, of the General Court of Connecticut, brought
this plan to the attention of the Commissioners, and they directed that due allowance should be made for the diet and education of John Mynor out of the corporation stock. (*Ibid.*, I, 265, foot-note.)

[1] In 1669, the Court, being solicited, expressed their approval of Mr. John Black-
bach's endeavors at "gospelizing" the natives. (*Ibid.*, II, 111.) Daniel Gookin,
Indian agent of the Massachusetts colony, writes, in 1674, that "sundry years
since," Mr. Abraham Purson, pastor of the church at Branford, preached the gospel to some Indians in those parts, and that he was encouraged in the work by the
Commissioners of the United Colonies. James Fitch, pastor of the church at Nor-
wich, writes to Gookin this same year, that the Connecticut Indians are in general
without inclination to learn the Word of God; but that he has under his care about
thirty of the Mohegans, whose children for two years past he has been teaching to
read. (*Mass. Hist. Col.*, First Series, I, 207–209.) In 1671, the work of Mr. Fitch
was gratefully acknowledged by the Court, and it decided to move the Commissioners of the United Colonies to allow him "suitable encouragement." (*Conn. Col.
Rec.*, II, 158; see also foot-note and p. 576.)

[2] *Ibid.*, V, 7.   [3] *Ibid.*, VI, 15.

children are still in danger to continue heathens : Which to prevent,

Be it enacted by the Governor, Council and Representatives, in General Court assembled, and by the authority of the same, that every person in this colony that hath taken, or shall take, any of the Indian children of this or the neighboring governments into the care of their families, are hereby ordered to use their utmost endeavor to teach them to read English, and also to instruct them in the principles of the Christian faith by catechising of them, together with other proper methods. And the selectmen and grand-jurors in the respective towns shall make diligent inquiry, whether the Indian children that are or may be put out as above, are by their masters or mistresses that have the care of them, instructed and taught as abovesaid. And if upon inquiry the said officers shall find that any such master or mistress hath neglected their duty herein, after due warning given, then said officers, or any two of them, shall inform the next assistant or justice of the peace, upon which the said authority shall summon such master or mistress so informed against, to appear before them ; and if upon examination it appear that said master or mistress hath neglected to instruct any Indian child or children put to them as aforesaid, they shall be fined at the discretion of said assistant or justice, not exceeding the sum of forty shillings, to be to the use of the school in the town where the master or mistress lives." [1]

In 1728 the Assembly granted £15 to Captain John Mason for the encouragement and support of his school among the Mohegans of New London township.[1] Five years previously the Court had consented to the settlement of Mason among these Indians, and had urged him " to set up a school among them and acquaint them in the Christian religion." [2] In 1729 the grant was renewed.[3] In 1742, upon advice of the Rev. Mr.

[1] *Ibid.*, VII, 102–103. [2] *Ibid.*, VII, 181.
[3] *Ibid*, VI, 429. [4] *Ibid.*, VII, 242.

Addams, the Assembly appropriated £12 for repairing the schoolhouse at Mohegan.[1] Ten years later, the Assembly was again addressed on the same subject. " Upon the memorial of the Rev. Messrs. Eliphalet Addams and David Jewet, representing to this Assembly that the society in England for propagating the gospel amongst the natives have, by their commissioners at Boston, been at great pains and cost on that head, and that the memorialists, by their order and at their expense, have provided a good school-master to teach and instruct the youth among the Mohegan Indians, &c.; representing that the school-house at Mohegan is in a shattered condition, and not suitable for the school-master and his family to live in: praying this Assembly to grant a sum of money to be applied for the building a small addition to said school-house, for the comfortable support of the school-master, and also for repairing said house, &c.: Resolved by this Assembly, that the treasurer of this colony be, and he is hereby ordered, to pay out of the treasury unto the Rev. Messrs. Eliphalet Addams and David Jewet the sum of one hundred and fifty pounds in bills of credit of the colony of Rhode Island or Province of New Hampshire, to be employed for the building a lean-to to the school-house in Mohegan, and for repairing said house. It is also recommended by this Assembly to the Indians at Mohegan whose children are to be instructed, that they contribute by their labor, or in some other way, to the accomplishment of this necessary work."[2] In 1755, Benjamin Uncas, sachem of the Mohegan Indians, and other members of the tribe petitioned the Assembly to grant £25 or £30 old tenor, to provide dinners for their children at school, and the Assembly accordingly ordered 50 s. lawful money to be paid over to Adonijah Fitch and the Rev. Mr. David Jewet for that purpose.[3] In 1757, Robert Clelland, schoolmaster of the Mohegan Indians, represented to the Assembly that the old school house, in

---

[1] *Ibid.*, VIII, 509.   [2] *Ibid.*, X, 115–116.

[3] *Ibid.*, X, 384.

which he lived, needed repairing to the extent of £7. The Assembly ordered that such a sum should be expended under the direction of the Rev. Mr. Jewet.[1] In 1760, the Assembly, in answer to a memorial of school-master Clelland stating that the salary which he was allowed by the commissioners of the evangelizing society was inadequate for his support, granted him £40 for his extraordinary service of eight years to the Mohegan Indians.[2] The next year Clelland petitioned in behalf of his pupils, and the Assembly appropriated £6 to be expended on their dinners while at school.[3] In October 1762, the school-master petitioned for both himself and his pupils, and was granted £21 10 s. by the Assembly, £15 in consideration of his services for the past three years and £6 10 s. in payment of the sum that he had advanced the Indian children for food.[4] The following May, on petition of the school-master, the Assembly granted £7 for school dinners.[5] In 1766, Clelland was allowed £15 for his services during the preceding three years.[6] In 1774, the Assembly granted on petition £10 7s. 11d. to William Hubbard and Zachary Johnson, £6 for the support of a school-master in the Mohegan school house and the remainder in payment of the sum which had been advanced by the petitioners in repairing the said school house.[7]

About 1733, an Indian school seems to have been established at Farmington, and to have secured the attendance of Indians from other towns.[8] In 1733, he legislature, on the advice of the pastor of the town of Farmington, appointed Capt. William Wadsworth and Capt. Josiah Hart of that town to provide during the winter for the dieting of the Indian youth in attendance upon the Indian town school.[9] The following

---

[1] *Ibid.*, XI, 34.   [2] *Ibid.*, XI, 414.   [3] *Ibid.*, XI, 517.
[4] *Ibid.*, XII, 100.   [5] *Ibid.*, XII, 169.   [6] *Ibid.*, XIII, 485–6.
[7] *Ibid.*, XIV, 246.

[8] *History of New Britain, with Sketches of Farmington and Berlin*, p. 215; · David N. Camp, A. M., *New Britain*, 1889.

[9] *Rec.*, VII, 471.

May, 24 £ 16s, 3d, was paid out by the Court to this committee for their winter's dieting of the Indian lads [1] and a similar
order was passed for the winter of 1734–5.[2]   In October, 1735,
the order was again renewed [3] and in the following spring
Capt. Wadsworth was paid £28 for the work.[4]

At this same session of the Assembly, a more general provision for Indian education was made by an act " directing
that there shall be a contribution, and the money thereby
raised, to be improved for the civilizing, &c. of the Indians, and
a sum granted for the instructing the Nahantick Indians in the
town of Lyme in the county of New London.   Notwithstanding that the first settlers of this colony, from time to time, by
persons skilled in the Indian tongue, endeavored to gain the said
natives to a belief of the Christian religion, yet the said Indians
did generally refuse the same; but of late the Indians have
desired to be instructed in the Christian religion,[5] which this
government, as well as many pious persons therein, have encouraged: And to the end that so good a work may be fur-
thered, be it enacted by the Governor, Council and Representatives, in General Court assembled, and by the authority
of the same, that at the next public Thanksgiving that shall be
appointed in this colony, there shall be a contribution attended
in every ecclesiastical society or parish in this government,
and that the money that shall be raised thereby shall be improved for the civilizing and Christianizing of the Indian
natives in this colony, (exclusive of the Moheags, who are
already provided for;) and that his Honor, the Governor, send
forth his order to the ministers of the respective parishes
accordingly; and the Governor and Council, for the time being, are hereby appointed to receive the said contribution, and
they are hereby directed carefully to improve the same for the

[1] *Ibid.*, VII, 491.   [2] *Ibid.*, VII, 509.

[3] *Ibid.*, VIII, 6.   [4] *Ibid.*, VIII, 8.

[5] Many of the Connecticut Indians participated in the Great Revival.   Trumbull's
History, II, 144.

end abovesaid; and they shall give an account of their doings therein to this Assembly, that so further care from time to time may be taken. And whereas this Assembly are now informed that the said Nahantick Indians desire their children may be instructed, thereupon it is resolved that, the colony treasurer do pay out of the public treasury unto Messrs. Thomas Lee, of Lyme, and Stephen Prentiss, of New London, the sum of £15, who are appointed to receive the same, and therewith they shall hire some suitable person to instruct the said children to read, and also in the principles of the Christian religion, and also render an account to this Assembly of their disbursements of the money aforesaid.[1] The above order of the Court seems to have been effective, for in May, 1737, the Court appointed a committee to receive from the Governor the money that had been contributed by the different societies " for the civilizing and Christianizing the colony's Indians." [2]

In 1741 one of these Indians, Atchetoset, represented to the Assembly that he and his family wished to be instructed in the Christian religion, but that he was unable to pay for the cost of schooling and dieting his children. Accordingly the Court ordered the Governor to instruct the Rev. Mr. Anthony Stoddard and Lieut.-Col. Preston to see to the " victualling " and the schooling and religious training of Atchetoset's children, and the Governor was furthermore directed to pay over £20 of the money that had been previously contributed, to the above gentlemen for this purpose.[3]

In October, 1750, one Martin Kellogg, of Stockbridge, stated to the Assembly that some of the Indians of the Six Nations had come to him to be instructed in reading, and that there seemed to be " an opportunity to bring them in the way of receiving the Gospel ;" but that necessary provision for their victualling and clothing was lacking. Whereupon the Assembly appointed

[1] *Rec.*, VIII, 37–38.
[2] *Ibid.*, VIII, 93.
[3] *Ibid.*, VIII, 372–3.

a committee to take the matter in charge and to draw upon
the public treasury to the extent of £250 "old tenor."[1]   In
October, 1751, this committee was further empowered to draw
upon the treasury to the extent of £500 old tenor.[2]

In May, 1763, the Rev. Mr. Eleazar Wheelock, pastor of the
Second Church in Lebanon, presented a memorial to the Assembly " representing that for some years past he has had
under his care and tuition several youths of the Indian tribes,
at present increased to more than twenty in number, with a
view to their being by proper discipline and instruction fitted
for missionaries, school-masters, interpreters, &c., among their
own people, and that though his past success therein has so
recommended his design as to excite the charity and liberality
of divers worthy persons in support of almost all the past expenses, yet the present aspect of said undertaking seeming to
merit as well as require some further assistance, he was induced to ask the favor and countenance of this Assembly
therein." Whereupon the Assembly, "seriously considering
the present new and extraordinary prospect (by the blessing
of Heaven on his Majesty's arms) doth greatly encourage an
attempt to promote Christian knowledge and civility of manners among the Indian natives of this land, . . . grant and
order a brief throughout this colony, recommending it to all
inhabitants charitably and liberally to their ability to contribute to such pious and important purposes, and that the
moneys so collected, be by the persons therewith intrusted, delivered to John Ledyard of Hartford, John Whiting of New Haven, David Gardiner of New London, David
Rowland of Fairfield, Samuel Gray of Windham, and Elisha
Sheldon of Litchfield, Esquires, each county's collections to
their own respective receivers; which receivers are hereby
directed to deliver the same to the treasurer of this
colony. . . .

" And it is further resolved, that said Mr. Wheelock do at his

[1] *Ibid.*, IX, 570, and X, 32–33.   [2] *Ibid.*, X, 66.

discretion, as occasion may be, apply to Jonathan Trumble, Daniel Edwards and George Wyllys, Esquires, for such moneys, parcel of such contributed sum as he shall apprehend to be necessary; which said committee, or any two of them, are hereby appointed, authorized and directed, to draw orders on said Treasurer for such sum or sums thereof as shall be shown to them to be useful and necessary in the then present exigencies of said affair, until the whole is exhausted.

" Provided nevertheless, that if the state and circumstances of said undertaking by any means hereafter become so altered, as in the opinion of said last mentioned committee, to render the further prosecution or support of said affair impracticable or doubtful whether it may answer the good end and design, in such case they are hereby directed to desist drawing as aforesaid, and by the earliest opportunity to advise this Assembly thereof, to the end such further order in the premises be taken as the present emergencies may recommend. Always provided such moneys be ultimately and wholly applied to the pious design of propagating the gospel among the heathen.

" And it is further ordered, that printed copies of this Act be seasonably delivered to the several ministers of the gospel within this colony, who are hereby also directed to read the same in their respective congregations, and thereon appoint a time for making such collection." [1]

In the following autumn, the Assembly ordered the ministers to suspend the publication of the aforesaid brief, having heard that where it had already been published, the collections had been small on account of an outbreak among the Western Indians, and that most of the ministers "apprehensive of the ill success of the charitable design," had appealed, through the Governor, for the advice of the legislature.[2]

In May, 1766, the Assembly complied with a request of Mr. Wheelock and renewed the brief throughout the colony.[3]

[1] *Ibid.*, XII, 151–152. [2] *Ibid.*, XII, 193. [3] *Ibid.*, XII, 490–1.

YALE COLLEGE

About 1698, the Rev. Mr. John Pierpont, of New Haven, the Rev. Mr. Andrew of Milford, and the Rev. Mr. Russel of Branford,[1] began to agitate the question of the founding of a college in Connecticut.[2] In 1701, they and their associates petitioned the legislature for a charter, representing " that from a sincere regard to, and zeal for, upholding the Protestant religion, by a succession of learned and orthodox men, they had proposed that a collegiate school should be erected in this colony, wherein youth should be instructed in all parts of learning, to qualify them for public employments in church and civil state, and that they had nominated ten ministers to be trustees, partners or undertakers for the founding, endowing and ordering the said school."[3] This petition, which was signed by a large number of the ministers and principal men of the colony, was granted by the legislature at its session in October, 1701.[4]

ACT FOR A COLLEGIATE SCHOOL[5]

" Whereas several well disposed and public spirited persons,

[1] These three clergymen had all lived in the old New Haven colony, and they had all been graduated at Harvard College. Mr. Pierpont married the grand-daughter of Mr. Davenport,

[2] *Yale College*, I, 13, 15. William L. Kingsley, New York, 1879.

[3] Quoted in Trumbull's History, I, 500.

[4] The charter is dated October 9th, the opening day of the session ; but it was probably granted on October 16th. See *Biographical Sketches of the Graduates of Yale College with Annals of the College History*, I, 3. Franklin B. Dexter, M. A., New York, 1885.

[5] The promoters of the College were doubtful concerning the Assembly's right of incorporation. In view of this uncertainty, Secretary Addington and Judge Sewall, of Massachusetts, who were in part responsible for the draft of the charter, wrote, on October 6, 1701, to Mr. Thomas Buckingham : " We on purpose gave your academy as low a name as we could that it might the better stand in wind and weather, not daring to incorporate it, lest it should be liable to be served with a writ of *quo warranto*." *An Historical Discourse, pronounced before the graduates of Yale College, August 14, 1850*, with an appendix, by Theodore D. Woolsey.

of their sincere regard to and zeal for the upholding and propagating of the Christian Protestant religion, by a succession of
learned and orthodox men, have expressed by petition their
earnest desire that full liberty and privelege be granted unto
certain undertakers, for the founding and suitably endowing
and ordering a collegiate school, within this his Majesty's
Colony of Connecticut, wherein youth may be instrncted in the
arts and sciences, who through the blessing of Almighty God,
may be fitted for public employment both in church and civil
state. To the intent therefore that all due encouragement be
given to such pious resolutions and that so necessary and
religious an undertaking may be set forward, supported and
well managed : Be it enacted by the Governor and Company of
the said colony of Connecticut in General Court assembled, nd
it is enacted and ordained by the authority of the same, that
there be and hereby is full liberty, right and privilege granted
unto Mr. James Noyes of Stonington, Mr. Israel Chancie of
Stratford, Mr. Thomas Buckingham of Saybrook, Mr. Abraham
Pierson of Kenelworth, Mr. Sam. Mather of Windsor, Mr. Tim.
Woodbridge of Hartford, Mr. James Pierpont of New Haven,
Mr. Sam. Andrew of Milford, Mr. Joseph Webb of Fairfield,
Mr. Noadiah Russell of Middletown, being all reverend ministers of the gospel and inhabitants within this said colony,
proposed to stand as trustees, partners or undertakers for the
said school, to them and their successors, to erect, form, direct,
order, establish, improve, and at all times, in all suitable ways,
for the future to encourage the said school in such convenient
place or places, and in such form, manner, and under such
orders and rules, as to them shall seem meet and most conducive to the aforesaid end thereof. so as such rules or orders
be not repuguant to the laws of the civil government : as also
to employ the moneys of any other estate which shall be

App., No. IV, 91 ; see also p. 97 for an interesting comparison of the Massachusetts draft and the legislative act. The whole phraseology of this document bears
out this aim. See Steiner's *Hist. of Educ. in Conn.*, p. 70.

granted by this Court, or otherwise contributed to that use, according to their discretion for the benefit of the said collegiate school from time to time and all times henceforward.

"And be it further enacted by the authority aforesaid, that the before named trustees, partners or undertakers, together with such others as they shall associate to themselves (not exceeding the number of eleven, or at any time being less than seven, provided also that the persons nominated or associated from time to time to fill up the said number, be ministers of the gospel inhabiting within this colony and above the age of forty years) or the major part of them, the said James Noyes, Israel Chancie, etc. . . . undertakers, and of such persons so chosen and associated as above said, and at any time hereafter, have and shall have henceforth the oversight, full and complete right, liberty, power and privilege, to furnish, direct, manage, order, improve and encourage from time to time, and in all times hereafter, the said collegiate school so erected and formed by them, in such ways, orders and manner and by such persons, rector, master and officers appointed by them, as shall according to their best discretion be most conducible to attain the aforementioned end thereof.

"And moreover it is ordered and enacted by the authority aforesaid, that the said James Noyes, etc., undertakers, trustees or partners, and the said persons taken from time to time into partnership, or associated as aforesaid with themselves, shall have and receive (and it is hereby given and granted unto them) the full and just sum of one hundred and twenty pounds in country pay [£60 sterling] to be paid annually and at all times hereafter (until this Court order otherwise) to them, and such person, or persons, only as they shall appoint and empower to receive the same ; to be faithfully disposed of by the said trustees, partners, or undertakers, for the end aforesaid, according to their discretion ; which said sum shall be raised and paid in such ways and manners, and at such a value as the country rates of this colony are and have been usually raised and paid.

" It is also further enacted by the authority aforesaid, that the said undertakers and partners and their successors be and hereby are further empowered to have, accept, acquire, purchase or otherwise lawfully enter upon, any lands, tenements and hereditaments to the use of the said school, not exceeding the value of five hundred pounds per annum, and any goods, chattels, sum or sums of money whatsoever as have heretofore already been granted, bestowed, bequeathed, or given, or as from time to time shall be freely given, bequeathed, devised or settled by any person or persons whatsoever upon and to and for the use of the said school towards the founding, erecting, or endowing the same, and to sue for, recover and receive all such gifts, legacies, bequests, annuities, rents, issues, and profits arising therefrom, and to employ the same accordingly ; and out oɪ the estate, revenues, rents, profits and incomes accruing and belonging to said school to support and pay as the said undertakers shall agree and see cause, the said rector or master, tutors, ushers, or other officers, their respective annual salaries or allowances ; as also, for the encouragement of the students, to grant degrees or licenses as they or those deputed by them shall see cause to order and appoint." [1]

In 1703 there were from 15 to 20 college students[2] under the tuition of Rector Pierson at Killingworth. Accordingly in October 14 of that year the General Court orders and enacts, " That no scholar being a student in the Collegiate School, shall be entered in the public list of male persons, nor be rated for his head; and if any such scholar be entered, his or their names shall be taken out again; and that the persons of all such scholars shall be exempted from watching and warding and all other such public service during the whole time that they shall continue in the said school."[3] Later in the month,

---

[1] *Conn. Col. Rec.*, IV, 363-5. [2] Dexter's Annals, I, 13.

[3] *Conn. Col. Rec.*, IV, 440. This order is the more significant in view of the French and Indian war, which was at that time making heavy drains upon the colony.

the Governor and Council grant the trustees permission to raise money by brief throughout the colony for the maintenance of a tutor and the promotion of a college building. " Further more the Governor and Council considering the very hopeful progress the reverend trustees have already made in the said affair, and the comfortable appearance that the said school under the present conduct of the said trustees will (through the divine blessing) conduce to the advancing of the the interest of religion and general good of this colony, do therefore hereby recommend the aforesaid approved measure to all persons within the said colony, not doubting but there will be in all a general readiness in their respective stations, and according to their respective circumstances to forward so good a work." [1]

There is no record of the result of this recommendation. For the next ten years, however, the Collegiate School continued in a disorganized and impoverished condition.

In 1712 the Assembly under an act for encouragement of learning [2] increased the appropriation to the Collegiate School for that year by about 25 per cent. [3]

In October, 1714, the Upper House of Assembly passed a bill granting £200 towards a college building, but the Lower House refused to concur and referred the matter to the next session. [4] In May, on a representation of the trustees, the Lower House " taking it into their serious consideration are fully satisfied of the real necessity of a suitable house being provided for the entertainment of the school. And do therefore order that for the encouragement of so good a work as building a convenient house for said school, a brief be sent

---

[1] *Ibid.*, IV, 454.   [2] See p. 99.

[3] *Ibid.*, V, 353. One hundred pounds in money or bills of credit was the appropriation in lieu of £120 country pay. " Country pay " consisted of certain commodities accepted by the government as lawful for the payment of taxes, but rated at fifty per cent. above their hard money value. (Dexter's Annals, I, 109.)

[4] Dexter's Annals, I, 143.

unto the several towns and parishes in this colony for the asking the contribution of the well affected to religion and learning among us."[1]   The Upper House amended this bill by making a special apppropriation of £100 from the colony treasury for the object in hand. The Lower House refused to accept this amendment and the bill fell through.[2] At the next session of the legislature in October, 105,793 acres of land which had come into the possession of Connecticut in the settlement of the boundary line between it and Massachusetts, were ordered by the Assembly to be sold and five hundred pounds of the proceeds were appropriated to the trustees of the Collegiate School " for the building a college house."[3]

The location of this house was in dispute among the trustees and students of the college. From 1707[4] to 1716 collegiate instruction had been carried on at Saybrook, but in 1716 some of the students alleged discontent with the instruction and general conditions at Saybrook and gathered together under Tutor Elisha Williams at Wethersfield.[5] In May of that year two of the Hartford trustees represent to the General Court that " as the generous concern which this honored Court have expressed for the promoting of learning in the people under their government, especially in that encouragement which they have given for the erecting and subsisting a collegiate school in this colony, is matter of great satisfaction to all such as reflect thereon and do rightly understand the true interests of a people; so, on the other hand, the present declining and unhappy circumstances in which that school lies, and the apparent hazard of its being utterly extinguished

[1] *Ibid.*   [2] *Ibia.*, I, 144.

[3] *Conn. Col. Rec.*, V, 528–9.

[4] During the rectorship of the Rev. Mr. Pierson, 1702–1707, instruction was given at the rector's own house at Killingsworth, and commencements were held at Saybrook, 9 miles distant, in a house donated for the purpose by a citizen of the town. (Dexter's Annals, I, 6.)

[5] Dexter's Annals, I, 148–9.

unless some speedy remedy be applied, affords but a melancholy speculation to such as are acquainted with it."[1] In view of the prospects[2] which were offered to the school by the town of Hartford, the trustees further petition the Assembly to aid in its location at that place. This memorial was acted upon by the Assembly which met at Hartford on May 10th, 1716. "Upon the representation of the Reverend Mr. Timothy Woodbridge and Mr. Thomas Buckingham and others, that the collegiate school at Saybrook is in a languishing condition, and moving to this Assembly for a committee to hear from them the circumstances thereof: It is resolved by this Assembly, that the several gentlemen, the trustees of the said school, be forthwith notified that this Assembly desire the said trustees to meet in this place on Wednesday next, that they may show to this Assembly the difficulties, and what may by them be thought expedient to be done therein, in order to the further proceedings of this Assembly for the better advantage of the said collegiate school."[3] The trustees who obeyed the above summons persuaded the Assembly to wait until the following October, promising that if they had not unanimously agreed on a place for a college by the next commencement, they would let the legislature name one.[4] In October, the majority of the trustees chose New Haven for the college site, and arrangements were made accordingly.[5] But in May, 1717, Mr. Woodbridge of Hartford again petitioned the Assembly to fix a place for the college.[6] Where-

---

[1] *Conn. Col. Rec.*, V, 550, foot-note.

[2] It was urged that Hartford was in the centre of the colony, and surrounded by many considerable towns; that distinguished persons in Massachusetts had promised to contribute and to send their sons to Hartford; that 6 or 7 hundred pounds had been raised there for the college, and other donations were expected.

[3] *Ibid.*, V, 550-1.

[4] Dexter's Annals, I, 150.   [5] *Ibid.*, I, 160, 162-3,

[6] On December 18, 1716, the annual town meeting of Hartford passed resolutions instructing the deputies of the town in the next General Assembly to offer a remonstrance against the settlement of the collegiate school at New Haven. It

upon the Lower House " resolved that it may be most for the public good and the health of the collegiate school to have it settled in some place at or near Connecticut River." [1] At the next meeting of the legislature, [2] on a motion of the Lower House, [3] the Trustees were summoned, on October 14th, to appear and give an account of their proceedings. The majority report stated that New Haven had been fixed upon for the college site, on account of the conveniency of its situation, the cheapness of subsistence there, and the larger amount of the contributions of particular gentlemen in that town " without which (notwithstanding the sums granted by the colony) we could not go through with so chargeable a work." [4] On October 24th, the Assembly took this report, together with the minority report of the Hartford trustees, into consideration. The Upper House agreed on the majority report. The Lower House voted in favor of Middletown, a town midway between Hartford and New Haven. [5] Thirty-five votes were cast for Middletown, 32 for New Haven, and 6 for Saybrook. [6] At the request of the trustees a joint meeting of both Houses was convened on October 26th, and the whole controversy was reviewed, point by point. The result is thus described by Tutor Johnson, an eye witness of the proceedings:

" The Upper House all as one man agreed that they would advise the trustees settling the school at New Haven to go on with it, esteeming their cause just and good, and they sent it

was urged that "the counties of Hartford and New London, being more in number than the rest of the government and paying the greatest part of the money given for subsisting the collegiate school, and having furnished the said school with the greater number of scholars, had reason to expect that in appointing the place of the school, good respect should be had to them therein." (*Ibid.*, I, 161.)

[1] *Conn. Col. Rec.*, VI, 30, foot-note.

[2] At this session Mr. Elisha Williams, deputy rom Wethersfield, was clerk of the House.

[3] Kingsley's History, I, 44. [4] Dexter's Annals, I, 173.

[5] *Ibid.*, I, 174. [6] Kingsley's History, I, 44.

down to the Lower House, where there was great throes and
pangs and controversies and mighty strugglings; at length
they put it to a vote, and there were six more [36 to 30] for
the side of New Haven than the contrary; . . . . And thus at
length the up-river party had their will, in having the school
settled by the General Court, though sorely against their will,
at New Haven, but many owned themselves fairly beat."[1]
This decision stands as follows in the colonial records: "A
question being put, whether under the present circumstancs
of the affairs of the collegiate school, the reverend trustees
be advised to proceed in that affair and finish the house they
have built in New Haven for the entertainment of the scholars belonging to the collegiate school: Resolved in the affirmative."[2] It was also resolved by this Assembly, "that in
lieu of one hundred and twenty pounds in pay formerly
granted by this Court for the encouragement of the collegiate
school, and to be drawn out of the public treasury, there shall
be the sum of one hundred pounds in bills of public credit
distributed among those that have instructed the scholars belonging to the collegiate school, the year past, both at
Weathersfield, New Haven and Saybrook, in proportion, according to the number of scholars taught by them."[3]   To
"the reverend trustees sent for by this Assembly five
shillings per diem during their attendance" were allowed.[4]

In spite of the above settlement, the tutor and students at
Wethersfield continued in that place during the winter of
1717–18; and at the May session of the legislature, in Hart
ford, the discontented faction reopened the controversy.[5]   In
answer to their petition the Lower House " considering the
great dissatisfaction of the country in general, do conclude,
that in order to [the college] flourishing and having the support

[1] Quoted by Dexter, *Annals*, I, 175.

[2] *Conn. Col. Rec.*, VI. 30.

[3] *Ibid.*, VI, 38.   [4] *Ibid.*, VI, 38.

[5] Dexter's Annals, I, 175, 176.

of this government, it must be settled some where near Connecticut River, and that for the present and until it be so settled, the hundred pounds granted to the tutors shall be divided between the tutors at Wethersfield, Saybrook and New Haven, according to the proportion of scholars under their tuition; and that it be recommended to the reverend trustees, that the commencements be interchangeably one year at Wethersfield, and one at New Haven, till it be further settled to the satisfac- of the Assembly." This order was passed by 35 against 21 votes.[1]

The Upper House refused to concur in this measure, voting that "the place of the school was fully determined already by the indisputable vote of the trustees, and the subsequent advice of the Assembly there upon."[2]

In September, the new college building[3] was opened and the Upper House accepted the trustees' invitation to hold its meetings in the college library. At this session the legislature planned to put an end to the sectional quarrels about the college under

"AN ACT FOR THE ENCOURAGEMENT OF YALE[4] COLLEGE."

"Whereas some difficulty and misunderstanding happened in this colony upon the fixing the Collegiate School and building the house for it at New Haven: therefore, for a final conclusion of said difference and misunderstandings, and for preventing the unhappy consequences that might ensue, and

---

[1] *Conn. Col. Rec.*, VI, 30, foot-note.

[2] Kingsley's History, I, 45.

[3] This building had been designed by Governor Saltonstall. (Dexter's Annals, I, 160.) He subscribed £50 to its building. (Kingsley's History, I, 45.) The total cost of the hall was £1,000 sterling. (*Ibid.*)

[4] At the commencement in 1718 the new building was christened Yale College in honor of Elihu Yale, of England, who, at the solicitation of agent Dummer, of Connecticut, Cotton Mather of Massachusetts, etc., had recently sent over £200 for a collection of books for the collegiate school. (Dexter's Annals, I, 177). The name was not formally given to the corporation until the charter of 1745.

for the introducing a good and happy agreement in this, as well as in all our public affairs: It is resolved by this Assembly, that the following proposals be concluded upon as an expedient for those ends, and it is hereby agreed and enacted,

I. That the annnal salary allowed out of the public treasury to said collegiate school for the past year shall be distributed the tutors at New Haven, Weathersfield, and Saybrook, in proportion to the scholars under their tuition.

II. That the scholars who performed their exercise at Weathersfield, shall have their degree at New Haven, without further examination; and all scholars entered in the school at Weathersfield shall be admitted to the same standing in the school at New Haven.

III. That there shall be five hundred pounds allowed for the building of a State House at Hartford; which money shall be procured by the sale of lands belonging to this colony, and put into the hands of such committee as this Assembly shall appoint for the use. And it is ordered that the scholars at Weathersfield come down to the school at New Haven.

IV. That fifty pounds be procured by the sale of such lands as above said, and given to the town of Saybrook, for the use of the school in said town.

V. That the Governor and Council be desired to give (at the desire of the said trustees of said college), such orders as they think proper, for removing the books belonging to the said college, [1] left at Saybrook, to the library provided for the placing them in Yale College at New Haven.

VI. That the several particulars above mentioned that relate to the said college be recommended by the Governor and Council in the name of this Assembly, to the trustees of the

---

[1] In 1700 the ten founders of the College met together at Branford and donated 40 volumes in folio to the collegiate school. In 1713 Sir John Davie and certain non-conformist ministers of Devon sent over 170 volumes, and in 1714 agent Dummer procured about 800 books for the school. (Kingsley's History, I, 20, 37.)

said school, for their observation, and that said college be carried on, promoted and encouraged at New Haven, and all due care taken for its flourishing." [1]

The bill for this act as it originally passed in the Upper House provided that £1000 should be procured from a sale of the public lands, of which sum £800 were appropriated to Hartford and £200 to the college trustees for the completion of the college house. [2]

Governor Saltonstall and Council experienced no little difficulty in carrying out the orders concerning the removal of the college books from Saybrook and the College students from Wethersfield. On October 28th, after ordering arrears of allowances for the years 1716 and '18 to be paid by the colony treasurer to Mr. John Prout, treasurer of the College, the Governor and Council also directed " that the secretary write an order on Mr. Daniel Buckingham, [3] of Saybrook, requiring him to deliver to the rector of Yale College, or his order, the books and papers belonging to that college, which were by direction of the trustees of the same left in his house, when the said college was removed to New Haven, and which he has held in his keeping since that time; and that the said order be inclosed in the forementioned letter to the rector." [4]

At a meeting of the Governor and Council in Saybook, December 2, the Governor communicated to the board of trustees the report made by the Rev. Mr. Samuel Russell and Mr. Thomas Rugles, trustees of Branford and Guilford, who had been appointed by the rector of the College to execute the board's order for the removal of the college books. The trustees reported that on November 11th, they demanded the books and papers from Mr. Buckingham, who refused to deliver

[1] *Conn. Col. Rec.*, VI, 83–4.

[2] Kingsley's History, I, 47.

[3] Son of the former pastor of Saybrook, in whose house the College had been partly domiciled. (Dexter's Annals, I, 200.)

[4] *Conn. Col. Rec.*, VI, 90–91.

them, " declaring he did not know that he had any books belonging to Yale College, but when he did, and should receive
authentic orders, he would deliver them."

After hearing this report, the board resolves, " that the said
Buckingham refusing to deliver the said books and papers
upon the said order given pursuant to the said act of the Assembly, has a manifest appearance of great misdemeanor and
contempt of authority; and that a precept be issued to the
sheriff of the county of New London, signed by Capt. Christopher Christophers, clerk of the Council, by order of this board,
commanding him in his Majesty's name to arrest the said
Daniel Buckingham, and have him before the Governor and
Council, to-morrow morning at ten of the clock, at the house
of Major John Clark in Say Brook, to be examined concerning
his said misdemeanor and contempt, and dealt with as the law
directs."[1]   Accordingly the following day the recalcitrant
Buckingham was brought before the board by the sheriff, and
after a statement of the whole affair was read to him, he was
asked " what he had to say, in defence of his refusal to render
the said books according to order, and for his treating the order of this board and the act of the Assembly with such contempt, answered that he could only say as he had done, and as
was declared in the above said return.

It was thereupon declared to him, that the collegiate school
to which the books and papers demanded did belong, was
erected by this government; that they had put the said school
into the care of divers trustees, and had settled and approved
of their carrying on the affairs of the said school at New
Haven, as also of the name of Yale College, given to the said
collegiate school; and had not only directed the trustees in the
removal of the books and papers belonging to it, to the room
prepared for them in Yale College at New Haven, but had provided particularly that the necessary orders for the removal of
them should be given by the Governor and Council; and that

[1] *Ibid.*, VI, 92.

since he had accepted the charge or keeping of the said books and papers, he was thereby an under-officer or servant of the said school, in the nature of a library keeper, and was absolutely under the will of the trustees or masters of the said school, to render the said books to their order and to the use of the said school, as there should be occasion or as they should be required of him by order of the government; and that its unaccountable for any one entrusted in like manner to keep the said books from the use of the said school. And this board, pursuant to the aforesaid act of Assembly, did moreover require of him the said Buckingham, as entrusted with the keeping of the said books, now to deliver them to this board, that they might give order for the safe conveyance of them to the library in Yale College; which he, the said Bnckingham, refused to do, still saying that he did not know he had any books belonging to Yale College. And it appearing to this board that the books and papers belonging to Yale College are at this present time in the dwelling house of the said Daniel Buckingham, in a chamber of the said house, where they were brought by order of the trustees with consent of said Buckingham, to be kept safe for the use of the said college; and that the said Buckingham, in contempt of the aforesaid order for the rendering of them, designing to hold them from said school, and prevent the said trustees of said college, and students therein, from the use of the said books and papers, whereby the declared resolution of the General Assembly to encourage the said school, and the aforesaid act will be greatly defeated, and the orders they have given for that end become ineffectual, ordered, that a precept be made to the sheriff of the county of New London, requiring him to demand the said books, and upon his refusal, to enter into the said house and chamber, and deliver and cause them to be delivered to the rector of the said college, Mr. Samuel Andrew, or to either of the gentlemen, viz. Mr. Samuel Russell of Branford, or Mr. Thomas Ruggles of Guilford, by him

appointed to receive them.[1] Ordered, That the said Buckingham to give bond with sureties, in the sum of one hundred
pound, to the public treasury of this colony, for his appearance
at the General Court to be holden at Hartford in next May, to
answer for his misdemeanor and contempt, in refusing to deliver the said books and papers, according to the aforesaid act
of Assembly, and also for his good behavior in the meantime,
and that he stand committed until he give bond as aforesaid.
And the said Daniel Buckingham as principal, and Nathaniel
Chapman and Joseph Dudley as sureties, acknowledge themselves bound jointly and severally to the public treasury of
this colony, in a recognizance of one hundred pounds, that the
said Daniel Buckingham shall appear at the General Court to
be holden at Hartford in May next, to answer for his aforesaid
misdemeanor and contempt, and that he shall be of good behavior in the meantime."[2]

In accordance with the order of Assembly, in December,
1718, the rebellious Wethersfield students came to the college
at New Haven, but within a month they returned to Wethersfield, alleging dissatisfaction with their instruction. Governor
Saltonstall called a special meeting of the Council at New
Haven on March 11, 1719, to consult with the trustees on this
affair.[3] Both Mr. Woodbridge and Mr. Buckingham, of
Hartford, refused to attend this meeting. Mr. Woodbridge
was reported by one member of the Council to have said that
" he had not advised the scholars in their going to or coming
from New Haven, and therefore should not concern himself in
that business." Mr. Buckingham was also reported to have
said that " he had long ago declared to the trustees that he
would never contend any more with them in the affairs of the

---

[1] The fulfillment of this order was in part frustrated by the people of Saybrook,
who broke the carts and turned loose the oxen intended for the transportation of
the books. About 260 volumes are said to have been destroyed. (Dexter's Annals,
I, 200. See also *Conn. Col. Rec.*, VI, 100.)

[2] *Ibid.*, VI, 93–94.   [3] *Ibid.*, VI, 98.

College and therefore . . . thought he should not attend the meeting proposed." It was also reported that four of the elder scholars at Wethersfield having been notified by Mr. Pitkin of the Council of the appointed meeting and bidden to attend "to show their grievance, in order to their being redressed," answered "that they understood that Mr. Woodbridge and Mr. Buckingham would not be there, and could not tell whether they should be there or not." The Governor and Council then proceeeded from the Council Chamber to Yale College hall, where they were received by the rector and trustees of the College. Then "the Governor acquainted the rector that the government which had with great satisfaction founded the said college at first by their charter, and had lately professed, with such solemnity, their desire and firm resolution to contribute to its prosperity, could not but take notice of what had lately happened, in the desertion of such a number of the students, in so uncommon a manner, and that he had no other information of it than by common fame, yet that was grown so loud, and was by many evil-minded persons industriously spread abroad, both to the injury of this college and to the great disturbance of peace and good order in the government, that he judged it necessary on that occasion to appoint this meeting, that having a right understanding of the management of the said deserters which had occasioned so much disorder, proper measures might be taken to redress what should be found amiss, and prevent the like for the future, and particularly all needful support and encouragement given to the said College. To which the Rev. Rector made a brief reply, wherein he took suitable notice of the care the government took for the prosperity of the College; and added that the only pretended cause which he knew of, of the aforementioned desertion, was the insufficiency of one of the tutors: but he doubted not it would be found, upon inquiry, most unreasonable." [1]

---

[1] *Ibid.*, VI, 98–100.

Two days later the affairs of the College were again discussed at a meeting of the Council and trustees. "Upon consideration had of the state of the College, the trustees present did declare, that Mr. Johnson, against whose learning it has been reputed that the deserting scholars had objected, had been for some years improved as a tutor in the said college, and was well known to be a gentleman of sufficient learning, and that they cannot but look upon it as a very unworthy part in them, if any of those that have deserted the College have endeavored to scandalize a gentleman in such a manner, whom much more competent judges highly esteem a man of good learning, and in that respect very well accomplished for the charge he is in. And further they declared, that they had been endeavoring to procure a rector to reside at the College, though their endeavors hitherto had been unsuccessful; and were of the opinion that it was highly necessary to procure immediately some gentleman to be resident there, as a rector *pro tempore*, till the latter end of May next, who should take the charge of the College, with a tutor under him, to assist in the tuition of the students; which they hoped would put the affairs of the College into a desirable state, and give entire satisfaction to all that wished for the prosperity of it. And the gentlemen of the Council, being unanimously of opinion that no expedient could conduce more to the benefit of the College and satisfaction of all, recommended it to the trustees that they would proceed to make choice of a person to reside in the College as a rector *pro tempore*; that he might be as soon as possible obtained. The Rev. Rector, Mr. Samuel Andrew, Mr. Samuel Russell, and Mr. Thomas Ruggles, trustees, etc., personally communicated to this board, that according to the recommendation made them from hence, to consider of some fitting person who might be obtained to reside as a rector in Yale College, they had considered that matter, and resolved that the Rev. Mr. Timothy Cutler, minister of Stratford, was a person of those qualifications that they could not but think him very proper to take charge of the tuition and government of the students in Yale College, from this present time to the last Wednesday of May or the first Wednesday of June next in the quality of a rector to reside there; and that they had pitched upon him for that end, and designed to procure his residence there forthwith. To which the Rev. Mr. Davenport[1] added particularly for himself, that he did with the rest of the gentlemen before mentioned fully concur in his opinion of Mr. Cutler's qualifications for that service, but had some scruple of removing him from the church, which he doubted might be attended with unhappy consequences, as to the affairs of that church and town in particular; wherefore he could not tell how to concur with them in their election of him to this service, unless it be considered strictly as under the limitation to that time set, viz., the last Wednesday in May, or first of June. And the gentlemen thereupon desired the advice of this board, who after consideration had, did advise them, that if the trustees could by any means obtain the Rev. Mr. Cutler to come and reside in Yale College, and take the charge of a rector upon him for the time limited, it would prove an expedient universally acceptable to the colony, as it was to this board, and to all persons who have been under any uneasiness respecting the state of that college, and prove a good means to put an end to the contentions, which are unhappily arisen, for want of such a person residing there. And that although the church and town of Stratford must be allowed to be unwilling altogether to part with their reverend pastor, who is worthy of their great respect and honor, yet for so short a time, and for so great and general advantage, as its hoped his residing at Yale College may prove, we can't but think that they will be persuaded to deny themselves, and be satisfied with that provision to supply his desk which you may be able to make for them. And we cannot but add our assurance, that if you may be succeeded so far as to gain him to at-

---

[1] Trustee from Stamford.

tend the proposed service, it will give a particular satisfaction to the Assembly ; and they will be encouraged to come into the consideration of, and favor the measures which, after that, may be thought best to supply the College with an acceptable resident rector for the future." [1]

The Assembly which was convened in the following May [2] resolved " that for the encouragement of Yale College, there be sold, by a trustee empowered by this Assembly for that end, so much for the country land as shall amount to the sum of three hundred pounds ; which money shall be put into the hands of such commissioners as shall be appointed by this Assembly, who shall pay to the trustees of the College the sum of forty pounds annually for the space of seven years next. Provided no other income that may happen to appertain to said college be sufficient for the encouragement of said college before the said seven years be expired. Provided also, that said committee shall not sell any lands in large farms where there is conveniency for a township." [3] Subsequently it was ordered " that the committee appointed for the sale of the land in the town of Staford, or any three of them, be and are hereby empowered to sell the land appointed by this Court to to be sold for the encouragement of Yale College, and take care that the money to be made by the said sale, given to the said college, be paid into the treasury of the said college." [4]

Mr. Timothy Cutler accepted his call to the College, and in the autumn of 1719 was formally appointed rector. One

---

[1] *Ibid.*, VI, 100–102.

[2] At this session the disaffected Hartford faction made a final attack upon Yale College. Woodbridge and Buckingham were returned as deputies from Hartford, and through them an attempt was made to displace Governor Saltonstall, the zealous supporter of the College, at the annual election of Governor. (Dexter's Annals, I, 202 ; *Conn. Col. Rec.*, VI, 106, foot-note.)

[3] *Ibid.*, VI, 125–6.

[4] *Ibid.*, VI, 130. In October, 1720, the Assembly ordered that the remainder of this grant should be given by the committee into the treasury of the College " as soon as conveniently they may." (*Ibid.*, VI, 214–5.)

month later the legislature freed him from all his taxes as long as he continued in office. [1]

In May, 1721, the Assembly agreed that, "whereas, there is great need of providing a suitable dwelling house for the use of the rector of Yale College : It is ordered by this Assembly, that there be a brief or collection of money made in each town of this Colony, and applied to that end."[2] The following month the Governor appointed July 23 the time for this subscription."[3] In October, 1721, it was provided by the Assembly "that what shall be gained by the impost on rum for two years next coming, [4] shall be applied to the building of a rector's house for Yale College."[5] In May, 1722, another appropriation was made by the legislature to further the building of the rector's house. "Whereas, it appears by the result of several audits that there are two articles of debt to the Colony, viz., twenty pounds in the hands of Mr. Lucass, a gentleman of Antigua, and the other is an article of slops left in the hands of Mr. Foxcraft, commissary of Anapolis, to the value of seventy-nine pounds, seven shillings, which we have long endeavored to obtain and are become desperate; And whereas, it is suggested that if the government would grant them (in case they can be recovered) to the support of the college in New Haven, those who are concerned in them might possibly be prevailed with not to withhold them from such a pious use : It is therefore considered and resolved, that if by direction of the Governor and Council those sums, or any part of them, can be gained, they shall be paid into the treasury of the said college, to be improved by the trustees thereof, to the benefit of said college, and particularly to the carrying on the building of the rector's house, if it shall be wanting to that end. Always provided, that the government

[1] *Ibid.*, VI, 159.   [2] *Ibid.*, VI, 256.   [3] *Ibid.*, VI, 260.
[4] This impost amounted to over £300, "probably in bills of credit." (Dexter's Annals, I, 259.)
[5] *Ibid.*, VI., 283.

be at no charge in recovering the money."[1]   The following
October, on a petition of the trustees, the Assembly re-enacted
the above provision, and furthermore empowered the trustees
to recover the debt from the commissary of Annapolis, "although it should be of greater value than the sum abovesaid."[2]
At this session, the trustees successfully petitioned for the
grant of a common seal, a provision which had been cautiously
omitted in the original charter to the collegiate school.[3]
A year and a half later the trustees again brought the college
charter to the attention of the legislature, and an Act in explanation of and addition to the Act for erecting a Collegiate
School in this Colony was passed by the Assembly.

"Whereas, pursuant to the powers and privileges granted to
cetrain trustees for erecting a collegiate school in this colony,
entitled An Act for a Collegiate School, the said trustees have
erected the said school in the town of New Haven, which
school is now known by the name of Yale College; And
whereas it appears to this Assembly, that an explanation and
enlargement of the powers and privileges granted by said act
is necessary for the carrying on the affairs of the said college,
for want of which it has labored under great difficulties,[4] very
much to the prevention of that order and good education which
is to be desired there : Be it therefore enacted by the Governor,
Council and Representatives, in General Court assembled, and
by the authority of the same, that the said act, which provides
that the number of the said trustees be not under seven nor
above eleven, is not to be understood or taken so as to be re
strictive of the power of the said trustees never to choose
any person to be a trustee when there is, of such persons as
have been chosen and acted as trustees, eleven persons living

---

[1] *Ibid.*, VI, 325.   [2] *Ibid.*, VI, 337–8.   [3] *Ibid.*, VI, 340.

[4] The differences which arose among the trustees in the removal of the College
from Saybrook to New Haven are here referred to; likewise the more recent
religious controversy which had occurred between the trustees and Rector Cutler
and Tutor Browne. See below.

in the colony or elsewhere; but that, in case any person so chosen be by Providence incapacitated from attending that service, or shall himself decline the same, through the necessity of his own affairs or for any other such reason as he shall judge requisite, the trustees, in any of their meetings lawfully called, may be understood to have, and it is hereby enacted and declared that they shall be taken to have, full power, by the majority of such meeting, to proceed to the choice of another trustee in the room of any such person. And it is hereby further declared and enacted to be the true intent and meaning of the act aforesaid, that the said trustees shall be empowered, and they are hereby declared to have power, to meet together for considering, advising about and resolving upon, all matters belonging to the trust of the said college committed unto them as aforesaid, and to agree and conclude, order and determine, concerning them, by the majority of the said meeting; and by the same majority to choose and appoint a clerk, who shall, in a fair book prepared for that end, register and carefully preserve the acts of all such meetings. And whereas it has been doubted wnat number of the said trustees may be looked upon as a sufficient or full meeting, in as much as there is not in the aforesaid act any express mention made of any meeting of the said trustees: It is therefore, to prevent all scruple of that kind for the future, hereby provided and declared, that due notice being given to the trustees, by consent of any three of them, of a meeting of the trustees desired at any time or place, any seven or more of the trustees present at such time and place shall be esteemed a full meeting. And it is hereby declared and enacted, that in all such meetings so called, or otherwise as the said trustees in any such full meeting shall agree, all affairs under the care of the said trustees shall be determined by the majority of such meeting. And whereas it has been found inconvenient that in the election of persons to be trustees, the trustees' election by the aforesaid act should be limited and restrained so as that the person who shall be chosen must necessarily be forty years of age : It is hereby declared and enacted, that for the future the said trustees in any election of a person into that trust shall not be esteemed or held obliged by said act to choose such persons as shall be above forty years of age, but may choose such persons otherwise qualified according to said act, provided he is thirty years of age. And it is further hereby allowed, enacted, granted and provided, that whosoever shall be chosen and made a rector of the said college shall, by virtue thereof, become a trustee of the same, and be so esteemed and taken during his continuance in the said rectorship." [1]

In May, 1724, the legislature was pleased to grant a further request of the trustees under an act " to enable the trustees of Yale College to exchange certain lands." These lands consisted of a farm of 600 acres in the township of Killingly which had been donated to the college in 1701 by Major James Fitch, member of the Council. [2] The title to this property was disputed, but the parties interested declared their willingness to give other lands equal in value and quantity in exchange for the Killingly farm, and the legislature was therefore appealed to by the trustees to legalize this transaction. [3] A request, however, of the trustees for a renewal of the appropriation of the tax on rum was refused on motion of the Lower House. [4]

In 1722 Rector Cutler made a formal acknowledgement of his conversion to the Episcopal persuasion and his resignation was consequently called for by the trustees. For the next four years different members of the board presided over the College. In September, 1725, Rev. Elisha Williams, pastor of Newington parish in Wethersfield, was called to the rectorship, and the trustees successfully petitioned the Assembly to recom-

---

[1] Ibid., VI, 416–417.
[2] Kingsley's History, I, 22.
[3] Conn. Col. Rec., VI, 446–7. See also Ibid., VI, 372.
[4] Dexter's Annals, I, 290.

pense his parishioners by freeing them from their country rates. "This Assembly rejoiced in the good providence that conducted the reverend trustees to fill up the vacancy of a rector in a said college with a gentleman so agreeable to the country, and so very acceptable to the Assembly;[1] and do enact that when the said Mr. Elisha Williams shall remove to New Haven into the service of rector in Yale College, according to appointment of the said reverend trustees, that Newington, or the inhabitants of said parish, shall be freed from paying their country tax for the space of four years next coming, on condition that the money be improved towards settling another minister in said parish."[2] The following May, the trustees informed the Assembly that "they had prevailed with the reverend Mr. Elisha Williams to remove from his parish at Newington to Yale College," and urged that "the people of Newington ought to be considered with respect to the disbursements they have made in settling Mr. Williams amongst them." It was therefore ordered by the Assembly, "that the treasurer pay out of the public treasury to the inhabitants of Newington the sum of one hundred pounds and sixteen shillings, in satisfaction of part of the sum the trustees agreed the said inhabitants should have as a recompence for their said disbursements; provided the said Mr. Williams be settled in the trust of rector of the said college."[3]

In October, 1727, a motion was carried in the Upper House to free Mr. Williams from taxation during his continuance in the rectorship, but the Lower House refused to concur.[4] At

---

[1] Mr. Williams had been a member of the legislature in 1718. After his resignation from the rectorship in 1739, he was again returned to the House of Representatives, and served as Speaker of the House during 5 of the 22 sessions in which he was a member of that body. (Dexter's Annals, I, 632.) See p. 125.

[2] *Conn. Col. Rec.*, VI, 569–570.

[3] *Ibid.*, VII, 24.

[4] Dexter's Annals, I, 365. In October, 1729, Rector Cutler petitioned in his own behalf on this subject; but the Lower House persisted in its refusal. (*Ibid.*, I, 401.)

this session, in answer to a petition of the trustees, the Assembly granted the College the impost " on rum " for one year.[1] In 1728 on account of the " pressing circumstances of Yale College" fifty pounds in bills of public credit is advanced by the government out of its yearly allowance to the Collge.[2] In May, 1729, upon a memorial of the trustees, the sum of £80 a year for the term of two years is appropriated to the College.[3] In October, 1730, on account of the depreciation of the bills of credit, this extra grant is increased to £100 and continued for another year.[4] In 1732, upon a memorial of the trustees, the Assembly appropriated 1500 acres to the " benefit and behoof" of the College. This grant was made up of 300 acres in each of the five townships which had recently been laid out east of the Housatonic river.[5] Six years later £40 was allowed to the trustees for laying out these " college farms,"[6] and the surveys which were then made were accepted and patents granted for them by the legislature.[7] In 1733 the Assembly orders a special appropriation of £100 to be paid to the College for the year past and a like approprlation is made for the current year.[8] This grant is renewed for one year in 1734;[9] for three years, in 1735,[10] and again for three years, in 1738.[11]

In 1735, a committee appointed by the Assembly, upon the memorial of the trustees, to view the state of Yale College, report that " it will be best that the roof, with some part of the backside and ends, also the kitchen, the doors and back windows, be all mended, the aforesaid new colored, and the fences erected." Whereupon the Assembly appoints Capt. Isaac Dickerman and Mr. John Ponderson a committee to oversee the work, and order them to draw fifty pounds out of the treasury of the colony, and to lay their accounts before the Assembly in the following May.[12] In May the report of the com-

[1] *Ibid.*, VII, 133.   [2] *Ibid.*, VII, 178.   [3] *Ibid.*, VII, 229.

[4] *Ibid.*, VII, 302.   [5] *Ibid.*, VII, 412–13.   [6] *Ibid.*, VIII, 203.

[7] *Ibid.*, VIII, 345-6.   [8] *Ibid.*, VII, 472.   [9] *Ibid.*, VII, 523.

[10] *Ibid.*, VIII, 24.   [11] *Ibid.*, VIII, 203.   [12] *Ibid.*, VIII, 15.

mittee was received by the Assembly and an additional appropriation of fifty pounds was made.[1] The following October, £53 18s, 3d, was paid to the committee on repairs, which sum was stated to be payment in full for the work done;[2] but later in the month Messrs. Dickermann and Ponderson were empowered to make further repairs and granted £25 to that end.[3] In October, 1738, Mr. Ponderson laid his final account before the Assembly. It was approved and Mr. Ponderson was given the sum of £5 8s, 9d, "the balance of said account."[4]

In the readjustment of the rates of taxation which was made in the colony in 1737, the rector, tutors and students, "until the expiration of the time for taking their second degree," were freed from poll taxes,[5] and at the same time the estate of the rector of Yale College was included in a provision which exempted the estates of all settled ministers from taxation.[6] Three years later the rector, tutors and students were also exempted from all military service.[7]

In 1739, Rector Williams resigned and Rev. Mr. Thomas Clap, pastor of the church in the first society of Windham, was chosen rector, and the trustees petitioned the Assembly in behalf of the society of Windham "to allow said society the sum of £310[8] for the satisfaction of their temporal damages." The Assembly forthwith granted this petition.[9]

In 1740, the trustees address the Assembly on the subject of needed building and repairs, and that body resolves "that the

[1] *Ibid.*, VIII, 37.
[2] *Ibid.*, VIII, 66.
[3] *Ibid.*, VIII, 75.
[4] *Ibid.*, VIII, 206.
[5] *Ibid.*, VIII, 131-2.
[6] *Ibid.*, VIII, 133.

[7] *Ibid.*, VIII, 379. England declared war against Spain in 1739, and military preparations were in order in all the American colonies.

[8] This sum was half the amount that the society had given to Mr. Clap at the time of his settlement as minister 14 years previous. Fourteen years was considered about half the usual term of a minister's service. (Kingsley's History, i, 65.)

[9] *Conn. Col. Rec.*, VIII, 308.

college house of the said college shall be repaired at the charge of this colony as soon as may be, which repairs shall be by new shingling the roof, clap-boarding the backside, ground-silling, if need be, and making necessary repairs of the windows, and in other parts where they are defective. And Mr. John Punderson and Mr. Daniel Edwards are hereby appointed to take care of and procure the said repairs to be made as reasonable as may be, and to render an account of their doings in that affair to this Assembly. And his Honor the Governor[1] and Nathaniel Stanly, Esq., shall draw out of the public treasury of this colony such sums of bills of public credit as they shall judge necessary for the purpose aforesaid, and deliver the same to said committee for the use aforesaid, taking their receipt therefor. And it is further resolved by this Assembly, that the other matters in the report aforesaid, respecting the building a new house for the entertainment of the students in said college, be referred to the consideration of this Assembly at their sessions in May next."[2]   There is no evidence that the subject of a new college building was considered in the subsequent May session of the Assembly, but in October, 1741, the trustees again petition the legislature concerning necessary repairs, and it is: "Ordered, that there be erected on the backside of the rector's house a small kitchen of about sixteen feet square, beside the chimney place, and one story high, and that such repairs as are necessary be made about the rector's house, and there be erected a good and decent new fence about the yard before the rector's house, and from thence by the street northward to the corner; and Messrs. Daniel Edwards and Samuel Mix,[3] of New Haven, are ap-

[1] In 1741, Governor Talcott having died, Mr. John Hitchcock was associated with Nathaniel Stanley in the above affair. (*Ibid.*, VIII, 442.)

[2] *Ibid.*, VIII, 345.

[3] In May, 1743, Edwards and Mix showed to the Assembly that " by some oversight, nothing had been allowed for their services," and prayed " to be remembered respecting that matter." Whereupon the Assembly allowed them £12 for " their trouble and service." (*Ibid.*, VIII, 530.)

pointed hereby to take care of and procure the said work to be done in the best and most convenient manner, and as reasonably as may be, and to render an account of their doings in that affair to this Assembly ; and Nathaniel Stanly, Esq., and Capt. John Marsh, are hereby ordered to draw out of the public treasury of this colony such sums of bills of credit as they shall judge necessary for the purpose aforesaid, and de- liver the same to the said committee, for the use aforesaid, taking their receipt therefor."[1] Later in the month, Nathaniel Stanley, Daniel Hitchcock, John Ponderson and Daniel Ed- wards are appointed a committee to make up accounts " con- cerning what hath been expended, and to give order for what money shall be found due and further needful to finish said repairs."[2] At this session thirty pounds per annum " in bills of credit of the new tenor, or other bills equivalent thereunto "[3] are granted to the College for three years.[4] In October, 1743, in response to a memorial from the trustees, the annual grant to the College is increased to £100 " lawful money."[5] In October, 1744, the trustees report that the rector's house is again in need of repairs and the Assembly resolve that " both roof and sides be new covered, the sides colored and the win- dows filled with sash glass ; and Capt. John Hubbard and Mr. Samuel Mix, of New Haven, are hereby appointed a committee to take care of and procure said work to be done and lay their accounts thereof before this Court before their sessions in May next. And this Assembly orders the treasurer of this colony to pay and deliver to the said committee the sum of two hun-

---

[1] *Ibid.*, VIII, 436–7.   [2] *Ibid.*, VIII, 442.

[3] In 1740 a new issue of paper money had been made to meet war expenses. The ratio between this so called new tenor and the outstanding paper issues or old tenor was 2 and ½ to one. (*A Historical Account of Connecticut Currency, Continental Money, and the Finances of the Revolution*, pp. 56, 59. Henry Bronson, M. D. Pub. in New Haven Hist. Coll., vol. I. New Haven, 1865.)

[4] *Rec.* VIII, 436.   [5] *Ibid.*, VIII, 553.

dred pounds in bills of credit, old tenor, to be improved for that purpose."[1]

At this session " an act for the more full and complete establishment of Yale College in New Haven, and for enlarging the powers and privileges thereof " was passed " by the Governor and Company of his Majesty's Colony in New England in America." " Whereas, upon the petition of several well disposed and public spirited persons, expressing their desire that full liberty and privilege might be granted unto certain undertakers, for the founding, suitably endowing, and ordering a collegiate school within this colony, wherein youth might be instructed in the arts and sciences, the Governor and Company of the said colony in General Court assembled at New Haven, on the 9th day of October in the year of our Lord one thousand seven hundred and one, granted unto the Rev. Messrs. James Noyes, Israel Chauncey [etc.] (who were proposed to stand as trustees, partners or undertakers for the said society), and to their successors, full liberty, right and privilege, to erect, form, direct, order, establish, improve, and at all times in all suitable ways to encourage the said school in some convenient place in this colony, and granted sundry powers and privileges for the attaining the end aforesaid: And whereas, the said trustees, partners and undertakers, in pursuance to the aforesaid grant, liberty, license, founded a collegiate school at New Haven, known by the name of Yale College, which has received the favorable benefactions of many liberal and piously disposed persons, and under the blessing of Almighty God has trained up many worthy persons for the service of God in the State as well as in the Church: And whereas the General Court of this colony, assembled at New Haven the tenth day of October, in the year of our Lord one thousand seven hundred and twenty-three, did explain and enlarge the aforesaid powers and privileges granted to the afore-

---

[1] *Ibid.*, IX, 62. In July, 1745, this appropriation was increased by £100 old tenor. (*Ibid.*, IX, 153.)

said partners, trustees or undertakers, and their successors, for the purpose aforesaid, as by the respective acts, reference thereto being had, more fully and at large may appear: And whereas the Rev. Messrs. Thomas Clap, Samuel Whitman, Jared Elliot, Ebenezer Williams, Jonathan Marsh, Samuel Cook, Samuel Whittelsey, Joseph Noyes, Anthony Stoddard, Benjamin Lord, and Daniel Wadsworth, the present trustees, partners and undertakers of the said school, and successors of those before mentioned, have petitioned that the said school with all the rights, powers, privileges and interests thereof, may be confirmed, and that such other additional powers and privileges may be granted as shall be necessary for the ordering and managing of the said school in the most advantageous and beneficial manner, for the promoting all good literature in the present and succeeding generations: Therefore, Governor and Company of his Majesty's said English Colony of Connecticut, in General Court assembled, this ninth day of May in the year of our Lord one thousand seven hundred and forty-five, enact, ordain and declare, and by these presents it is enacted, ordained and declared: That the said Thomas Clap, Samuel Whitman, Jared Eliot, Ebenezer Williams, Jonathan Marsh, Samuel Cook, Samuel Whittelsey, Joseph Noyes, Anthony Stoddard, Benjamin Lord, and Daniel Wadsworth, shall be an incorporate society, or body corporate and politic, and shall hereafter be called and known by the name of The President and Fellows of Yale College in New Haven; and that by the same name they and their successors shall and may have perpetual succession, and shall and may be persons capable in the law to plead and be impleaded, defend and be defended, and answer and be answered unto, and also to have, take, possess, acquire, purchase or otherwise receive, lands, tenements, hereditaments, goods, chattels or other estates, and the same lands, tenements, hereditaments, goods, chattels or other estates to grant, demise, lease, use, manage or improve, for the good and benefit of the said college, according to the tenor of the donation and their discretion. That all gifts, grants, bequests and donations of lands, tenements or hereditaments, of goods and chattels, heretofore made to or for the use, benefit and advantage of the collegiate school aforesaid, whether the same be expressed to be made to the president or rector and the rest of the incorporate society of Yale College, or to the trustees or undertakers of the collegiate school in New Haven, or to the trustees by any other name, style or title whatsoever, whereby it may be clearly known and understood that the true intent and design of such gifts, grants, bequests and donations was to or for the use, benefit and advantage of the collegiate school aforesaid, and to be under the care and disposal of the governors thereof, shall be confirmed, and the same are hereby confirmed and shall be and remain to, and be vested in the president and fellows of the college aforesaid and their successors, as to the true and lawful successors of the original grantees. That the said president and fellows and their successors shall and may hereafter have a common seal to serve and use for all causes, matters and affairs of them and their successors, and the same to alter, break and make new, as they shall think fit. That the said Thomas Clap shall be, and he is hereby established the present president, and the said Samuel Whitman, Jared Eliott, Ebenezer Williams, Jonathan Marsh, Samuel Cook, Samuel Whittelsley, Joseph Noyes, Anthony Stoddard, Benjamin Lord, and Daniel Wadsworth, shall be, and they are hereby established, the present fellows of the said college; and that they and their successors shall continue in their respective places during life, or until they, or either of them, shall resign or be removed or displaced, as in this act is hereby expressed. That there shall be a general meeting of the president and fellows of said college in the college library. on the second Wednesday of September annually, or at any other time and place which they shall see cause to appoint, to consult, advise and act in and about the affairs and business of the said college; and that on any special emergency the president or any two of the fellows or any four of the fellows may appoint a meeting at the said college, provided they give notice thereof to the rest by letters sent and left with them or at the places of their respective abode five days before such meeting; and that the president and six fellows or in case of the death, absence or incapacity of the president, seven fellows convened as aforesaid, (in which case the eldest fellow shall preside,) shall be deemed a meeting of the president and fellows of said college; and that in all the said meetings the major vote of the members present shall be deemed the act of the whole and where an equi-vote happens the president shall have a casting vote. That the president and fellows of said college and their successors, in any of their meetings assembled as aforesaid, shall and may from time to time, as occasion shall require, elect and appoint a president or fellow in the room and place of any president or fellow who shall die, resign or be removed from his office, place or trust, whom the said Governor and Company hereby declare for any misdemeanor, unfaithfulness, default or incapacity, shall be removable by the president and fellows of the said college, six of them at least concurring in such act; and shall have power to appoint a scribe or register, a treasurer, tutors, professors, steward, and all such other officers and servants usually appointed in colleges or universities, as they shall find necessary, and think fit to appoint, for the promoting good literature and the well ordering and managing the affairs of said college, and them or any of them at their discretion to remove, and to prescribe and administer such forms of oaths (not being contrary to the laws of England or of this colony) as they shall think proper to be administered, to all the officers, instructors of the said college, or to such and so many of them as they shall think proper, for the faithful execution of their respective places, offices and trusts. That the present president and

fellows of said college and their successors, and all such
tutors, professors and other officers as shall be appointed for the
public instruction and government of said college, before they
undertake the execution of their respective offices and trusts,
or within three months after, shall publicly in the college hall
take the oaths and prescribe the declaration appointed by an
Act of Parliament made in the first year of King George the
First, entitled an Act for the further security of his Majesty's
person and government and the succession of the Crown in the
heirs of the late Princess Sophia, being Protestants, and for
extinguishing the hopes of the pretended Prince of Wales and
his open and secret abettors : that is to say, the president before the Governor, Deputy Governor, or any two of the Assistants of this colony, for the time being, and the fellows, tutors
and other officers before the president for the time being, who
is hereby empowered to administer the same; an entry of all
which shall be made in the records of the said college. That
the president and fellows shall have the government, care and
management of said college, and all the matters and affairs
thereunto belonging, and shall have power, from time to time as
occasion shall require, to make, ordain and establish all such
wholesome and reasonable laws, rules and ordinances, not repugnant to the laws of England, nor the laws of this colony,
as they shall think fit and proper, for the instruction and education of the students, and ordering, governing, ruling, and
managing the said college, and all matters, affairs and things
thereunto belonging, and the same to repeal and alter, as they
shall think fit; (which shall be laid before this Assembly as
often as required, and may also be repealed or disallowed by
this Assembly when they shall think proper.)   That the president of the said college, with the consent of the fellows, shall
have power to give and confer all such honors, degrees or
licenses as are usually given in colleges or universities, upon
such as they shall think worthy thereof.   That all the lands
and rateable estate belonging to the said college, not exceeding

the yearly value of five hundred pounds sterling, lying in this government, and the persons, families and estates of the president and professors, lying and being in the town of New Haven, and the persons of the tutors, students, and such and so many of the servants of said college as give their constant attendance on the business of it, shall be free and exempted from all rates, taxes, military service, working at highways, and other such like duties and services. And for the special encouragement and support of said college, this Assembly do hereby grant unto the president and fellows and their successors, for the use the of the said college, in lieu of all former grants, one hundred pounds silver money, at the rate of six shillings and eight pence per ounce, to be paid in bills of public credit, or other currency equivalent to the said hundred pounds (the rate or value thereof to be stated from time to time by this Asembly,) in two equal payments in October and May annually: this payment to continue during the pleasure of this Assembly.[1] In full testimony and confirmation of this grant and all the articles and matter therein contained, the said Governor and Company do hereby order that this Act shall be signed by the Governor and Secretary, and sealed with the public seal of this colony, and that the same, or a duplicate or exemplification

---

[1] This annual grant varied from year to year, according to petitions of the corporation. In October, 1746, £262, 10s. old tenor, were granted (*Ibid.*, IX, 256); in May, 1747, £85 14s. 3d. new tenor, for the preceding half year (*Ibid.*, IX, 315); in October, 1747, £85 14s. 3d. new tenor, for the first half of the current year (*Ibid.*, IX, 323); in May, 1748, £107 3s. new tenor (*Ibid.*, IX, 375); in *October, 1748, £107 3s. new tenor (*Ibid.*, IX, 386); in October, 1749, £233 7s. new tenor, for the preceding half year and the first half of the current year (*Ibid.*, IX, 464); in May, 1750, £116 13s. 6d. new tenor (*Ibid.*, IX, 535-6); in October, 1850, £116 13s. 6d. new tenor (*Ibid.*, IX, 550); in May, 1751, £116 13s. 6d. new tenor (*Ibid.*, X, 7); in October, 1751, £116 13s. 6d. new tenor (*Ibid.*, X, 48); in May, 1752, £114 6s. new tenor (*Ibid.*, X, 77-78); in October, 1752, £114 6s. new tenor (*Ibid.*, X, 134); in May, 1753, £114 5s. 9d. new tenor (*Ibid.*, X, 187); in October, 1753, £50 "lawful money" (*Ibid.*, X, 229); in May, 1754, £50 "lawful money" (*Ibid.*, X, 274); in October, 1754, £50 "lawful money" (*Ibid.*, X, 323.)

thereof, shall be a sufficient warrant to the said president and fellows, to hold, use, and exercise all the powers and privileges therein mentioned and contained."[1]

The above charter was mainly the work of President Clap. His original draft was slightly amended by Colonel Fitch of the Council to whom it had been sent by the trustees " for his perusal and best thoughts upon it." [2] In addition to the favor of the legislature in passing this act of incorporation, President Clap received the support of that body in a breach of religious discipline which occured about that time in Yale College. Two students who had been expelled from the College on account of sympathy with the so-called Separatist movement which had been exciting the whole of New England, petitioned the Assembly for redress from the college authorities. Their petition was rejected by the Old Light majorities of both Houses.[3]

In May, 1747, the long standing effort of the trustees to obtain a new college hall was finally successful. " Upon the memorial of the President and Fellows of Yale College in New Haven, representing that the present college house is not large enough to entertain one half of the students, and that there is a necessity of a new house of about one hundred and ten feet in length and thirty-eight feet in breadth and three stories high besides the garrets, praying this Assembly to take the matter into their consideration at this time, and grant that money necessary for the building of such an house may be raised in such a manner as under the present circumstances of the government may be thought most convenient: Resolved by this

---

[1] *Ibid.*, IX, 113–118.

[2] Dexter's Annals, I, 754–5.

[3] *Ibid.*, I, 772. Before this occurrence, in May, 1742, the legislature had already supported the ecclesiastical discipline of the College in accepting the report of a committee which had been appointed to consider a reference made by Governor Law to "the unhappy circumstances of the College." This report was favorable to the corporation in its expulsion of one David Brainard from the student body on the charge of censure of the religious state of the College. (Woolsey's Discourse, App. XI, p. 106–7.)

Assembly, that there be a public lottery of fifty thousand pounds old tenor concerted and drawn in the usual and proper form of public lotteries, at New Haven in the county of New Haven, and that fifteen per cent. be deducted out of each prize for building of said house and charge of said lottery. And it is further ordered and enacted, that the said affair of the lottery shall [be] forth with proceeded upon, and that Capt. John Hubbard, Mr. Samuel Mix and Mr. Chauncey Whittelsey, all of New Haven, be the directors and managers thereof. And the money which shall be raised by the lottery as aforesaid shall remain in the hands of the aforesaid directors and managers of said affair, to be disposed of in erecting a college as aforesaid, according to such orders as shall be given by this Assembly from time to time." [1] About £775 sterling were cleared [2] from this lottery and at the request of the President and Fellows of Yale College the Assembly of October, 1747, appointed a committee to see that this sum was properly delivered to the officers of the college. [3] This money was found insufficient for the purpose in hand and the corporation petitioned the Assembly for an additional amount. Accordingly in October, 1749, the Assembly granted £4000 in bills of credit, old tenor, " for the carrying on and finishing the building." [4]

In October, 1750, a committee of the Assembly who had been " desired to view the College, and to see what repairs were necessary to be made," show " that it is necessary to take down and rebuild the kitchen chimney in part or whole, and to cover the back side, to mend the floors and make new window frames, and to put pillars under the girts, beside some other smaller repairs," etc. Whereupon the Assembly appointed Captain John Hubbard and Mr. Samuel Mix " a committee to make the aforesaid reparations and emendations in

[1] *Conn. Col. Rec*, IX, 279-280.

[2] Dexter's Annals, II, 140.   [3] *Conn. Col. Rec.*, IX, 325.

[4] *Ibid.*, IX, 492-3. This sum amounted to £363 sterling, and was the proceeds of a French prize taken by a Connecticut frigate. (Dexter's Annals, II, 227.)

the said college, and to improve such proper persons as they shall see fit for the purpose aforesaid, and to draw their orders on the treasurer of this colony for all such sums as shall be necessarily expended for making such reparations."[1] Mr. Hubbard's accounts were approved in May, 1752, and a balance of £627 19 s. 2d, old tenor, was paid over to him.[2]

In 1751, the new college hall was still unfinished, and so on petition of the corporation the Assembly appoint a committee to inspect the " college house . . . so far as it is already carried on, and the expenses of it, and to make some estimates of the future charges which shall be necessary, and consider and propose the most proper measures in order to defray them."[3] The committee report, " that they have inspected the said college house, and inquired into the expenses already incurred in building said college house, and find that there is now due from said corporation for work already done, the sum of £1764 17 s 3d, in bills of credit, old tenor, over and above the several sums already obtained by the lottery, grants of this Assembly, and donations made by private gentlemen, and that by their estimate there will be needed to complete and furnish said house the sum of £6,000 0s, 0d, old tenor bills." Whereupon the Assembly appoint William Pitkin and Joseph Buckingham, Esqrs. a committee, to receive of the treasurer of the colony bonds from sundry persons in the colony, payable in bills of credit either of the Connecticut or the neighboring governments, to the value of £7764 17s 3d, old tenor, and to deliver the same to Thomas Clap, President of Yale College. The Assembly also authorized President Clap " by himself or his substitutes, to ask, sue for, recover and receive, the money due on such bonds, to be by the said president and fellows improved towards the finishing said college house."[4] The building was opened in September, 1752, and at the following Commencement it was named Connecticut Hall.[5]

---

[1] *Ibid.*, IX, 580.   [2] *Ibid.*, X, 97.   [3] *Ibid.*, X, 46.   [4] *Ibid.*, X, 46–47.

[5] The translation of the dedication that was pronounced in Latin at the ceremony

In October, 1754, upon a memorial of President Clap, the Assembly order Colonel Gurdon Saltonstall and Major Jabez Hamlin, the commissaries of the colony, to turn over the balance of their accounts, about the sum of £3,800 old tenor[1] to the Rev. Mr. Clap " to be by him improved towards finishing the new college house, called Connecticut Hall," and President Clap is directed " to proceed, as soon as may be consistent with prudence and good discretion" and to lay his accounts before the Assembly "when he hath expended what said sums amount to."[2]

In view of the ecclesiastical controversies which were rife in the third and fourth decades of this century, and in which, as we have seen, the students as well as the faculty of Yale College had become engaged, the corporation began to agitate the establishment of a separate chair of divinity in the College, as a means towards orthodoxy. On October 19, 1752, a committee that had been appointed to consider the propriety of governmental co-operation in this plan, recommended that £10,000 old tenor should be obtained from a sale of colony lands on Housatonic River, and appropriated to the support of a professor of divinity. The Lower House, apparently distrustful of the orthodoxy of the College, refused to accept this recommendation.[3]

The following year, the question came up again in Assembly. A joint committee of both Houses reported in favor of a donation to a divinity professorship of the income for ten years from £1,000 worth of colony lands, and of a general contribution by all the church to that object. The Lower House agreed only to the second of these proposals.[4] " Whereas one

reads thus: " Whereas, through the favor of Divine Providence, this new college house has been built by the munificence of the colony of Connecticut, in perpetual commemoration of so great generosity this neat and decent building shall be called " Connecticut Hall." (Kingsley's History, I, 77–8.)

[1] Of this sum £250 sterling were eventually realized. (Dexter's Annals, II, 354.)

[2] *Conn. Col. Rec.*, X, 322.   [3] Dexter's Annals, II, 303.   [4] *Ibid.*, II, 321.

principal end proposed in erecting and supporting Yale College in New Haven was, to supply the churches of this colony with a learned, pious and orthodox ministry, to which purpose it is requisite that the students of the said college should have the best instructions in divinity and the best patterns of preaching set before them: And whereas the settling a learned, pious and orthodox professor of divinity in the said college would greatly tend to promote that good end and design: And whereas the present incomes of the said college are but in part sufficient to support such a professor: This Assembly being desirous to promote and encourage such a good design, do hereby grant and allow of and order a general contribution to be made in all the religious societies in this colony, and recommend the same both to ministers and people, and order that the money raised thereby be remitted to the president of said college, to be improved by the corporation towards the support of such a professor."[1]   At this same session, in view of the demands of students of the Episcopal denomination in the College, the trustees put the question to the legislature "whether all the students of College shall be obliged to attend the public worship on the Lord's Day, together in one place, as heretofore." The point was merely referred to a committee; no answer seems to have been given to the trustees.[2]

In May, 1754, the Lower House expressed its disapproval of the ecclesiastical doings in the College by dissenting from the usual semi-annual grant to that institution. Later, however, upon reconsideration, the grant was passed.[3] But in the spring of the following year, the Lower House persisted in dissenting from the regular appropriation on the pretext of large current expenses on account of the French War.[4] The

---

[1] *Conn. Col. Rec.*, X, 213.   [2] Dexter's Annals, II, 320.   [3] *Ibid.*, II, 322.

[4] *Ibid.*, II, 337. Mr. Dexter and Mr. Kingsley explain this action on the ground that the " New Lights " in the Assembly had always been inimical to President Clap, and that he had also alienated the " Old Lights," about two-thirds of the Lower House, by the establishment of the college church and the exaction of a declaration of faith from the college officers.

grant was never renewed. During the remainder of President Clap's administration until his resignation in 1766, much opposition both from within and without the College was shown to his rigid and arbitrary management of that institution. From 1758 to 1763 four distinct appeals were made to the legislature, through the fellows, the graduates and the students of the College, to examine into the college church, whose setting up was held to be " an infringement on the order and rights of the regular churches, . . . and a daring affront to legislative power;" and also into the rate of tuition and the system of fines and punishments administered to the student body.[1] The last attack was in the shape of a memorial addressed to the Assembly and signed by nine gentlemen, in which it was urged that the legislature by right of being founder of the College, should send a committee of visitation to rectify existing abuses.[2] The arguments of this memorial were met so ably by President Clap, that they failed to move the Assembly to action and the independence of the corporation was preserved.[3]

In May, 1762, the President and Fellows petitioned the legislature for aid in the erection of the College chapel whose foundation had been laid the preceding year. At this time the Lower House refused to grant the petition;[4] but upon its renewal in 1765 the legislature agreed to pay the deficit in the college treasury to the account of the new chapel,— a matter of £327 11s, 8d, " lawful money."[5] In October, 1766, the appeal of the corporation for legislative aid is again successful. " On the memorial of the President[6] and Fellows of Yale College in New Haven, showing the necessity of sufficient funds to enable them to support the officers needful for the instruc-

---

[1] *Ibid.*, II, 507, 564–5, 723–4. [2] *Ibid.*, II, 777–8.
[3] *Ibid.*, II, 780–1. [4] *Ibid.*, II, 724.
[5] *Conn. Col. Rec.*, XII, 438–9.

[6] President Clap resigned in September, 1766, and Rev. Mr. Naphtali Daggett became President, *pro tem.*

tion, government and well-being of that society; praying for such aid and assistance as will enable them to support that important interest, so as to answer the true and great ends of its institution ; a committee appointed to take the affairs into consideration, etc., have reported that they find the want of sufficient funds complained of is occasioned by the payment of considerable sums out of the college treasury towards building the chapel, finishing a house for a professor of divinity and for his support, also by the inability of the tenants, the great decrease of the number of students, and the withdrawal of the usual annual grant from this Assembly; that they are of opinion that it is necessary the College be furnished with the following officers, supported with the salaries to their offices severally annexed, viz :

A President, at £150 per annum.

A Professor of Divinity, £113 6s. 8d.

A Senior Tutor, £65 1s. 4d.

3 Junior Tutors, at £57 1s. 4d. each, £171 4s.

That the revenues of College are not sufficient therefor, and that there will be wanting to pay off the debts of the College and support it the current year, the sum of £159 12s. 0d. which they recommended to be paid to said president and fellows out of the impost duty on rum collected by the naval officers of the ports of New London and New Haven; and further, that it be recommended to said president and fellows that their laws be revised and printed in English as well as Latin, and one book of their laws lodged in the Secretary's office; and that the government of said college be as near like parental, and as few pecuniary mulcts as the circumstances thereof will admit; and that the steward in making up his quarter bills insert the punishment of each scholar with the offence for which the same was imposed, for the parents' information; and that in order for the continual support of college their accounts be annually laid before the General Assembly of this colony in the October sessions: Resolved by this As-

sembly, that the matters and things herein before mentioned to
be reported by said committee be accepted and approved, saving that there be but two junior tutors, and that the salary
provided for the third, viz. £57 1 s. 4d. be deducted out of the
said sum of £159 12s. 0 d. And the naval officer of the port
of New Haven is hereby accordingly ordered to pay to the
treasurer of said college the remaining sum, being £102, 10s,
8 d. out of said duty on rum, or so much thereof as he hath
money arising thereon in his hands. And in case he, said
naval officer, have not sufficient, the naval officer of New London is ordered to pay the residue thereof to said treasurer, for
the use and purposes aforesaid."[1]

In October, 1767, the accounts of the College were presented
to the Assembly in accordance with the recommendations of
the preceding year. The corporation report that the College
is in debt £159 8s, 6d, " including a balance of £49 8s, 6d, due
towards finishing the chapel, and that some repairs of the old
college and coloring the windows of the new college and
chapel are now necessary, the cost of which is computed at
£63 11s, 6d." Two hundred and twenty-three pounds out of
the duties on rum are accordingly voted by the Assembly to
the College.[2]

In October, 1768, the President and Fellows report that the
expenses of the College during the past year have exceeded
the revenue by £122 16s, 10d, and " that several things are
wanting to put the College in a reputable condition, and some of
them necessary, such as finishing the new library and entries
of the brick college, a decent fence to the college yard, and
more convenient kitchen and dining room." The Assembly
therefore grants £182 16s, 10d " to be improved for payment
of said debt and finishing the new library."[3]

In October, 1769, the corporation report a debt of £226 11s,
11d, " which they have no way of discharging "; and the As-

[1] *Ibid.*, XII, 513-14.   [2] *Ibid.*, XII, 529-530.   [3] *Ibid.*, XIII, 103-4.

sembly grants for this purpose £83 4s, 11d, to be paid out of the impost duties on rum.[1]

In October, 1770, the corporation report a debt of £216 4s, 6d, and the Assembly grant them an equivalent sum to be paid in bills of credit out of the colony treasury.[2]

In May, 1772, the Assembly grants lottery privileges to certain of the inhabitants of New Haven for the extension of a wharf in their harbor on condition that "the wharfage of such part of said wharf as shall be built with said moneys so to be raised to be taken on all shipping that shall moor at the same according to the rates that shall from time to time be imposed and laid by the proprietors aforesaid be and the same hereby is appropriated to the use of Yale College in said New Haven, after expending such part thereof as shall be necessary in maintaining the same in good and sufficient repair."[3]

In October, 1772, a committee was appointed by the Assembly to inspect the state of the College. "Whereas promoting and encouraging literature and useful arts in the collegiate school in this colony is of the greatest public importance, and for that end is become necessary to establish such durable supports as shall best answer the great purposes of founding said school, and to grant them such powers as shall best answer the ends designed: Therefore, Col. Jabez Hamblin, Mr. James Hillhouse, Majr. Samuel Holden Parsons, Ebenezer Silliman, Esq., Col. Jabez Fitch and Col. John Williams are appointed to join with such gentlemen as the Upper House shall appoint, to take into consideration the state of education and learning in said school, the government, laws and constitution of the same, to look into the several donations at any time made for the support of said school, the revenues arising therefrom, and the state in which they now are, and to consider and devise the most effectual measures to render the institution most extensively useful and the support thereof permanent and

---

[1] *Ibid.*, XIII, 261.   [2] *Ibid.*, XIII, 396.   [3] *Ibid.*, XIII, 622–3.

lasting, and to confer with the president and fellows of said college concerning the same, and to make report to this or some future Assembly." This order was concurred in by the Upper House, who joined the Hon. Matthew Griswold, Roger Sherman and Abraham Davenport, Esqs. to the above committee.[1] Upon the report of this committee that the College is in debt £180 10s, 9d, the Assembly appropriates that sum to the college treasury.[2]

In May, 1774, the Assembly grants the College £107 7 s, 6d, in payment of its debt for the year 1772–73.[3]

---

[1] *Ibid.*, XIV, 36.   [2] *Ibid.*, XIV, 63.   [3] *Ibid.*, XIV, 328.

NEW HAMPSHIRE

In 1641 those settlements in New Hampshire which had been planted by Mason and Gorges, and by emigrants from Massachusetts and England, passed under the jurisdiction of the Massachusetts Company, and were accounted members of the Massachusetts colony until the year 1679.[1] In this year New Hampshire became a royal province. In 1685 it was re-united to Massachusetts under Governor Dudley, and with the

---

[1] During this period New Hampshire towns were naturally subject to the school legislation of the Massachusetts government. In 1680 there were only 4 towns in New Hampshire; Portsmouth, settled by Mason and Gorges colonists, in 1623, counted 120 rateable persons and 71 voters ; Dover, settled about the same time, by the same company and later by Massachusetts emigrants, counted 61 voters ; Hampton, settled in 1638 by emigrants from England and Massachusetts, 124 rateables and 57 voters, and Exeter, settled at the same time by Antinomian exiles from Massachusetts, 66 rateables and 20 voters. (*Provincial Papers, Documents and Records, relating to the Province of New Hampshire*, I, 424, 426-8. Edited by Nathaniel Bouton, D. D. Concord, 1867. *The History of New Hampshire*, pp. 8-9, 37, 38. Jeremy Belknap, A. M. Philadelphia, 1784. *The Annals of Portsmouth*, p. 65. Nathaniel Adams. Portsmouth, 1825.)

" At a public town meeting held the 5, 2 mo., 58, it is agreed by the selectmen together with the town, that £20 per annum shall be yearly raised for the maintenance of a school-master in the town of Dover, that is to say, for the teaching of all the children within the township of Dover, the said schoolmaster having the privilege of all strangers out of the township aforesaid. The said master also to have to read, write, cast account . . . as the parents shall require." (*Dover Town Records*, given in *Provincial Papers of N. H.*, I, 234, foot-note.)

" The selectmen of this town of Hampton have agreed with John Legat for this present year ensuing, to teach and instruct all the children of or belonging to our town, both male and female (which are capable of learning) to write and read and cast accounts (if it be desired), as diligently and carefully as he is able to teach and instruct them. And so diligently to follow the said employment at all such time and times this year ensuing, as the weather shall be fitting for the youth to come together to one place to be instructed. And also to teach and instruct

exception of a short period of union with Massachusetts under charter government, the same royal governor presided over both colonies until 1741. Their legislatures however remained distinct.

In 1693 the New Hampshire legislature passed the first general enactment in the province concerning education. It was " enacted and ordained that for the building and repairing of meeting houses, ministers' houses, school houses and allowing a salary to a schoolmaster in each town within this province, the selectmen, in the respective towns, shall raise money by an equal rate and assessment upon the inhabitants. —and every town within this province (Dover only excepted during the war) shall from and after the publication hereof, provide a schoolmaster for the supply of the town, on penalty of ten pounds ; and for neglect thereof, to be paid one-half to their Majesties, and the other half to the poor of the town." [1]

them once in a week, or more, in some orthodox catechism provided for them by their parents or masters.

And in consideration hereof we have agreed to pay, or cause to be paid, unto the said John Legat the sum of £20, in corn and cattle and butter, at price current, as payments are made of such goods in this town, and this to be paid by us quarterly . . . John Legat entered upon schooling the 21 day of the 3 month, 1649." (*Town Records*, given in *an Historical Address*, delivered at Hampton, New Hampshire, December 25, 1838, by Joseph Dow, A. M. App. Note F. p. 44. Concord, 1839.)

In 1669 Dover, Exeter and Portsmouth contributed to Harvard College, Dover, £32 15s. ; Exeter, £10, and Portsmouth, £60 per annum for 7 years. (Quincy's *History of Harvard University*, I, App. XXIII, 508.) With this gift the inhabitants of Portsmouth sent the following address to the General Court :

" Humbly sheweth that seeing by your means (under God) we enjoy much peace and quietness, and very worthy deeds are done to us by the favorable aspect of the government of this colony upon us, we accept it always and in all places with all thankfulness ; and although we have articled with yourselves for exemption from public charges, yet we never articled with God and our own consciences for exemption from gratitude, which to demonstrate while we were studying, the loud groans of the sinking college, in its present low estate, came to our ears, the relieving of which we account a good work for the house of our God, and needful for the perpetuating of knowledge, both religious and civil, among us, and our posterity after us, and therefore," etc. (*Rec. of Mass.*, IV, Pt. II, 433.)

[1] Cited by Nathaniel Bouton in his address on the *History of Education in*

In 1714, this provision was in part re-enacted in an Act for the maintenance and supply of the ministry.

[Section III.] "And it is hereby further enacted and ordained, that for building and repairing of meeting-houses, ministers' houses, school-houses, and allowing a salary to a school-master, of each town within this province; the selectmen in their respective towns shall raise money by an equal rate and assessment upon the inhabitants, in the same manner as in the present act directed for the maintenance of the minister; and every town within this province shall from and after the publication hereof provide a school-master for the supply of the town."[1]

In 1719 and 1721 more specific legislation on the same subject took place.

"AN ACT FOR THE SETTLEMENT AND SUPPORT OF GRAMMAR
SCHOOLS.

"Be it enacted by his Excellency the Governor, Council, and Representatives, in General Assembly convened, and by the authority of the same: That every town within this province, having the number of fifty householders, or upwards, shall be constantly provided of a school-master to teach children and youth to read and write. And where any town or towns have the number of one hundred families, or householders, there shall also be a grammar school set up and kept in every such town, and some discreet person of good conversation, well-instructed in the tongues, shall be procured to be master thereof; every such school-master to be suitably encouraged and paid by the inhabitants. And the selectmen of such towns respectively are hereby impowered to agree with such school-masters for salary, and to raise money by way of rate

New Hampshire, p. 11 ; but I am unable to find any reference to this law in the published laws of the colony or in the *Index to the Laws of New Hampshire*. Manchester. 1886.

[1] *Acts and Laws of his Majesty's Province of New Hampshire*, p. 58. Portsmouth. 1761.

upon the inhabitants to pay the same. And if any town qualified as aforesaid shall neglect the due observance of this act for
the procuring and settling of any such school-master, as aforesaid, by the space of six months, every such defective town
shall incur the penalty of twenty pounds, for every conviction
of such neglect, upon complaint made to the court of quarter
sessions of the peace; which penalty shall be towards the support of such school or schools within this province, where
there may be most need, at the discretion of the aforesaid
court, to be levied by warrant from the court in proportion
upon the inhabitants of such defective town, which warrant
shall be directed to the selectmen of such town, and paid in to
the treasurer of this province, for the end aforesaid. And in
default of payment thereof within three months from the date
of such warrant, then execution to be issued against the said
inhabitants. And if any town that may attain to the number
above mentioned do suppose themselves uncapable of complying with this act, they shall apply themselves to the court of
general sessions of the peace within this province, who are
hereby empowered to determine the same."[1]

"AN ACT IN ADDITION TO THE ACT FOR THE SETTLEMENT AND SUPPORT OF GRAMMAR SCHOOLS.

" Whereas the selectmen of sundry towns within this province
often neglect to provide grammar schools for their respective
towns, whereby their youth lose much of their time, to the
great hindrance of their learning; for remedy whereof: Be it
enacted by his Excellency the Governor, Council, and Representatives, in General Assembly convened, and by the authority of the same, that not only each town, but each parish
within this province consisting of one hundred families, shall
be constantly provided with a grammar school; and the selectmen of such towns and parishes respectively are hereby empowered to agree with such school-masters for salary, and to

---

[1] *Ibid.*, p. 120.

supply such school with sufficient fuel for fire as there shall be occasion, and to raise money by way of rate upon the inhabitants, to pay the same. And further, it is enacted by the authority aforesaid, that so often as it happens that any such town or parish, as aforesaid (after publication hereof), is destitute of a grammar school for the space of one month, the selectmen of such town or parish shall forfeit the sum of twenty pounds[1] for every such neglect, to be paid out of their own estates, and to be applied towards the defraying the charges of the province."[2]

Between 1680 and 1775 over 100 towns[3] were incorporated in New Hampshire, and Nathaniel Bouton, who discoursed in 1833 to the New Hampshire Historical Society on the history of education in New Hampshire, says that he had concluded after an extended examination of the records of these towns, that one lot was invariably reserved for a school in all the grants of the Masonian proprietors, of Massachusetts and of

---

[1] In 1771 this fine, together with the similar fine on towns failing to keep schools, which was provided for in the foregoing act, was reduced to £10 in view of the appreciation which had taken place in the provincial currency. (*Acts and Laws*, p. 260. Portsmouth, 1771.)

[2] *Ibid.*, p. 121.

[3] In a large number of these towns there were less than 50 inhabitants, and education was neglected. (Bouton's *History of Education*, pp. 13–14.) Belknap writes of the administration of the school law :

"Formerly when there were but few towns, much better care was taken to observe the law concerning schools than after the settlements were mutiplied ; but there never was uniform attention paid to this important matter in all places. Some towns were distinguished for their carefulness, and others for their negligence. When the leading men in a town were themselves persons of knowledge and wisdom, they would provide the means of instruction for children; but where the case was otherwise, methods were found to evade the law. The usual way of doing this was to engage some person to keep a school for a few weeks before the court term, and discontinue it soon after." (*History of New Hampshire*, III, 288–9.)

The school records of some of these towns, Chester, Charlestown, Canterbury, Concord, Keene, etc., given in the collections of the *New Hampshire Historical Society*, bear out the above statements.

Governor John Wentworth 2nd; bnt that in those charters issued to most of the Vermont towns and to Holderness, Chesterfield, Westmoreland, Walpole, Keene, Charlestown and Westminster, by Governor Benning Wentworth, there is no mention of this school grant.[1]

In 1758 a convention of Congregational ministers met at Somersworth, New Hampshire, and having taken " into consideration the great advantages which may arise to Church and State from the erecting an academy or college," unanimously voted to petition Governor Benning Wentworth for a charter for that purpose. Their aims were thus definitely stated. " We . . . beg leave to present a request to your Excellency in behalf of literature, which proceeds not from any private or party views in us, but our desire to serve the government and religion by laying a foundation for the best instruction of youth. We doubt not your Excellency is sensible of the great advantages of learning, and the difficulties which attend the education of youth in this province, by reason of our distance from any of the seats of learning, the discredit of our medium, etc. We have reason to hope that by an interest among our people, and some favor with the government, we may be able in a little time to raise a sufficient fund for erecting and carrying on an academy or college within this province." [2] . . . The following year, the committee to whom the petition had been entrusted, reported that the Governor had manifested some unwillingness to grant a charter agreeable to the convention, but that they hoped that maturer consideration on his part and the advice of his Council would lead him to a change of view.[3]

In 1762 this society of ministers, abandoning their own project, endorsed that of Dr. Eleazer Wheelock for the education

---

[1] *History of Education in New Hampshire*, p. 15.

[2] *The History of Dartmouth College.* p. 16. Baxter Perry Smith. Boston, 1878.

[3] *Ibid.*, p. 17.

of Indian youth. In 1754 Dr. Wheelock had started an Indian school at Lebanon, Connecticut. The money that was collected for this school in England was put into the hands of a board of trustees, whose president was the Earl of Dartmouth. In 1761 the Massachusetts legislature granted aid to this school, and the next year the legislature of New Hampshire followed its example. On June 17, 1762, it was voted that the Hon. Henry Sherburne and Mishech Weare, Esquires, Peter Gilman, Clement March, Esq., Capt. Thomas W. Waldron and Capt. John Wentworth, be a committee to consider of the subject matter of Rev. Mr. Eleazar Wheelock's memorial for aid of his school. On the favorable report of this committee the legislature made a grant to the school of fifty pounds per annum for five years. This grant was not continued beyond the first or second year.[1]

The developement of the Indian school necessitated the choice of a site for buildings. Dr. Wheelock writes in 1763 that among other offers Governor Wentworth had offered a tract of land in the western part of the province of New Hampshire for the use of the school.[2] Five years later Wheelock's agent reported that the Governor[3] " appeared very friendly to the design—promised to grant a township, six miles square, to the use of the school, provided it should be fixed in that province, and that he would use his influence that his Majesty should give the quit-rents to the school, to be free from charge of fees except for surveying." [4] After two unsuccessful applications to the Connecticut legislature for an act of incorporation, a royal charter was obtained in 1769 through Governor Wentworth, and the following year the school, now formally called Dartmouth College, was established at Hanover,[5] New Hampshire.

[1] *Ibid.*, p. 22.   [2] *Ibid.*, p. 29.

[3] John Wentworth, who succeeded his uncle, Benning Wentworth, in 1763.

[4] *Ibid.*, pp. 35-6.

[5] A list of proposed donations which determined the location of Dartmouth

CHARTER OF DARTMOUTH COLLEGE.

George the third by the grace of God, of Great Britain, France and Ireland, King, defender of the faith, etc.

To all to whom these presents shall come, greeting : Whereas it hath been represented to our trusty and well beloved John Wentworth Esq., Governor and Commander-in-chief, in and over our Province of New Hampshire, in New England in America, that the Rev. Eleazar Wheelock of Lebanon, in the colony of Connecticut, in New England aforesaid, now Doctor in Divinity, did, on or about the year of our Lord, one thousand seven hundred and fifty-four, at his own expense, on his own estate and plantation, set on foot an Indian Charity School and for several years through the assistance of well disposed persons in America, clothed, maintained and educated a number of the children of the Indian natives, with a view to their carrying the gospel in their own language, and spreading the knowledge of the great Redeemer among their savage tribes, and hath actually employed a number of them as missionaries and schoolmasters in the wilderness for that purpose, and by the blessing of God upon the endeavors of said Wheelock, the design became reputable among the Indians, insomuch that a larger number desired the education of their children in said school, and were also disposed to receive missionaries and schoolmasters in the wilderness, more than could be supported by the charitable contributions in these American colonies. Whereupon the said Eleazar Wheelock thought it expedient that endeavor should be used to raise contributions from well disposed persons in England, for the carrying on and

College at Hanover, is given in an appendix in Smith's History, pp. 442-4. Heading the list are :

"The King's most gracious Majesty, by advice of his Excellency, John Wentworth, Esq., his Majesty's Governor of the Province of New Hampshire, and of his Council, a charter of the township of Landaff, about 24,000 acres.

Honorable Benning Wentworth, Esq., late Governor of New Hampshire, 500 acres, on which the college is fixed in Hanover." The King gave £200 of the £9,494 7s. 7½d. which was raised for the school in England. (*Ibid.*, p. 409.)

extending said undertaking, and for that purpose said Eleazar Weeelock requested the Rev. Nathaniel Whitaker, now Doctor in Divinity, to go over to England for that purpose, and sent over with him the Rev. Sampson Occom, an Indian minister, who had been educated by the said Wheelock. And to enable the said Whitaker, to the more successful performance of said work on which he was sent, said Wheelock gave him a full power of attorney, by which said Whitaker solicited those worthy, and generous contributors to the charity, viz. the right Hon. Wm. Earl of Dartmouth, the Hon. Sir Sidney Stafford Smythe, Knight, one of the barons of his Majesty's court of Exchequer, John Thornton, of Clapham, in the county of Surrey, Esq., Sam Roffey, of Lincoln's Innfields, in the county of Middlesex, Esq. Charles Hardey, of the parish of St. Mary-le-bonne, in said county, Esq. Daniel West, of Christ's Church, Spitalfields, in the county aforesaid, Esq., Samuel Savage, of the same place, gentleman ; Josiah Robarts, of the parish of St. Edmund the King, Lombard Street, London, gentleman, and Robert Keen, of the parish of St. Botolph, Aldgate, London, gentleman ; to receive the several sums of money which should be contributed, and to be trustees to the contributors to such charity ; which they cheerfully agreed to. Whereupon, the said Whitaker did, by virtue of said power of attorney, constitute and appoint the Earl of Dartmouth, Sir Sidney Stafford Smythe, John Thornton, Samuel Roffey, Charles Hardy, and Daniel West, Esqs., and Samuel Savage, Josiah Robarts, and Robert Keen, gentleman, to be trustees of the money which had then been contributed, and which should by his means be contributed for said purpose ; which trust they have accepted, as by their engrossed declaration of the same under their hands and seals, well executed fully appears, and the same hath also been ratified by a deed of trust, well executed by said Wheelock. And the said Wheelock further represents, that he has, by the power of attorney, for many weighty reasons, given full power to the said trustees, to fix

upon and determine the place for said school, most subservient
to the great end in view. And to enable them understand-
ingly to give the preference, the said Wheelock has laid
before the said trustees the several offers which have been
generously made in the several governments in America to
encourage and invite the settlement of said school among
them for their own private emolument, and for the increase of
learning in their respective places, as well as for the furtherance of the general design in view. And whereas a large
number of the proprietors of lands in the western part of this
our Province of New Hampshire, animated and excited thereto
by the generous example of his Excellency their Governor,
and by the liberal contributions of many noblemen and gentlemen in England, and especially by the consideration that
such a situation would be as convenient as any for carrying on the great design among the Indians; and also considering that without the least impediment to the said design,
the same school may be enlarged and improved to promote
learning among the English, and be a means to supply a
great number of churches and congregations which are likely
soon to be formed in that new country, with a learned and
orthodox ministry, they the said proprietors have promised
large tracts of land for the uses aforesaid, provided the school
shall be settled in the western part of our said Province.
And they the said right Hon., Hon. and worthy trustees
beforementioned, having maturely considered the reasons
and arguments in favor of the several places proposed, have
given the preference to the western part of our said Province,
lying on Connecticut River, as a situation most convenient for
said school. And the said Wheelock has further represented
a necessity of a legal incorporation, in order to the safety and
well-being of said seminary, and its being capable of the tenure
and disposal of lands and bequests for the use of the same.
And the said Wheelock has also represented, that for many
weighty reasons, it will be expedient, at least in the infancy of

said institution, or till it can be accommodated in that new country, and he and his friends be able to remove and settle by and round about it, that the gentlemen whom he has already nominated in his last will (which he has transmitted to the aforesaid gentlemen of the trust in England) to be trustees in America, should be of the corporation now proposed. And also as there are already large collections for said school in the hands of the aforesaid gentlemen of the trust in England, and all reason to believe from their signal wisdom, piety and zeal, to promote the Redeemer's cause (which has already procured for them the utmost confidence of the kingdom) we may expect they will appoint successors in time to come, who will be men of the same spirit, whereby great good may and will accrue many ways to the institution, and much be done by their example and influence to encourage and facilitate the whole design in view; for which reasons said Wheelock desires that the trustees aforesaid, may be vested with all that power therein which can consist with their distance from the same. Know ye therefore that we, considering the premises and being willing to encourage the laudable design of spreading Christian knowledge among the savages of our American wilderness. And also that the best means of education be established in our province of New Hampshire, for the benefit of the said province, do, of our special grace, certain knowledge and mere motion, by and with the advice of our council for said province, by these presents will, ordain, grant and constitute that there be a college erected in our said province of New Hampshire, by the name of Dartmouth College, for the education and instruction of youths of the Indian tribes in this land, in reading, writing, and all parts of learning, which shall appear necessary and expedient, for civilizing and christianizing the children of pagans, as well as in all liberal arts and sciences, and also of English youths, and any others. And the trustees of said college may, and shall be, one body corporate and politic in deed, action and name, and shall be called, named, and distinguished by the name of the trustees of Dartmouth College. And further, we have willed, given, granted, constituted and ordained, and by this our present charter, of our special grace, certain knowledge and mere motion, with the advice aforesaid, do for us, our heirs and successors forever, will, give, grant, constitute, and ordain, that there shall from henceforth and forever, be in the said Dartmouth College a body politic, consisting of trustees of Dartmouth College. And for the more full and perfect erection of said corporation and body politic, consisting of trustees of Dartmouth College, we, of our special grace, certain knowledge and mere motion, do, by these presents, for us, our heirs and successors, make, ordain, constitute and appoint, our trusty and well-beloved John Wentworth, Esq., governor of our said province, and the governor of our said province of New Hampshire, for the time being, and our trusty and well-beloved Theodore Atkinson, Esq., now president of our council of our said province, George Jaffrey and Daniel Pierce, Esqs., both of our said council, and Peter Gilman, Esq., now speaker of our House of Representatives in said province, and Wm. Pitkin, Esq., one of the Assistants of our colony of Connecticut, and our trusty and well-beloved Eleazar Wheelock, of Lebanon, Doctor in Divinity, Benjamin Pomeroy, of Hebron, James Lockwood, of Weathersfield, Timothy Pitkin and John Smalley, of Farmington, and Wm. Patten of Hartford, all of our said colony of Connecticut, ministers of the gospel (the whole number of said trustees consisting, and hereafter forever to consist, of twelve and no more) to be trustees of said Dartmouth College, in this our province of New Hampshire. And we do further, of our special grace, certain knowledge and mere motion, for us, our heirs and successors, will, give, grant and appoint that the said trustees and their successors shall, forever hereafter, be in deed, act and name, a body corporate and politic, and that they, the said body corporate and politic, shall be known and distinguished in all deeds, grants, bargains, sales, writings, evidences or otherwise however, and in all courts forever hereafter plead and be impleaded by the name of the trustees of Dartmouth College. And that the said corporation by the name aforesaid, shall be able and in law capable for the use of said Dartmouth College, to have, get, acquire, purchase, receive, hold, possess and enjoy, tenements, hereditaments, jurisdictions and franchises for themselves and their successors, in fee simple or otherwise however, and to purchase, receive, or build any house or houses, or any other buildings, as they shall think needful and convenient for the use of said Dartmouth College, and in such town in the western part of our said province of New Hampshire, as shall, by said trustees, or the major part of them be agreed upon, their said agreement to be evidenced, by an instrument in writing under their hands ascertaining the same. And also to receive and dispose of any lands, goods, chattels and other things of what nature soever, for the use aforesaid. And also to have, accept and receive any rents, profits, annuities, gifts, legacies, donations or bequests of any kind whatsoever for the use aforesaid: so nevertheless, that the yearly value of the premises do not exceed the sum of six thousand pounds sterling. And therewith or otherwise to support and pay, as the said trustees, or the major part of such of them as are regularly convened for that purpose, shall agree; the president, tutors, and other officers and ministers of said Dartmouth College, and also to pay all such missionaries and schoolmasters as shall be authorized, appointed and employed by them for civilizing, christianizing, and instructing the Indian natives of this land, their several allowances, and also their respective annual salaries or allowances, and also such necessary and contingent charges, as from time to time shall arise and accrue, relating to said Dartmouth College. And also to bargain, sell, let or assign lands, tenements, hereditaments, goods or chattels, and all other things whatsoever, by the name aforesaid, in as full and ample a manner, to all intents and purposes as a natural person or other body corporate or politic, is able to do by the laws of our realm of Great Britain, or of said province of New Hampshire. And further, of our special grace, certain knowledge and mere motion, to the intent that our said corporation and body politic may answer the end of their erection and constitution, and may have perpetual succession and continuance forever, we do for us, our heirs and successors, will, give and grant unto the said trustees of Dartmouth College, and to their successors forever, that there shall be once a year, and every year, a meeting of said trustees, held at said Dartmouth College, at such time as by said trustees, or the major part of them, at any legal meeting of said trustees shall be agreed on. The first meeting to be called by the said Eleazar Wheelock, as soon as conveniently may be, within one year next after the enrollment of these our letters patent, at such time and place as he shall judge proper. And the said trustees, or the major part of any seven or more of them, shall then determine on the time for holding the annual meeting aforesaid, which may be altered as they shall hereafter find most convenient. And we do further ordain and direct, that the said Eleazar Wheelock shall notify the time for holding the first meeting to be called as aforesaid, by sending a letter to each of said trustees, and causing an advertisement thereof to be printed in the "New Hampshire Gazette," and in some public newspaper printed in the colony of Connecticut. But in case of the death or incapacity of said Wheelock, then such meeting to be notified in manner as aforesaid, by the Governor or Commander in chief of our said Province for the time being. And we also, for us, our heirs and successors, hereby will, give and grant unto the said trustees of Dartmouth College aforesaid, and to their successors forever, that when any seven or more of the said trustees or their successors are convened and met together for the service of said Dartmouth College, at any time or times, such seven or more shall be capable to act as fully and amply to all intents and purposes, as if all the trustees of said college were personally present; and all affairs and actions whatsoever, under the care of said trustrees, shall be determined by the majority or greater number of those seven or more trustees, so convened and met together. And we do further will, ordain and direct, that the president, trustees, professors, and tutors, and all such officers, as shall be appointed for the public instruction and government of said college, shall, before they undertake the execution of their respective offices or trusts, or within one year after, take the oaths and subscribe the declaration, provided by an act of Parliament, made in the first year of King George the first, entitled, " An Act for the further security of his Majesty's person and government, and the succession of the crown in the heirs of the late Princess Sophia being Protestants, and for the extinguishing the hopes of the pretended Prince of Wales, and his open and secret abettors," that is to say, the president before the Governor of our said Province for the time being, or by one empowered by him to that service, or by the president of our council, and the trustees, professors, tutors and other officers, before the president of said college, for the time being, who is hereby empowered to administer the same ; an entry of all which shall be made in the records of the said college. And we do for us, our heirs and successors, hereby will, give, and grant full power and authority to the president, hereafter by us named, and to his successors, or in case of his failure, to any three or more of said trustees, to appoint other occasional meetings, from time to time, of the said seven trustees, or any greater number of them, to transact any matter or thing necessary to be done, before the next annual meeting, and to order notice to the said seven or any greater number of them, of the times and places of meetings for the services aforesaid, by a letter under his or their hands of the same, one month before said meeting. Provided always, that no standing rule or order be made or altered, for the regulation of said college, or any president or professor be chosen or displaced, or any other matter or thing transacted or done, which shall continue in force after the then next annual meeting of said trustees as aforesaid. And further, we do by these presents, for us, our heirs and successors, create, make, constitute, nominate and appoint our trusty and well beloved Eleazar Wheelock, Doctor in Divinity, the founder of said college, to be president of said Dartmouth College, and to have the immediate care of the education and government of such students, as shall be admitted into said Dartmouth College, for instruction and education ; and do will, give and grant to him in said office, full power, authority and right, to nominate, appoint, constitute and ordain by his last will, such suitable and meet person or persons as he shall choose, to succeed him in the presidency of said Dartmouth College; and the person so appointed by his last will, to continue in office, vested with all the powers, privileges, jurisdiction and authority of a president of said Dartmouth College, that is to say, so long as until such appointment, by said last will, shall be disapproved by the trustees of said Dartmouth College. And we do also for us, our heirs and snccessors, will, give and grant to the said trustees of Dartmouth College, and to their successors forever, or any seven or more of them, convened as aforesaid, that in case of the ceasing or failure of a president, by any means whatsoever, that the said trustees do elect, nominate and appoint such qualified person, as they, or the major part of any seven or more of them, convened for that purpose, as above directed, shall think fit, to be president of said Dartmouth College, and to have the care of the education and government of the students as aforesaid. And in case of the ceasing of a president as aforesaid, the senior professor or tutor, being one of the trustees, shall exercise the office of a president, until the trustees shall make choice of, and appoint a president as aforesaid ; and such professor or tutor, or any three or more of the trustees, shall immediately appoint a meeting of the body of the trustees for the purpose aforesaid. And also, we do will, give and grant to the said trustees, convened as aforesaid, that they elect, nominate and appoint, so many

tutors and professors, to assist the president in the education and government of the students belonging thereto as they
the said trustees shall, from time to time, and at any time think
needful and serviceable to the interests of the said Dartmouth
College. And also that the said trustees, or their successors,
or the major part of any seven or more of them, convened for
that purpose as above directed, shall at any time displace and
discharge from the service of said Dartmouth College, any or
all such officers, and elect others in their room and stead as
before directed. And also that the said trustees or their successors, or the major part of any seven of them which shall
convene for that purpose as above directed, do from time to
time as occasion shall require, elect, constitute and appoint a
treasurer, a clerk, an usher and a steward, for the said Dartmouth College, and appoint to them, and each of them, their
respective businesses and trust; and displace and discharge
from the service of said college, such treasurer, clerk, usher
or steward, and elect others in their room and stead; which
officers so elected as before directed, we do for us, our heirs
and successors, by these presents constitute and establish in
their respective offices, and do give to each and every, of them,
full power and authority, to exercise the same in said Dartmouth College, according to the directions and during the
pleasure of the said trustees, as fully and freely as any like
officers in any of our universities, colleges, or seminaries of
learning, in our realm of Great Britain, lawfully may or ought
to do. And also, that the said trustees or their successors, or
the major part of any seven or more of them, which shall convene for that purpose, as is above directed, as often as one or
more of said trustees shall die, or by removal or otherwise
shall, according to their judgment become unfit or incapable
to serve the interests of said college, do, as soon as may be,
after the death, removal, or such unfitness or incapacity of
such trustee or trustees, elect and appoint such trustee or trustees as shall supply the place of him or them so dying, or be-

coming incapable to serve the interests of said college; and every trustee so elected and appointed, shall, by virtue of these presents, and such election and appointment, be vested with all the powers and privileges which any of the other trustees of said college are hereby vested with. And we do further will, ordain and direct, that from and after the expiration of two years from the enrollment of these presents, such vacancy or vacancies shall be filled up unto the complete number of twelve trustees, eight of the aforesaid whole number of the body of the trustees shall be resident and respectable freeholders of our said Province of New Hampshire, and seven of said whole number shall be laymen. And we do further of our special grace, certain knowledge and mere motion, will, give and grant unto the said trustees of Dartmouth College that they and their successors, or the major part of any seven of them which shall convene for that purpose as above directed, may make, and they are hereby fully empowered from time to time fully and lawfully to make and establish such ordinances, orders and laws, as may tend to the good and wholesome government of the said college, and all the students and the several officers and ministers thereof, and to the public benefit of the same, not repugnant to the laws and statutes of our realm of Great Britain or of this our province of New Hampshire (and not excluding any person of any religious denomination whatsoever from free and equal liberty and advantage of education, or from any of the liberties and privileges or immunities of the said college on account of his or their speculative sentiments in religion, and of his or their being of a religious profession different from the said trustees of the said Dartmouth College), and such ordinances, orders and laws which shall as aforesaid be made, we do by these presents, for us, our heirs and successors, ratify, allow of and confirm, as good and effectual to oblige and bind all the students and the several officers and ministers of said college. And we do hereby authorize and empower the said trustees of Dartmouth

College, and the president, tutors and professors by them elected and appointed as aforesaid, to put such ordinances, laws and orders into execution to all intents and purposes. And we do further of our special grace, certain knowledge and mere motion, will, give and grant unto the said trustees, of said Dartmouth College, for the encouragement of learning and animating the students of said college to diligence and industry, and a laudable progress in literature, that they and their successors, or the major part of any seven or more of them convened for that purpose as above mentioned, do by the president of said college for the time being, or any other deputed by them, give and grant any such degree or degrees to any of the students of the said college, or any others by them thought worthy thereof, as are usually granted in either of the universities or any other college in our realm of Great Britain; and that they sign and seal diplomas or certificates of such graduations to be kept by the graduates as perpetual memorials and testimonies thereof. And we do further of our special grace, certain knowledge and mere motion, for us, our heirs and successors, by these presents give and grant unto the trustees of said Dartmouth College and to their successors, that they and their successors shall have a common seal under which they may pass all diplomas or certificates of degrees, and all other affairs of business of and concerning the said college, which shall be engraven in such form and with such an inscription as shall be devised by the said trustees for the time being, or by the major part of any seven or more of them convened for the service of said college as is above directed. And we do further for us, our heirs and successors, give and grant unto the trustees of said Dartmouth College and their successors, or the major part of any seven or more of them convened for the service of said college, full power and authority from time to time to nominate and appoint all other officers and ministers which they shall think convenient and necessary for the service of the said college not herein particularly named

or mentioned; which officers and ministers we do hereby impower to execute their offices and trusts as fully and freely as
any one of the officers and ministers in our universities or colleges in our realm of Great Britain lawfully may or ought to do.
And further, that the generous contributors to the support of
this design of spreading the knowledge of the only true God
and Saviour among the American savages, may from time to
time be satisfied that their liberations are faithfully disposed of
in the best manner for that purpose, and that others may in
future time be encouraged in the exercise of the like liberality
for promoting the same pious design; it shall be the duty of
the President of said Dartmouth College and of his successors,
annually or as often as he shall be thereunto desired or
requested, to transmit to the Right Hon., hon. and worthy gentlemen of the trust of England before mentioned, a faithful
account of the improvements and disbursements of the several
sums he shall receive from the donations and bequests made
in England through the hands of the said trustees, and also
advise them of the general plans laid and prospects exhibited,
as well as a faithful account of all remarkable occurrences, in
order if they shall think expedient that they may be published.
And this to continue so long as they shall perpetuate their board
of trust, and there shall be any of the Indian natives remaining
to be proper objects of that charity. And lastly, our express
will and pleasure is, and we do by these presents for us our
heirs and successors, give and grant unto the said trustees of
Dartmouth College and to their successors forever, that these
our letters patent or the enrolment thereof in the Secretary's
office of our province of New Hampshire aforesaid, shall be
good and effectual in law to all intents and purposes against
us our heirs and successors, without any other license, grant or
confirmation from us our heirs and successors hereafter by the
said trustees to be had and obtained, notwithstandiug the not
writing or misrecital, not naming or misnaming the aforesaid
offices, franchises, privileges, immunities, or other the premises

or any of them, and notwithstanding a writ of *ad quod damnum* hath not issued forth to enquire of the premises or any of them before the ensealing hereof, any statute, act, ordinance or proviso, or any other matter or thing to the contrary notwithstanding. To have and to hold, all and singular the privileges, advantages, liberties, immunities, and all other the premises herein and hereby granted and given, or which are meant, mentioned, or intended to be herein and hereby given and granted unto them the said trustees of Dartmouth College and to their successors forever. In testimony whereof we have caused these our letters to be made patent, and the public seal of our said province of New Hampshire to be hereunto affixed. Witness our trusty and well-beloved John Wentworth, Esq., Governor and Commander-in-Chief in and over our said province, etc., this thirteenth day of December, in the tenth year of our reign, and in the year of our Lord one thousand seven hundred and sixty-nine.

J. WENTWORTH.

By his Excellency's command
with the advice of Council.

THEODORE ATKINSON, Secretary."[1]

On April 13, 1771, an Act was passed by the New Hampshire legislature for establishing and making passable a road from the Governor's house in Wolfborough to Dartmouth College in Hanover. Its preamble reads: " Whereas the opening and making of roads through the various parts of the province, is of great public utility; and the making of a road to Dartmouth College will greatly promote the design of that valuable institution; be it therefore enacted, etc." [2]

[1] Given in Smith's *History of Dartmouth College*, pp. 457–464.

[2] *Acts and Laws*, p. 266. Portsmouth, 1771.

RHODE ISLAND

The educational records of the central government of Rhode Island are extremely scant. They consist of the usual provision for the military exemption of schoolmasters, of an act of incorporation for a denominational college and a grant of lottery privileges for the establishment of a town school.

In a revision of the militia laws which was made at a session of the Assembly held at Newport in 1718, all schoolmasters were stated to be among those persons who were exempted from bearing arms in the "train-bands or companies" of the colony.[1]

In July, 1763, a number of gentlemen of the Baptist persuasion were called to meet together at the house of Deputy Governor Gardner in Newport to consult about the establishment of a Baptist College in Rhode Island. This meeting was brought about through the efforts of James Manning, a representative of the Philadelphia Baptist Association.[2] The Association designed that the Baptists should have the chief government of the projected institution, but that other denominations should also be represented in the corporation. A draft of a charter drawn up by Dr. Stiles[3] of the Congregational church of Newport and a petition[4] signed by 62 prominent citizens were presented

---

[1] *Acts and Laws of his Majesty's Colony of Rhode Island and Providence Plantations in America*, p. 86. Boston, 1719.

[2] *History of Brown University*, with illustrative documents, p. 120. Reuben A. Guild. Providence, 1867.

[3] President of Yale College in 1778.

[4] The preamble of this petition with the exception of one clause was incorporated in the final draft of the charter. The omitted clause read "and whereas there is a confessed absence of polite and useful learning in this colony, your petitioners," etc. (*Ibid.*, p. 122.)

to the legislature at its August session in 1763. On a motion
of Mr. Jenckes, member from Providence and a Baptist, the
consideration of this charter was postponed to the next session
of the legislature on the ground that the draft that had been
presented gave more power to the Congregationalists than to
the Baptists. In October, 1763, a second draft was presented,
but on account of sectarian bickerings and quarrels in the Assembly, the incorporation was again deferred.[1] Finally in February, 1764, the following act of incorporation was passed by the
legislature: "Whereas institutions for liberal education are
highly beneficial to society, by forming the rising generation to
virtue, knowledge and useful literature, and thus preserving in
the community a succession of men duly qualified for discharging the offices of life with usefulness and reputation; they have
therefore justly merited and received the attention and encouragement of every wise and well-regulated state; and whereas,
a public school or seminary, erected for that purpose, within
this colony, to which the youth may freely resort for education in the vernacular and learned languages and in the liberal
arts and sciences, would be for the general advantage and
honor of the government; and whereas, Daniel Jenckes, Esq.,
Nicholas Tillinghast, Esq., Nicholas Gardner, Esq., Col. Josias
Lyndon, Col. Elisha Reynolds, Peleg Thurston, Esq., Simon
Pease, Esq., John Tillinghast, Esq., George Hazard, Esq., Col-
Job Bennett, Nicholas Easton, Esq., Arthur Fenner, Esq., Mr.
Ezekiel Gardner, Mr. John Waterman, Mr. James Barker, Jr.,
Mr. John Holmes, Solomon Drown, Esq., Mr. Samuel Winsor,
Mr. Joseph Sheldon, Charles Rhodes, Esq., Mr. Nicholas
Brown, Col. Barzillai Richmond, Mr. John Brown, Mr. Gideon
Hoxsey, Mr. Thomas Eyres, Mr. Thomas Potter, Jr., Mr.
Peleg Barker, Mr. Edward Thurston, Mr. William Redwood,
Joseph Clarke, Esq., Mr. John G. Wanton and Mr. Thomas
Robinson, with many other persons, appear as undertakers in
the valuable design; and thereupon, a petition hath been pre-

[1] *Ibid.*, pp. 126–7.

ferred to this Assembly, praying that full liberty and power may be granted unto such of them, with others, as are hereafter mentioned, to found, endow, order and govern a college, or university, within this colony; and that, for the more effectual execution of this design, they may be incorporated into one body politic, to be known in the law, with the powers, privileges and franchises, necessary for the purpose, aforesaid. Now, therefore, know ye, that, being willing to encourage and patronize such an honorable and useful institution, we, the said Governor and Company, in General Assembly convened, do for ourselves and our successors, in and by virtue of the power and authority, within the jurisdiction of this colony, to us by the royal charter granted and committed, enact, grant, constitute, ordain and declare, and it is hereby enacted, granted, constituted, ordained and declared, that the Hon. Stephen Hopkins, Esq., the Hon. Joseph Wanton, Jr., Esq., the Hon. Samuel Ward, Esq., the Hon. William Ellery, Esq., John Tillinghast, Esq., Simon Pease, Esq., James Honyman, Esq., Nicholas Easton, Esq., Nicholas Tillinghast, Esq., Darius Session, Esq., Joseph Harris, Esq., Francis Willet, Esq., William Logan, Esq., Daniel Jenckes, Esq., George Hazard, Esq., Nicholas Brown, Esq., Jeremiah Niles, Esq., Joshua Babock, Esq., Mr. John G. Wanton, the Rev. Edward Upham, the Rev. Jeremiah Condy, the Rev. Marmaduke Brown, the Rev. Gardner Thurston, the Rev. Ezra Stiles, the Rev. John Greaves, the Rev. John Maxon, the Rev. Samuel Winsor, the Rev. John Gano, the Rev. Morgan Edwards, the Rev. Isaac Eaton, the Rev. Samuel Stillman, the Rev. Samuel Jones, the Rev. James Manning, the Rev. Russel Mason, Col. Elisha Reynolds, Col. Josias Lyndon, Col. Job Bennet, Mr. Ephraim Bowen, Joshua Clarke, Esq., Capt. Jonathan Slade, John Taylor, Esq., Mr. Robert Shettel Jones, Azariah Dunham, Esq., Mr. Edward Thurston, Jr., Mr. Thomas Eyres, Mr. Thomas Hazard and Mr. Peleg Barker, or such, or so many of them as shall, within twelve months from the date hereof, accept of this trust, and qualify themselves as hereinafter directed, and their successors, shall be forever hereafter one body corporate and politic, in fact and name, to be known in law by the name of Trustees and Fellows of the College or University, in the English Colony of Rhode Island and Providence Plantations, in New England, in America; the trustees and fellows, at any time hereafter, giving such more particular name to the college, in honor of the greatest and most distinguished benefactor, or otherwise, as they shall think proper; which name, so given, shall, in all acts, instruments and doings of said body politic, be superadded to their corporate name, aforesaid, and become a part of their legal appellation, by which it shall be forever known and distinguished;[1] and that, by the same name, they and their successors, chosen by themselves, as hereafter prescribed, shall, and may, have perpetual succession; and shall, and may, be persons able and capable in the law, to sue and to be sued, to plead and to be impleaded, to answer and to be answered unto, to defend and to be defended against, in all and singular suits, causes, matters, actions and doings, of what kind soever; and also to have, take, possess, purchase, acquire, or otherwise receive and hold lands, tenements, hereditaments, goods, chattels, or other estates; of all which they may, and shall, stand and be seized, notwithstanding any misnomer of the college, or the corporation thereof; and by whatever name, or however imperfectly the same shall be described in gift, bequests, and assignments, provided the true intent of the assignor or benefactor be evident; also the same to grant, demise, aliene, use, manage, and improve, according to the tenor of the donations, and to the purposes, trusts, and to which they shall be seized thereof, and full liberty, power, and authority is hereby granted unto the said trustees and fellows, and their successors, to found a college, or university, within this colony, for promoting the liberal arts, and universal literature; and with the monies, estates and

---

[1] Name changed to Brown University in 1804.

revenues of which they shall from time to time become legally seized, as aforesaid, to endow the same; and erect the necessary buildings and edifices thereof, on such place within this colony as they shall think convenient; and generally to regulate, order, and govern the same, appoint officers, and make laws, as hereinafter prescribed; and hold, use, and enjoy all the liberties, privileges, exemptions, dignities, and immunities, enjoyed by any college, or university, whatever. And furthermore, that the said trustees and fellows, and their successors, shall, and may, forever hereafter have a public seal, to use for all causes, matters, and affairs whatever of them and their successors, and the same seal to alter, break, and make anew, from time to time, at their will and pleasure; which seal shall always be deposited with the president, or senior fellow. And furthermore, by the authority aforesaid, it is hereby enacted, ordained and declared that it is now, and at all times hereafter shall continue to be, the unalterable constitution of this college, or university, that the corporation thereof shall consist of two branches, to wit: that of the trustees, and that of the fellowship, with distinct, separate and respective powers; and that the number of the trustees shall, and may be, thirty-six; of which, twenty-two shall forever be elected of the denomination called Baptists, or Antipaedobaptists; five shall forever be elected of the denomination called Friends, or Quakers; four shall forever be elected of the denomination called Congregationalists, and five shall forever be elected of the denomination called Episcopalians; and that the succession in this branch shall be forever chosen and filled up from the respective denominations in this proportion, and according to these numbers, which are hereby fixed, and shall remain to perpetuity immutably the same; and that the said Stephen Hopkins, Joseph Wanton, Samuel Ward, William Ellery, John Tillinghast, Simon Pease, James Honyman, Nicholas Easton, Nicholas Tillinghast, Darius Sessions, Joseph Harris, Francis Willett, Daniel Jenckes, George Hazard, Nicholas Brown,

Jeremiah Niles, John G. Wanton, Joshua Clarke, Gardner Thurston, John Greaves, John Maxson, John Gano, Samuel Winsor, Isaac Eaton, Samuel Stillman, Russell Mason, Elisha Reynolds, Josias Lyndon, Job Bennet, Ephraim Bowen, John Taylor, Jonathan Slade, Robert Shettell Jones, Azariah Dunham, Edward Thurston, Jr., and Peleg Barker; or such, or so many of them as shall qualify themselves, as aforesaid, shall be, and they are hereby declared and established the first and present trustees. And that the number of the fellows, inclusive of the president (who shall always be a fellow), shall, and may be, twelve; of which, eight shall be forever elected of the denomination called Baptists, or Antipaedobaptists; and the rest indifferently of any or all denominations; and that the Rev. Edward Upham, the Rev. Jeremiah Condy, the Rev. Marmaduke Brown, the Rev. Morgan Edwards, the Rev. Ezra Stiles, the Rev. Samuel Jones, the Rev. James Manning, William Logan, Esq., Joshua Babcock, Esq., Mr. Thomas Eyers, and Mr. Thomas Hazard, or such, or so many of them as shall qualify themselves, as aforesaid, shall be, and they are hereby, declared the first and present fellows and fellowship, to whom the president, when hereafter elected (who shall forever be of the denomination called Baptists, or Antipaedobaptists), shall be joined to complete the number. And, furthermore, it is declared and ordained, that the succession in both branches shall at all times hereafter be filled up and supplied according to these numbers, and this established and invariable proportion from the respective denominations, by the separate election of both branches of this corporation, which shall at all times sit and act by separate and distinct powers; and in general, in order to the validity and consummation of all acts, there shall be in the exercise of their respective, separate and distinct powers, the joint concurrence of the trustees and fellows, by their respective majorities, except in adjudging and conferring the academical degrees, which shall forever belong, exclusively, to the fellowship, as a learned faculty. And furthermore, it is constituted, that the instruction and immediate government of the college, shall forever be, and rest, in the president and fellows, or fellowship. And furthermore, it is ordained, that there shall be a general meeting of the corporation on the first Wednesday in September, annually, within the college edifice, and until the same be built, at such place as they shall appoint, to consult, advise and transact the affairs of the college or university; at which, or at any other time, the public commencement may be held and celebrated; and that on any special emergencies, the president, with any two of the fellows, or any three of the fellows, exclusive of the president, may convoke, and they are hereby empowered to convoke an assembly of the corporation, on twenty days' notice; and that in all meetings, the major vote of those present of the two branches, respectively, shall be deemed their respective majorities, aforesaid; provided, that not less than twelve of the trustees, and five of the fellows, be a quorum of their respective branches; that the president, or, in his absence, the senior fellow present, shall always be moderator of the fellows; that the corporation, at their annual meetings, once in three years, or oftener, in case of death or removal, shall, and may choose a chancellor of the university, and treasurer, from among the trustees, and a secretary from among the fellows; that the nomination of the chancellor shall be in the trustees, whose office shall be only to preside as a moderator of the trustees; and that in his absence, the trustees shall choose a moderator for the time being, by the name ot vice chancellor; and at any of their meetings, duly formed, as aforesaid, shall, and may be, elected a trustee or fellow, or trustees, or fellows, in the room of those nominated in this charter, who may refuse to accept, or in the room of those who may die, resign, or be removed. And furthermore, it is enacted, ordained and declared, that this corporation, at any of their meetings regularly convened, as aforesaid, shall and may elect and appoint the president and professors of languages and the several parts of literature; and upon the demise of him or them, or either of them, their resignation or removal from his or their office, for misdemeanor, incapacity, or unfaithfulness, (for which he or they are hereby declared removable by this corporation), others to elect and appoint in their room and stead; and at such meeting, upon the nomination of the fellows, to elect and appoint tutors, stewards, butlers, and all such other officers usually appointed in colleges or universities, as they shall find necessary, and think fit to appoint for the promoting liberal education, and the well ordering the affairs of this college; and them, or any of them, at their discretion to remove, and substitute others in their places; and in case any president, trustee or fellow, shall see cause to change his religious denomination, the corporation is hereby empowered to declare his or their place or places vacant, and may proceed to fill up it or them, accordingly, as before directed; otherwise, each trustee and fellow, not an officer of instruction, shall continue in his office during life, or until resignation. And further, in case either of the religious denominations should decline taking a part in this catholic, comprehensive and liberal institution, the trustees and fellows shall, and may, complete their number, by electing from their respective denomination, always preserving their respective proportions herein before prescribed and determined; and all elections shall be by ballot or written suffrage; and that a quorum of four trustees and three fellows may transact any business, excepting placing the college edifice, election of trustees, president, fellows and professors; that is to say: so that their acts shall be of force and validity until the next annual meeting, and no longer. And it is further enacted and ordained by the authority aforesaid, that each trustee and fellow, as well those nominated in this charter, as all that shall heaeafter be duly elected, shall, previous to their acting in a corporate capacity, take the engagement of allegiance prescribed by the law of this colony to His Majesty, King George the Third, his heirs

and rightful successors to the crown of Great Britain; which
engagement shall be administered to the present trustees and
fellows, by the Governor or Deputy Governor of this colony,
and to those from time to time hereafter elected by their respective moderators, who are hereby empowered to administer
the same. And still more clearly to define and ascertain the
respective powers of the two branches, on making and enacting
laws,—It is further ordained and declared, that the fellowship
shall have power, and are hereby empowered from time to
time, and at all times hereafter, to make, enact and publish all
such laws, statutes, regulations and ordinances, with penalties,
as to them shall seem meet, for the successful instruction and
government of the said college or university, not contrary to
the spirit, extent, true meaning and intention of the acts of the
British Parliament, or the laws of this colony; and the same
laws, statutes and ordinances to repeal; which laws, and the
repeals thereof, shall be laid before the trustees, and with their
approbation, shall be of force and validity, but not otherwise.
And further, the trustees and fellows, at their meetings aforesaid, shall ascertain the salaries of the respective officers, and
order the monies assessed on the students for tuition, fines and
incidental expenses, to be collected by the steward, or such
other officer as they shall appoint to collect the same; and the
same, with their revenues, and other college estates in the
hands of the treasurer, to appropriate in discharging salaries
and other college debts; and the college accounts shall be
annually audited and adjusted in the meeting of the corporation.
And furthermore, it is hereby enacted and declared, that into
this liberal and catholic institution, shall never be admitted
any religious tests; but on the contrary, all the members
hereof, shall forever enjoy full, free, absolute, and uninterrupted
liberty of conscience; and that the places of professors, tutors,
and all other officers, the president alone excepted, shall be
free and open for all denominations of Protestants; and that
youth of all religious denominations shall, and may, be freely

admitted to the equal advantages, emoluments, and honors of the college or university; and shall receive a like, fair, generous, and equal treatment during their residence therein, they conducting themselves peaceably, and conforming to the laws and statutes thereof; and that the public teaching shall, in general, respect the sciences; and that the sectarian differences of opinions, shall not make any part of the public and classical instruction; although all religious controversies may be studied freely, examined and explained by the president, professors and tutors, in a personal, separate, and distinct manner, to the youth of any or each denomination; and above all, a constant regard be paid to, and effectual care taken of, the morals of the college. And furthermore, for the honor and encouragement of literature, we constitute and declare, the fellowship, aforesaid, a learned faculty; and do hereby give, grant unto, and invest them and their successors with, full power and authority, and they are hereby authorized and empowered, by their president, and in his absence, by the senior fellow, or one of the fellows appointed by themselves at the anniversary commencement, or at any other times, and at all times hereafter, to admit to, and confer any and all the learned degrees, which can or ought to be given and conferred in any of the colleges or universities in America, or any such other degrees of literary honor as they shall devise, upon any and all such candidates and persons as the president and fellows, or fellowship, shall udge worthy of the academical honors; which power of conferring degrees, is hereby restricted to the learned faculty, who shall, or may, issue diplomas, or certificates, of such degrees, or confer degrees by diplomas, and authenticate them with the public seal of the corporation, and the hands of the president and secretary, and of all the professors, as witnesses, and deliver them to the graduates as honorable and perpetual testimonies. And furthermore, for the greater encouragement of this seminary of learning, and that the same may be amply endowed and enfranchised with the same privileges, dignities

and immunities, enjoyed by the American colleges and Euro-
pean universities,—We do grant, enact, ordain and declare,
and it is hereby granted, enacted, ordained and declared, that
the college estate, the estates, persons, and families of the
president and professors, for the time being, lying and being
within the colony, with the persons of the tutors and students,
during their residence at the college, shall be freed and exempted from all taxes, serving on juries, and menial services;
and that the persons, aforesaid, shall be exempted from bearing arms, impresses and military services, except in case of in-
vasion. And furthermore, for establishing the perpetuity of
this corporation, and in case that at any time hereafter, through
oversight, or otherwise, through misapprehensions and mis-
taken constructions of the powers, liberties and franchises
herein contained, any laws should be enacted, or any matters
done and transacted by this corporation contrary to this
charter,—It is hereby enacted, ordained and declared, that all
such laws, acts and doings, shall be in themselves null and
void; yet, nevertheless, the same shall not, in any courts of
law, or by the General Assembly, be deemed, taken, inter-
preted, or adjudged into an avoidance, defeazance, or forfeiture of this charter; but that the same shall be, and remain
unhurt, inviolate, and entire unto the said corporation, in perpetual succession; which corporation may, at all times, and
forever hereafter, proceed, and continue to act; and all their
acts, conformably to the powers, tenor, true intent and meaning of the charter, shall be, and remain in full force and
validity; the nullity and avoidance of any such illegal acts, to
the contrary in any wise, notwithstanding. And lastly, we
the Governor and Company, aforesaid, do, for ourselves, and
our successors, forever, hereby enact, grant and confirm unto
the said trustees and fellows, and to their successors, that this
charter of incorporation, and every part thereof, shall be good
and available in all things in the law, according to our true
intent and meaning; and shall be construed, reputed, and ad-

judged in all cases most favorably on the behalf and for the best benefit and behoof of the said trustees and fellows, and their successors, so as most effectually to answer the valuable ends of this most useful institution.   In full testimony of which grant, and of all the articles and matters therein contained, the said Governor and Company do hereby order, that this act shall be signed by the Governor and Secretary, and sealed with the public seal of this colony, and registered in the colony's records; and that the same, or an exemplification thereof, shall be a sufficient warrant to the said corporation to hold, use and exercise all the powers, franchises, and immunities herein contained."[1]

There was much contention among the towns of the colony concerning the location of Rhode Island College.   It was finally established at Providence.   Thereupon the discontented contestants of Newport sent in a petition to the legislature for the founding of another college in that town.   A charter was granted to the Newport petitioners by the Lower House by a vote of twenty majority.   The Upper House, however, influenced by a counter-petition of the corporation of Rhode Island College, refused to concur in this measure.

Provision for elementary and secondary education seems to have been wholly entrusted by the legislature to the town governments,[3] and to charitable persons and corporations.

---

[1] Records of the Colony of Rhode Island and Provincial Plantations in New England, VI, 385-391.   Edited by John R. Bartlett.   Providence, 1862.

[2] Guild's History of Brown University, p. 204-6.

[3] A schoolmaster was called in 1640 by a town vote to keep a public school in Newport.   One hundred and four acres were granted to him, and 100 acres were appropriated to the building of a school house.   (History of the State of Rhode Island and Providence Plantations, I, 145-6.   Samuel G. Arnold.   New York, 1859.)

In 1663 the town of Providence voted 100 acres of upland and 6 acres of meadow to the maintenance of a school.   (Ibid., I, 282.)

Over a century later, in 1767, Governor Bowen drew up a plan for a system of free public schools for the town ; but it was rejected " by the poorer sort of the people " of the town.   (History of Higher Education in Rhode Island, p. 26.   William H. Tolman, Ph. D.   Washington, 1894.)

At a session held at Warwick in October, 1721, an act was passed "to redress the misemployment of lands, goods, and stocks of money, heretofore given to certain charitable uses . . . by several well disposed persons, to and for the relief of the poor, and bringing up of children to learning." This act empowered the town council to enforce the carrying out of all such pious trusts according to the will of the donors.[1] In May, 1774, the legislature incorporated the charitable Baptist Society of the town of Providence. The charter empowers the grantees to receive and hold donations, legacies, assignments, etc., for the use and " support of pastors, relief of the poor, in schooling their children . . . or any other religious uses in said church and congregation."[2] At this same session the lottery act above referred to was passed by the Assembly. " Whereas, a number of the inhabitants of East Greenwich, preferred a petition, and represented unto this Assembly, that there is, at present, but one school house in the compact part of the said town ; and that another is necessary for the education of youth ; and thereupon prayed this Assembly, that a lottery may be granted, to raise the sum of $600, to be applied towards the purchasing a lot, and building a public school house in the said town ; and that Preserved Pearce, Esq., Mr. Oliver Arnold and Mr. John Reynolds, all of East Greenwich ; and Silas Casey, Esq., and Mr. Isaac Tripp, Jr., both of Warwick, may be appointed directors of the said lottery ; on consideration whereof,—It is voted and resolved, that the prayer of the foregoing petition be, and the same is hereby, granted, on the usual conditions provided, that no charge accrue to the Colony, thereby."[3]

[1] *The Charter and Laws of the Colony of Rhode Island and Providence Plantations in America*, pp. 122–4. Newport, 1730.

[2] *Rhode Island Schedules*, p. 9.

[3] *Rhode Island Col. Rec.*, VII, 242.

NEW NETHERLANDS AND NEW YORK

In 1621, a quasi-public corporation known as the Dutch West India Company was granted a monopoly of trade on the coasts of Africa and America by the States-General of the United Netherlands. Under its charter the Company possessed sovereign rights of government; only the appointment of its chief governors and its declarations of war or peace were subject to the approval of the States-General. In return for these privileges of trade and government the Company was bound to advance the interests of its colonies.[1] Care for the religious and educational welfare of those colonies it shared with the State Church of Holland through the Classis of Amsterdam.[2]

In 1623, the Company sent over its first shipload of colonists to settle on the Hudson and Delaware rivers.[3] In the following year a Director and Council were established in the colony by the Company and given supreme legislative and executive authority.[4]

In 1629, as an inducement to immigration, the Company issued a so-called charter of exemptions and privileges to all patroons, masters or private persons willing to plant colonies in New Netherland. To such colonists the charter granted exemption from taxation for a period of ten years and privileges of land holdings, trade and self-government. In return, among other stipulations, was the following:

" XXVII. The patroons and colonists shall in particular, and

[1] *History of New Netherlands*, pp. 89, 90. Edmund B. O'Callaghan, New York, 1846.

[2] *History of the State of New York*, I, 614. John R. Brodhead, New York, 1874.

[3] *O'Callaghan's History*, pp. 99, 100.   [4] *Ibid.*, p. 101.

in the speediest manner, endeavor to find out ways and means whereby they may support a minister and school master, that thus the service of God and zeal for religion may not grow cool and be neglected among them, and they shall, for the first, procure a comforter of the sick there." [1] This provision was reembodied in section 28 of of the New Project of Freedoms and Exemptions drawn up between 1630 and 1635 by the States-General to all persons of condition in the Netherlands, qualifying as lords and patroons of New Netherland.[2] A wider provision for education was contained in the articles drawn up in 1638 by the chamber of Amsterdam, the division of the West India Company having the New Netherlands in special charge, for the colonization and trade of that country.

" 8. Each householder and inhabitant shall bear such tax and public charge as shall hereafter be considered proper for the maintenance of clergymen, comforters for the sick, schoolmasters, and such like necessary officers ; and the Director and Council there shall be written to touching the form hereof, in order, on receiving further information hereupon, it be rendered the least onerous and vexatious."[3] In a new charter of freedoms and exemptions granted to the colonists by the Company in 1640, the Company appears to take upon itself the aforesaid responsibilities. " And no other religion shall be publicly admitted in New Netherland except the Reformed, as it is at present preached and practiced by public authority in the United Netherlands; and for this purpose the Company shall provide and maintain good and suitable preachers, schoolmasters and comforters of the sick." [4] This ruling of the Company seems to have not been readily effected, for in 1644 the Company's Board of Accounts, in a report suggesting measures by which the decay in New Netherland can be prevented, " population increased, agriculture advanced and that country

---

[1] *New York Colonial Documents,* II, 557. Edited by E. B. O'Callaghan M. D., LL. D., Albany, 1858. See also *Ibid.,* I, 405.

[2] *Ibid.,* I, 99.   [3] *Ibid.,* I, 112.   [4] *Ibid.,* I, 123.

wholly improved for the Company's benefit," present among other estimates for the salaries of necessary officers and servants an estimate of 360 florins per annum for one schoolmaster, precentor and sexton ;[1] and five years later in a popular remonstrance addressed to the States-General by the New Netherland colonists, the following statement occurs in the account which they gave of the grievous lack of church property in the colony : " The plate has been a long time passed around for a common school, which has been built with words, for, as yet, the first stone is not laid ; some materials have only been provided.   However the money given for the purpose hath all disappeared and is mostly spent, so that it falls somewhat short : and nothing permanent has as yet been effected for this purpose."[2]   In this same memorial which enumerates the reasons for the decay of the country and suggests measures for its relief, the following criticism appears : " Care ought to be taken of the public property, both ecclesiastical and civil. . . . . It is doubtful but Divine worship must be entirely intermitted in consequence of the clergyman's departure, and the Company's inability.   There ought to be also a public school provided with at least two good teachers, so that the youth, in so wild a country, where there are so many dissolute people, may first of all, be well instructed and indoctrinated, not only in reading and writing, but also in the knowledge and fear of the Lord.   Now, the school is kept very irregularly, by this one or that, according to his own fancy, as long as he thinks proper."[3]

In 1647, Director-General Stuyvesant had taken the same subject into consideration, and among those propositions which he presented to his Council, six months after his arrival in the colony, for the reform of his predecessor's neglect and mismanagement, occurs the following :

" 5thly. Whereas, by want of proper place, no school has been kept in three months, by which the youth is spoiled, so is

[1] *Ibid.*, I, 155.   [2] *Ibid.*, I, 300.   [3] *Ibid.*, I, 317.

proposed, where a convenient place may be adapted to keep the youth from the street and under a strict subordination."[1] It was consequently decreed by the Council, to wit, Van Dincklagen, vice-director, Van Dyck, fiscal, Van Trinkoven, secretary, and La Montagne, Adraen Keyser and Captain Bryant Newton, councilors, that as this point was of particular interest to the commonalty, it should be proposed to the nine Tribunes, so that the best means might be employed at the smallest expense of the commonalty.[2] In accordance with this decision, Stuyvesant wrote to the representatives of the people:[3]

" 3rdly. Not less necessary than the former article is the building of a new school and dwelling-house for the school-master, for the benefit of the commonalty and the education of the youth. We are inclined to bear personally and in behalf of the Company a reasonable proportion, and continue to do so in the future, and promote this glorious work. Meanwhile, it is required to make some previous arrangement to provide a convenient place during next winter, either in one of the out-houses belonging to the Attorney-General's Department, to which I should give the preference, or any other convenient place as may be approved by the church wardens."[4] The Nine Men do not seem to have responded to the suggestions of the Governor and Council, and so in August, 1649,

---

[1] *Albany Records*, VII, 106. These MS. records have been inaccessible to the writer, and this reference and several others to them in the following pages have been taken from D. J. Pratt's able compilation, "The Annals of Public Education in the State of New York," Albany, 1872.

[2] *Ibid*, VII, 106.

[3] These representatives constituted an advisory board of nine men, who had been chosen by Stuyvesant from 18 men elected by the people of Manhattan, Brooklyn, Amerfoort and Pavonia, "in order that the government of New Amsterdam might continue and increase in good order, justice, police, population, prosperity and mutual harmony, and be provided with stronger fortifications, a church, a school, etc." (*O'Callaghan's History*, II, 37.)

[4] *Alb. Rec.*, VII, 107, 108.

upon the resignation of schoolmaster Cornelessin,[1] Stuyvesant writes to the Classis of Amsterdam " for a pious, well-qualified and diligent schoolmaster " on the plea that " nothing is of greater importance than the right, early instruction of youth."[2] This application was probably referred by the Classis to the Directors of the West India Company,[3] who wrote to Stuyvesant as follows : " Jan. 27, 1649. We will make use of the first opportunity to supply you with a well-instructed schoolmaster, and shall inform ourselves about the person living at Haarlem, whom your Honor recommended."[4] " Feb. 16, 1650. We appoint, at your request, a schoolmaster [William Verstius], who shall also act as comforter of the sick. He is considered an honest and pious man, and shall embark at the first opportunity."[5] "April 15, 1650. The schoolmaster for whom you solicited, comes in the same vessel with this letter. The Lord grant that he may for a long time exemplify the favorable testimony which he carried with him from here, to the edification of the youth."[6]

In 1650, Secretary Van Tienhoven writes in behalf of the Amsterdam Chamber in answer to the Remonstrance to which reference has already been made, and which was presented directly to the States-General by the delegates of the commonalty.[7] "Although the new schoolhouse, toward which the commonalty contributed something, has not yet been built, it is not the Director, but the church wardens who have charge of the funds. The Director is busy providing materials. Meanwhile a place has been selected for a school, of which Jan Cornelissen has charge. The other teachers[8] keep school

---

[1] *Brodhead's History*, I, 507. [2] *Ibid.*, I, 508.

[3] *Pratt's Annals*, p. 9. [4] *Alb. Rec.*, IV, 17.

[5] *Ibid.*, IV, 23. [6] *Ibid.*, IV, 30. [7] *Brodhead's History*, I, 511.

[8] Private schoolmasters, of whose existence in the colony there are records from the year 1633. (*History of the School of the Reformed Protestant Dutch Church in the City of New York*, pp. 29, 35, foot-note. Henry W. Dunshee, New York, 1853.) The public or common school referred to in the above citations was the church school.

in hired houses, so that the youth are not in want of schools
to the extent of the circumstances of the country.[1] Tis true
there is no Latin school nor academy; if the commonalty require such, they can apply for it and furnish the necessary
funds . . . The question is, are the Company or the Directors
obliged to have constructed any buildings for the people out
of the duties paid by the trader in New Netherland on exported goods, particularly as their High Mightinesses granted
those duties to the Company to facilitate garrisons, and the
payment of the expenses attendant thereupon, and not for
building hospitals and orphan asylums, churches and school-
houses for the people. In New England there is no impost or
duty on imports or exports, but every one is assessed by the
local government according to his means, and must pay to the
extent of his property and as the magistrates tax him, for
. . . erection of schools and salaries of teachers. If they
[the colonists] are such patriots as they appear to be, let them
be leaders in generous contributions for such laudable objects,
and not complain when the Directors requested a collection
toward the erection of a church and school."[2] This document
together with others bearing upon the situation in New
Netherland were handed over to a committee of the States-
General for consideration. This committee submitted a "pro-

---

[1] In certain observations on the colonization of New Netherland, etc., which Van
Tienhoven furnished to the States-General on February 22, 1650, he enumerated
the following persons as necessary to colonists :

A superintendent to every 250 farmers.

" A clergyman ; or in his place provisionally, a comforter of the sick, who could
also act as schoolmaster."

A surgeon.

A blacksmith.

Three or four house carpenters.

One cooper.

One wheelwright.

Other tradesmen who " follow with them." (*N. Y. Col. Doc.*, I, 361. See
also 370.)

[2] *N. Y. Col. Doc.*, I, 423, 424, 425, 431.

visional order " for the government of New Netherland, which
they recommended the States-General with the consent of a
majority of the Directors of the Company to enact.[1] In the
sixth section of this plan, the committee advise that three
ministers shall be settled in New Netherland; "and the commonalty shall be also obliged to have the youth instructed by
good schoolmasters."[2]

In April, 1652, the Company made provision for another
school in the colony. In a letter to the Director-General, the
Company directors write : " We give our consent above all this,
that one public school may be established, for which one
school-master would be sufficient, and he might be engaged at
250 florins annually. We recommend you Jan de la Montagne,
whom we have provisionally favored with the appointment.
Your Honor may appropriate the city tavern for this purpose,
if this is practicable."[3] In this year, as a result of numerous
petitions and memorials from the colonists to the home government, the settlement at Manhattan was created a municipality,
with right to elect one schout fiscal or treasurer, two
burgomasters and five schepens,[4] and two years later the Dutch
towns on Long Island were also granted municipal privileges.
A district court was established for these Long Island towns
with authority to regulate roads, to build churches and schools,
etc.[5] But the Governor and Council continued both in theory
and practice to exert a local as well as a general control over
the affairs of the colony. In May, 1654, the Burgomasters of
New Amsterdam obtained permission from the Directors of
the Company to manage the finances of the city. At the same
time they were required to pay all the public salaries out of
the excise tax.[6] They failed, however, to meet this require-
ment, and in spite of a formal assurance which they made to
the Director and Council to support certain civil and ecclesi-

[1] *Brodhead's History*, I, 513. [2] *N. Y. Col. Doc.*, I, 389. [3] *Alb. Rec.*, IV, 68.
[4] *Brodhead's History*, I, 540.   [5] *Ibid.*, I, 580.   [6] *Ibid.*, I, 588.

astical officials,—" a foresinger to act also as school-master," being among the latter,—tax collection and payment of the official salaries were resumed by the provincial government.[1]

The following extracts from the records of the council and the municipality of New Amsterdam show in detail the scope and methods of the Provincial Government's administration of educational questions. On January 26, 1655, "William Verstius, schoolmaster and chorister in this city, [New Amsterdam] solicited the Council by a petition, as he had completed his service, and whereas there were now several persons fully competent to acquit themselves in this charge, that he might be favored with his dismission, and permitted to return to Holland in the first ship. On which petition was given the apostil, that it would be communicated to the Consistory and Ministers."[2]

[In Council, March 23, 1655.] "Whereas William Vestius, chorister and schoolmaster of this city, hath several times earnestly solicited leave to depart for the Fatherland, so is his request granted him; and in consequence thereof, have the noble Lords of the Supreme Council, with the consent of the respected Consistory of this city, appointed Harmanus Van Hoboocken as chorister and schoolmaster of this city, at thirty-five guilders per month, and one hundred guilders annual expenditures; who promises to conduct himself industriously and faithfully, pursuant to the instructions already given, or hereafter to be given.

(Signed) NICASIUS DE SILLE, LA MONTAGNE."[3]

[In Council, August 11, 1655.] "A petition being read of Harman van Hoboocken, now the chorister in this city, soliciting, as he is burthened with a wife and four small children, without possessing any means for their sustenance, that his salary may be paid to him monthly, or, at least, quarterly, so is, after deliberation, given as apostil as long as the

---

[1] *Ibid.*, I, 590.   [2] *Alb. Rec.*, X, 6.   [3] *Ibid.*, X, 29, 30; XXV, 133.

supplicant remains in service, he may depend on the punctual payment of his salary." [1]

The records of the burgomasters and schepens of New Amsterdam, for February 21, 1656, contain this minute : " The schout having exhibited, in conformity to instructions from the Honorable Director General and Council, the request of the schoolmaster, Harman van Hoboocken, in court, they endorse. Said schoolmaster shall communicate to the burgomasters and schepens what he is allowed for each child per quarter, pursuant to instructions from the General and Council, which being done, further order shall be taken on petitioner's request." [2]

[In Council, February 19, 1658,] "On motion the Attorney-General is commanded, to go the house of Jacob Van Corler, who has, since some time, arrogated to himself to keep school, and to warn him that Director General and Council have deemed it proper to send him a supersedeas, till he shall have solicited and obtained from the Director General and Council an act in propria forma." [3] This action drew forth the following protest on March 5, from the municipality of New Amsterdam.

" TO THE RIGHT HONORABLE, DIRECTOR GENERAL AND COUN-
CILLORS OF NEW NETHERLAND.

" Right Honorable Sirs—The burgomasters and schepens of the city of Amsterdam, in New Netherland, represent with all respect, that some burghers and inhabitants of the above-named city, have presented a certain petition to this Court, whereof copy is hereunto annexed, remonstrating that your

---

[1] *Alb. Rec.*, X, 81.

[2] *The Records of New Amsterdam*, II, 39   Edited by Berthold Fernow, New York, 1897.   See also *Ibid.*, II, 219-20.   On November 4, 1856, the municipality granted Hoboocken's petition for school lodgings by empowering him to charge a rental of 100 guilders per annum to the account of the city.

[3] *Alb. Rec.*, XIV, 114.

Honors were pleased to notify Jacob Corlaar, through the Fiscal Nicasius de Sille, not to keep any school; and as they, the petitioners, find themselves greatly interested thereby, as their children forget what the above-named Jacob van Corlaar had to their great satisfaction previously taught them in reading, writing and cyphering, which was much more than any other person, no one excepted; therefore, they request that the above-named Corlaar may be allowed again to keep school; and although the above-named burgomasters and two schepens have spoken verbally thereon to your Honors, and your Honors were not pleased to allow it, for reasons thereunto moving your Honors, they therefore, in consequence of the humble supplication of the burghers and inhabitants aforesaid, again request that your Honors may be pleased to permit the above-named Corlaar again to keep school, which doing, we remain your Honors subjects,

THE BURGOMASTERS AND SCHEPENS."[1]

The above petition was read in Council March 19, 1658, and it was decided that "school-keeping and the appointment of schoolmasters depend absolutely from the jus patronatus in virtue of which Director-General and Council interdicted school-keeping to Jacob van Corlaar, as having arrogated it to himself without their orders, in which resolution they do as yet persist."[2]

[In Council, March 26, 1658,] "Being presented a petition of Jacobus van Corler, soliciting the permission to keep school within this city, and to instruct children in reading and writing. For weighty reasons influencing the Director-General and Council, the apostil was nihil actum."[3]

[In Council, July 30, 1658,] "A petition being presented of Jan Lubberts, soliciting, that he might be permitted to keep school, to instruct in reading, writing and arithmetic. . . .

---

[1] *New Amsterdam Rec.*, II, 348.

[2] *Alb. Rec.*, XIV, 151. [3] *Ibid.*, XIV, 158. See also *N. A. Rec.*, II, 348.

The petition is granted, provided he conducts himself as such a person ought to do." [1]

On August 16, 1660, the following petition to keep a school was granted in Council: "To the Honorable, Respectful, Valiant Director-General and Council in New Netherland: Shows with all due and submissive reverence Jan Juriaense Becker, your supplicant, that he, through the caprices of the unsteady fortune since a short time—not knowing why—has been compelled to become a tavern keeper—for which he nearly sacrificed all what he possessed and whereas, the supplicant is apprehensive that many difficulties, and even poverty is threatening him and his family—so is it, that the supplicant, imploring addresses himself to your Honor, soliciting most humbly, that it may please your Honor to regard with pity the supplicant, being an old Company's servant, and to employ him as a writer in the service of the Company, either in the Esopus,—here or anywhere else, whereever your Honor might deem it proper—or—if your Honor cannot employ him at this time in their service—that then the supplicant might be permitted to keep school, to instruct the youth in reading and writing, etc. Expecting a favorable apostil, he remains

Your Honor obedient servant,

J. BECKER." [2]

[In Council, October 27, 1661.] "Whereas, Harman van Hoboocken, before schoolmaster and chorister, was removed because another was sent to replace him by the Lords Directors and the Consistory, [3] solicits to be employed again in one

---

[1] *Alb. Rec.*, XIV, 318.   [2] *Ibid.*, XXIV, 374, 375.

[3] Evert Pietersen, concerning whom the Amsterdam Chamber writes to the Director-General and Council under date of May 2, 1661: "Whereas, we have deemed it necessary to promote religious worship, and to read to the inhabitants the word of God, to exhort them, to lead them in the ways of the Lord, and console the sick, that an expert person was sent to New Netherlands, in the city of New Amsterdam, who at the same time should act there as chorister and schoolmaster; so it is, that we, upon the good report which we have received about the person of Evert Pietersen, and confiding in his abilities and experience in the

or other manner in the Company's service, so is he engaged as adelborst,[1] and allowed 10 guilders per month and 175 for board, from 27th Oct., 1661. Nota: Whereas the aforesaid Harman is a person of irreproachable life and conduct, so shall he be employed on the bouwery of the Director-General as schoolmaster and clerk, with this condition, that the Director-General, whenever his service might be wanted for the Company as adelborst, shall replace him by another expert person."[2]

On September 21, 1662, the Council granted the following petition: "To the Noble, Great and Respected the Director-General and Council in New Netherland: Shows reverently,

aforesaid services, together on his pious character and virtues, have, on your Honor's recommendation, and that of the magistrates of the city of New Amsterdam, appointed the aforesaid person as consoler of the sick, chorister and schoolmaster, at New Amsterdam, in New Netherland, which charge he shall fulfill there, and conduct himself in these with all diligence and faithfulness; also, we except that he shall give others a good example, so as it becomes a pious and good consoler, clerk, chorister and schoolmaster; regulating himself in conformity to the instructions which he received here from the Consistory, and principally to the instructions which he received from us, which he shall execute in every point faithfully: Wherefore, we command all persons, without distinction, to acknowledge the aforesaid Evert Pietersen as consoler, clerk, chorister and schoolmaster in New Amsterdam, in New Netherland, and not to molest, disturb or ridicule him in any offices, but rather to offer him every assistance in their power, and deliver him from every painful sensation, by which the will of the Lord and our good intentions shall be accomplished." (*Ibid.*, VIII, 321.)

On May 9, the Directors write that Mr. Pietersen, who has been engaged "as schoolmaster and clerk, upon a salary of 36 guilders per month, and 125 guilders annually for his board," has already embarked for New Netherland. "And whereas, he has solicited to be supplied with some books and stationery, which would be of service to him in that station, so did we resolve to send you a sufficient quantity of these articles, as your Honor may see from the invoice. Your Honor ought not to place all these at his disposal at once, but from time to time, when he may be in want of these, when his account ought directly to be charged with its amount; so, too, he must be charged with all such books of which he may be in want as a consoler of the sick, which he might have obtained from your Honor, which afterward might be reimbursed to him, whenever he, ceasing to serve in that capacity, might return these; all these must be valued at the invoice price." (*Ibid.*, IV, 373.)

[1] A sergeant or something above a common soldier.   [2] *Ibid.*, XIX, 383.

Johannes Van Gelder, a citizen and inhabitant of this city, how that he, supplicant, being tolerebly acquainted with reading and writing, it has happened that several of the principal inhabitants of this city advised and encouraged him too, to open a public school, and consequently induced the supplicant, who looks out for a living in an honorable way, to adopt their advice—in the hope that he shall execute this task to their satisfaction who shall make use of his service—but as this is not permitted, except that an admission is previously obtained, so he addresses himself to your Honors, requesting their admission for this exercise—viz—keeping a public school —which doing, etc.

Your Honors' subject and servant,

JOHANNES VAN GELDER." [1]

[In Council, December 31, 1665,] "Andreas Hudde appeared before the Director-General and Council, and solicited a license to keep school, received for answer that the Council shall ask upon his proposal the opinion of the Minister and the Consistory." [2]

All the records that have been so far quoted refer to elementary education. In 1658 the West India Company cooperated with Director Stuyvesant and the city of New Amsterdam in a plan for secondary education. On May 20, the Company Directors write to Stuyvesant: " The Rev. Driesius [3] mentioned to us more than once that it might, in his opinion, be serviceable if a Latin school was established, in which the youth might be instructed—in which he was willing to engage his service; and whereas, we do not disapprove this plan, as we thought its communication proper, that your Honor, if you considered it proper to make an experiment of such an establishment, might advice us in what manner such an institution might be carried into effect to the greatest

---

[1] *Ibid.*, XX, 215.   [2] *Ibid.*, IX, 309.

[3] The Rev. Samuel Drisius, of Leyden, was settled as minister in New Amsterdam, in 1652. (*Brodhead's History*, I, 537.)

advantage for the community, and with the least expense to the Company."[1] The Directors write to Stuyvesant again on this matter on April 25, 1659: " Our earnest exertions[2] to provide your city with a Latin schoolmaster shall, we expect, be placed beyond doubt by the arrival of Alexander Carolus Curtius, who was before a Professor in Lithuania, whom we have engaged[3] for this purpose, allowing him an annual salary of 1,500 florins . . . boarding included, besides one hundred more as a gift, to purchase merchandise, of which he may dispose to his advantage at his arrival, as you will see from the enclosed extract of our resolutions, and the copy of our contract with him . . The books which the schoolmaster required to instruct the youth in the Latin language, will not be made ready from the unexpected departure of the vessels, wherefore this must be postponed to the next opportunity."[4]

On July 23, Director Stuyvesant and the Council announce the arrival of Alexander Carolus Curtius to the Company. To this point they write : " We hope and confide that the com-

---

[1] *Alb. Rec.*, IV, 268.

[2] The Directors were undoubtedly spurred on to "earnest exertions " by the letter which was written to them on September 19, 1658, by the burgomaster and schepens of New Amsterdam . . . " Further, laying before your Honors the great augmentation of the youth in this province and place . . . and though many of them can read and write, the burghers and inhabitants are nevertheless inclined to have their children instructed in the most useful languages, the chief of which is the Latin tongue ; and as there are no means so to do here, the nearest being at Boston, in New England, a great distance from here, and many of the burghers and inhabitants of this place and neighborhood having neither the ability nor means to send their children thither, we shall therefore . . . humbly request that your Honors would be pleased to send us a suitable person for master of a Latin school . . . not doubting but were such person here, many of the neighboring places would send their children hither to be instructed in that tongue, hoping that increasing from year to year, it may finally attain to an academy, whereby this place arriving at great splendor, your Honors shall have the reward and praise next to God, the Lord, who will grant His blessing to it. On your Honors sending us a schoolmaster, we shall endeavor to have constructed a suitable place or school . . . " (*N. A. Rec.*, III, 15, 16.

[3] On April 10, 1659. See *Ibid.*, VIII, 201, 202.   [4] *Ibid.*, IV, 303, 305.

munity shall reap great benefits from it for their children, for which we pray that a bountiful God may vouchsafe his blessing. The state of this new institution shall be ere long communicated to your Honors."[1]

On December 22, 1659, the Directors write to Stuyvesant: "The complaints which have been made by the Latin schoolmaster or rector shall, in our opinion, in great part be removed. Now henceforward the payment is made according to the value of Holland currency. If to this sum is added that which he receives from his pupils annually,[2] then it would seem to be adequate for the sustenance of a single individual, more so, as his salary from time to time must be increased by the increase of the youth whose parents cannot decently neglect to reward his endeavors which he bestows on the instruction of their children. In this your Honor ought to assist him, and recommend him to the parents, as the circumstance of time may permit."[3]

On April 16, 1660, the Directors send further instructions about the Latin schoolmaster: "As we have been informed that Rector Curtius is practising physic, and did solicit that we would provide him with an herbarium, which would be to

---

[1] *Ibid.*, XVIII, 19, 20.

[2] Curtius was allowed by the Director-General and the burgomasters of New Amsterdam to take 6 guilders per quarter for each pupil. In 1660 the Burgomasters hear that contrary to this order he is taking one beaver, valued at eight guilders, for each boy per quarter. They consequently warn him that unless he conform to the aforesaid order they will keep from him the yearly stipend of 200 guilders which is granted to him by the city. Cited by Pratt in *Annals*, p. 26, from *N. A. Rec.*, III, 427, 428, but not given in published records. In 1661, Schoolmaster Curtius refused to pay the excise tax, arguing that in Holland professors, preachers and rectors were exempt, and that the Director-General had also granted him exemption. But the Burgomasters decided that the rector should pay the excise. (*N. A. Rec.*, III, 253.) Later in the year Curtius petitions the Court to allow him 600 guilders a year " on condition of receiving no contribution from the youth." This petition is referred by the Court to the Director General and Council. (*Ibid.*, III, 344.)

[3] *Ibid.*, IV., 325.

him of great service, so we send him this book by the present opportunity, which your Honor will deliver to him. But the book ought to remain the property of the Company; so, too, the books which have been lately transmitted. Your Honor ought to make a memorandum of all these articles, so that it may not be forgotten."[1]

In 1661, Dr. Curtius having shown himself inadequate was dismissed from his position by the Company Directors[2] and returned to Holland. Dr. Aegidius Luyck aspired to take his place as rector of the Latin school, and on July 30, 1663, sent in the following petition to the Director-General and his Council: "Shews with all humble reverence, that whereas I, undersigned, called for the private instruction of the Director-General's childrens, sometimes have by a few inhabitants here, who saw and heard the full satisfaction; be it said without the least arrogance, of the aforesaid Honorable Lord, upon the good method of inculcating the first principles of the Latin and Greek languages, as in writing, arithmetic, catechising and *honorum morum praxis*, with respect to his children, and even by his Hon. seriously solicited to request that I might be employed in the Rectoratum of this city, and his Hon. fully acquainted with the necessity of having the youth in a now rising place, and that several who in behalf of their children submitted before to troubles and expenses, under the former Doctor, now should be compelled to sacrifice all their prospects, or at a yet greater expense send their children to the Patria. So his Honor deemed it proper to employ me for this end, promising that he would advise and recommend it to the Lord Directors, so that a salary might be allowed to me. With this looking forward I remain satisfied, returned to the school, and exerted every nerve so that the number of my disciples was increased to twenty, among whom were two from Virginia and two from Fort Orange, and ten or twelve more from the two aforesaid places were expected, while others were intended to board with

[1] *Alb. Rec.*, IV, 341, 342.   [2] *Dunshee's History*, p. 53.

me. But while I was waiting with patience for an answer from
the Directors, I nevertheless did not receive it, without knowing its cause. I offer, notwithstanding, cheerfully to continue
in my service, but solicit most earnestly and humbly that the
Director-General, with his High and Faithful Council, that it
may please them to provide me with a decent salary, so as I
cannot doubt, it shall meet their aprobation, as well knowing
that I cannot hire on the small payment which is received
from the disciples, and as a laborer deserve his wages, and if I
might obtain a favorable resolution, my ardour and zeal to acquit myself well of my duty must be of course increased, by
which I am encouraged to remain.

> Your Hon. humble and obedient servant,
>
> AEGIDIUS LUYCK."[1]

On August 9, a vote was taken on this petition in Council,
and Dr. Luyck was told that he should first address himself
to the Directors of the West India Company.[2] Director Stuyvesant was pleased to set down his full opinion on the matter
as follows: " My advice on the request of the Rev. Ægidius
Luyck is, that I condescend to acquiesce in the majority of
votes. Nevertheless, being of opinion that the instruction of
the youth, with well regulated schools, is not less serviceable
or less required than even church service, that the many
proofs, too, of the supplicant's piety, talents and diligence in
instructing children, and his more than common progresses,
which have been during five quarters of a year such, that they
far excel the instructions of the late rector, Alexander Carolus
Curtius, as will be attested by the ministers of the holy word
of God, and other competent judges, to which ought to be
added, that such a plan is contributing effectually to increase
the renown of this place and school—and really an actual
advantage, so well for our youth as for our inhabitants, as by
example the increase of the school from Virginia and elsewhere—for these and other reasons, partly already explained

[1] *Alb. Rec.*, XXI, 257, 258.   [2] *Ibid.*

in that petition, it would be my advice, that aforesaid Ægidius
Luycke, to encourage him in his service, ought to enjoy the
quality and salary which the Lords Directors of the Privileged
West Indian Company, Department of Amsterdam, granted to
the first Latin schoolmaster, Alexander Carolus Curtius. If
not absolutely, at least with decent intercession and recommendation, under the aforesaid Lords Directors."[1] The foregoing decision of the Council called forth another appeal[2]
from Dr. Luyck and a petition[3] from the Burgomasters of New
Amsterdam in his behalf. To the Burgomasters' petition the
following answer was given in Council, August 16, 1663:
"The Director General and Council are, with the supplicants,
of opinion that the continuation and encouragement of the
Latin school is necessary, and, as it is customary in our
Fatherland, that such persons by the cities which make use of
them are engaged, so are the supplicants authorized by this,
to allow such a salary to the aforesaid Rev. Luyck as they

[1] *Ibid.*, XXI, 259.

[2] *Alb. Rec.*, XXI, 269, 270. In this second letter, Dr. Luyck states that he has
already addressed the Company on the subject of the rectorship, and that he under-
stands that the question is left by the Company Directors to the decision of the
Director General and Council.

[3] "Whereas, on your Honor's recommendations, and our letters last year written to the Directors, the aforesaid Rev. Luyck was requested to act here as schoolmaster in the Latin language, in lieu of the late Rector Curtius, on such a salary
as should be allowed to him by the Directors, of which he has no information that any
conclusive step was made, so is it that we, experiencing the good instruction and
discipline of our youth, deem ourselves obliged humbly to solicit your Honors that
it may please them to grant the supplicant a disposition on his written request,
with granting him such a salary as your Honors in their wisdom and discretion
shall deem proper. So that the supplicant's growing zeal, to the detriment of your
Honors and that of our children and the youth of this city with that sent hither
from other places, may not be cooled, but rather daily may be increased, to the renown and glory of this city—by our neighbors and other further remote places—
in the hope that this our just request shall be maturely considered by your Honors,
so that your Honor shall favor the aforesaid Luyck with an ordinary and competent salary, by which we shall feel ourselves obliged, and remain. . . ." (*Ibid.*,
XXI, 271, 272.)

shall deem reasonable,[1] of which salary Director-General and
Council, provisionally upon the approbation of the Noble
Directors, shall pay the half."[2]

By the treaty which was signed at Hartford in 1650 between
Director Stuyvesant and the Commissioners of the United
Colonies, the western part of Long Island was assigned to the
Dutch and the eastern part to the English.[3] During the next
few years, several of the towns which lay west of Oyster Bay,
the division point of the Island, sent in petitions to the central
government of New Netherland on the subject of schools and
schoolmasters. On October 16, 1655, the Director-General
and Council passed an ordinance authorizing the magistrates
of Midwout[4] to lay out that village on condition that "5 @ 6
lots be reserved for public buildings, such as for the sheriff,
minister, the secretary, schoolmaster, village tavern and public
court house."[5] Three years later the magistrates of Midwout
apply to the provincial government for further directions for
the administration of the lots which had been appropriated to
the church in Midwout. They furthermore suggest that 50
acres be appropriated " to the maintenance of a school, church
service, etc." The Council agree to this plan.[6]

In 1661 ten of the inhabitants of Middleburgh present the following petition to Director Stuyvesant : " That whereas God
hath been pleased of late years to deprive us of Middleburrow,
of Long Island, of the public means of grace & salvation, and
also of education of our children, in scholastical discipline, the
way to true happiness, but yet God in mercy of late hath provided for us a help meet for the discipline of education of our children, and by the same person help in the Sabbath exercises,

---

[1] The salary agreed upon was the equivalent of 1000 guilders in seawant.
(*Ibid.*, XXI, 273.)   [2] *Ibid.*

[3] *Brodhead's History*, I, 519.   [4] Flatbush, L. I.

[5] *Laws and Ordinances of New Netherland*, 1638–1674, p. 199. Compiled by
Edmund B. O'Callaghan, Albany, 1868.

[6] *Alb. Rec.*, XIV, 73, 74, 75.

we, therefore, who never gave nor consented to the giving of the housing, and lands, built and fenced in, and also dedicated for the use of the public dispensation of God's word unto us, we humbly intreat your Honorable Lordship, that this our said schoolmaster, Richard Mills by name, may be by your Lordship's order possessed of the said housing and lands for his use and ours also, for our children's education and the Sabbath exercise, the which God doth require, and we have need for us and our children thereof: As the housing now stands, it is like all to go to wreck and ruin, the fences falling down, the house and barn decaying and wanting repair, and Francis Dowtye [1] doeth not repair it, nor the town, as it stands between him and them, will not repair it, and by this means is like to come to nothing in a short time; and so we and your Lordship also, by this means, shall be disappointed; therefore our humble request is to your Lordship, is, that this, our schoolmaster, and at present our souls' help in dispensing God's word to us and our children every Lord's day, may be settled in it, to enjoy it without any molestation from Francis Doughty, or any of his, for so long time our God shall be pleased to continue him amongst us, or to provide another for us, thus knowing that your Lordship is as willing, to further our souls' good as well as our bodies', we rest your Lordship's humble petitioners & loyal subjects."

In answer to this petition, on February 18 the Director-General orders Francis Doughty to give "a quiet possession unto the present schoolmaster, Mr. Richard Mills, of the house and land, being with our knowledge, consent and help, built for the public use of the ministry, and by these means it may, nor cannot be given and transported for a private heritage." [2]

On July 4, 1661, the Schout and Schepens of Breuckelen

---

[1] Mr. Doughty had married the widow of Rev. John Moore, minister of Middleburgh. Moore died died in 1657, and his family continued to live in the parsonage which served also as a church and schoolhouse. (*Pratt's Annals*, p. 29.)

[2] *Alb. Rec.*, XIX, 13, 14.

respectfully represent "to the Right Honorable Director-General and Council of New Netherland:" "that they found it necessary that a court messenger was required for the Schepens' Chamber, to be occasionally employed in the village of Breuckelen and all around where he may be needed, as well as to serve summons, as also to conduct the service of the church, and to sing on Sundays; to take charge of the school, dig graves, etc., ring the bell, and perform whatever else may be required   Therefore, the petitioners, with your Honors' approbation, have thought proper to accept for so highly necessary an office, a suitable person who is now come before them, one Carel van Beauvois, to whom they have hereby appropriated the sum of 150 florins, besides a free dwelling; and whereas, the petitioners are apprehensive that the said C. v. Beauvois would not and cannot do the work for the sum aforesaid, and the petitioners are not able to promise him any more, therefore the petitioners, with all humble and proper reverence, request your Honors to be pleased to lend them a helping hand, in order thus to receive the needful assistance." In answer to this petition the Director and Council agreed to "pay 50 guilders in wampum annually, for the support of the precentor and schoolmaster in the village of Breuckelen." [1]

On December 20, 1663, a similar agreement was entered into between the provincial government and the town of Bushwick. "Appeared in Council, commissaries of the village of Bushwyck, notifying how that they in their village were in great want of a person who would act as clerk and schoolmaster, to instruct the youth; and whereas there was proposed to them the person of Boudewyn Maenhout, from Crampen de Lek, that they had agreed with him, viz.: that he should officiate as clerk and keep school for the instruction of the youth, for which he should receive 400 florins in seawant annually, besides house rent, they solicited therefore, that this

[1] *Ibid.*, XIX, 194.

transaction might be approved by the Director-General and Council in New Netherland, and that the Company would contribute annually something to facilitate the payment of said salary. Which being taken in consideration by the Director-General and Council in New Netherland, the engagement of the person and the agreement with the aforesaid Boudewyn Maenhout is hereby approved, provided that he shall previously be examined by the Rev. Ministers of this city, and if they deem him competent for the task, then shall annually be paid by the Company, to render it more easy to aforesaid village to pay that salary to the aforesaid Boudewyn 25 florins heavy money."[1]

About this time petitions from the towns of New Amsterdam, Bergen and New Harlem were also directed on the same subjects to the central government. On February 2, 1662, the Burgomasters of New Amsterdam petition for the gift of a certain lot in the Brewer Street for the building of a "good schoolhouse for the benefit of the inhabitants of this city." The Director and Council, however, "deem it, for various reasons, more proper that the schoolhouse be constructed on a part of the present church yard."[2]

On December 17, 1663, the sheriff, commissaries and schoolmaster of the town of Bergen were summoned to appear in Council on a matter which is fully set forth in the petition which was presented by them to the Director and Council. "Shew reverently, the sheriff and commissaries of the village of Bergen, which they presume, is known to your Honors, that before the election of the commissaries, ye were solicited for Michael Jansen, deceased, to be favored with the appointment of a clerk who should at the same time keep school, to instruct the youth, the person of Engelbert Steenhuysen, who possessed the requisite abilities, so is it that the sheriff and commissaries now a year past proposed it to the community, who then approved it, and resolved to engage him not only as

---

[1] *Ibid.*, XX, 297.   [2] *Ibid.*, XX, 39.

clerk but with the express stipulation that he, besides this function, was to keep school, which the aforesaid Steenhuysen engaged to do, and did so during five quarters of a year, for which was allowed him 250 florins in seawant annually, besides some other stipulations, besides the school money, so as reason and equity shall demand. Now is it so, that the aforesaid Engelbert Steenhuysen, whereas he has a lot and house and a double farm, situated in the jurisdiction of the village of Bergen, is, by the complaints of the majority of the community, obliged with the other inhabitants, to provide for the sustenance of a soldier, by which the aforesaid Engelbert Steenhuysen considers himself highly aggrieved, and so resigned his office, pretending that a schoolmaster and clerk ought to be exempted from all taxes and burthens of the village, which he says is the common practice through the whole Christian world, which by the sheriff and commissaries, is understood can only take place when such a clerk or schoolmaster does not possess anything else but the schoolwharf [lot], but by no means, when as a schoolmaster in possession of a house and lot, and a double farm, that he, in such a case, should pay nothing from his lot and lands; and the community at large is of the same opinion, as he receives his salary as clerk, and not only is obliged to act well in his capacity as clerk, but even to look out and procure himself a proper and convenient place to keep school, which he thus far neglected, and pretends that the community must effect this, so that he may keep his school in it. They cannot perceive how Engelbert Steenhuysen can be permitted to resign his office, when he neglected to notify his intention a half year before, wherefore the supplicants address themselves to your Honor, humbly soliciting them to insinuate to the aforesaid Engelbert Steenhuysen to continue in his service this second year—and to decline, if the aforesaid Eng. Steenhuysen is or is not obliged, by his possession of a lot and farm, to provide in the maintenance of a soldier, so well as the other inhabitants." After the plaintiffs and defendant were heard at length, it was agreed that schoolmaster Steenhuysen should serve his time, "agreeably to the contract mentioned in said petition, so as he ought to do."[1]

On December 15, 1663, the commissaries of New Harlem petition as follows : " Gentlemen : With reverence and due submission shew your noble, great and respectful supplicants, subjects residing in N. Haerlem . . . having seen and experienced, from Sabbath to Sabbath, the small success of the public congregation, and fully believing that better care might be taken of the interests of religion, and the whole worship with more decency performed, if a clerk and schoolmaster on a fixed salary could be engaged, so that the word of God might be heard, an edifying sermon read, catechising introduced, and the sick be visited, it seemed, therefore, to the supplicants of your Honors, whose office is to attend to the common welfare and advantage of aforesaid village, . . . to be their duty to speak with the congregation on this subject, and to endeavor to persuade Jean de la Montagne, an inhabitant of that place, to save expense, that he would accept this office by permission. Wherefore they deemed it proper to address your Honor as the patrons of the church of Jesus Christ, and humble . . . to solicit that it might please them to consent, both to the establishment of that office and the appointment of said person for the benefit of the church of God, and the not less necessary instruction of the children, but considering . . . their present utter inability to provide a competent and decent salary, and that it was not in their power to collect more for his sustenance than 24 schepel corn, they are now most reverently soliciting that it may please your Honor agreeably to their usual discretion, to contribute something for a decent salary and the better encouragement of " [etc.] . . . A grant of 50 guilders per annum from the Company's treasurer was the answer of Director and Council to the above petition.[2]

[1] *Ibid.*, XXI, 439, 440.   [2] *Ibid.*, XXII, 11.

On March 17, 1664, was enacted the only general measure for education which was passed during the whole existence of the provincial government of New Netherlands.

" Ordinance of the Director-General and Council of New Netherland, for the better and more careful instruction of youth in the principles of the Christian religion.

"Whereas it is highly necessary and most important that the youth from childhood up be instructed not only in reading, writing and arithmetic, but especially and chiefly in the principles and fundamentals of the Reformed religion, according to the lesson of that wise king, Solomon, —train up a child in the way he shall go, and when he is old he will not depart from it,—so that in time such men may proceed therefrom, as may be fit to serve their Fatherland as well in the Church as in the State. This then, being taken into particular consideration by the Director-General and Council of New Netherland, because the number of children is through the merciful blessing of the Lord, considerably increasing here, they have deemed it necessary, in order that so useful and God-acceptable a work may be the more effectually promoted, to recommend and command the schoolmasters, as we do hereby, that they shall appear in the church, with the children committed to their care and intrusted to them, on Wednesday before the commencement of the sermon, in order, after the conclusion of Divine Service, that each may in the presence of the reverend ministers and the elders who may be present, examine his scholars as to what they have committed to memory of the Christian commandments and catechism, and what progress they have made; after which performance, the children shall be dismissed for that day, and allowed a decent recreation." [1]

In 1664, Charles II, King of England granted to his brother, the Duke of York, all the land lying between the Connecticut River and Delaware Bay and in the same year a govenor was

---

[1] *Laws and Ordinances of New Netherland*, p. 461.

commissioned and sent over by the Duke of York to take possession of this territory. Shortly after the surrender of Manhattan, Governor Nicolls notified the inhabitants of Long Island to send two delegates from each town to a convention at Hempstead, on February 28th, 1665. At this convention, a body of laws which had been " collected out of the several laws now in force in his Majesty's American colonies and plantations" was presented by the Govenor and confirmed by the delegates.[1] Among these laws was the following provision for

"CHILDREN AND SERVANTS.

" The constable and overseers are strictly required frequently to admonish the inhabitants of instructing their children and servants in matters of religion and the laws of the country. And that the parents and masters do bring up their children and apprentices in some honest lawful calling, labor or employment. And if any children or servants become rude, stubborn or unruly, refusing to hearken to the voice of their parents or masters, the constable and overseers (where no justice of peace shall happen to dwell within ten miles of the said town or parish) have power upon the complaint of their parents or masters to call before them such an offender, and to inflict such corporal punishment as the merit of their fact in their judgment shall deserve, not exceeding ten stripes, provided that such children and servants be of sixteen years of age." [2]

The " Duke's Laws " originally obtained only in the shire of Yorkshire, i. e., Long Island, Staten Island and Westchester County, and did not go into effect in New York until 1674; from that time they probably continued in effect until 1691.[3] Meanwhile, Dutch laws and usages seem to have continued in force.

On October 12, 1665, the Governor licensed one John Shutte "for teaching of the English tongue at Albany." " Whereas,

---

[1] *The Colonial Laws of New York*, I, 6, 7, Albany, 1894.

[2] *Ibid.*, I, 26.   [3] *Ibid.*, Historical Note, I, p. xii.

the teaching of the English tongue is necessary in this government; I have, therefore, thought fit to give license to John Shutte to be the English schoolmaster at Albany. And, upon condition that the said John Shutte shall not demand any more wages from each scholar than is given by the Dutch to their Dutch schoolmasters, I have further granted to the said John Shutte that he shall be the only English schoolmaster at Albany."[1]

On May 16, 1670, Governor Francis Lovelace, who had been commissioned Nicolls' successor in 1667, granted a similar license to Jan Jurians Beecker "to be schoolmaster at Albany." "Whereas, Jan Jurians Beecker had a grant to keep the Dutch school at Albany for the teaching of youth to read and to write, the which was allowed of and confirmed to him by my predecessor, Colonel Richard Nicolls. Notwithstanding which several others not so capable, to undertake the like some particular times and seasons of the year when they have no other employment, where by the scholars removing from one school to another do not only give a great discouragement to the master who makes it his business all the year, but also are hindered and become the more backwards in their learning for the reasons aforesaid, I have thought fit that the said Jan Jurians Beecker, who is esteemed very capable that way, shall be the allowed schoolmaster for the instructing of the youth at Albany and parts adjacent; he following the said employment constantly and diligently and that no other be admitted to interrupt him. It being to be presumed that the said Beecker for the youth, and Jacob Joosten, who is allowed of for the teaching of the younger children are sufficient for that place."[2] There is one other record of Governor Lovelace's supervision of education.

"An order made on behalf of Mr. Charlton for getting in his

---

[1] *The Annals of Albany*, IV, 16.   Joel Munsell, Albany, 1853.

[2] *Ibid.*, V, 15-16.

money from the Town of Hempstead, for teaching school there."

"Whereas, I am given to understand that the major part of your town did, at a public meeting contract with Richard Charlton to keep a school to instruct the children and youth there to write and read, the which he hath performed for the whole time of the contract, yet divers of the town, although they have received the benefit thereof, do refuse, or too long delay, the payment contracted for; these are to require you to cause speedy payment to be made unto him, according to your contract, that persons of that calling be not discouraged, otherwise he will have good remedy against you at law to your greater charge and disparagement. Given under my hand at Fort James, in New York this 21st day of March 1671.

FRAN. LOVELACE.

To the Justices of the Peace, Constable and Overseers at Hempstead."[1]

During the re-occupation of New York by the Dutch from July 30, 1673 to October 22, 1674, the Governor-General and his Council issued an ordinance on October 1, " explaining the duties and powers of the schout and schepens of Midwout, Amesfoort, Breuckelen, New Utrecht, Gravesend and Bushwyck." The ordinance contained the following provision: "9. The sheriff and schepens shall have power to conclude on some ordinances for the welfare and peace of the inhabitants of their district, such as laying highways, setting off lands and gardens, and in like manner, what appertains to agriculture, observance of the Sabbath, erecting churches, schoolhouses, or similar public works." Similar instructions were sent to Flushing, Hemsted, Middleburgh, Jamaica, Oysterbay, Southampton, Southold, Seatalcot, Huntington and East Hampton on L. I., to Swanenburg, Hurley and Marbletown, in the Esopus, to Elizabethtown, Woodbridge, Shrewsbury,

---

[1] *General Entries in Office of Sec'y of State*, IV, 117, given in *Annals of Public Education*, pp. 58, 59.

Newarke, Bergen, Piscattaway and Middletown behind Achter Cul, and to Staten Island and Westchester.[1] In the above general ordinance it was provided that all orders of any importance on the part of the respective sheriff and schepens, should be presented before publication to the chief magistrate for his approval. Not long after the passing of this ordinance, the officials of the town of Bergen appealed to the central government concerning a school controversy which had arisen in their town.

"At a Council holden in Fort Wm. Hendrick, the 24 December, 1673. Present—Anthony Colve, Governor-General, Cornelis Steenwyck, Councillor." "The schout and magistrates of the town of Bergen requesting that the inhabitants of all the settlements dependent on them, of what religious persuasion soever they may be, shall be bound to pay their share towards the support of the precentor and schoolmaster, etc., which being taken into consideration by the Governor and Council, it is ordered: That all the said inhabitants, without any exception, shall, pursuant to the resolution of the magistrates of the town of Bergen, dated 18th December, 1672, and subsequent confirmation, pay their share for the support of said precentor and schoolmaster."[3]

"In a Council, holden in Fort Willem Hendrick, this 24 of May, 1674. Present—Governor-General Colve, Councillor Cornelis Steenwyck and Secretary Nicholaes Bayard, assumed Councillor." "The schout and magistrates of the town of Bergen, complaining by petition, that some of the inhabitants of their dependent hamlets, in disparagement of the previous order of the Governor-General and Council, dated the 24th December last, obstinately refuse to pay their quota to the support of the precentor and schoolmaster. Ordered: The Governor-General and Council persist in their previous man-

---

[1] *Laws and Ordinances of N. N.*, pp. 478–480.

[3] *N. Y. Col. Doc.*, II, 672–3.

date of the 24th December last and order the schout to proceed to immediate execution against all unwilling debtors."[1]

"At a Council held in Fort Willem Hendrick, 15th June, 1674. Present—Governor-General Anthony Colve, Councillor Cornelis Steenwyck, Fiscal Willem Knyff, and Secretary Nicholas Bayard as assumed Councillors." " On petition of Lourens Andries and Joost van der Linde, agents for the inhabitants of Mingagqué and Pemrepogh, requesting to be excused from contributing to the support of the schoolmaster at Bergen, &c. Ordered: Copy hereof to be furnished the magistrates of the town of Bergen to answer the same."[2]

"At a Court held in Fort Willem Hendrick, on the 5th of July, 1674. Present—as on May 24, 1674." " The Governor and Council of New Netherland, having seen the complaint of the town of Bergen against the inhabitants of the villages of Pemrepogh, Mingagquy, &c., and the answer given by them, in regard to what the inhabitants of Pemrepogh and Mingagquy aforesaid, owe for the support of the schoolmaster and precentor of the town of Bergen, it is after due inquiry resolved and ordered, that the inhabitants of Pemrepogh and Mingagquy, shall promptly pay their share for the support aforesaid, on pain of proceeding against them with immediate execution."[3]

In 1686, Thomas Dongan was commissioned royal governor of New York. Among his instructions was the following: " 38. And we do further direct that no schoolmaster be henceforth permitted to come from England and to keep school within our province of New York without the license of the said Archbishop of Canterbury. And that no other person now there or that shall come from other parts be admitted to keep school without your license first had." [4] Similar instructions

---

[1] *Ibid.*, II, 714.   [2] *Ibid.*, II, 720.   [3] *Ibid.*, II, 730.

[4] *Ibid.*, III, 372. Until 1700, teachers' licenses were uniformly granted by the provincial authority. In that year the municipality of Albany "admitted " one Bogardus as schoolmaster for the city. (*Pratt's Annals*, p. 75.)

were given to Governor Sloughter, on January 31, 1689,[1] to
Governor Fletcher, on March 7, 1692,[2] to the Earl of Bellamont,
on August 31, 1697,[3] and to Governor Hunter, on December
27, 1709.[4] In these cases the Bishop of London was named
as licenser instead of the Archbishop of Canterbury.[5] In one
instance the gubernatorial license seems to have been held un-
necessary. In the charter granted by William III. to the
the Reformed Dutch Church the following " concession " is
made. " And our will and pleasure further is, and we do hereby declare that, that the ministers of said church, for the time
being, shall and may, by and with the consent of the elders
and deacons of the said church, for the time being, nominate
and appoint a schoolmaster and such other under officers as
they shall stand in need of." [6]

In 1689 the so-called Leisler rebellion occurred. The struggle between the Dutch democracy and the English aristocracy
left its mark upon the school records of the time.

" To the honorable Major Richard Ingoldsby, Commander in
chief of their Majesties' Province of New York, &c. The humble
request of Rudolphus Varick, minister, and Joseph Hegeman,
elder of the Dutch Church in Flatbush, humbly showeth : That
in the late rebellion, Joannes Van Eckelen the then clerk and
schoolmaster of Flatbush hath always been a very great zealot for
the faction of Leisler &c., as may appear to your Honor, your-

---

[1] *N. Y. Col. Doc.*, III, 688.   [2] *Ibid.*, III, 821.
[3] *Ibid.*, IV, 288.   [4] *Ibid.*, V, 135.

[5] In 1685. the Bishop of London proposed to the Lords of Trade that he should
be given all ecclesiastical jurisdiction in the West Indies, and "that no schoolmaster coming from England be received without license from his Lordship, or
from other His Majesty's plantations without they take the governor's license."
The Board approved of these suggestions, and "the like instructions were given
to other governors." (*Ibid.*, VII, 362, 363.) A precedent seems to have been
established at this time, which was continued as a more or less settled policy during the remaining period of British control.

[6] *Dunshee's History of the School of the Reformed Prot. Dutch Church*, pp.
56–57.

self having taken letters out of his pocket at the City Hall, which he was carrying to Leisler into the fort, and was very active in raising men in the country to withstand their Majesties' forces. Especially the aforesaid Joanes Van Eckelen hath been always opposing the minister and church council in their endeavors for supporting the government for the crown of England and enticing people to the party of Leisler, contrary to all their admonitions, publicly defaming the aforesaid minister, setting the common people against him, offering his service to drag him out of his house, by violence, to a pretended court, as also procuring the apprehension and fining of the aforesaid elder for about thirty pounds, because he endeavored to have hindred their committing hostilities on the English towns on Long Island. Upon the considerations and others too long to rehearse, besides other complaints as to his service in the aforesaid office, the church council did dismiss the aforesaid Joanes van Ekelen and did forbid him more to officiate, but choose in his place one Joannes Schenck, a fitter person and well affected to the present government. Now your petitioners give your Honor to understand that said Joanes van Ekelen hath clandestinely and without any of their knowledge procured a license from your Honor, whereby he again sets up school in defiance of their church and accustomed privileges, refusing to obey the civil power, but daily affronting them, whereby he draws many of the late faction to his side, to the manifest scandal of their Majesties' present government, and since it hath never been accustomed to have two schoolmasters in that small town heretofore, your petitioners humbly pray your Honor that said Joanes van Ekelen may be forbid farther to teach school in Flatbush and that your honor would please to authorize Joanes Schenck to be the only schoolmaster there, for the reasons abovesaid, and your petitioners shall ever pray for your Honor's health and happiness.

JOSEPH HEGEMAN, elder.   RUDOLPHUS VARICK."[1]

[1] *N. Y. Col. MSS.*, XXXVIII, 4. Given in Pratt's *Annals*, p. 73.

The above petition was granted at a Council held at Fort William Henry, September 26, 1691.[1]

"To the Right Honorable Major Richard Ingoldsbey Esq., Commander-in-Chief of the Province of New York, and the Honorable Council. The humble petition of Jaques Cortlejouir, Justice of the peace, and Rudolphus Varick, minister of the gospel in Kings County, humble sheweth: That in the time of the late disorders within the province one Meyndert Coerten lately attained of high treason was marching with some ill men from New Utrecht towards the fort against the King's forces, under your Honor's command, who then did threaten Joost De Baane the schoolmaster and reader of said town, to turn him out of that employ because he refused to side with them in their rebellion, and although the said justice and minister since that time have endeavored to hinder the same, yet nevertheless some of those ill effected persons without any cause given, but in contempt of the authority, have forced the said Joost de Baane to forsake the place, although the land out of which the schoolmaster and reader of the town is maintained, was given to the town, by the said justice, out of his proper estate. Wherefore the petitioners have thought it their duty to become humble suppliants in behalf of the said Joost de Baane, humble offering to your Honors that it would tend much to the peace and quiet of the said town that your Honors would be pleased to order, that the said Joost de Baane be continued in the said employ as schoolmaster and reader of the said town, and that he be allowed his salary as formerly from the 14th of April last, since which time he was causeless turned out."[2] The Council resolved on July 16, 1692, that "a license be granted unto the said Joost de Bane to be schoolmaster of New Utrecht, and that he is entitled to, and ought to receive, the salary belonging to the reader and schoolmaster of said

---

[1] *Council Minutes* (MS. in office of Sec'y of State), VI, 55. Text of order given in Pratt's *Annals*, p. 73.

[2] *N. Y. Col. MSS.*, XXXVIII, 154. Given in Pratt's *Annals*, p. 74.

town from the 14th of April last; and the justices be wrote to
and required to suffer none other to officiate in the quality of
a schoolmaster in the said town without a license from the
government, nor in the quality of reader, but by the appointment of the minister." [1]

As a result of the conclusion of the French and Indian War
in 1697, Governor Bellamont opened negotiations with the
Indians of the Five Nations. Among other plans which he
advanced at these Albany conferences, was that of religious
education. His promises to supply the tribes with ministers
from England and the neighboring country were cordially received by the Indians. [2] A more definite proposition, however,
proved unacceptable. At the fourth conference on August 29,
1700, Lord Bellamont promised to engage the minister at
Albany to learn the Indian tongue, so that they might be
better served in the work of the gospel. The Governor also
stated, " I hope in a little time to have the Bible translated
into your language and to have some of your children taught
to read, so that you may have the comfort and edification of
God's word, which I am sure will be hugely pleasing to you
when your children are able to read it to you. Now that
I am upon this subject, I wish you would send two or three
Sachems' sons out of each nation to be kept at school
at New York, where I will take care to have them taught to
write and read both English and Indian, and they shall be well
clothed and dieted at the King's charge, and after three or four
years that they are perfect in their writing and reading, they
shall return home to you and other boys shall come in their
places; by which means you will always have those among
you that will understand English and will be serviceable to you
upon many occasions." [3] This offer was passed over by the
Sachems on the ground that they were not masters of their
children. " That is a matter," they said, " that relates to our

---

[1] *Council Minutes MS.*, VI, 111. Given in Pratt's *Annals*, p. 74.

[2] *N. Y. Col. Doc.*, IV, 727-8, 729-730, 732-3.　　　　[3] *Ibid.*, IV, 734.

wives, who are the sole disposers of their children ,ile they
are under age."[1]

Governor Bellamont's successor, Edward Lord Viscount
Cornbury, seems to have conceived generous plans for educa-
tiion in the colony. In his opening address on October 20,
1702, to the General Assembly, a body composed of 21 representatives from the counties of New York, Richmond, Westchester, King's, Queen's, Suffolk, Ulster and Albany, the manor
of Rensselaer Wyck and the Borough of Westchester, Cornbury
urged the legislators to prepare a good bill " for the erecting of
public schools in proper places," and assured them that such a
bill, as well as all others for the good of the country and the
preservation and encouragement of the people, would always
receive his " ready compliance." [2] Accordingly on October 30,
the House voted that a " public free-school " should be erected,
and it was ordered: " That Major Jackson do acquaint the town
of Hempstead, that a public free-school is designed to be
erected, and to enquire of them, what encouragement they will
allow towards the same, within the bounds of that township;
and that he make report thereof to the House Friday next." [3]
On that day, November 6, Major Jackson reports that Hempstead had voted in general town meeting to grant 100 acres of
land "for encouragement of a free-school to be erected in
the township . . . with conveniences of watering near the
East Meadow Point, and also . . . liberty for timber for building, fencing and fire-wood with other conveniences to be had
within the township."[4] On November 10, the House voted
that " the city and county of New York have leave to bring in a
bill to raise £50 per annum for a free-school," and Mr. French
and Mr. De Lancey were ordered to bring in a bill accordingly.[5] On November 14, Mr. French presented to the House a

---

[1] *Ibid.,* IV, 738.

[2] *Journal of the General Assembly of the Colony of New York,* I, 145. New
York, 1764.

[3] *Ibid.,* I, 148.   [4] *Ibid.,* I, 150.   [5] *Ibid.,* I, 151.

bill entitled "An Act to enable the Mayor, Alderman and commonalty of the city of New York to raise £50 per annum, for seven years, towards maintaining a schoolmaster, within the said city of New York." [1]   On November 17, the bill was sent to committee where it received some amendments. [2]   It was reported to the House on November 19, passed by that body and sent up to the Council for concurrence. [3]   On November 20 the committee of the Council [4] to whom the bill had been committed, reported that the bill as it stood was contrary to the Governor's instructions relating to the licensing of schoolmasters and that it should be returned to the House for amendment. [5]   But on the House tartly insisting that the amendment should proceed from the Council, [6] the following proviso was drawn up by the committee of the Council for insertion in the bill.   " Provided always that such schoolmaster, if chosen from England, then to be licensed by the Right Reverend father in God, the Lord Bishop of London, and approved of by the governor or commander-in-chief of this province for the time being.   And in case any fit person shall be here found for the discharge of that duty, as well as upon any vacancy that may hereafter happen upon the death, absence or disability of such schoolmasters, that then and in such case, the Common Council of the city of New York, for the time being shall and may recommend to the governor or commander-in-chief of this province for the time being such fit person, qualified as aforesaid, for license and approbation, which is always to be had and obtained before such schoolmaster be instituted to the salary aforesaid, any thing herein contained to the contrary thereof in any wise not withstanding." [7]   When the bill was returned

---

[1] *Ibid.*, I, 152.   [2] *Ibid.*, I, 153.   [3] *Ibid.*

[4] The Council consisted of Governor Cornbury, Wm. Smith, S. S. Broughton, Rip Van Dam, Caleb Heathcote, John Bridges.

[5] *Journal of the Legislative Council of the Colony of New York*, I.   Albany, 1861.   [6] *Journal of Assembly*, I, 155.

[7] *Council Journal*, I, 186.

to the House with the above amendment, the House desired a conference of the committees of both Houses.[1] In this conference the above amendment was amended as it stands in the bill as it was finally passed by both House and Council and assented to by the Governor on November 27, 1702.[2]

"AN ACT FOR ENCOURAGEMENT OF A GRAMMAR FREE SCHOOL IN THE CITY OF NEW YORK.

"The Mayor, Alderman and Commonalty of the City of New York having represented unto the General Assembly of this province the great necessity there is of having a free school in the said city, for the education and instruction of youth and male children; that such pious and necessary work may receive due encouragement, be it enacted by his Excellency the Governor and Council and Representatives convened in General Assembly, and by authority of the same, that there shall be hereafter elected, chosen, licensed, authorized, and appointed one able, skilful and orthodox person to be schoolmaster for the education and instruction of youth and male children of such parents as are of French and Dutch extraction, as well as of the English, may come and be instructed in the languages or other learning usually taught in grammar schools. And for the encouragement of such schoolmaster, be it further enacted by the authority aforesaid, that henceforward annually there shall be in the said city assessed, levied, collected and paid for the space or term of seven years, the sum of fifty pounds current money of New York for the maintenance of the said schoolmaster, which said sum of fifty pounds shall be assessed, levied, collected and paid by such persons, at such times, in such manner and proportions, and under such penalties respectively as is provided for the assessing levying, collecting and paying of the sum of one hundred pounds per annum for the minister of New York, by an act of Assembly intitled, an Act for settling a ministry, and raising a maintenance for them

---

[1] *Journal of Assembly,* I, 155.   [2] *Ibid.,* I, 157, 158.

in the City of New York, County of Richmond, Westchester and Queens County, made in the fourth year of King William and Queen Mary. Provided always, that such schoolmaster shall, from time to time, as a vacancy happens, be chosen and recommended by the Common Council of the said city for the time being, in order to be licensed and approved by the right Honorable the Bishop of London or the Governor or Commander-in-chief of this province for the time being, anything herein contained to the contrary thereof in any ways notwithstanding." [1]

About two months after the passage of this act, the Common Council of the city of New York petitioned Governor Cornbury to use his influence with the Bishop of London and the Society for the Propagation of the Gospel for the procurement of a schoolmaster, the Council being of the opinion that there was no available person in the city " proper and duly qualified to take upon him the office of schoolmaster of said city." [2] The Council also desired that the so-called King's Farm should be appropriated to the projected school. In answer to this petition, Mr. George Muirson was " preferred " by the Governor as city schoolmaster. [3] He was duly licensed for this post by the Governor, who also attended to the payment of his salary.

" To Mr. George Muirson, greeting :

" I do hereby authorize and impower you to teach and keep school within the city of New York, and to instruct all children with whom you shall be entrusted in the English, Latin and Greek tongues or languages and also in the arts of writing and arithmetic. You are therefore carefully and diligently to discharge the duty of a schoolmaster in the said city and you are to receive and enjoy all such privileges and advantages

---

[1] *The Colonial Laws of New York*, I, 516-7. Albany, 1894.

[2] *Minutes of the N. Y. Common Council* (MSS.), II, 517, 519, 520. Given in Pratt's *Annals*, pp. 85-6.

[3] *The Documentary History of the State of New York*, III, 113. Edited by E. B. O'Callaghan, M. D., Albany, 1850.

as to the office and place of a schoolmaster doth or may belong. Whereof the mayor, all her Majesty's justices of peace and other officers within the said city, are hereby required to take notice and govern themselves accordingly. Given under my hand and seal at arms at Fort Anne in New York, this twenty-fifth day of April, 1704.   CORNBURY."[1]

"To WILLIAM PEARTREE, ESQ^R, MAYOR OF THE CITY OF NEW YORK :

"You are hereby directed and required to pay, or cause to be paid, unto Mr. George Muirson, schoolmaster of the city of New York, the sum of five and twenty pounds, for half a year's salary due and ending the second Tuesday in January next, for which this shall be your sufficient warrant. Given under my hand and seal at Fort Anne in New York, this twentieth of October, 1704.   CORNBURY."[2]

The following licenses demonstrate that Governor Cornbury made frequent use of his supervisory prerogative over the schoolmasters of the province.

"I do hereby authorize and impower you, Andrew Foucautt, to teach an English and French school within the City of New York, and to instruct all children where with you shall be entrusted for the purpose in the said languages, as also in the art of writing, arithmetic, &c. You are therefore carefully and diligently to discharge the duty of a schoolmaster in the said city, and to receive and enjoy all such privileges and advantages as to the office and place of a schoolmaster doth and may belong and appertain."[3] . . . . Dated September 13, 1703.

"To THE WORTHY MR. ELIAS NEAU, GREETING :

"Reposing special trust and confidence in your ability, prudence and integrity, have nominated, constituted and appointed,

---

[1] *Deeds* (MS) *in office of Sec'y of State*, X, 5. Given in Pratt's *Annals*, p. 87. In 1705 Muirson went to England, and Mr. Andrew Clark was appointed by the Common Council, and licensed by the Governor in his stead. (*Ibid.*, p. 88.)

[2] *N, Y. Col. MSS.*, I, 19. Given in Pratt's *Annals*, p. 87.

[3] *Deeds* (MS.), IX, 736. Given in Pratt's *Annals*, p. 90.

and do hereby nominate, constitute and appoint you, the said
Elias Neau, to be catechist in the city of New York, and do
hereby give and grant unto you full license and power to catechise all children, Indians, negroes and other persons within
the said city. Given under my hand and seal at Fort Anne in
New York this twenty-fourth day of August, 1704.

"CORNBURY."[1]

"EDWARD VISCOIMT CORNBURY [ETC.] TO STEPHEN GASHERIS,
  GREETING :
"You are hereby empowered and licensed to read the service of the Dutch church at Kingstown, in the county of
Ulster, from time to time, until you receive further orders from
me; and you are likewise hereby empowered and licensed to
keep a writing and reading school at Kingstown aforesaid,
until you receive further orders from me to the contrary.
Given under my hand at Kingstown, this tenth day of August,
in the third year, &c., annoque, Dom. 1704."[2]

"To HENRY LINDLEY, GREETING :
"I do hereby authorize and empower you to keep and teach
school within the town of Jamaica, in Queens County, and to
instruct all children with whom you shall be entrusted in the
English and Latin tongues, or languages, and also in the art
of writing and arithmetic, for and during my pleasure. Given
under my hand and seal at Fort Anne, in New York, this 18th
day of April, 1705.   CORNBURY."[3]

A license similar to the above was granted to Mr. Alexander
Baird on March 6, 1706, for the town of Hempstead, in
Queens County.[4] On June 23, 1705, Elias Bon Repos was
licensed to keep school within the town of New Rochell, West-
chester County.[5] Governor Hunter renewed this license on
December 12, 1712.[6] On August 29, 1705, Mr. John Wood

[1] *Deeds*, X, 27. Given in Pratt's *Annals*, p. 91.

[2] *N. Y. Col. MSS.*, XLIX, 165. Given in Pratt's *Annals*, p. 91.

[3] *Deeds*, X, 94. Given in Pratt's *Annals*, p. 91.

[4] *Deeds*, X, 171.   [5] *Ibid.*, X, 65.   [6] *Ibid.*, X, 326.

was licensed to keep a dancing school and Mr. Prudent De La Fayole, a French school, in New York City.[1] On December 5, 1705, Thomas Huddleston was licensed to teach English, writing and arithmetic in Jamaica, Queens County.[2] On April 17, 1706, Mr. James Jeffray was authorized to keep and teach school in New York City.[3] On May 1, 1706, Mr. Edward Fitzgerald was given the same right in Westchester County.[4] In July, 1712, one Allane Jarratt obtained from Governor Hunter a license " to teach writing, arithmetic and navigation and other parts of the mathematics to all such persons as shall be desirous to be instructed therein within this city or province of New York," during the Governor's pleasure.[5]

About 1704, the Society for the Propagation of the Gospel in Foreign Parts became very active in its missionary services to New York. In consequence, the Provincial Government appears to have thrown off for a term of years all educational responsibilities. In addition to supplying ministers and schoolmasters to the province, the Society undertook in 1729, to establish a library in New York. On September 23, 1728, the Society's secretary wrote to Governor Montgomery desiring him to advise the legislature to determine upon a proper place for the large and valuable donation which the Society intended to give to the use of the clergy and gentlemen of New York, Jersey, Pennsylvania and Connecticut. It was also suggested that the government should pass an act for the preservation of this projected library. This letter was laid before the House on June 24, 1729. The House passed a vote of thanks to the Society for " prefering it [New York] before any of his Majesty's other plantations . . . to reposite a library, in which will not only redound to the reputation of this colony but be vastly useful and beneficial to the inhabitants thereof." It was then ordered that the Mayor and Common Council of the city of New York should report upon the facilities at their

---

[1] *Ibid.*, X, 66.   [2] *Ibid.*, X, 82.   [3] *Ibid.*, X, 112.   [4] *Ibid.*, X, 114.
[5] *Deeds*, X, 319, 310. Given in *Annals*, pp. 93-4.

disposal for the library.[1] On June 27, Mayor Lurting reported in behalf of the Common Council that they were "truly sensible of the great advantages which may arise from so generous and seasonable a present" and that they were "zealously disposed" to provide a large room for the accommodation of the library. The Mayor's letter was ordered to be entered at large upon the journal of the House and the Governor was requested to forward the original with a copy of the minutes of the House to the venerable Society and "to assure them that this House is heartily disposed to pass an act, for the due preservation of the works when here."[2] The books were sent over by the Society, but the promise of the Assembly does not seem to have been kept.[3]

It was not until 1732 that the legislature renewed any direct interest in education. On October 3 of that year a petition of "sundry gentlemen" was presented to the House to bring in a bill to establish a perpetual support for a master to teach Latin and Greek, and it was ordered: "That leave be given to bring in a bill for encouraging a public school, to teach Latin, Greek, arithmetic and the mathematics, in the city of New York; and that for the encouragement of a schoolmaster for that purpose, the unappropriated money, to rise by the Act for licensing hawkers and peddlers, until the first day of December, 1737, be applied for that end; and that the said city make up the income of that fund annually, during that time, to the sum of . . . . pounds; and that in consideration thereof, the said schoolmaster shall be obliged to teach gratis, the number of . . . . children."[4] Accordingly on October 5, Mr. De Lancey introduced a bill on the aforesaid subject.[5] On October 10, the bill was read a second time and committed to a

---

[1] *Journal of the Assembly*, I, 601.   [2] *Ibid.*, I, 602.

[3] *The History of the late Province of New York*, I, 262. By the Hon. William Smith. Collections of the New York Historical Society, First Series, vol. IV, New York, 1829.

[4] *Journal of Assembly*, I, 645.   [5] *Ibid.*, I, 646.

committee of the whole House.[1] On October 12, Mr. Garritsen reported that the committee "had gone through the bill, and made several amendments, and added several clauses thereto." The report was accepted and the bill was passed and sent to the Council for concurrence.[2] On October 14, the bill was passed by the Council without amendment and was assented to by the Governor.[3]

"An Act to encourage a public school in the City of New York for teaching Latin, Greek and Mathematics.

"Whereas, good learning is not only a very great accomplishment but the properest means to attain knowledge, improve the mind, morality and good manners and to make men better, wiser and more useful to their country as well as to themselves. And whereas the City and Colony of New York abounds with youths of a genius not inferior to other countries, it must undoubtedly be a loss to the public and a misfortune to such youths if they are destitute of the opportunity to improve their capacities by a liberal education. And whereas the Mayor and Alderman and a great number of the principal inhabitants of the said City of New York have by their petition to General Assembly set forth that one Mr. Alexander Malcolm has, by keeping of a private school within the said City given a satisfactory proof of his abilities to teach Latin, Greek and the mathematics ; but as the income of that school does at present fall short of a comfortable support for himself and his family, they humbly pray he may have a suitable encouragement to keep a public school amongst us under such regulations and restrictions as may answer that end. And altho' the not rightly applying of a temporary salary heretofore allowed for a free school, has been the chief cause that an encouragement for the like purpose has ever since been neglected; but in as much as the present circumstances afford a better prospect, and to the end our youth may not be deprived of the benefits before mentioned be it enacted by his Excellency the Governour the Council and

[1] *Ibid.*, I, 647.　　　[2] *Ibid.*, I, 648.　　　[3] *Council Journal*, I, 624–5, 626.

the General Assembly, And it is hereby enacted by the authority of the same that there shall be one public school established and kept in the City of New York to teach Latin, Greek and all the parts of mathematics from the first day of December next ensuing to the first day of December which will be in the year one thousand seven hundred and thirty seven and that the above named Alexander Malcolm shall be the master thereof during that time under the regulations and restrictions, and for the reward and encouragement here in after mentioned. Be it further enacted by the same authority that the above named school master or the school master of such school for the time being, shall for and in consideration of the encouragement here in after mentioned, be and hereby is obliged during the time aforesaid to provide at his own cost and charge in the said City of New York a proper and convenient house or room and there in during the time and term aforesaid (Sundays and usual Holydays only excepted) to teach gratis and without any farther or other reward or consideration from any person whatever than what is allowed to him by this Act, in the best manner he is able the Latin and Greek languages, arithmetic and all the other branches of the mathematics, or in such of them as the said school master shall be ordered and directed by the persons hereinafter vested with the power to give such orders and directions the number of twenty youths in the proportion following, that is to say. For the City and County of New York, ten. For the City and County of Albany, two. For King's County, one. For Queen's County, one. For Suffolk County, one. For Westchester County, one. For Richmond County, one. For Orange County, one. For Ulster County, one. And for Dutchess County, one. Be it further enacted by the authority aforesaid that the youths so to be taught, are to be recommended in manner following, that is to say; for the cities and counties of New York and Albany, by the respective mayors, recorders and alderman thereof. And for the several Counties by the Justices at the General Sessions of the Peace to be held for those Counties respectively. And in such Recommendations under their hands they are respectively to certify the name and names of such youth, their age (which is not to be under fourteen years) and that they have been well instructed in reading and writing of English. And in such certificate is to be added a command to the schoolmaster for the time being, to receive such youth as a scholar; who is accordingly to receive them them in his school, and to teach him or them in such manner as he by such certificate or order shall be directed. And the persons aforesaid are hereby impowered and directed not only to grant such certificates and orders gratis, but in like manner from time to time to supply such vacancies, as shall or may happen in the said school in the said number of youths by death or otherwise during the continuance of the said Act. And be it enacted by the same authority that if the said Mr. Malcolm or the schoolmaster for the time being shall at any time during the term aforesaid refuse to receive or teach the youths sent to him for that purpose in the manner above mentioned, it shall absolutely barr him of the reward by this Act allowed to him. Provided the number of such youths do not exceed the number herein before limited; nor shall it be deemed a default in him if either of the said cities or any of said counties shall at any time recommend or send a less number than they hereby have a right to do. And to the end the school hereby intended may be duely and orderly kept and the aforesaid scholars well instructed. Be it further enacted by the same authority that the Justices of the Supreme Court, the Rector of Trinity Church and the Mayor, Recorder and Aldermen of the City of New York for the time being or the major part of them shall be and hereby are impowered constituted and appointed visitors of the said school for the term aforesaid and vested with a power to remove the master for the time being for misbehaviour or neglect of his duty

and upon his removal to elect appoint and establish another
in his place; as also when ever the master's place is void by
any other means whatsoever during the term aforesaid the
visitors aforesaid or the major part of them are hereby further
authorized and impowered to elect appoint and establish master
in such place so become void; and the master so by them
elected appointed and established shall be entitled to the salary
or reward hereby intended for the master aforesaid. Provided and be it enacted by the same authority that the before
named Alexander Malcolm hereby appointed master of the said
public school, shall not be removed during the term aforesaid
except for misbehaviour or neglect of his duty in the keeping
of the said school or in teaching of the youth in the manner
aforesaid. And that the said Mr. Malcolm or the school master
for the time being of the public school before mentioned
may be enabled to provide a proper school and be encouraged to teach the said number of youth in manner as
aforesaid be it enacted by the same authority that after the
money already appropriated in and by the act entitled
An Act for reviving an Act entitled An Act for licencing
hawkers and pedlars within this Colony and for paying the
sum of sixty pounds unto Richard Bradley Esq'r passed
this present session shall be paid and discharged out of that
fund; all the residue of the money that shall arise from thence
forward until the first day of December which will be in the
year one thousand seven hundred and thirty seven by virtue of
the said act shall be and hereby is applied for and towards the
encouragement of such schoolmaster as aforesaid. And for the
orderly and effectual paying of the same to him, the treasurer
of this colony shall be and hereby is enjoined yearly and every
year during the continuance of the said act to state an account
of that fund deducting out of the money that has already
arisen or may arise thereby six pence in the pound for his
receiving and paying the same, as likewise what by the said
act and a former act he has been directed to pay out of the

same; which account so stated he is hereby further enjoined annually, between the first and the tenth day of December to deliver unto his Excellency the Governor who is thereupon requested to issue warrants in Council for so much as by such account shall appear in the treasury by the virtue of that fund payable to the said Mr. Malcolm or to the schoolmaster for the time being; which warrants the said Treasurer is hereby likewise directed from time to time to pay and discharge out of the said fund accordingly. And for a further encouragement to the said schoolmaster or the schoolmaster for the time being, be it enacted by the authority aforesaid that over and above the sum or sums of money annually to be raised in the city of New York by virtue of an act entitled An Act for settling a ministry and raising a maintenance for them in the city of New York, counties of Richmond, Westchester and Queen's county passed in the fourth year of King William and Queen Mary there shall at the same time in the same manner and by the same persons be assessed levied and collected and yearly paid to the treasurer of the said city during the continuance of this act the sum of £40 current money of this colony besides the charge of collecting and paying the same, for which sum so to be annually paid during the said term the Mayor of the said city for the time being in Common Council convened is yearly to issue warrants for the same on the said City Treasurer payable quarterly to the above named Mr. Malcolm or the schoolmaster for the time being. And the said Mayor the said Treasurer and all persons who are to assess levy and collect the above mentioned tax for the minister and poor are hereby strictly charged and commanded to act conformable to the intent and meaning of this clause. Always provided and be it further enacted by the same authority that whenever the fund of hawkers and pedlers shall during the term aforesaid happen to exceed the sum of £40 per annum such over-plus shall remain in the Treasury, so nevertheless as that the said sallary for the whole five years out of the said fund does not fall short of the sum of £200 anything to the contrary thereof notwithstanding. And be it further enacted by the authority aforesaid that this act shall be deemed a public act and accepted as such in all courts and by all officers within this colony." [1]

The above act expired by its own limitation in 1737, and consequently on October 18, Mr. Simon Johnson moved for leave to bring into the House a bill for its continuance.[2] On November 30 the House resolved itself into a committee of the whole House upon the bill to continue the school act of 1732; "after some time spent therein a motion was made by David Jones, Esq., and the question was put, whether Mr. Malcolm, the Latin schoolmaster, be allowed forty pounds per annum out of the moneys to arise by virtue of the Act for licensing hawkers and peddlers within this colony.

" For the Affirmative.	For the Negative.
Col. Matthews,	Adolph Philipse, Esq.,
Capt. Livingstone,	Col. Beekman,
Mr. Abraham Lot,	David Jones, Esq.,
James Alexander, Esq.,	John Walter, Esq.,
Mr. Speaker [Lewis Morris, Jr],	Col. Hicks,
Col. Schuyler,	Col. Chambers,
Capt. Winne,	Mr. Tur Boss,
Capt. Brat,	John Lecount, Esq.,
Johannis Lot, Esq.,	Mr. Hardenbergh,
Mr. Verplank,	David Pierson,
Col. Philipse [Frederick],	Major Platt,
Col. Morris [Lewis Morris, sen.],	Major Mott.
Col. Rensselaer.	

It's carried in the affirmative [by a majority of one.] A motion was made, and the question was put, whether Mr. Malcolm, the Latin schoolmaster, be allowed forty pounds per annum from the city of New York.

[1] *Col. Laws*, II, 103.

[2] *Journal of Assembly*, I, 718.

For the Affirmative.	For the Negative.
[The same as on the former motion, except Mr. Abraham Lot also], Mr. Hardenbergh, Col. Hicks, David Jones, Esq., David Pierson.	[The same as on the former motion, except David Jones, Esq., Col. Hicks, Mr. Hardenbergh and David Pierson, also,] Mr. Abraham Lot.

It's carried in the affirmative [by a majority of seven.] A motion was made, and the question was put, whether Mr. Malcolm's salary be continued for a longer period than one year? It's carried in the negative." [1]

On December 1 the House resolved itself into a committee of the whole House on this bill and, after "some time spent therein Mr. Speaker resumed the chair and Simon Johnson, Esq., reported from the committee that they had gone through the bill, altered the title, made several amendments and added several clauses thereto." [2] The report was agreed to by the House and the bill was passed without amendment by the Council, [3] and assented to by the Governor under the title of an Act for the further encouragement of a public school in the city of New York for teaching Latin, Greek and Mathematics. [4] In a report made by Lieutenant-Governor Clarke to the Lords of Trade on June 2, 1738, after enumerating among the acts passed at the last session of Assembly the above act and the Act for licensing peddlers, etc., the Governor writes: "Being confident that public schools for the education of youth will always find countenance from your Lordships I will lay the two last bills before you without any further remarks in their favor. I wish the Assembly had made the reward greater than it is like to be, from the last of these bills. That money was applied before to the like use, but fell short of the

---

[1] *Ibid.,* I, 727.   [2] *Ibid.,* I, 728.   [3] *Council Journal,* I, 705.

[4] *Col. Laws,* II, 973–977. The only significant difference in this act from the act of 1732, besides the difference in its duration already referred to, is the fixing of the minimum age limit of "recommended scholars" at nine instead of fourteen years of age.

sum intended, nor could the schoolmaster get any redress though he petitioned for it or got some of his friends to move the House in his behalf. It is not likely it will bring in more now. However the master having at present no other way of living is obliged to submit."[1]

The following account bears out the Governor's statement in this matter. On December 6, three days prior to the passage of the school bill by the Upper House, Schoolmaster Malcolm stated to the Lower House that of the £400 allowed him for 5 years by the Act of 1732, he had received only £284 17s. 6d. This shortage was due to a deficiency in the license fund from which one-half of his salary was ordered to be drawn. He then proceeded to beg the honorable House to order the payment of the money due him "and relieve him from the difficulty of so great a disappointment." After a debate upon this petition, the question was put "whether the aforesaid £115 2s. 6d. be a debt due from this colony?" The question wa_ carried in the negative by a vote of 16 to 7. A motion was then made and carried by a vote of 16 to 8 for the rejection of the petition.[2]

Three years later Alexander Malcolm sent in another petition to the Assembly on the same subject. At this time the arrears of salary in 1738 were figured at £111 2s. 6d. A motion was made and the question was put whether Mr. Malcolm had set forth an equitable demand in his petition. The motion was carried by a vote of 14 to 9.[3] An act was subsequently passed by the legislature to pay £111 7s. 2d. to Mr. Malcolm out of the license fund.[4]

KING'S COLLEGE.[5]

In 1697 Governor Fletcher leased to the Episcopal Church in New York a certain part of the Governor's demesne called

---

[1] *N. Y. Col. Doc.*, VI, 118.   [2] *Journal of Assembly*, I, 730.
[3] *Ibid.*, I, 788.   [4] *Col. Laws*, III, 86-7.
[5] In 1784 re-named Columbia College.

the King's Farm.   This lease was vacated by Governor Bellomont, who thereby called down upon himself the anger of the
colonial church.   In writing in justification of his action to the
Lords of Trade on April 13, 1699, Governor Bellomont ob-
serves: " Mr. Attorney General assures me that in Colonel
Dongan's time, he, to make his court to King James, desires
this farm might be appropriated to the maintenance of a Jesuit
school; but King James (bigot though he was) refused, saying
that he would not have his governors deprived of thier conveniences."[1]   Bellomont's successor, Governor Cornbury, proved
to be of a different mind concerning this property and
through his influence it came into the possession of the corporation of the parish of Trinity Church.   At a meeting of the
church wardens and vestry on February 19, 1703, "it being
moved, which way the King's Farm which is now vested in
Trinity church should be let to farm, it was unanimously
agreed that the Rector and church wardens should wait upon
my Lord Cornbury, the Governor, to know what part thereof
his Lordship did design towards the college which his Lordship designs to have built, and thereupon, to publish placarts for
the letting there of at the public outcry, tothe highest bidder."[2]
Nothing came of the Governor's plans for a college.   Whether
or not the promoters of the grammar school acts which were
passed in the first half of the 18th century had in mind, as it
has been supposed, purposes for an institution of higher learning it is difficult to ascertain.   At any rate no direct legislation
for a college occurred in the colony until 1746.

On October 23 of that year it was ordered in the Lower
House that " a bill be brought in for raising the sum of £2,250
by a public lottery . .   for the advancement of learning and
towards the founding of a college;" and Mr. Cruger and Capt.

---

[1] *N. Y. Col. Doc.*, IV, 490.

[2] *Record*, I, 43.   Given in *The Origin and Early History of Columbia College*, p. 7.   George H. Moore, LL. D., New York, 1890.

Richards were appointed a committee to attend to the matter.[1]

On October 28 Mr. Cruger reported that the committee or the whole House to whom the bill had been committed had " made several amendments and added a clause thereto."[2] On the following day the bill as amended was passed by the Lower House and sent up to the Council. On November 8 the bill was passed by the Upper House without amendment,[3] and on December 6 it was assented to by the Governor.[4] The preamble of this Act reads as follows: " In as much as it will greatly tend to the welfare and reputation of the Colony that a proper and ample foundation be laid for the regular education of youth, and as so good and laudable a design must readily excite the inhabitants of this colony to become adventurers in a lottery of which the profits shall be employed for the founding a college for that purpose. Be it enacted, etc."[5] Section 14 reads: " And that the purpose of founding the said college may not be obstructed by any other application of the moneys to arise from the profits of the said lottery, be it enacted by the authority aforesaid, that each and every Representative in General Assembly, for the time being, who shall hereafter in General Assembly move or consent to the applying or appropriating the said moneys to any other purpose whatever, than the founding the college aforesaid, shall be and hereby is declared and made forever incapable of sitting and voting in this or any future General Assembly, and new writs shall issue accordingly."[6]

On February 23, 1748, Mr. Cruger moved for leave to bring in a bill in the Lower House for raising £2,250 by a public

---

[1] *Journal of the Votes and Proceedings of the General Assembly of the Colony of New York*, II, 128. New York, 1766.   [2] *Ibid.*, II, 129.

[3] *Journal of the Legislative Council of New York*, 1743–1775, p. 952. Albany, 1861.   [4] *Ibid.*, p. 959.

[5] *The Colonial Laws of New York*, III, 607. Albany, 1894.

[6] *Ibid.*, III, 614–15.

lottery for a further provision towards founding a college, etc.[1]
In committee of the whole House the amount of the sum to be
raised was amended to £1,800.[2]   The bill as thus amended was
passed by the Council without further change on March 25
and assented to by the Governor,[3] on April 8th.[4]   Its provisions
were re-enacted on October 28,[5] as it had expired the preceding month without a sufficient number of contributors having
been secured for the drawing of the lottery.[6]   This act, together
with two of the three subsequent college lottery acts, contains a
provision similar to that of Section 14 of the preceding act on
the same subject.[7]

On November 7, 1851, the Lower House ordered Capt.
Richard and Mr. Nicoll to prepare and bring in a bill for vesting in trustees the sum of £3,443 18s. raised by way of lottery
for erecting a college.[8]   The bill was brought in, amended by
a committee of the whole House, passed and on November 14
sent up to the Council.[9]   On November 18 the Council resolved into a committee on the bill, amended it and returned
it to the Lower House, where the amendments of the Council
were accepted.[10]

"*An Act for vesting in trustees the sum of three thousand
four hundred and forty-three pounds, eighteen shillings raised
by way of lottery for erecting a college within this colony.*
Whereas the sum of £3,443 18s. has been raised within this
colony by way of lottery for erecting a college, for the education of youth within the same, which sum being not conceived
sufficient without further additions to answer the said end of

---

[1] *Journal of the Gen. Ass.*, II, 226.   [2] *Ibid.*, II, 228, 230.

[3] Governor Clinton complained, however, that the commissioners named in this
act had been appointed without his being consulted. (*N. Y. Col. Doc.*, VII,
685.)

[4] *Council Journal*, pp. 1012, 1015.   [5] *Ibid.*, p. 1029.

[6] *Colonial Laws of N. Y.*, III, 731.   [7] *Ibid.*, III, 686–7.

[8] *Journal of Gen. Ass.*, II, 321.   [9] *Ibid.*, II, 323.

[10] *Council Journal*, 1085–86.

erecting, completing and establishing a college for the advancement of useful learning, it is conceived necessary that trustees be appointed as well for the setting at interest the said sum of £3,443 18s. already raised for the said purpose, as for receiving the contributions and donations of such persons as may be charitably disposed to be benefactors and encouragers of so laudable an undertaking. Be it therefore enacted by his Excellency the Governor, the Council, and the General Assembly, and it is hereby enacted by the authority of the same, that the eldest Councilor residing in this colony,[1] the Speaker of the General Assembly, and the Judges of the Supreme Court, [the Mayor of the City of New York, and the Treasurer of this colony for the time being,][2] together with James Livingston Esquire, Mr. Benjamin Nicol, and Mr. William Livingston or the survivor or survivors of them the said James Livingston, Benjamin Nicol and William Livingston, shall be and hereby are appointed trustees for managing[3] the said sum of £3,443 18s. and for managing[4] any other sum or sums of money, lands, goods or chattels, which may be contributed or given by any person or persons whatsoever to be employed to the said use and purpose of erecting, completing and establishing a college for the advancement of learning within this colony. All which said sum and sums of money they the said trustees [and the major part of them and of the survivors of them][2] shall be and hereby are impowered, required and directed to put out at interest, yearly and every year, together with the interest arising thereon, until the same shall be employed for the use and purpose of erecting or establishing a college for the advancement of learning within this colony, in such manner as shall by some Act or Acts hereafter to be passed for that purpose be directed. And be it further enacted by the authority aforesaid, that if

---

[1] Amended by the Council from " President of the Council."

[2] The parentheses indicate Council amendment.

[3] Amended from " receiving and taking into their hands."

[4] Amended from " receiving."

any lands, tenements or hereditaments shall be given by any person or persons whatsoever towards founding the said college, the aforesaid trustees and the major part of them and of the survivors of them shall be, and hereby are enabled to let the same to farm to the best advantage, for advancing the said undertaking [rendering the rent to the treasurer of this colony, for the time being for the use and purpose aforesaid.]¹ And be it further enacted by the authority aforesaid that the treasurer of this colony shall and he is hereby required and directed [to pay to the borrowers such sum and sums of money aforesaid, from time to time, as shall be specified in the securities by them to be given, with the consent of the major part of the trustees aforesaid or of the survivors of them, which securities shall be in the names of two or more of the trustees aforesaid consenting, with conditions for the payment of the money and interest therefrom arising, to the treasurer of this colony for the time being for the use and purpose aforesaid and such securities given as aforesaid shall be to the said treasurer good vouchers and discharges for the sums paid thereon by him and therein mentioned.]¹ And be it further enacted by the authority aforesaid, that the aforesaid trustees shall be and hereby are enabled to receive proposals from any of the cities or counties within this colony, which shall be desirous of having the said college erected within their said cities or counties, touching the placing or fixing the same therein respectively. And the said trustees [and every of them] shall be and hereby are required to render a just and true account on oath of all their proceeding in the premises, to the Governor, Council and General Assembly, when by them or any of them, thereunto required."²

On November 9, 1752, two days before the close of the session, the Lower House resolved, *nemine contradicente*, to take

---

¹ The parentheses indicate Council amendment.

² *Col. Laws*, III, 842–44.

into consideration at their next meeting "the establishing a seminary for the education of youth" within the colony.[1] At the convening of the legislature on May 30, 1753, Governor Clinton observed in his opening address to the Assembly: "The resolution you made at the close of the last session for establishing a seminary for the education of youth within this colony is laudable and worthy your diligent persecution and most serious attention."[2]

On June 6 the Lower House ordered Mr. Cruger and Mr. Livingston to prepare another lottery bill in aid of the projected college and on the same day a bill for raising £1,125 was presented.[3] After amendment by the House in committee of the whole,[4] the bill was sent on June 13 to the Council, where it was passed without amendment on June 25.[5] On July 4 it was signed by the Governor.[6] On the same day the Governor also signed a bill which provided for the continuance of the excise duty until 1767. The Act furthermore directed that "whereas it has been the intention of the legislature for several years past to establish a seminary within this colony for the education of youth in the liberal arts and sciences, and as, at present, no other means can be devised," £500 of the excise revenue is to be paid annually for seven years by the colony treasurer to the trustees of the projected college, who are to distribute that sum "in salaries for the chief master or head of the seminary by whatever denomination he may be hereafter called, and for such and so many other masters and officers, uses and purposes concerning the establishment of the said seminary as the said trustees shall from time to time in their discretion think needful." The trustees are also directed to ascertain the tuition fees of the college and to be ready at all times to report thereon to the government.[7]

The day before this Act was passed the Assembly having

[1] *Journal of Gen. Ass.*, II, 336. [2] *Ibid.*, II, 337. [3] *Ibid.*, II, 339.
[4] *Ibid.*, II, 340. [5] *Council Journal*, p. 1117. [6] *Ibid.*, p. 1123.
[7] *Col. Laws*, III, 908–910.

been " informed that a report had been raised and industriously propagated that in case the money raised by lottery for erecting a college . . . should prove insufficient for that purpose, the General Assembly intend to supply the deficiency by a tax on the people, that the said college, if erected, was to be supported and maintained by taxes; and that the sum of £500 appropriated out of the excise fund for establishing a seminary of learning . . . was to be repaid . . . by a tax on the people . . . *Resolved, nemine contradicente*, that the said report is groundless, false and malicious, and is calculated and intended to raise and infuse jealousies into the minds of the good people of this colony of their Representatives in General Assembly and other sinister purposes." [1]

On November 1, 1754, the Lower House was informed that the college trustees were in attendance to make a majority and a minority report to the House, and it was moved that these reports should be entered at large upon the journal of the House.   The motion was carried in the affirmative, 14 to 8.   The majority report signed by John Chambers, Daniel Hosmanden, Edward Holland, James Livingston, Benjamin Nicoll and A. de Peyster, gave an account of the disposition of the lottery funds on the part of the trustees and likewise stated that an offer had been made to them by the rector and inhabitants of the city of New York in communion with the Church of England to give a reasonable quantity of the church farm for the erecting and use of a college, and that no proposal had been made to them by any other person for that purpose. Trustee William Livingston in his minority report protested against certain doings of the major part of the trustees which they had not set down in their report to the legislature.   He stated that in the preceding month of May the trustees had petitioned the Governor for a charter of incorporation.   They had also declared in this address that they were willing to accept the offer of Trinity church with its accompanying con-

[1] *Journal of the Gen. Ass.*, II, 350.

ditions that the Master of the college be a member of the Established Church, and that the liturgy of that church be the " constant morning and evening service, used in that college forever." William Livingston set down 20 articles of objection against the implication of this petition and the draft of the charter which the other trustees had drawn up. He urged that the establishment of the Church of England liturgy in the college without the consent of the legislature would be unjust to the other denominations whose representatives had already voted for the support of the college; that no religious tests had been prescribed by the legislature for the college officers; that in the legislature only lay the power to accept gifts of land for the locating of the college, and that they alone had the right to incorporate that institution.[1]

On November 6, the House resolved, " *nemine contradicente,* that this House will not consent to any disposition of the moneys raised by way of lottery for erecting and establishing a college . . . than by act or acts of the legislature of this colony, hereafter to be passed for that purpose." [2] At the same time leave was given to Mr. Livingston to bring in a bill of incorporation. On November 26, the day appointed for the third reading of the bill, Captain Walton moved, in view of the facts that the bill was of the utmost consequence to the people with respect to both their religious and civil liberties and that the advanced season of the year did not allow of its receiving that attention that its vast importance required, that its further consideration should be postponed to the next session and that in the meantime it should be printed for the benefit of constituents. And it was so ordered.[3] On this same day Mr. Cruger moved for leave to bring in a bill for raising £1125 by lottery for the college.[4] The motion was debated and then carried in the

---

[1] *Journal of Gen. Ass.*, II, 395-402.   [2] *Ibid.*, II, 404.

[3] *Ibid.*, II, 412-13.

[4] This was a measure to provide for the re-enaction of the lottery bill of July 4, 1753, which had already been re-enacted on December 12, 1753. (*Council Journal*, 1144.)

affirmative, 12 to 9.[1] On November 28, the day appointed for the second reading of this bill, Mr. Livingston moved its postponement to the next meeting of the legislature; but the motion was lost by a vote of 12 to 14.[2] The House then resolved itself into a committee of the whole upon the bill. A motion of Mr. Livingston that the whole amount of the money arising from the lottery should remain in the hands of the managers of the lottery, no part being given over to the trustees, was lost by a vote of 12 to 15. A motion of Mr. Nicoll that the clause providing for the expulsion from the House of any member who might move or consent to the appropriation of the lottery money to any other purpose except that of the college might be struck out, was carried by a vote of 16 to 11.[3] The bill was signed by the Governor on December 7.[4] Meanwhile, the Governor had also signed the charter that was desired by the majority of the trustees.

" GEORGE THE SECOND, by the grace of God, of Great Britain, France, and Ireland, King, Defender of the Faith, etc. To all whom these presents shall come, Greeting : Whereas, by several acts of the Governor, Council, and General Assembly of our Province of New York, divers sums of money have been raised by public lotteries, and appropriated for the founding, erecting, and establishing a college in our said government, for the education and instruction of youth in the liberal arts and sciences : And Whereas, the rector and inhabitants of the city of New York in communion of the Church of England as by law established, for the encouraging and promoting the same good design, have set apart a parcel of ground for that purpose, of upwards of three thousand pounds value, belonging to the said corporation, on the west

---

[1] *Journal of Assembly*, II, 419.   [2] *Ibid.*, II, 421.

[3] *Ibid.*, II, 422. On November 27, 1756, an act was passed which incorporated this motion, and extended its application to similar provisions in the lottery acts of 1746, 1748 and 1753. (*Col. Laws*, IV, 105–6.)

[4] *Council Journal*, 1181.

side of the Broadway, in the west ward of our city of New
York, fronting easterly to Church street, between Barclay
street and Murray street, four hundred and forty foot; and from
thence running westerly, between and along the said Barclay
street and Murray street, to the North river; and also, a street,
from the middle of the said land, easterly to the Broadway, of
ninety foot, to be called Robinson street. And have declared
that they are ready and desirous to convey the said land in
fee, to and for the use of a college, intended and proposed to
be erected and established in our said province, upon the
terms in their said declaration mentioned : And Whereas, our
loving subjects, the trustees, appointed in and by an act of the
Governor, Council, and General Assembly of our said Province
of New York, entitled an Act for vesting in trustees the sum
of three thousand four hundred and forty three pounds,
eighteen shillings, by way of lottery, for erecting a college
within this colony, esteeming the said lands offered and set
apart by the said rector and inhabitants of the city of New
York, in communion of the Church of England, as by law
established, the most convenient place for the building, erecting and establishing a college, in our said province, have, by
their humble petition, presented to our trusty and well-beloved
James De Lancey, Esq., our Lieutenant-Governor and Commander-in-Chief of our said Province of New York, in Council,
prayed our letters patent of incorporation for the better establishing, erecting, and building a college, on the said lands, and
the more effectually governing, carrying on, and promoting
the same, and instructing of youth in the liberal arts and
sciences : Wherefore, We, being willing to grant the reasonable request and desire of our said loving subjects, and to encourage the said good design of promoting a liberal education
among them, and to make the same as beneficial as may be,
not only to the inhabitants of our said Province of New York,
but to all our colonies and territories in America : Know Ye,
that We, considering the premises, do of our especial grace,

certain knowledge, and mere motion, by these presents, will, grant, constitute, and ordain, that when, and as soon as the said rector and inhabitants of the city of New York, in communion of the Church of England, as by law established, shall legally convey and assure the said herein before mentioned lands to the corporation, or body politic, erected and made by these our letters patent, that there be erected and made on the said lands, a college, and other buildings and improvements, for the use and conveniency of the same, which shall be called and known by the name of King's College, for the instruction and education of youth in the learned languages, and liberal arts and sciences; and that in consideration of such grant, to be made by the rector and inhabitants of the city of New York, in communion of the Church of England, as by law established, the president of the said college, for the time being, shall forever hereafter be a member of, and in communion with the Church of England, as by law established; and that the governors of the said college, and their successors, forever, shall be one body corporate and politic, in deed, fact and name, and shall be called, named and distinguished, by the name of the Governors of the College of the Province of New York, in the City of New York, in America, and them and their successors, by the name of the Governors of the College of the Province of New York, in the City of New York, in America, one body corporate and politic, in deed, fact and name, really and fully, we do for us, our heirs and successors, erect, ordain, make, constitute, declare and create by these presents, and that by that name, they shall and may have perpetual succession : And we do for us, our heirs, and successors, for the continuance and better establishment of the said college, will, give grant, ordain, constitute and appoint, that in the said college, to be erected and built upon the lands aforesaid, there shall from henceforth forever be a body corporate and politic, consisting of the Governors of the College of the Province of New York, in the City of New York, in America;

and for the more full and perfect erection of the said corporation and body politic, consisting of the Governors of the College
of the Province of New York, in the City of New York, in
America, we do will, grant, ordain, constitute, assign, limit and
appoint, by these presents, the most Reverend Father in God,
our trusty and well beloved Thomas, Lord Archbishop of
Canterbury, and the most reverend the Lord Archbishop of
Canterbury for the time being; the right honorable Dunk, Earl
of Halifax, first Lord Commissioner for Trade and Plantations
for the time being; our now Lieutenant Governor and Commander-in-chief of our said Province of New York, and the
Governor or Commander-in-chief of our said Province for the
time being; the eldest Councilor of our said province now and
for the time being; the Judges of our Supreme Court of
Judicature of our said province now and for the time being;
the Secretary of our said province now and for the time being;
the Attorney General of our province now and for the time being; the Speaker of the General Assembly of our said province
now and for the time being; the Treasurer of said province now
and for the time being; the Mayor of our city of New York in
our said province now and for the time being; the rector of
Trinity Church in our said city of New York now and for the
time being; the senior minister of the Reformed Protestant
Dutch Church in our said city now and for the time being; the
minister of the ancient Lutheran Church in our said city now
and for the time being; the minister of the French Church
in our said city now and for the time being; the minister
of the Presbyterian Congregation in our said city for
the time being; the president of the said college, appointed by
these presents, and the president of the said college for the
time being, to be chosen as herein after is directed, and twenty
four other persons, who shall be called and named, and are
hereby called and named, the Governors of the College of the
Province of New York, in the City of New York in America;
and for that purpose we have elected, nominated, ordained,

constituted, limited and appointed, and by these presents do, for us, our heirs and successors, elect, nominate, ordain, constitute, limit, and appoint, the said most Reverend Father in God, Thomas, Lord Archbishop of Canterbury, and the Lord Archbishop of Canterbury for the time being; the right honorable Dunk, Earl o Halifax, first Lord Commissioner for Trade and Plantations for the time being; our now Lieutenant Governor and Commander-in-chief of our Province of New York, and the Governor or Commander in chief of our said Province for the time being; the eldest Councilor of our said Province now and for the time being; the Judges of our Supreme Court of Judicature of our said Province now and for the time being; the Secretary of our said Province now and for the time being; the Attorney General of our said Province now and for the time being; the Speaker of the General Assembly of our said Province now and for the time being; the Treasurer of our said Province now and for the time being; the Mayor of our said city of New York now and for the time being; the rector of Trinity Church in our said city now and for the time being; the senior minister of the Reformed Protestant Dutch Church in our said city now and for the time being; the minister of the ancient Lutheran Church in our said city now and for the time being; the minister of the French Church in our city now and for the time being; the minister of the Presbyterian Congregation in our said city for the time being; the president of the said college, appointed by these presents, and the president of the said college for the time being; and Archbishop Kennedy, Joseph Murray, Josiah Martin, Paul Richard, Henry Cruger, William Walton, John Watts, Henry Beekman, Philip Ver Planck, Frederich Philipse, Joseph Robinson, John Cruger, Oliver De Lancey, James Livingston, Esquires, Joseph Read, Nathaniel Marston, Joseph Haynes, John Livingston, Abraham Lodge, David Clarkson, Leonard Lispenard and James De Lancey the younger, gentlemen, to be the present governors of the said college; and we do by these presents ordain and appoint

our well beloved Samuel Johnson, Doctor of Divinity, to be the
first and present president of the said college, for and during
his good behaviour; and do will that he and the president for
the time being after him, who shall also hold his office during
good behaviour, shall have the immediate care of the education
and government of the students that shall be sent to and admitted into the said college for instruction and education, according to such rules and orders as shall be made by. the
governors of the said college; and they are by these presents made and constituted a body corporate and politic,
by the said name of the Governors of the College of the Province of New York, in the City of New York, in America; and
they and their successors, by the said name of the Governors
of the College of the Province of New York, in the City
of New York, in America, be, and for ever hereafter shall
be, a body politic and corporate, in deed, fact and name,
and shall be capable and able in law to sue and be sued,
implead and be impleaded, answer and be answered unto,
defend and be defended, in all courts and places, before us, our
heirs and successors, and before all and any the judges, justices,
officers and ministers of us, our heirs and successors, in any
court or courts, place and places whatsoever, in all and all
manner of actions, suits, complaints, pleas, causes, matters and
demands whatsoever, and of what kind or nature soever, in as
full, ample manner and form as any of our other liege subjects
of our said Province of New York can or may sue and be
sued, implead and be impleaded, defend and be defended, by
any lawful ways and means whatsoever. And, also, that they
and their successors, by the said name of the Governors of the
College of the Province of New York, in the City of New York,
in America, be, and forever hereafter shall be a body corporate,
capable and able in law to purchase, take, hold, receive, enjoy
and have any messuages, houses, lands, tenements and hereditaments, and real estate whatsover, in fee simple, or for term of
life, or lives, or years, or in any other manner howsoever, for

the use of the said college; provided always, the clear yearly value thereof do not exceed the sum of two thousand pounds sterling; and also goods, chattells, books, moneys, annuities, and all other things of what nature and kind soever. And, also, that they and their successors, by the same name of the Governors of the College of the Province of New York, in the City of New York, in America, to and for the use of the said college, shall and may have full power and authority to erect and build any house or houses, or other buildings, as they shall think necessary or convenient; and also to give, grant, bargain, sell, demise, assign, or otherwise dispose of all or any messuages, lands, tenements, rents and other hereditaments, and real estate, and all goods, chattells, money and other things whatsoever, as to them shall seem fit, either in the payment of the salary or salaries of the president, fellows and professors of the said college, or any other officers or ministers of the same, at their will and pleasure; excepting always, and it is, nevertheless, our true intent and meaning that the said governors of the said college for the time being, and their successors, or any of them, shall not do or suffer to be done, at any time hereafter, any act or thing whereby or by means whereof the lands set apart and offered to be conveyed by the rector and inhabitants of the city of New York, in communion of the Church of England as by law established, for the use of the college, or any part thereof, shall be vested, conveyed, or transferred, to any other person, contrary to the true meaning hereof, other than by such leases as are hereafter mentioned: Our will and pleasure is, therefore, and we do for us our heirs and successors will and ordain, that no grant or lease of the said land, or any part thereof, shall be made by the said governors of the said college which shall exceed the number of twenty-one years, and that either in possession or not above three years before the end and expiration or determination of the estate or estates in possession. And we do by these presents will, ordain and direct, that the

said governors of the said college (except always the Lord
Archbishop of Canterbury for the time being, and our
first Lord Commissioner for Trade and Plantations) do, at
their first meeting, after the receipt of these our letters patents,
and before they proceed to any business of and concerning the
said college, take the oaths appointed to be taken by an act
passed in the first year of our late Royal Father's reign, entitled, [an Act for the further security of his Majesty's person
and government, and the succession of the Crown, in the heirs
of the late Princess Sophia, being Protestants, and for extinguishing the hopes of the pretended Prince of Wales, and his
open and secret abettors], and make and subscribe the declaration mentioned in an Act of Parliament made in the twenty
fifth year of the reign of King Charles the second, entitled,
[an Act for preventing dangers which may happen from popish
recusants]; as also, an oath, faithfully to execute the trust reposed in them, as members of the said corporation, which oaths
we authorize and empower the justices of our Supreme Court
of Judicature, for our said Province of New York for the time
being, any or either of them to administer; and that when, and
as often as any person or persons, either by his office or place
in our said government, or elsewhere, (except always the Lord
Archbishop of Canterbury for the time being, and our first
Lord Commissioner for Trade and Plantations for the time
being), or by choice of the said governors of the said college,
shall become, or be chosen a member or members of the said
corporation, they shall, before they are admitted, or enter into
the said office or trust, take the said oaths, and subscribe the
said declaration to be administered to them in the manner above
directed. And we do further will, ordain, and direct, that the
governors of the said college, shall yearly, and every year hereafter, forever, on the second Tuesday in the month of May, in
every year, meet together in our said city of New York, for
the better taking care of, and promoting the interest of the
said college; and that the said governors of the said college

or any fifteen or more of them being met, shall be a legal meeting of the said corporation, and they, or the major part of them so met, shall have full power and authority to adjourn from day to day, as the business of the said college may require, and to do, execute, and perform, all and every act and acts, thing and things whatsoever, which the said governors of the said college are, or shall by these, our letters patent, be authorized and impowered to do, act, or transact, in as full and ample manner, as if all and every of the members of the said corporation were present. And we do will, ordain, and direct, that as our right trusty and well beloved Thomas, Lord Archbishop of Canterbury, and the Lord Archbishop of Canterbury for the time being, and our said first Lord Commissioner for Trade and Plantations, and the first Lord Commissioner for Trade and Plantations for the time being, cannot attend the meetings of the said corporation, they and each of them shall, from time to time, have full power and authority to appoint a proxy, in writing, under their hand and seal, which person or persons so appointed by them, and each of them shall and may represent them, and each of them, respectively, according to such appointment, and shall have full power to vote and act as a governor or governors of the said corporation, at any and every meeting of the said corporation, as fully and amply as if they, the constituents, and each of them were present at every such meeting or meetings ; and in case any other meeting or meetings of the said governors of the said college shall, at any time or times, be judged and deemed necessary for the carrying on and promoting of the business and interest of the said college, or the government thereof, by any five members of the said corporation, we do, by these presents, authorize and impower such five members, by writing, under their hands, to direct the clerk of the said corporation to give notice of the day appointed by them, for such meeting, at the said city of New York, by advertising the same in one or more of the public newspapers, at least, seven days before such meeting; and, that at such meeting, the said clerk, before entering on any business, shall certify such notification, under his hand, to the Board then met; provided, always, fifteen or more of the said members shall be then met together, which said fifteen or more members, so met, in pursuance of such notification, shall be a legal meeting of the said governors of the said college; and they, or the major part of them so met, shall have full power and authority to adjourn from day to day, as the business of the said college may require, and to do, transact, and perform, all matters and things whatsoever, that the said governors of the said college are, or shall be authorized and impowered to do, by these presents. And, of our further grace, certain knowledge, and mere motion, to the intent that the said corporation and body politic, may answer the end of their erection and constitution, and may have perpetual succession and continue forever, we do for us, our heirs, and successors, give and grant unto the said governors of the said college of the Province of New York, in the city of New York in America, and to their successors for ever, that when and as often as they or any fifteen or more of the said members of the said corporation or of their successors shall be met together at their said yearly meeting herein before appointed, or at any other meeting upon notification, as aforesaid, for the service of the said college, that the Governor or Commander in chief of our said Province of New York, and, in his absence, the first person in rank in our said government, who holds his place as a governor of the said corporation by his office, place, or dignity, and, in the absence of such, the eldest governor or member of the said corporation then present, such seniority to be taken according as they are named in this charter, during the lives of the present governors, and after their death, the seniority to be taken and accounted as they have been a longer or shorter time governors of the said corporation, shall preside at such meeting from time to time, and that at such meeting or meetings from time to time, they or the major part of them so met, shall have full power and authority to elect,

nominate, and appoint any person to be president of the said
college in a vacancy of the said presidentship for and during
his good behaviour; provided, always, such president elect or
to be elected by them, be a member of, and in communion with
the Church of England, as by law established; and also, to
elect one or more fellow or fellows, professor or professors,
tutor or tutors, to assist the president of the said college
in the education and government of the students belonging to
the said college, which fellow or fellows, professor or professors,
tutor or tutors, and every of them, shall hold and enjoy their
said office or place, either at the will and pleasure of the governors of the said corporation, or during his or their good
behaviour, according as shall be agreed upon between such
fellow or fellows, professor or professors, tutor or tutors, and
the said governors of the said college, provided, always, such
fellow or fellows, professor or professors, tutor or tutors, before
they or either of them enter into or take upon themselves such
office, do take the oaths and subscribe the declaration herein before directed, to be taken and subscribed by the governors of the
said colleges before they enter upon their said respective offices;
and that when and as often as any or either of the said offices
shall become vacant by death or otherwise, the said governors
or the major part of any fifteen or more of them so met as
aforesaid, shall have full power to elect, nominate and appoint,
other or others in their places, upon the same proviso or condition as aforesaid; and, also, to elect, nominate and appoint,
upon the death, removal, refusal to qualify, or other vacancy
of the place or places, of any governor or governors of the
said corporation not holding his office or place as a member
of the same, by the virtue of any other station, office, place,
or dignity, from time to time, other or others in their
places or stead as often as such vacancy shall happen, which
governor or governors so from time to time elected and appointed, shall, by virtue of these presents, and of such election
and appointment be vested with all the powers, authoritys, and

privileges, which any governor of the said corporation is hereby invested with. And, we do further, of our especial grace, certain knowledge, and mere motion, for us, our heirs, and successors, grant and ordain that when and often as the pressident of the said college, or any fellow, professor or tutor holding his place during good behaviour shall misdemean himself in his or their said offices, and thereupon a complaint or charge in writing of such misdemeanour shall be exhibited against him or them by any member of the said corporation, at any meeting or meetings of the said corporation met and convened as aforesaid, that it shall be lawful for the said members of the said corporation then met, or the major part of them from time to time, upon examination and due proof, to suspend or discharge such president, fellow, professor, or tutor, from his said office, and other or others in his or their place or places to appoint; and, we do further for us, our heirs, and successors, will and grant that the said governors of the said college, or the major part of any fifteen or more of them convened and met as aforesaid, shall and may, from time to time, as occasion may require, elect, constitute, and appoint, a treasurer, clerk and steward, for the said college, and to appoint them and each of them their respective business and trusts, and to displace and discharge from the service of the said college such treasurer, clerk, or steward, and to elect other or others in their places and stead; and such treasurer, clerk and steward, so elected and appointed, we do for us, our heirs, and successors, by these presents constitute and establish in their offices, and do give them full power and authority to exercise the same in the said college, according to the direction and during the pleasure of the said governors of the said college, or the major part of any fifteen or more of them convened as aforesaid, as fully and freely as any other the like officers in any of our universities or any of our colleges in that part of our kingdom of Great Britian called England, lawfully may and ought to do. And we do further, of

our especial grace, certain knowledge, and mere motion, give
and grant unto the said governors of the said college, that they
and their successors, or the major part of any fifteen or more
of them convened and met together in manner aforesaid, shall
and may direct and appoint what books shall be publicly read
and taught in the said college, by the president, fellows, professors, and tutors, and shall and may, under their common
seal, make and set down, and they are hereby fully impowered,
from time to time, to make and set down in writing, such laws,
ordinances, and orders, for the better government of the said
college, and students and ministers thereof, as they shall think
best for the general good of the same, so that they are not
repugnant to the laws and statutes of that part of our kingdom
of Great Britian called England, or of our said province of New
York, and do not extend to exclude any person of any religious
denomination whatever from equal liberty and advantage of
education, or from any the degrees, liberties, privileges, benefits, or immunities of the said college, on account of his
particular tenets in matters of religion ; and such laws, ordinances and orders, which shall be so made as aforesaid, we do
by these presents, for us, our heirs, and successors, ratify,
confirm, and allow, as good and effectual to bind and oblige
all and every the students and officers and ministers of the said
college ; and we do hereby authorize and impower the said
governors of the said college, or the major part of any fifteen
or more of them, at any of their meetings convened as aforesaid,
and the president, fellows, and professors for the time being, to
put such laws, ordinances, and orders, in execution, that is to
say, such as inflict upon any student the greater punishments
of expulsion, suspension, degradation, and public confession,
by the governors of the said college, or the major part of any
fifteen or more of them, convened and met together as aforesaid only ; and such as inflict the lesser punishments, by the
president, fellows and professors, or any of them, according to
the true intent of such laws, ordinances, and orders, as shall

be made in pursuance of these presents for that purpose. And we do further will, ordain, and direct, that there shall be for-ever hereafter public morning and evening service constantly performed in the said college, morning and evening forever, by the president, fellows, professors, or tutors, of the said college, or one of them, according to the liturgy of the Church of England as by law established, or such a collection of prayers out of the said liturgy, with a collect peculiar for the said college, as shall be approved of from time to time by the governors of the said college, or the major part of any fifteen or more of them convened as aforesaid: and we do further will and grant, that the said governors of the said col-lege for the time being, or the major part of any fifteen or more of them convened as aforesaid, shall have full power and lawful authority to visit, order, punish, place and displace, the treasurer, clerk, steward, students, and other officers and min-isters of the said college, and to order, reform, and redress, all and any the disorders, misdemeanors and abuses in the persons aforesaid, or any of them, and to censure, suspend, or deprive them, or any or either of them, so always, that no visitation, act, or thing, in or concerning the said college, be made or done by any person or persons whatsoever but as is herein before directed and declared. And we do further, of our especial grace, certain knowledge, and mere motion, will, give and grant, unto the said governors of the said college, that for the encourage-ment of the students of the said college to diligence and industry in their studies, that they and their successors, and the major part of any fifteen or more of them convened and met together as aforesaid, do, by the president of the said college, or any other person or persons by them authorized and appointed, give and grant any such degree and degrees to any the students of the said college, or any other person or persons by them thought worthy thereof, as are usually granted by any or either of our universities or colleges in that part of our king-dom of Great Britian called England, and that the president, or such other persons to be appointed for that purpose as aforesaid, do sign and seal diplomas or certificates of such degree or degrees, to be kept by the graduates as a testimonial thereof. And further, of our especial grace, certain knowledge, and mere motion, we do for us, our heirs, and successors, will, give and grant, unto the said governors of the said college, and their successors, that they shall and may have one common seal, under which they shall and may pass all grants, diplomas, and all other writings whatsover, requisite, necessary, or convenient to pass under the seal of the said corporation; which seal shall be engraven in such form and with such devices and inscriptions as shall be agreed upon by the said governors of the said college, or the major part of any fifteen or more of them that shall be convened for the service of the said college, in the manner above directed; and by these our letters patent it shall and may be lawful for them and their successors, at any of their meetings convened as aforesaid, as they shall see cause, to break, change, alter, and new make the same, or any other common seal, when and as often as to them shall seem convenient. And we, further, for us, our heirs, and successors, give and grant unto the said governors of the said college, and their successors, or the major part of any fifteen or more of them convened as aforesaid, full power and authority, from time to time, and at all times hereafter, to nominate and appoint all other inferior officers or ministers which they shall think convenient and necessary for the use of the college, not herein particularly named or mentioned, which officers and ministers we do hereby impower to excute their respective offices or trusts, during the will and pleasure only of the governors of the said college, or the major part of any fifteen or more of them convened as aforesaid, as fully and freely as any other the like officers or ministers in and of our universities or any other college in that part of the kingdom of Great Britain called England may or ought to do. And, lastly, of our express will and pleasure, and mere motion, we do, for us, our heirs, and successors, give and grant unto the said governors of the said college, and to their successors for ever, that these our letters patent, being entered of record, as is herein after particularly expressed, or the enrollment thereof, shall be good and effectual in the law, to all intents and purposes, against us, our heirs, and successors, without any other license, grant or confirmation from us, our heirs or successors, hereafter by the said Governors of the said college to be had or obtained, notwithstanding the not reciting or misrecital, or not naming or misnaming, of the aforesaid offices, franchises, privileges, immunities, or other the premises, or any of them ; and notwithstanding a writ *ad quod damnum* hath not issued forth to inquire of or concerning the premises, or any of them, before the ensealing hereof, any statute, act, ordinances, or provision, or any other matter or thing to the contrary thereof in any wise notwithstanding; to have, hold, and enjoy, all and singular, the privileges, liberties, advantages and immunities, and all and singular other the premises herein or hereby granted, or meant, mentioned, or intended to be herein and hereby given and granted unto them, the said Governors of the said College of the Province of New York, in the City of New York, in America, and to their successors forever. In testimony whereof, we have caused these our letters to be made patent, and the great seal of our Province of New York to be hereunto affixed, and the same to be entered of record in our Secretary's office of our said Province, in one of the books of patents there remaining. Witness our trusty and well-beloved James De Lancy, Esq., our Lieutenant Governor, and Commander-in Chief in and over our Province of New York, and the territories depending thereon, in America, in, by, and with the advice and consent of our Council of our said Province, this thirty-first day of October, in the year of our Lord one thousand seven hundred and fifty-four, and of our reign the twenty-eighth." [1]

[1] Charters, Acts and Official Documents, pp. 10–24, compiled by John B. Pine, New York, 1895.

On May 13, 1755, the Governors of the College of the Province of New York petitioned Governor De Lancey for an additional charter providing for the establishment of a professorship in divinity of the Reformed Protestant Dutch Church.[1] This charter was granted on May 30, 1755.

"George the Second, by the grace of God, of Great Britain, France and Ireland, Defender of the Faith and so forth, to all to whom these presents shall come, greeting.

"Whereas our loving subjects, the Governors of the College of the Province of New York, in the City of New York, in America, by their humble petition presented to our trusty and well-beloved James De Lancey, Esq.; our Lieutenant-Governor and Commander-in-chief of our said Province of New York, in Council, have set forth, that although by our letters patent of incorporation, bearing date the thirty-first day of October last past, the sole power of electing professors in said college is vested in the said governors: Yet the said petitioners humbly conceived, that it would tend to the prosperity of the college, and the increase of the number of students, if provision could be made for establishing a professorship in divinity in the same, for the instruction of such youth as may intend to devote themselves to the sacred ministry, in those churches in this province that are in communion with, and conform to the doctrine, discipline and worship established in the United Provinces, by the National Synod of Dort; and any other students that may be desirous to attend his lectures: And therein did humbly pray, that an additional charter might be granted them for that purpose; and that the nomination of such professor, from time to time, be in the ministers, elders and deacons of the Reformed Protestant Dutch church in the City of New York.

"And whereas upon the surrender of this our province by the Dutch, in the year of our Lord one thousand six hundred and sixty-four, it is provided by the eighth article of surrender,

[1] 1 *Ibid.*, p. 25.

that the Dutch here shall enloy the liberty of their consciences in divine worship and church discipline. And we being willing and desirous, that all our loving subjects, the members of the Reformed Protestant Dutch churches, who are very numerous in our government of New York, should always continue as they have hitherto done, to enjoy the liberty of their consciences in divine worship and church discipline, and that they may always have learned pastors and teachers to instruct and assist them therein; as also to promote the prosperity ot the aforesaid college, and the increase of the number of students therein. Know ye, that of our especial grace, certain knowledge, and mere motion, we have willed, granted, constituted and appointed, and by these presents, do will and grant to the Governors of the College of the Province of New York, in the City of New York, in America, and to their successors, that from time to time, and at all times hereafter forever, there may, and shall be in the said college, a professor of divinity of the Reformed Protestant Dutch Church, for the instruction of such youth as may intend to devote themselves to the sacred ministry in those churches, in this our Province of New York, that are in communion with, and conform to the doctrine, discipline and worship established in the United Provinces, by the National Synod of Dort; and any other students that may be desirous to attend his lectures.

"And we do by these presents, will, give, grant and appoint, that such professor shall be from time to time, and at all times hereafter, nominated, chosen and appointed by the ministers, elders and deacons of the Reformed Protestant Dutch Church in the City of New York, for the time being, when they shall see fit to make such nomination, choice and appointment. And they are hereby fully empowered and authorized to make such nomination, choice and appointment; and they are hereby required to certify such nomination, choice and appointment, to the governors of the said college, under their corporation seal: Provided always, such professor so to be chosen from time to time by them, be a member of, and in communion with the said Reformed Protestant Dutch Church. And thereupon the governors of the said college, and the president thereof for the time being, shall, and are hereby required and commanded to receive and admit him accordingly: Anything in our herein beforementioned charter of incorporation to the contrary notwithstanding. Which professor of divinity, we will and direct, shall, before he enter into or take upon himself such office, take the oaths and subscribe the declaration directed in our charter aforesaid, for the other professors and officers of the said college to take, before one of the judges of our supreme court of judicature for our said Province of New York, who is empowered and authorized to administer the same.

"And we do further will, ordain and grant, that the said professor of divinity, shall hold his said place or office during his good behavior, or during will and pleasure, according to such agreement as shall be made between him and the said minister, elders and deacons of the Reformed Protestant Dutch Church, at the time of his nomination and appointment, and be entitled unto, and have, exercise and enjoy the same, and like powers, privileges, and authorities in the said college, as other professors of and in the same do or may have, hold, exercise, or enjoy in the same. And also shall demean and conform himself to such rules, laws and regulations as the other professors in the said college are or shall be obliged to conform unto, and regulate themselves by. And in case he shall misdemean himself in said office, he shall be liable to be suspended or discharged from the same, in the same manner as other professors of and in the said college are or may be suspended or discharged, by virtue of our aforesaid charter of incorporation."[1]

On June 12, 1755, the Governors of the College of the Province of New York petitioned the Lower House to vest in their body the money which had been raised by lotteries and excise

[1] *Ibid.*, pp. 26–28.

duty for the benefit of the college and also to grant them "such further and other assistance and encouragement, the better to enable them to carry on the useful work aforesaid, as to the honorable House shall seem reasonable and consistent with the public good." A motion was made and carried by a vote of 11 to 9 to postpone the consideration of this petition to the next session of the legislature.[1] At that time, however, the petition was not brought up for discussion, for on December 18, in response to a counter petition presented by William Livingston and two others, the House stated that the governors of the college had not, as the counter petitioners supposed, applied to the legislature for an act of incorporation nor for a legislative appropriation of the college funds,[2] and it was not until the following year, on November 29, 1756, that an appropriation bill was passed by the House.[3] This bill, which was passed by the Council on November 30, and signed by the governor on December 1,[4] vests one-half[5] of the money raised by lotteries for the college plus interest and profits in the governing board of the college " to be disposed of by them in such manner as to them shall seem best for the advancement of learning." The annual appropriation of £500 from the excise revenue together with all tutition fees which had become due were also to be handed over to the governors, and the trustees appointed in the acts of 1751 were discharged from all further trust.[6]

In 1762, the governors of the college sent an agent to England to solicit subscriptions for the college. A royal brief was obtained for a joint collection with the College, Academy and Charitable School of Philadelphia. On October 6, 1762, arch-

---

[1] *Journal of Gen. Ass.*, II, 446–7.   [2]*Ibid.*, II, 468.   [3]*Ibid.*, II, 520.

[4]*Council Journal*, pp. 1287–1289. Governor Hardy writes to the Board of Trade on February 26, 1757, that he passed this act " to reconcile the differences that had arisen about the college." (*N. Y. Col. Doc.*, VII, 217.)

[5] The other half was appropriated to the purchasing of land for the erection of a pest house for New York City and for the building of a gaol in this city.

[6] *Col. Laws*, IV, 160–2.

bishop Secker writes to President Johnson that there had been considerable opposition to his college in the King's Council; but that he had obtained twice as much from the King for the New York college as for the Philadelphia institution, "because the former is a royal foundation and hath no other patron."[1]

In 1764 an application was made to the King for a grant of land in behalf of the New York college, but although it received the approval of the Lords of Trade,[2] no grant was made by the Crown.[3] Eight years later the Governors of King's College petitioned King George the Third to remit their quit rents and to incorporate their seminary as a university "with such privileges and such an establishment of professors as his Majesty shall approve."[4] Nothing came of this petition; but the Governors persisted in their plan.

On August 22, 1774, Lieutenant-Governor Colden writes to Governor Tryon in England: "The Governors of King's College in New York have desired that the draft which they have made of a royal charter may pass through my hands to your Excellency.[5] I make no doubt you will use your influence with the ministry in order to obtain it. The dissenters from the Church of England have the sole education, not only in all the seminaries of learning in the New England colonies,

---

[1] *N. Y. Col. Doc.*, VII, 507.   [2] *Ibid.*, VIII, 297.

[3] President Johnson, in writing to Archbishop Secker, in April, 1762, remarks in reference to the illiberality of the New York Colonial authorities on the general subject of educational grants : " It is a great pity, when patents are granted, as they often are, for large tracts of land, no provision is made for religion or schools. I wish therefore instructions were given to our governors never to grant patents for townships or villages, or large manors, without obliging the patentees to sequester a competent portion for the subject of religion and education." (*Ibid.* VII, 497.)

[4] *Ibid.*, VIII, 296.

[5] Before Governor Tryon's departure from New York, King's College conferred the degree of doctor of law upon him. (*History of the New Netherlands, Province of New York, and State of New York*, I, 451. William Dunlap, New York, 1839.)

but likewise in New Jersey and other colonies. It therefore seems highly requisite that a seminary on the principles of the Church of England be distinguished in America by particular privileges, not only on account of religion, but of good policy, to prevent the growth of republican principles which already too much prevail in the colonies."[1] In the royal instructions that were given to Governor Tryon on May 4, 1775, previous to his return to New York, reference was made to this subject of university incorporation in the following terms: "The King has no doubt that the religious communities in New York, as well the dissenters as those of the Established Church, are fully satisfied of his Majesty's gracious intentions to afford them all reasonable support and protection. . . . . . What is now requested, however, by the Reformed Dutch and Presbyterian Churches and by the members of King's College, involves constitutional questions of great difficulty, and it is more especially necessary that the charter proposed in the latter case should have the fullest consideration before any step is taken upon it. To that end I have received the King's commands to lay the draft of that charter transmitted to you by Mr. Colden, before the Privy Council in order that it may be put into such a train of examination as shall be judged necessary, but I do not think it likely that their Lordships will be induced to advise the King to grant a charter which is to have the effect to increase the number of members in the House of Representatives without the consent and concurrence of that House; in other respects, the charter does not appear to me to be liable to any material objection.[2]

[1] *N. Y. Col. Doc.*, VIII, 486.

[2] *Ibid.*, VIII, 573-4.

NOTE.—The above chapter was already in press when my attention was drawn to the fact that a bill was proposed in the New York Assembly in 1691 "to appoint a school-master for the educating and instructing of children and youth, to read and write English in every town in the Province." (Journal of Assembly, I, 7.)

PENNSYLVANIA

In 1681, William Penn received a grant from Charles the Second of a tract of land lying between the fortieth and forty-third parallels of latitude, bounded on the East by the Delaware River and extending westward five degrees of longitude. For this territory Penn, in accordance with his charter rights of absolute proprietor, drew up a frame of government which was published in England in May, 1682. The twelfth and thirteenth provisions of this document read as follows:

" Twelfth. That the Governor and Provincial Council shall erect and order all public schools, and encourage and reward the authors of useful sciences and laudable inventions in the said province.

" Thirteenth. That for the better management of the powers and trust aforesaid, the Provincial Council shall from time to time divide itself into four distinct and proper committees, for the more easy administration of the affairs of the province, which divides the seventy-two into four eighteens, every one of which eighteens shall consist of six out of each of the three orders or yearly elections, each of which shall have a distinct portion of business, as followeth : First, a committee of plantations, to situate and settle cities, ports, market-towns and high-ways, and to hear and decide all suits and controversies relating to plantations. Secondly, a committee of justice and safety, to secure the peace of the province, and punish the mal-administration of those who subvert justice to the prejudice of the public or private interest. Thirdly, a committee of trade and treasury, who shall regulate all trade and commerce according to law, encourage manufacture and country growth, and defray the public charge of the province. And fourthly, a committee of manners, education and arts, that all wicked and scandalous living may be prevented, and that youth may be successively trained up in virtue and useful knowledge and arts.[1] The quorum of each of which committees being six, that is, two out of each of the three orders or yearly elections as aforesaid, making a constant and standing council of twenty-four, which will have the power of the Provincial Council, being the quorum of it, in all cases not excepted in the fifth article; and in the said committees and standing Council of the province, the Governor, or his deputy, shall or may preside as aforesaid; and in the absence of the Governor or his deputy, if no one is by either of them appointed, the said committees or Council shall appoint a president for that time, and not otherwise; and what shall be resolved at such committee, shall be reported to the said council of the province, and shall be by them resolved and confirmed before the same shall be put in execution; and that these respective committees shall not sit at one and the same time, except in cases of necessity."[2]

Penn arrived in his province in October, 1682, and in the following month issued writs for the election of members to a General Assembly.[3] Accordingly, on December 4, a body of seven representatives elected by the freeholders of the province

---

[1] William Penn gave expression to his great solicitude for education in several of his writings. The following passage embodying his idea of the relation between government and education is quoted by Proud in his *History of Pennsylvania*, vol. I, p. 11: " If we would preserve our government, . . . we must secure the youth. This is not to be done but by the amendment of the way of their education, and that with all convenient speed and diligence. I say, the government is highly obliged. It is a sort of trustee for the youth of the kingdom, who, though now minors, yet will have the government, when we are gone . . . If this be done, they will owe more to your memories for their education than for their estates."

[2] *Charters and Laws of the Province of Pennsylvania*, 1682–1700, pp. 95, 96. Compiled by Geo. Stoughton, B. M. Nead, Tho. McCamant, Harrisburg, 1879.

[3] Seven representatives were ordered to be returned from each of the six counties. There is, however, no evidence of the exact number of persons who actually constituted the First Assembly. (See *Charters and Laws*, Appendix B, p. 474.)

met together at Chester, "alias Upland." The Proprietary's Frame of Government was confirmed and the so-called Great Body of Laws, which was based on ninety bills presented to the Assembly by the Proprietary was enacted. Chapter 60 was as follows: "Chap. LX. And be it, &c. That the laws of this province, from time to time, shall be published and printed, that every person may have the knowledge thereof. And they shall be one of the books taught in the schools of this province, and territories thereof."[1]

On March 10th, 1863, a second Assembly met at Philadelphia consisting of 72 Councilmen and Assemblymen. To this Assembly a second frame of government was presented, which, in limiting the Council to 19 members, the Governor and 3 Representatives from each county, abolished the division of the Council into the four standing committees provided for by the first frame or charter. In their stead, it was provided: "Eleventh. That one-third of the Provincial Council residing with the Governor, shall with the Governor from time to time have the care of the management of all public affairs, relating to the peace, justice, treasury, trade and improvement of the province and territories, and to the good education of youth and sobriety of the manners of the inhabitants therein as aforesaid."[2] The tenth provision of the charter of 1683 was identi-

---

[1] *Ibid.*, p. 123. The action of a Council held at Philadelphia, May 23, 1683, at which Governor Penn and Councilmen Chr. Taylor, Wm. Clark, Ralph Withers, Jo. Harrison, Lasse Cock, Jno. Symcock and Wm. Haigne were present, witnesses to the problematical administration of this law. "It was proposed to have an attested copy of the laws printed. After some debate, the Governor put the question, and it was carried in the negative, they should not be printed. It was then moved that an attested copy under the Secretary's hand should be transmitted to the president and clerk of each respective county, for the people to have the course to for their information, and that the people may have copies of the copy from the president and clerk, so as it be attested to by two justices as authentic. After a short debate, the Governor put the question . . . Passed in the affirmative." (*Colonial Records*, Minutes of the Provincial Council, I, 74. Philadelphia, 1852.)

[2] *Charters and Laws*, p. 157.

cal with the twelfth provision of the charter of 1682. Among the 81 bills drawn up by the Council and passed by the House at this session was the following:

CHAPTER CXII.

" And to the end that poor as well as rich may be instructed in good and commendable learning, which is to be preferred before wealth, Be it &c. that all persons in this province and territories thereof, having children, and all the guardians or trustees of orphans, shall cause such to be instructed in reading and writing; so that they may be able to read the Scriptures; and to write by that time they attain to twelve years of age; and that then they be taught some useful trade or skill, that the poor may work to live, and the rich, if they become poor, may not want. Of which every county court shall take care; and in case such parents, guardians, or overseers shall be found deficient in this respect, every such parent, guardian or overseer, shall pay for every such child, five pounds, except there should appear an incapacity in body or understanding to hinder it."[1]

Ten months later, December 26, 1683, the administration of this law came under consideration at a Couucil held at Philadelphia, at which Governor Penn and Councilmen Thos. Holmes, Wm. Clayton, Wm. Haigue and Lasse Cock were present. " The Governor and Provincial Council, having taken into their serious consideration the great necessity there is of a school-master for the instruction and sober education of youth in the town of Philadelphia, sent for Enoch Flower, an inhabitant of the said town, who for twenty years past hath been exercised in that care and employment in England, to whom having communicated their minds, he embraced it upon these following terms: to learn to read English, 4 s by the quarter, to learn to read and write, 6 s. by the quarter, to learn to read, write and cast account, 8 s. by the quarter; for board-

---

[1] *Ibid.*, p. 142.

ing a scholar, that is to say, diet, washing, lodging and schooling, ten pounds for one whole year."[1]

On the 17th of the following month, at a Council composed
of Governor Penn and Councilmen James Harrison, John
Symcock, Chris. Taylor, Lasse Cock, Wm. Biles, Wm. Clayton and Thos. Holmes, the following proposals were made :
"A law proposed for making of several sorts of books, for
the use of persons in this Province.

"Proposed that care be taken about the learning and instruction of youth, to wit: a school of arts and sciences."[2]

There is no evidence that either of the above plans was
presented by the Council to the Assembly which met in
May, 1684. In fact, during the ensuingnine years, so great
was the spirit of hostility between the Council and the
House, that there was scant legislation of any kind, and
"neglect and miscarriage of government" furnished an argu-
ment for the royal abrogation of the proprietary charter,
which occurred in 1692.[3] The same year, Colonel Benjamin
Fletcher, Governor of New York, was likewise commissioned
royal Governor of Pennsylvania. Within a month after his
arrival at Philadelphia in 1693, a General Assembly was convened, consisting of eight Councilmen, appointed by the Governor, and twenty Assemblymen, elected by the freeholders.
At this Assembly, after a lengthy controversy between the
Governor and Representatives concerning the confirmation of
the pre-established proprietary laws, under a bill called a Petition of Right, the Governor ordered "that all justices, sheriffs and constables and other officers in the Province of
Pennsylvania and country of New Castle should execute or
cause the same to be executed until their Majesties' pleasure,
should be further known."[4] Among the proprietary laws

---

[1] *Col. Rec.*, I, 91.   [2] *Ibid.*, I, 93.

[3] *The History of Pennsylvania*, I, 377. Robert Proud, Philadelphia, 1797.

[4] *Charters and Laws*, App. B, p. 551.

which were thus continued, the law for the education of youth, which had been enacted by the Assembly of 1683, was included with one qualification.

CHAPTER XXV.

" And to the end that the poor as well as the rich may be instructed in good and commendable learning, which is to be preferred before wealth, be it enacted by the authority aforesaid, that all persons in this province and territories hereof having children, and all guardians and trustees of orphans (*having sufficient estate and ability so to do*)[1] shall be instructed in reading and writing; so that they may be able, at least, to read the Scriptures, and write by the time they attain to twelve years of age. And that they be taught some useful trade and skill, that the poor may work to live and the rich, if they become poor may not want. Of which every county court shall take care. And in case such parents, guardians, overseers shall be found deficient in that respect, every such parent, guardian or overseer, shall pay for every such child, five pounds, except there should appear an incapacity in body or understanding to hinder it." [2]

Increasing hostility between the royal governor and the people and a reconciliation between the Crown and the Proprietary resulted in the restoration to Penn in August, 1694, of the full rights of proprietary government. At the second assembly, which was convened October 26, 1696, by Deputy Governor Markham, a new frame of government was drawn up by the Governor and accepted by the Assembly. In this act of settlement, the provisions for erection of public schools, encouragement of science and invention, and oversight of youthful education on the part of the Governor and Council, which had been contained in the charters of 1682 and 1683, but which had been omitted from the Petition of Right of 1693, were re-

---

[1] These words are italicized to indicate the aforesaid qualification.

[2] *Ibid*, p. 238.

newed.[1] The following year, Governor and Council were called upon to use their educational prerogative.

AT A COUNCIL HELD AT PHILADELPHIA, SATURDAY, 12TH FEBRUARY, 1697–8.

"Upon reading the petition of Samuel Carpenter, Edward Shippen, Anthony Morris, James Fox, and David Lloyd, William Southbee and John Jones, in these words, viz. To the Governor and Council of the Province of Pennsylvania and Territories thereof, sitting at Philadelphia, the tenth day of the twelfth month, Anno Domini, 1697–8. The humble petition of Samuel Carpenter, Edward Shippen, Anthony Morris, James Fox, David Lloyd, William Southbee and John Jones, in behalf of themselves and the rest of the people called Quakers, who are members of the Monthly Meeting, holden and kept at the new meeting house, lately built upon a piece of ground fronting the High street, in Philadelphia aforesaid, obtained of the present Governor by the said people, sheweth; That it hath been and is much desired by many, that a school be set up and upheld in this town of Philadelphia, where poor children may be freely maintained, taught and educated in good literature, until they are fit to be put out apprentices, or capable to be masters or ushers in the said school. And for as much as by the laws and constitutions of this government, it is provided and enacted that the Governor and Council shall erect and order all public schools, and encourage and reward the authors of useful sciences and laudable inventions, in the said province and territories, therefore, may it please the Governor and Council to ordain and establish that at the said town of Philadelphia a public school may be founded, where all children and servants, male and female, whose parents,

---

[1] *Ibid.*, p. 251. With but one slight modification. In the Frame of '96, "Governor and Council" are to supervise public affairs, etc., instead [of " one-third of the Provincial Council residing with the Governor," together with the Governor, as was provided by the Frame of '83. In 1696, the Council was cut down from three to two representatives from each county.

guardians and masters be willing to subject them to the rules and orders of the said school, shall from time to time, with the approbation of the overseers thereof for the time being, be received or admitted, taught and instructed; the rich at reasonable rates, and the poor to be maintained and schooled for nothing. And to that end a meet and convenient house and houses, buildings and rooms, may be erected for the keeping of the said school, and for the entertainment and abode of such and so many masters, ushers, mistresses, and poor children, as by the order and direction of the said Monthly Meeting shall be limited and appointed from time to time. And also, that the members of the aforesaid Meeting for the time being, may, at their respective monthly meetings, from time to time make choice of, and admit such and so many persons as they shall think fit, to be overseers, masters, ushers, mistresses, and poor children of the said school, and the same persons, or any of them, to remove and displace, as often as the said Meeting shall see occasion. And that the overseers and school aforesaid, may forever stand and be established and founded in name and in deed, a body politic and corporate, to have continuance forever, by the name of the Overseers of the Public School founded in Philadelphia, at the request, costs and charges of the people of God called Quakers. And that they, the said overseers, may have perpetual succession, and by that name they and their successors may forever have, hold and enjoy, all the lands, tenements and chattels, and receive and take all gifts and legacies, as shall be given, granted or devised for the use and maintenance of the said school and poor scholars, without any farther or other license or authority from this government in that behalf; saving unto the chief Proprietor his quitrents out of the said lands. And that the said overseers, by the same name, shall and may, with consent of the said Meeting, have power and capacity to devise and grant, by writing, under their hands and common seal, any of the said lands and tenements, and to take and purchase any other lands, tenements or hereditaments, for the best use and advantage of the said school. And to prescribe such rules and ordinances for the good order and government of the same school, and of the masters, ushers, mistresses, and poor children successively, and for their and every of their stipends and allowances, as to the members of the said Monthly Meeting for the time being, or the major part of them, shall seem meet; with power also to sue and be sued, and to do, perform and execute all and every other lawful act and thing, good and profitable for the said school, in as full and ample manner as any other body politic or corporate, more perfectly founded and corporate, may do. The Governor and Council do grant this petition as is desired."[1]

This Quaker school which was established in 1689 through a suggestion, it has been said,[2] of the Proprietary to Thomas Lloyd, President of the Council, had already been brought to the formal notice of the Governor and Council at a Council held at Philadelphia, August 1, 1693, at which William Markham, Lieutenant-Governor, Patrick Robinson, secretary, and Andrew Robeson, Robert Turner and Lawrence Cock, Councilmen, were present. "Thomas Meaking, keeper of the free school in the town of Philadelphia, being called upon before the Lieutenant-Governor and Council, was told that he must not keep school without a license. Answered that he was willing to comply, and to take a license. Was therefore ordered to procure a certificate of his ability, learning and diligence, from the inhabitants of note in this town, by the sixteenth instant, in order to the obtaining a license, which he promised to do."[3]

The Friends' Free School was presumably chartered by the Governor in 1697, although no such charter is on record. It received additional charters from the Proprietary in 1701, 1708

---

[1] *Col. Rec.*, I, 531-3.

[2] See *History of Education in Pennsylvania*, p. 41.   James P. Wickersham, LL. D., Lancaster, 1886.

[3] *Col. Rec.*, I, 383.

and 1711, and came to be known as the "William Penn Charter School." The charter of 1711 reviews and amplifies the two preceding charters.

"Whereas, the prosperity and welfare of any people depend, in a great measure, upon the good education of youth, and their early instruction in the principles of true religion and virtue, and qualifying them to serve their country and themselves, by breeding them in reading, writing and learning of languages, and useful arts and sciences suitable to their sex, age and degree; which cannot be effected in any manner so well as by erecting public schools for the purposes aforesaid.

"And whereas, upon the petition of Samuel Carpenter, Edward Shippen, Anthony Morris, James Fox, David Lloyd, William Southby and John Jones, on behalf of themselves and others, to William Markham, my then Lieutenant-Governor, and to the Council of the said Province, on the first day of the twelfth month, in the year one thousand six hundred and ninety-seven, desiring that a public school for teaching and instructing children and servants, both male and female, might be founded in the town of Philadelphia, in this Province, to continue forever, under certain overseers, to be incorporated for that purpose, and to have perpetual succession, with several powers and privileges therein mentioned. My said then Lieutenant-Governor and Council did grant and order that such school should be founded and erected with the incorporation privileges and powers as desired; and such a school was accordingly founded in the town of Philadelphia.

"And whereas, several of the same petitioners having in the year one thousand seven hundred and one, made fresh application to me in Council, to confirm the said order and grant, I did, with the consent of my Provincial Council, and pursuant to the power vested in me by the late King Charles the Second, and to the laws of said province, by an instrument or patent, under my hand and my great provincial seal, bearing date the five and twentieth day of October in the said year, grant and confirm all and every request, matter and thing contained in the petition above mentioned, and did thereby found, ordain and establish the said public school to be kept forever, in the said town of Philadelphia, or in some convenient place adjacent, with power to frame and erect such and so many buildings, for the use and service of the said school and the entertainment of masters, ushers, mistresses and poor children, and to choose and admit such and so many masters, ushers, mistresses and poor children therein as they shall see meet, and I did by the same patent, for me, my heirs and successors, grant and ordain the said overseers to be a body politic and corporate, in name and deed, to continue forever, by the name of the Overseers of the Public School founded in Philadelphia, at the request, cost and charges of the people of God called Quakers, and that the said overseers and their successors should forever have, hold and enjoy, to the use of said school, all the messuages, lands, tenements and hereditaments, goods and chattels, and receive and take all gifts and legacies then before given, granted or devised, or that should be thereafter given, granted or devised, to the use and maintenance of the said school and masters, ushers, mistresses and poor children thereof, without further, or other leave, license or authority whatsoever from me, my heirs or successors, saving to me and them the respective quit-rents, duties and payments thereout reserved, and payable by their original grants and patents, and with full power to frame, make and prescribe such rules and ordinances, for the good order and government of the said school and of the masters, ushers, mistresses and poor children, with other privileges in the same patent expressed, or by the same patent, relation thereto being had, may appear.

"And whereas, at the further request of the several trusty and well beloved Friends, I did, by an instrument, or charter, under my hand and my greater provincial seal, bearing date the twenty-second day of the fifth month, called July, in the year of our Lord, one thousand seven hundred and eight, give and grant to Samuel Carpenter, Edward Shippen, and others, therein named and designated, full license, power and authority to build, erect, found and establish, in the said town of Philadelphia, or in the county of Philadelphia, one public school, to consist of such and so many masters, mistresses and ushers and teachers, and for maintaining, teaching and instructing such and so many poor children of both sexes in reading, work, languages, arts and sciences, as to the overseers therein named should seem meet; and that such public school should forever thereafter be incorporated and called the Public School founded in the town and county of Philadelphia, in Pennsylvania, at the request, cost and charges of the people called Quakers, and that there should be forever thereafter fifteen discreet and religious persons of the people called Quakers, overseers of the same public school, to be incorporated and made one body politic and corporate, by the name of the Overseers of the Public School, founded in the town and county of Philadelphia, in Pennsylvania, at the cost and charges of the people called Quakers, to have perpetual succession forever; in which last charter or instrument, I granted to the said overseers several powers, authorities and privileges, for the good government, improvement and support of such school, as by the said charter or instrument may appear.

"And whereas, it hath lately been represented to me by some of the said overseers that the good ends intended by erecting such school will be better answered and effected if the said corporation were made more extensive, and the powers and privileges granted to the said overseers were more enlarged.

"Now know ye that I being desirous to give all further due encouragement to so pious and useful an undertaking, do hereby, for me and my heirs, will and ordain that the public school erected and founded by either of the former grants, hereinbefore recited, shall forever hereafter be incorporated, called and known by the name of the Public School founded by charter in the town and county of Philadelphia, in Pennsylvania, and not by any other name, style or title whatsoever, and that fifteen discreet and religious persons shall be the overseers of the said school, who, and their successors, shall forever hereafter be one body politic and corporate in deed, name and law, to perpetual succession, and to be named and called by the name of the Overseers of the Public School, founded by charter in the town and county of Philadelphia, in Pennsylvania, and not by any other name, style or title whatsoever, and then by the said name, I do confirm and establish any name or names of the said school, or of the said overseers, in any former patent or charter by me granted, in any wise notwithstanding, and the same school by the name aforesaid, I do by these present erect, found, establish and confirm, to have continuance forever. And that the said pious foundation and undertaking may have and take better effect, and for the good government of the said school, and that the lands, tenements, rents, revenues, stock, goods, money and other things that have been given, granted, assigned and appointed, and which now are intended to be, or hereafter shall be given, granted, assigned or appointed, for the continual maintenance and support of the said school, may be well ordered, and be justly converted or employed to the use of the said school forever, I hereby will and ordain, and by these presents do assign, nominate, constitute and appoint my trusty and well beloved friends, Samuel Carpenter, the elder, Edward Shippen, Griffith Owen, Thomas Story, Anthony Morris, Richard Hill, Isaac Norris, Samuel Preston, Jonathan Dickinson, Nathan Stanbury, Thomas Masters, Nicholas Waln, Caleb Pusey, Rowland Ellis and James Logan to be the present overseers of said school. And I further will and ordain, for me and my heirs, that the above named overseers of the said school and their successors shall and may, by the said name of the Overseers of the Public School, founded by charter, in the town and county of Philadelphia, in Pennsylvania, be persons able and capable in law, to purchase, receive, obtain, retain, possess and enjoy

to them and their successors, overseers of said school
forever, for the use and benefit of the said school, any
manors, lands, tenements, revenues, rents, money, goods
and chattels, whatsoever of any person or persons whom-
soever. And that the said overseers and their successors
shall and may have a common seal, on one side whereof shall
be engraved my coat of arms, with this inscription, " Good Instruction is better than Riches," to be made use of and serve
for the business relating to the said school, and the possession
and revenues thereof. And that the said overseers and their
successors by the name aforesaid, shall and may sue and be
sued, plead and be impleaded, defend and be defended, answer
and be answered, in all manner of courts, pleas and demands
of what kind and nature soever they be, either in law or equity,
or of any transgression, offence, thing, cause or matter done or
committed, or to be done or committed, in, upon or about the
premises, or touching or concerning any thing specified in these
presents, in the same manner as any private persons, natives,
inhabitants or planters in Pennsylvania aforesaid, being persons able, and in law capable, may plead or may be impleaded,
defend or be defended, answer or be answered. And I do
hereby for me and my heirs, will, ordain and grant that the
houses and buildings already erected, for the use of the said
school, by virtue of any of the charters hereinbefore recited or
mentioned, shall be, remain and continue for uses, purposes
and services of the said school only, according to the design
and intention of the erectors thereof, unless the said overseers
herein nominated and appointed shall think fit otherwise to
employ the same, in pursuance of the powers granted by these
presents. And that the said overseers and their successors
shall and may from time to time, as they shall think convenient, and the increase of the inhabitants of the said town and
county of Philadelphia shall require, erect in any other place
or places within the said town and county, as they, or the
major part of them, shall think proper and convenient, any

number of houses or buildings, for places of instruction of said scholars, and for the dwelling and abode of masters, mistresses, ushers, teachers, scholars, officers and servants, belonging and to belong to such school. And I do by these presents, for me and my heirs, give and grant to the said overseers, and their successors forever, that they, or the major part of them, for the time being, shall have full power and authority to make, set down, establish and ordain such good and necessary statutes, orders, rules and ordinances in writing under their hands, and under their common seal, for the better ordering, ruling, governing and improving of the said school, school-masters, school-mistresses, ushers, teachers, scholars and servants, belonging to the same, for the time being, and their several allowances, stipends and wages, and of the houses, buildings, lands, possessions, revenues, incomes, rents, goods and chattels of the said school from time to time, with all other things whatsoever, unto the said school belonging, as to the increase or improvement of the rents, re-pairing of the premises, or any other matter or thing, that may tend to the good of the said school, as the overseers for the time being, or the major part of them, shall think meet and conven-ient, so as the said statutes, orders, rules and ordinances, be in no wise repugnant to the rights, privileges and jurisdiction of me and my heirs, as governors of the said province, nor contrary to, but as near as may be agreeable to, the laws and statutes of the said province: all of which statutes, orders, rules and ordi-nances, until they shall be repealed, or altered, by the same authority, I will and enjoin, by these presents, to be entirely obeyed, kept and observed from time to time forever hereafter, by the overseers, masters, mistresses, ushers, teachers, scholars, and other officers and servants, of or belonging to the said school, for the time being, and every of them. And I have fur-ther given and granted, and by these presents, for me and my heirs, do give and grant unto all and every person and persons, who now are, or hereafter shall be, owners of land, or inhabitants of Pennsylvania aforesaid, and territories thereunto belonging, special license, free power, and lawful authority, to give, grant, bargain and sell, alien and devise, demise, set and let unto the above named overseers of the said public school, and their successors, for the use and benefit of the said school, any manors, messuages, lands, tenements, hereditaments, sum or sums of money, goods or chattels whatsoever, saving to myself and my heirs, all quit-rents issuing, and to issue out of such manors, messuages, lands, tenements, and hereditaments provided nevertheless. And I do, for me and my heirs, ordain that the said overseers, for the time being, or any of them, or their successors, or any of them, shall not make any lease of any of the lands, tenements or hereditaments, of or belonging to the said corporation, which shall exceed the number of one and fifty years, in possession and not in reversion, and whereupon shall not be reserved, payable yearly or half yearly, during every such lease, the best and most improved rent that can be got for the same respectively at the time of making such lease or leases. And for the better government of the school, I do hereby, for me and my heirs, give and grant full license, power and authority, unto the said overseers of the said school, and their successors or the major part of them, from time to time, to nominate, place and displace, and visit the masters, mistresses, ushers, teachers, scholars and other inferior officers and servants of or belonging to the said schools, for the time being, and to order, reform and redress all or any disorders, misdemeanors, offences and abuses, done or committed by the person aforesaid, or any of them, according to the statutes and ordinances, which shall be made, ordained or appointed as aforesaid, as the said overseers for the time being, or the major part of them shall think fit. And that the said schoolmasters, mistresses, ushers, teachers, scholars and other officers and servants thereunto belonging, for the time being, shall be exempted, freed and discharged from all visitation and correction of or by any other person or persons whatsoever. And I. do hereby, for me and my heirs, ordain, grant and appoint, that when and so often as any overseers of the said school shall die, surrender or be removed from his or their place of overseer or overseers, for any misdemeanor, (in which case I will that any overseer, shall and may be removed by a majority of the overseers, for the time being, who shall be the only judges thereof,) then and so often, the residue of the said overseers shall remain, continue and be corporate by the name of the Public School founded by charter, in the town and county of Philadelphia, in Pennsylvania, to all intents and purposes, as if the whole number of overseers were in being. And also that then and so often it shall be lawful for the rest of the overseers, or the major part of them, and they are hereby directed and enjoined to nominate, elect and appoint, by an instrument, under their common seal, one or more discreet, religious persons in the room and place, rooms and places, of such overseer or overseers so dying, surrendering, or being removed, within forty days after such death, and due notice thereof, and after such surrender or removal, which person or persons so nominated, elected and appointed shall from thenceforth be, and be reputed and deemed an overseer or overseers of the said school, to all intents and purposes, according to the true intent and meaning of these presents. In testimony whereof I have set my hand, and caused the greater provincial seal of Pennsylvania to be affixed to these presents, Dated the nine and twentieth day of November, one thousand seven hundred and eleven.

Wm. Penn." [1]

These charters to a private educational agency are suggestive of a change of State policy concerning education. In December, 1699, the Proprietary returned to his province after an absence of sixteen years, and in 1701 he presented for the acceptance of the Assembly a new and, as it proved, final frame of government. In this charter, which continued in force until 1776, the provisions for education which had been made in the

---

[1] Given by Wickersham, pp. 44–48.

former charters were entirely omitted. The charters to the Friends' Public School and the following general Act, which was passed on May 28, 1715, point to the government's acceptance of private societies as proper educational agents :

CHAPTER CCIII.   AN ACT FOR EMPOWERING RELIGIOUS
SOCIETIES TO BUY, HOLD AND ENJOY LANDS,
TENEMENTS AND HEREDITAMENTS.

" Be it enacted by Charles Gookin, Esq., by the royal appro-bation Lieutenant-Governor, under William Penn, Esq., Pro-prietary and Governor-in-Chief of the Province of Pennsylvania, by and with the advice and consent of the freemen of the said province in General Assembly met, and by the authority of the same, that it shall and may be lawful to and for all religious societies or assemblies and congregations of Protestants, within this province, to purchase any lands or tenements for burying grounds, and for erecting houses of religious worship, schools and hospitals ; and by trustees, or otherwise, as they shall think fit, to receive and take grants or conveyances for the same, for any estate whatsoever, to and for the use or uses aforesaid, to be holden of the lord of the fee by the accustomed rents and services. And be it further enacted by the authority aforesaid, that all sales, gifts or grants made to any of the said societies, or to any person or persons in trust for them, or any of them, for or concerning any lands, tenements or heredita-ments within this province, for and in any estate whatsoever, to and for the use and uses aforesaid, shall be and are by this Act ratified and confirmed according to the tenor and true meaning thereof, and of the parties concerned therein. And where any gifts, legacies or bequests have been or shall be made by any person or persons to the poor of any of the said respective religious societies, or to or for the use or service of any meeting or congregation of the said respective societies, the same gifts and bequests shall be employed only to those charitable uses, or to the use of those respective societies or meetings, or to the poor people to whom the same are or shall be given or intended to be given or granted, according to what may be collected to be the true intent and meaning of the respective donors or grantors." [1]

A memorial addressed to the Lords of Trade and Plantations on December 9, 1718, by " William Penn, Proprietary and Governor of the Province of Pennsylvania, and several of his friends, in behalf of the people of that province, humbly sheweth: . . . The true reason of this Act [Chapter CCIII.] was to encourage in an infant colony, where there were no endowments, the building of hospitals, churches, and other places for religious worship, and charity schools for educating of youth, etc., without any other view that we can understand; but that if any lands or tenements, etc., are or shall be given to any such pious uses, they shall in such case be applied to that use, according to the intent of the donor, and to no other use whatsoever. Therefore, we hope the pious meaning of this Act will have that weight with the Lords of Trade to be by them favorably reported. It being the interest of persons of all persuasions that this law should pass without any view to this or that persuasion only, we hope will gain it the royal assent." [2] This plea, however, proved unsuccessful.

On July 9, 1719, the Board of Trade wrote to the Lords Justices, enumerating those laws which had been passed by the Pennsylvania legislature between 1712 and 1715 and which were proper to be repealed. Among these the above Act was included on the ground that it contained a clause "which confirms all sales, gifts or grants already made to those societies, which retrospect, we are of opinion, may probably be attended with ill consequences to purchasers, creditors and other persons." [3] Consequently, the law was repealed by the

---

[1] *Statutes at Large of Pennsylvania*, III, 37–38.

[2] *Ibid.*, III., App. IV., 448.

[3] *Ibid.*, III, App. IV, 463–4.

Lords Justices in Council on July 21, 1719. About eleven years later, a similar Act was passed by the colonial legislature.

CHAPTER CCCXX. AN ACT FOR THE ENABLING RELIGIOUS
SOCIETIES OF PROTESTANTS WITHIN THIS PROVINCE
TO PURCHASE LANDS FOR BURYING-GROUNDS,
CHURCHES, HOUSES FOR WORSHIP,
SCHOOLS, ETC.

" Whereas sundry religious societies of people within this province professing the Protestant religion have at their own respective costs and charges purchased small pieces of land within this province of Pennsylvania, and thereon have erected churches and other houses of religious worship, school-houses and almshouses, and enclosed part of the same lands for burying-grounds; and whereas the said lands were purchased and paid for by the said respective societies in the name or names of persons at that time being of or professing themselves to be of the same religious persuasion with the societies who made use of the names of the said persons as trustees for and in behalf of the said societies. And whereas some of the said trustees or their heirs, having afterwards changed their opinions and joined themselves to other religious societies of a different persuasion from the people by whom the said persons were at first entrusted, and upon pretext of their having the fee-simple of the lands so purchased in their names vested in them, have, contrary to the true intent and meaning of the first grant or gift, attempted by granting away the said lands, houses of religious worship and burying-grounds, to deprive the society of people in possession of the same of the right and use of the said houses of worship and burying-grounds, to the great disquiet and uneasiness of many of the good people of this province; and others, being entrusted in the like manner, may hereafter do the same:[1] For remedy whereof, and for the better securing

---

[1] See *Votes and Proceedings of the House of Representatives of the Province of Pennsylvania*, III, 145–47. Philadelphia, 1754. On the House Journal for

the several religious societies in the quiet and peaceable possession of their churches, houses of worship, school-houses and almshouses and burying-grounds within this province: Be it enacted by the Honorable Patrick Gordon, Esq., Lieutenant-Governor of the Province of Pennsylvania and of the Counties of New Castle, Kent and Sussex on Delaware, by and with the advice and consent of the representatives of the freemen of the said province in General Assembly met, and by the authority of the same, that all sales, gifts or grants made of any lands or tenements within the Province of Pennsylvania to any person or persons in trust for sites of churches, houses of religious worship, schools, almshouses and for burying-grounds or for any of them, shall be and are hereby ratified and confirmed to the person or persons to whom the same were sold, given or granted, their heirs and assigns, in trust, nevertheless, and for the use of the respective religious societies for whose use the same were at first sold, given, granted or purchased, according to the true intent and meaning of such gifts or grants; and that every sale, gift, grant or devise of any such trustee or trustees or any person or persons in whose name or names the said lands for erecting churches, houses of religious worship, schools, almshouses or burying-grounds within this province were purchased, taken or accepted, or the heirs or assigns of such trustees, shall be and are hereby declared to be for the sole use, benefit and behalf of the said respective societies, who have been in the peaceable possession of the same for the space of twenty-one years next before the tenth day of June, in the year of our Lord one thousand, seven hundred and thirty, or for whose use the same were at first given, granted or devised, and no other.   And be it further enacted by the authority aforesaid, that it shall and may be lawful to and for any religious society of Protestants within this province to purchase, take and re-

January 27, 1731, is entered in full a remonstrance of the Baptist Society of Philadelphia against the Episcopal Church of Philadelphia on the grounds mentioned in the above Act.

ceive by gift, grant or otherwise, for burying-grounds, erecting churches, houses of religious worship, schools and almshouses, for any estate whatsoever, and to hold the same for the uses aforesaid of the lord of the fee by the accustomed rents . . . Provided also, that this Act nor anything therein contained, shall be deemed or construed to impeach the just right or title which any person or persons may have to any of the lands or tenements hereinbefore mentioned, so that they prosecute such their right or claim within the space of three years next after the publication of this Act. Passed February 6, 1730–31." [1]

Concerning this Act, his Majesty's counsel at law, at the request of the Board of Trade in November, 1739, stated his objection as follows: " It seems to me that as this Act enables societies to purchase in mortmain without any restriction or limitation, though there is an Act in force in Great Britain against such purchases, it is on that account improper to be confirmed." [2]

The Act, however, was apparently never considered by the Crown, but allowed to become a law by lapse of time in accordance with the proprietary charter.

In 1731, through the influence of Benjamin Franklin, a small number of Philadelphia gentlemen subscribed the sum of £100 towards the founding of a circulating library. In 1742 this library society was incorporated by the Proprietaries of the province under the name of the Library Company of Philadelphia. Franklin and 74 associates were given full power to hold lands, to sue and be sued, etc., to have a common seal, and to meet and make laws for the government of the company, for the admission of new members, and for the appointment of all necessary officers. In the preamble of the charter the grantees are stated to " have, at a great expense, purchased a large and valuable collection of useful books, in order to erect a library for the advancement of knowledge and literature in the

---

[1] *Statutes at Large*, IV, 208–210. See also *Col. Rec.*, III, 394.

[2] *Statutes at Large*, III, App. V, 504.

city of Philadelphia," and, therefore, John Penn, Thomas Penn
and Richard Penn," true and absolute Proprietaries," proceed
to declare that " being truly sensible of the advantage that may
accrue to the people of this province by so useful an undertaking, and being willing to encourage the same, have given and
granted," etc.[1]

In 1740, certain citizens of Philadelphia of various religious
denominations built a hall for religious worship, and for the
special use of George Whitfield during his visits to Philadelphia. The building was also intended to serve as a charity
school for poor children. Nine years later the property was
vested in 24 trustees, with the additional object of the founding
of an academy. A private endowment of £800 per annum for
a term of 5 years was secured, and the city of Philadelphia
granted £200 to the institution with a promise of an annual
endowment of £100 for 5 years.[2] In 1753, a charter was
obtained from the Proprietaries.

CHARTER TO THOMAS LAWRENCE AND OTHERS, TO BE TRUSTEES
OF THE ACADEMY AND CHARITABLE SCHOOL IN THE
PROVINCE OF PENNSYLVANIA

" Thomas Penn and Richard Penn, true and absolute Proprietors and Governors-in-Chief of the Province of Pennsylvania
and Counties of New Castle, Kent and Sussex, on Delaware, to
all persons to whom these presents shall come, greeting:
Whereas, the well-being of a society depends on the education
of their youth, as well as, in great measure, the eternal welfare
of every individual, by impressing on their tender minds
principles of morality and religion, instructing them in the
several duties they owe to the society in which they live, and

---

[1] Charter given in *A Catalogue of the Books belonging to the Library Company of Philadelphia,* vol. I, pp. XIII–XV, Philadelphia, 1835.

[2] *Benjamin Franklin and the University of Pennsylvania,* pp. 234–76. Edited
by F. N. Thorpe, Ph. D. Bureau of Education. Circular of Information, No. 2,
1892.

one towards another, giving them the knowledge of languages, and other parts of useful learning necessary thereto, in order to render them serviceable in the several public stations to which they may be called. And whereas, it hath been represented to us by Thomas Lawrence, Wm. Allen, John Inglis, Tench Francis, William Masters, Lloyd Zachary, Samuel Mc-Call, junior, Joseph Turner, Benjamin Franklin, Thomas Leech, William Shippen, Robert Strettell, Philip Syng, Charles Willing, Phineas Bond, Richard Peters, Abraham Taylor, Thomas Bond, Joshua Maddox, William Plumstead, Thomas White, William Colemen, Isaac Norris and Thomas Cadwalader,[1] of our city of Philadelphia, gentlemen, that for the erecting, establishing and maintaining an academy within our said city as well to instruct youth for reward, as poor children, whose indigent and helpless circumstances demand the charity of the opulent part of mankind, several benevolent and charitable persons have generously paid, and by subscriptions promised hereafter to pay into their hands as trustees, for the use of the said academy, divers sums of money, which sums already paid, they, the said trustees, have expended in the purchase of lands well situated, and a building commodious for the uses aforesaid, within our said city, in maintaining an academy there, as well for the instruction of poor children on charity, as others whose circumstances have enabled them to pay for their learning, for some time past, and in furnishing the said academy with books, maps, mathematical instruments, and other necessaries of general use therein, according to the intentions of the donors. And whereas, the said trustees to facilitate the progress of so good a work, and to perfect and perpetuate the same, have humbly besought us to incorporate them and their successors. Now know ye, that we, favoring such pious, useful, generous, and charitable designs, hoping through the favor of Almighty God, this academy may prove a nursery of virtue

---

[1] Eleven of these trustees were likewise trustees of the Library Company.

and wisdom, and that it will produce men of dispositions and capacities beneficial to mankind in the various occupations of life; but more particularly suited to the infant state of North America in general, and for other causes and considerations us hereto especially moving, have granted, ordained, declared, constituted, and appointed, and by these presents we do, for us, our heirs, and successors grant, ordain, declare, constitute, and appoint, that the said Thomas Lawrence, [etc.,] and such others as shall be from time to time chosen, nominated or elected in their place and stead, shall be one community, corporation and body politic, to have continuance forever, by the name of the Trustees of the Academy and Charitable School in the province of Pennsylvania, and that by the same name, they shall have perpetual succession, and that they and their successors by that name, shall be capable in law to purchase, have, take, receive, and enjoy to them and their successors in fee and in perpetuity, or for any other or lesser estate or estates, any manors, lands, tenements, rents, annuities, pensions, or other hereditaments within the said province of Pennsylvania, or three lower counties of New Castle, Kent and Sussex, by the gift, grant, bargain, sale, alienation, enfeoffment, release, confirmation, or device of any person or persons, bodies politic or corporate, capable to make the same. And further, that they may take and receive any sum or sums of money or any kind, manner or portion of goods or chattels that shall to them be given, granted or bequeathed by any person or persons, bodies politic or corporate, capable to make a gift, grant or bequest thereof; and therewith to erect, set up, maintain, and support an academy or any other kind of seminary of learning in any place within the said province of Pennsylvania, where they shall judge the same to be most necessary and convenient for the instruction, improvement and education of youth in any kind of literature, erudition, arts and sciences, which they shall think fitting and proper to be taught. [Here follow provisions for a common seal, for corporate rights of suing, being sued, etc.] And further, in order to continue and perpetuate this community and corporation, we do grant, ordain and declare, that when any one or more of the present or future trustees of this academy and school shall remove his or their habitation or habitations, and shall dwell at a distance of five miles from the seat of the said academy at that time, or shall go and reside out of the province of Pennsylvania, although at a place nearer to the said academy than five miles, or shall happen to die or be otherwise disabled from performing the office and duty of a trustee or trustees, the other trustees shall, as soon after as they conveniently can, proceed to elect and choose one or more fit person or persons, then residing within five miles of the said academy, and within the said province, to fill the place or places of such absenting, deceased or disabled person or persons. And we do also, for us, our heirs and successors, give and grant to the said trustees and corporation and their successors, full power and authority in all time and times coming to make, ordain, and enact all such rules, ordinances, laws and statutes, and from time to time to alter and amend the same as they shall judge most convenient, reasonable and needful for the good government of the said community, the management of the affairs thereof, and the perfectual promotion of the good ends hereby intended; provided always, that the said rules, ordinances, laws and statutes be not repugnant to the laws and statutes then in force at the kingdom of Great Britain, or to the laws then in force in our said province of Pennsylvania."[1]

Two years later a confirmatory charter was granted. By this Act the name of the institution was changed to "The College, Academy and Charitable School," and in it certain amplifications, fitting to an institution assuming collegiate standing, were incorporated. . . . "And whereas the said trustees[2] have, by their petition to Robert Hunter

[1] Given in *Benj. Franklin and the University of Pennsylvania*, pp. 68-70.

[2] Alexander Stedman and John Mifflin had taken the places of Thomas Lawrence and Isaac Norris on the board of trustees.

Morris, Esq., our Lieutenant Governor and Commander-in-chief, in and over our said province of Pennsylvania and counties of New Castle, Kent and Sussex, on Delaware, repreented, that since our granting our said recited charter, the academy therein mentioned, by the blessing of the Almighty God, is greatly improved, being now well provided with masters not only in the learned languages, but also in the liberal arts and sciences, and that one class of hopeful students have now attained to that station in learning and science by which, in all well constituted seminaries, youth are entitled to their first degree, and which the said students are earnestly desirous to be admitted to; and that it is hoped, from the capacities and diligence of this class, they will hereafter merit admission to the higher degrees in the arts and sciences; from whence the said trustees reasonably expect a succession of youth in this college and academy, equally meritorious, and deserving of such public honors, which are at the same time the strongest incentives to, and the justest rewards of, diligence and merit; and therefore prayed an addition to our recited charter, to empower them and their successors, to admit deserving students to the usual degrees, and to confer such dignity on the masters in the said seminary, as shall seem meet and necessary for its good government and establishment upon this enlargement of the design, for the benefit both of the present and future times. And we being willing to grant this reasonable request of the said trustees, and to give all proper encouragement to an institution so happily begun, and hitherto so successfully carried on, for the benefit of our said province, as well as the neighboring provinces and colonies in America; Now know ye also, that we do hereby, for us, our heirs, and successors, give and grant full power and authority to the said trustees, and their successors, from time to time, and at all times forever hereafter, in such manner, and under such limitations, as they shall think best and most convenient, to constitute and appoint a provost and vice-provost of the said college and academy, who shall be severally named and styled Provost and Vice-Provost of the same. Also to nominate and appoint professors for instructing the students of the same seminary, in all the liberal arts and sciences, the ancient languages, and the English tongue, who shall be severally styled professor of such art, science, language or tongue, according to such particular nomination and appointment; which provost, vice-provost and professors, so constituted and appointed, shall be known and distinguished, as one body and faculty, by the name of the Provost, Vice-Provost and Professors of the College and Academy of Philadelphia, in the Province of Pennsylvania and by that name shall be capable of exercising such powers and authorities, as the said trustees and their successors shall think necessary to delegate to them, for the discipline and government of the said college, academy and charitable school; provided always, that the said trustees, the provost and vice-provost and each professor, before they shall exercise their several and respective powers or authorities, offices and duties, do and shall take and subscribe the three first written oaths, appointed to be taken and subscribed, in and by one act of Parliament, passed in the first year of the reign of our late sovereign Lord George the First, entitled, An Act for the Further Security of his Majesty's Person and Government, and the Succession of the Crown in the Heirs of the Late Princess Sophia, being Protestants, and for Extinguishing the Hopes of the Pretended Prince of Wales, and his Open and Secret Abettors; and shall also make and subscribe the declaration, appointed to be made and subscribed, by one other act of Parliament, passed in the twenty-fifth year of the reign of King Charles the Second, entitled, An Act for Preventing Dangers which may Happen from Popish Recusants: excepting only the people called Quakers, who, upon taking, making and subscribing the affirmations and declarations, appointed to be taken, made, and subscribed by the acts of General Assembly of the Province of Pennsylvania to qualify them for the exercise of civil offices, shall be admitted to the exercise of all and every the powers, authorities, offices and duties above mentioned, anything in this provision to the contrary notwithstanding; all which oaths and affirmations we do hereby authorize and empower the Lieutenant-Governor of our said province, or the Mayor or Recorder of the City of Philadelphia aforesaid, or any two justices of the peace, for the time being to administer. . . . And we do hereby, at the desire and request of the said trustees, constitute and appoint the Reverend William Smith, M. A. to be the first and present provost of the said college and academy, and the Reverend Francis Allison, M. A., to be the first and present vice-provost of the same, who shall also retain the name and style of Rector of the Academy, which offices the said persons shall have and hold only during the pleasure of the said trustees. And we do further, for us, our heirs and successors, authorize the said trustees and their successors to meet on such day or days, as they shall by their laws and statutes appoint, to examine the candidates for admission for degrees in the said college and academy, and also to transact, determine and settle all the business and affairs of the same. And we do will and ordain, that at all those meetings, such a number of members so met and convened, as shall by the laws and statutes be authorized to transact any particular affairs or business, and the majority of them shall have full power to transact, determine and settle such affairs and business, in as ample and effectual a manner as if all the said trustees were present; excepting always the nominating, constituting and discharging the provost, vice-provost and professors, or any of them; in all and every of which acts, there shall be thirteen at least of the members of the said corporation present and consenting. And we do further, for us, our heirs and successors, authorize and empower the said trustees and their successors, met from time to time as aforesaid, to make laws and statutes to regulate, ascertain and settle the precedence, powers and duties of the said provost, vice-provost, (or rector) and professors, in the execution of the laws made, or to be made, for the education of the youth, and the wholesome government of the said college, academy and charitable school; and also by these laws and statutes, in such manner and form as they shall think convenient, to empower the provost, vice-provost and professors for the time being, to make and execute ordinances, for preserving good order, obedience and government, as well among the students and scholars, as the several tutors, officers and ministers, belonging to the said college, academy and charitable school; and further, by the said laws and statutes, to enact all other matters and things, in and concerning the premises, which may by the said trustees and their successors, be thought conducive to the well-being, advancement and perpetuating the said college, academy and corporation; provided always, that the said laws be not repugnant to the laws and statutes then in force in the Kingdom of Great Britain; nor to the laws and statutes then in force in our said province of Pennsylvania. And we do further, for us, our heirs and successors, give and grant the trustees of the said college and academy, that for animating and encouraging the students thereof to a laudable diligence, industry, and progress in useful literature and science, they and their successors, met together on such day or days as they shall appoint for that purpose, shall have full power and authority, by the provost, and in his absence, by the vice-provost, and in the absence of both provost and vice-provost, by the senior professor, or any other fit person by them authorized and appointed, to admit any the students within the said college and academy, or any other person or persons meriting the same, to any degree or degrees, in any of the faculties, arts, and sciences, to which persons are usually admitted, in any or either of the universities or colleges in the kingdom of Great Britain. And we do ordain, that the provost, vice-provost, or other person appointed as foresaid, shall make, and with his name, sign diplomas or certificates of the admission to such degree or degrees, which shall be sealed with the public seal of the said corporation, and delivered to the graduates as honorable and perpetual testimonials thereof, provided always, and it is hereby declared to be our true meaning and express will, that no student or students, within the said college and academy, shall ever or at any time or times hereafter, be admitted to any such degree or degrees, until such students have been first recommended and presented as worthy of the same, by a written mandate, given under the hands of at least thirteen of the trustees of the said college and academy, and sealed with the privy seal belonging to the said corporation, after a public examination of such student or students in their presence, and in the presence of any other persons choosing to attend the same, to be had in the hall of the said college and academy, at least one whole month before the admission to such degree or degrees; and provided further, that no person or persons, excepting the students belonging to the said seminary, shall ever, or at any time or times, be admitted to any such degree or degrees, unless with the express mandate of at least two-thirds of the whole number of trustees, first to be obtained under their hands and the privy seal aforesaid and to the provost, vice-provost and professors of the said college and academy directed." [Here follows a provision for enabling the corporation to hold propreity to the extent of £5000 annual value.] [1]

The Reverend William Smith, who was appointed provost of the college in the above charter, belonged to the Church of England, and he and the institution which he represented seem to have fallen quickly into disfavor with the Assembly, a body made up mainly of Quakers and German sectarians. In 1758, Dr. Smith was arrested and imprisoned for three months by order of the Assembly on charge of implication in a libellous attack upon that body. During his imprisonment, Dr. Smith sent an appeal to the King and on June 26, 1759,

---

[1] Given in *Benj. Franklin and the University of Pennsylvania*, pp. 71–77.

the King in Council " declared his high displeasure at the unwarrantable behavior of the House of Representatives of Pennsylvania in assuming to themselves powers which do not belong to them, and invading both his majesty's royal prerogative and the liberties of the subject."[1] About this time the College, Academy and Charitable School of Philadelphia was indirectly attacked by the legislature.

" At a council held at Philadelphia, Tuesday, the 2d of June, 1759, the Governor laid before the Board a bill sent up to him by the House entitled, 'An Act for the more effectual suppressing of lotteries and plays,' which was read and taken into consideration. The members of Council acquainted the Governor they had been well informed, and believed it to be true, that this bill was principally intended to destroy the College, Academy and Charity School of this city, which was a most noble and useful institution; that some members of the House were known to have thrown all possible discouragements on it, and failing of success, they had probably fallen on this method to prohibit lotteries, from which of late the Academy had drawn its principal support. That eighty poor boys and forty poor girls were instructed gratis in the School to read, write and cast accounts, and the girls to sew and do all sorts of plain needle-work, under two masters and a mistress. That in the schools there were one hundred and thirty boys who were instructed in the Greek, Latin and English tongues, and were likewise taught at the same time writing and mathematics. And that in the College there were above twenty students who were instructed by able professors in all the higher branches of learning, oratory, Euclid, logic, ethics, natural and experimental philosophy ; that the expenses of professors and masters were very great, amounting to thirteen hundred pounds a year, and that all the sums they received from such scholars as paid did not exceed five hundred pounds a year, so that they were at an annual expense of eight hun-

[1] *Penn. Col. Rec.*, VIII, 442-7.

dred pounds, which at first they raised by subscription; but this proving too heavy upon a few individuals, who had subscribed largely towards the support of this useful seminary of learning, they have of late supported this expense by lotteries, which had been uprightly managed by people of the best credit in the province, and the prizes always paid with the utmost punctuality and honor. That there had been no lotterier carried on in this province other than for the most necessary and charitable purposes, viz., the fortification of the city, the defense of the province in time of war, and the finishing the Episcopal church of this city, all which were managed with the greatest uprightness." [1]

The Act for the more effectual suppressing of lotteries and plays was passed, however, on the twentieth of the same month.[2]   It was repealed by the King on September 2, 1760.[3]

During a visit to England in 1759, Dr. Smith secured from Proprietary Thomas Penn a deed for the college of one fourth of the manor of Perkasie in Bucks county, a matter of 2,500 acres.   Three years later, Smith obtained the royal permission to collect subscriptions in England for his institutions.[4]   He subsequently collected £6,921, of which sum Thomas Penn gave £500, and the King, £200.[5]   The Proprietaries gave in all

---

[1] *Ibid.*, VIII, 339–40. According to the Journal of the Assembly much pressure had been brought to bear for the suppression of plays. During the latter part of May addresses on the subject were presented to the legislature by the Quakers, the Baptists and the German Lutherans of the City of Philadelphia. And in answer to these petitions the Lower House appointed a committee on May 26, "to prepare and bring in a bill to prevent the exhibition of theatrical entertainments, and for suppressing of lotteries with this government." (*Votes and Proceedings*, V, 51-2.)

[2] *The Charters and Acts of Assembly of the Province of Pennsylvania*, II 109. Philadelphia, 1762.

[3] *Ibid.*, I, 162.

[4] Order in Council given in *Benjamin Franklin and the University of Pennsylvania*, pp. 77–9.

[5] *Penn. Col. Rec.*, VIII. 236–8.

£4,500 to the College, Academy and Charitable School of Phila-delphia. Their opinion of that institution is further shown in the joint letter written by them, the Archbishop of Canterbury and the Reverend Samuel Chandler to its trustees under date of April 9, 1764. "This institution you have professed to have been originally founded and hitherto carried on for the general benefit of a mixed body of people. In his Majesty's royal brief, it is represented as a seminary that would be of great use for raising up all instructors and teachers as well as for the service of the Society for Propagating the Gospel in Foreign Parts, as for other Protestant denominations in the colony. At the time of granting this collection, which was solicited by the Provost, who is a clergyman of the Church of England, it was known that there were united with him a vice-provost who is a Presbyterian, and a principal professor of the Baptist persua-sion, with sundry inferior professors and tutors, all carrying on the education of youth with great harmony; and people of various denominations have hereupon contributed liberally and freely. But jealousies now arising lest this foundation should afterward be narrowed and some party endeavor to ex-clude the rest, or put them on a worse footing than they have been from the beginning, or were at the time of this collec-tion, which might not only be deemed unjust in itself, but might likewise be productive of contentions un-friendly to learning and hurtful to religion; we would there-fore recommend it to you to make some fundamental rule or declaration to prevent inconveniencies of this kind."[1] On the following June, such a declaration was made and recorded by the trustees of the college.[2]

The State's policy of favoring charitable institutions by the granting of lottery privileges was reasserted several times after its temporary suspension in 1759. Chapter XVIII of the Acts

[1] Given in *Benj. Franklin and the University of Pennsylvania*, pp. 79-80.

[2] *Ibid.*, pp. 80-81.

of Assembly of 1766–7 was an "Act for raising by way of lottery, the sum of £490, 19s., to be applied to the payment of the arrears of debt, due for the building and finishing the German Lutheran Church in Earl township, in Lancaster county, and towards the erecting and building a school house to the same church." [1]

On February 18, 1769, the Assembly passed an Act giving ampler powers to the managers of a lottery for erecting a new school house for the High Dutch Reformed Congregation, etc. [2]

[1] *The Acts of Assembly of the Province of Pennsylvania.*   Philadelphia, 1775.

[2] *Laws of the Commonwealth of Pennsylvania*, I, 466.   Philadelphia, 1803.

DELAWARE

In 1682, William Penn found about 1,000 Swedes and 1,000 Dutch and English settled along the banks of the Delaware. The Swedes had made a permanent settlement on the west bank, at the mouth of the Christina Creek, in 1638; the Dutch captured this region in 1655, and in 1664 the English took possession. The governments of Sweden, Holland and England had all considered the subject of education in their respective settlements. In 1640 Queen Christina of Sweden granted to one Henry Hochhaumer the right to plant a colony in New Sweden. Article seven of this charter reads: "As regards religion, we are willing to permit that besides the Augsburg Confession, the exercise of the pretended reformed religion may be established and observed in that country; in such manner, however, that those who profess the one or the other religion, live in peace, abstaining from every useless dispute, from all scandal and from all abuse. The patrons of this colony shall be obliged to support at all times, as many ministers and schoolmasters, as the number of inhabitants shall seem to require; and to choose, moreover, for this purpose, persons who have at heart the conversion of the pagan inhabitants to Christianity."[1]

John Printz was commissioned Governor of New Sweden, August 15, 1642, and among the royal instructions given to him for the government of the colony was the following:

"XXVI. Before all the Governor must labor and watch that he renders in all things to Almighty God, the true worship which is his due, the glory, the praise and the homage

[1] *Pennsylvania Archives*, Second Series, V, 760. Harrisburg, 1877.

which belong to him, and take good measures that the divine service is performed according to the true confession of Augsburg, the Council of Upsal and the ceremonies of the Swedish Church, having care that all men, and especially the youth, be well instructed in all the parts of Christianity, and that a good ecclesiastical discipline be observed and maintained."[1]

After the seizure of Fort Christina by Governor Stuyvesant, the West India Company took control of the northern part of Delaware Colony and the City of Amsterdam, of the southern. In the draft of the conditions offered by the City of Amsterdam to emigrants to the Delaware, "to the end that the said colonists may gain their livelihood there safely, honestly and prosperously, the City aforesaid doth beforehand guarantee as follows:

" VII.   Said City shall cause to be erected about the market or in a more convenient place, a public building suitable for divine service; item, also a house for a school which can likewise be occupied by the person who will hereafter be sexton, psalm-setter and school master; the City shall besides have a house built for the minister.

" VIII.   The City aforesaid shall provisionally provide and pay the salary of a minister and school-master, unless their High Mightinesses or the Company think otherwise.

" X.   Concerning the Company's custom, the City shall agree therefore as favorable as possible, and especially that the duty to be paid in New Netherlands shall be employed in building and maintaining public works."[2]

The West India Company agreed to the above conditions, reserving only the duty on peltries to the exclusive use of the Company.[3]

School-master Evert Pietersen reached New Amstel with the first body of colonists from the City of Amsterdam on

---

[1] *Ibid.*, V, 773.   [2] *Ibid.*, V, 793, 794, 795.   [3] *Ibid.*, V, 795.

April 25, 1657, and on August 10, 1657, he reports to the Municipal Commissioners of Amsterdam that he has already begun to keep school, having 25 children.[1] In a return of moneys paid for the colony on the Delaware by the Amsterdam Commissioners, Pietersen is accounted to have received for his services as " comforter of the sick, etc.," a total of 1068 florins and 16 stivers; on March 18, 1661, 927 florins, 16 stivers; on March 23, 1661, 66 florins and on October 10, 1661, 75 florins.[2] In this last entry he is referred to as "late comforter of the sick, etc."

The royal grant to James, Duke of York, made in 1664, included all the territory between the Connecticut and the Delaware Rivers, and five days after the capitulation of New Amsterdam, Governor Nicolls sent a force to take possession of both sides of the Delaware River. A deputy-governor was appointed for New Castle (New Amstel) and the province of Delaware became an appendage to the province of New York. But the Dutch laws were probably continued in the province, for the Duke's code was not introduced until 1676. For the educational provision in those laws and for the instructions concerning education given to subsequent royal governors of New York and Delaware, the reader is referred to the history of the educational legislation and administration of the colony of New York.

In 1682 the Duke of York ceded the so-called three lower counties on the Delaware, New Castle, Kent and Sussex to William Penn. Until 1702 this country was an integral part of the province of Pennsylvania. In that year a separate legislature was elected by the three lower counties.

In 1743 the Delaware legislature passed an Act similar to[3] that passed by the Pennsylvania legislature in 1731 " for the

---

[1] *Ibid.*, V, 290.   [2] *Ibid.*, V, 419.

[3] The two Acts are identical in form and content, except that the retrospective clause of the Delaware act was for a period of 7 instead of 21 years.

enabling religious societies of Protestants . . . to purchase lands for burying grounds, churches, houses for worship, schools, etc."[1]

In 1772, the legislature passed an Act vesting the public lands and buildings of New Castle in a body   town trustees In Section 2 of this Act, a certain piece of land which had always been held " as ground dedicated and set apart for the use of the said town " and upon which the inhabitants intended to erect a school house and desired the same to be appropriated and applied to that use, was " settled upon and vested in David Finney, John Thompson, George Read, Thomas M'Kean and George Munroe, gentlemen, and the survivors and survivor of them, and the heirs and assigns of survivor, in trust nevertheless for the erecting a school house or school houses thereon, and to be for that use forever."[2]

---

[1] *Laws of the State of Delaware*, I, 271-4. New Castle, 1797.
[2] *Ibid.*, II., 516-7.

NEW JERSEY

UNDER the name of Nova Caesaria or New Jersey the Duke of York transfered in 1664 that part of his royal grant which lay between the Hudson River and the ocean on the east, and the Delaware River on the west and south, to two proprietaries in England. Ten years later West New Jersey came into the possession of William Penn and four other Quaker proprietors, and in 1682, East New Jersey was likewise disposed of to Quaker associates. The government of West Jersey consisted of a general elective assembly and an executive board of commissioners. Subsequently a single executive officer appointed by the Assembly was substituted for this board. Among the laws passed by the Assembly of West Jersey at a session held at Burlington, in 1682, was the following.

"VIII. And for the encouraging learning, for the better education of youth; Be it hereby enacted, and agreed by authority aforesaid, that the island called Matininuck Island, late in the possession of Robert Stacy, with all and every the appurtenances, is hereby given, and shall from hence forth for ever hereafter, be and remain to and for the use of the town of Burlington, and to others concerned therein, within the first and second tenths, the rents, issues and profits thereout and therefrom yearly arising to be by the overseers appointed or to be appointed in Burlington, employed for the maintaining of a school for the education of youth within the said town, and in the first and second tenths."[1]

In 1683, the 24 proprietors for East Jersey published certain

[1] *The Grants, Concessions and Original Coutributions of the Province of New Jersey*, compiled by Aaron Leaming and Jacob Spicer, p. 455. Philadelphia.

fundamental constitutions for the government of the province. They provided for a governor to be chosen from their own number to be represented in the colony by a deputy governor; for an assembly consisting of the proprietors or their deputies and 72 representatives elected by the inhabitants of the eight towns in the colony; and for a common council to be associated with the governor and to consist of the proprietors or their proxies and 12 freemen chosen from the members of the grand assembly, which " common council will thus consist of six and thirty, whereof they shall be three committees; twelve for the public policy, and to look to manners, education and arts; twelve for trade and management of the public treasury; and twelve for plantations and regulating of all things, as well as deciding all controversies relating to them. In each committee, eight shall be of the Proprietors, or their proxies, and four of the freemen. Each of these committees shall meet at least once a week, and all the thirty-six once in two months, and oftener, in such places and at such times as they shall find most convenient. And if it happen the number of freemen in the great council to be doubled, there shall also be twelve more of them to be added to the common council; in this common council and those several committees the one-half shall be a quorum, as in the former article." [1]

In 1688, the Jersey proprietaries surrendered their patents to the Crown, and for a short period East and West Jersey were annexed to New York. In 1690, under Governor Andros, the Proprietaries re-asserted their authority, and two years later Andrew Hamilton was appointed governor of both the Jerseys. During his administration two school bills were passed by the legislature. Chapter 3 of the laws passed at an Assembly held at Perth Amboy, East New Jersey, in 1693, reads as follows :

" Whereas the cultivating of learning and good manners tends greatly to the good and benefit of mankind, which hath

[1] *Ibid.*, p. 156.

hitherto been much neglected within this province; Be it therefore enacted by the Governor, Council and Deputies in grand Assembly now met and assembled, and by the authority of the same, that the inhabitants of any town within this province, shall and may by warrant from a justice of the peace of that county, when they think fit and convenient, meet together and make choice of three more men of the said town, to make a rate for the salary and maintaining of a schoolmaster within the said town, for so long time as they think fit. And the consent and agreement of the major part of the inhabitants of the said town, shall bind and oblige the remaining part of the inhabitants of the said town to satisfy and pay their shares and proportion of the said rate; and in case of a refusal or non-payment, distress to be made upon the goods and chattels of such person or persons so refusing or not paying, by the constable of the said town, by virtue of a warrant from a justice of the peace of that county. And the distress so taken to be sold at a public vendue, and the overplus, if any be after payment of the said rate and charges, to be returned to the owner." [1]

The bill of this Act was sent up by the House of Deputies to the Council on October 30, 1693. It was passed by that body on the same day, and was returned to the house. [2]

Chapter 5 of the laws passed at a session in Perth Amboy in 1695 was

AN ACT FOR REGULATING OF SCHOOLS

"Whereas there was an Act made Anno Domini 1693, for the establishing of schools in each respective town in this province, and by experience it is found inconvenient by reason of the distance of the neighborhood, the said Act directing no suitable way whereby all the inhabitants may have the benefit

---

[1] *Ibid.*, p. 328.

[2] *Record of the Governor and Council of East Jersey*, 1682–1703, pp. 165, 166. Jersey City, 1872.

thereof; Be it therefore enacted by the Governor, Council and Representatives in General Assembly now met and assembled, and by the authority of the same, that three men be chosen yearly and every year in each respective town in this province, to appoint and agree with a school master, and the three men so chosen shall have power to nominate and appoint the most convenient place or places where the school shall be kept from time to time, that as near as may be the whole inhabitants may have the benefit thereof."[1]

In 1702 New Jersey was reunited with New York as a royal province. In 1738 the two colonies were again separated. During this period there was constant strife between the Episcopal Governors and Councils and the Assemblies of Quaker and Dissenter constituencies. In 1745 Governor Morris was petitioned by representatives of the Presbyterian Synod of New York for a charter for a college.[2] The petitioners were refused. The following year, upon the death of Governor Morris, a similar petition was assented to by Andrew Hamilton, President of the Council and acting Governor. There is no official record of the charter which was then granted, but in a contemporary number of the Pennsylvania Gazette a summary of the document is given together with certain particulars about the new institution.

" These are to give notice to all concerned, that by his

---

[1] *The Grants, Concessions, etc.*, p. 358.

[2] About 1726, William Tennent, a Presbyterian clergyman, opened a small school for the study of divinity and the liberal arts on the southwest bank of the Neshaminy River in Pennsylvania. The success of this school and of others modeled upon it, led the Presbyterian Church to plan in 1739 for the erection of a college for the middle colonies. Three years later discussion arose between the presbyteries of New Brunswick and Philadelphia on the refusal of the latter to recognize the ecclesiastical training of Tennent's so-called Log Cabin College as adequate for admission into the Presbytery. A split in the church resulted, and the Synod of New York came into existence in 1745 as a union of the presbyteries of New York, New Brunswick and New Castle. See *The Planting of Princeton College*, p. 186. John DeWitt in *The Presbyterian and Reformed Review*, April, 1897.

Majesty's royal charter for erecting a college in New Jersey,
for the instructing of youth in the learned languages, and in
the liberal arts and sciences, bearing date October 22, 1746,
Messrs. William Smith, Peter Vanbrugh Livingston, William
Peartree Smith, gent, and Messrs. Jonathan Dickinson, John
Pierson, Ebenezer Pemberton and Aaron Burr, ministers of
the gospel, are appointed trustees of the said college, with
full power to any four or more of them, to choose five more
trustees to the exercise of equal power and authority in the
said college, with themselves. By virtue of which power, the
said trustees nominated in the charter, have chosen the Rev.
Messrs. Gilbert Tennent, William Tennent, Samuel Blair,
Richard Treat and Samuel Finley as trustees of the said college
of New Jersey. Which trustees, are by the said charter, constituted a body corporate and politic, both in fact and name,
with full power to act as such to all intents and purposes, and
rendered capable of a perpetual succession to continue forever.
By which royal charter, there is authority given to the major
part of any seven or more of the said trustees, and their successors convened for that purpose, to purchase, receive and
dispose of any possessions, tenements, goods, and chattels,
gifts, legacies, donations and bequests, rents, profits, and
annuities of any kind whatsoever, and to build any house or
houses, as they shall think proper, for the use of the said
college. And also by the said charter is given to the major
part of any seven or more of the said trustees and their successors, full power to choose, and at pleasure to displace, a
president, tutors, professors, treasurer, clerk, steward, and
usher, with any other ministers and officers as are usual in any
of the universities or colleges in the realm of Great Britain.
And also by the said charter is given to the major part of any
seven of the said trustees, and their successors, full power to
make any laws, acts and ordinances for the government of the
said college as are not repugnant to the laws and statutes of
the realm of Great Britain, nor to the laws of the province of

New Jersey; provided, that no person be debarred of any of the privileges of the said college on account of any speculative principles of religion; but those of every religious profession have equal privilege and advantage of education in the said college. And also by the said charter power, is given to the major part of any seven of the said trustees and their successors, by their president, or any other appointed by them, to give any such degrees as are given in any of the universities or colleges in the realm of Great Britain, to any such as they shall judge qualified for such degrees; and power to have and use a common seal to seal and confirm diplomas or certificates of such degrees, or for any other use which they shall think proper."[1]

In 1647 Jonathan Belcher was appointed royal governor of New Jersey. During the ten years of his administration he took great interest in the College of New Jersey. On March 21, 1747, he writes to Aaron Burr, one of the trustees: "You cannot be more thoughtful and solicitous for the growth and prosperity of my adopted daughter, our future Alma Mater, than I am."[2] On May 12, 1748, the Governor encloses the draft of a new charter for the College to James Logan of Philadelphia for his approval, with a request that he serve as the head of the trustees, being as he is "in the first class of learning of the English America."[3] The charter in question passed under the great seal of the province on October 22, 1746.

CHARTER OF THE COLLEGE OF NEW JERSEY

" George the Second, by the grace of God, of Great Britain, France and Ireland, king, defender of the faith, &c., to all to whom these presents shall come, greeting—

" Whereas sundry of our loving subjects, well-disposed and

---

[1] *Pennsylvania Gazette*, August 13, 1747, given in *Princeton College Bulletin*, pp. 1–2. February, 1891.

[2] *Archives of the State of New Jersey*, First Series, VII. 115–6. Edited by W. A. Whitehead, Newark, 1883.

[3] *Ibid.*, VII, 124–5.

public-spirited persons, have lately, by their humble petition, presented to our trusty and well-beloved Johnathan Belcher, Esquire, Governor and Commander in chief of our province of New Jersey in America, represented the great necessity of coming into some method for the encouraging and promoting a learned education of our youth in New Jersey, and have expressed their earnest desire that a college may be erected in our said province of New Jersey in America, for the benefit of the inhabitants of the said province and others, wherein youth may be instructed in the learned languages, and in the liberal arts and sciences. And whereas by the fundamental concessions made at the first settlement of New Jersey by the Lord Berkley and Sir George Carteret, then proprietors thereof, and granted under their hands and the seal of the said province, bearing date the tenth day of February, in the year of our Lord one thousand six hundred and sixty-four, it was, among other things, conceded and agreed, that no freeman within the said province of New Jersey should at any time be molested, punished, disquieted or called in question, for any difference in opinion or practice in matters of religious concernment, who do not actually disturb the civil peace of the said province; but that all and every such person or persons might, from time to time, and at all times thereafter, freely and fully have and enjoy his and their judgments and consciences, in matters of religion, throughout the said province, they behaving themselves peaceably and quietly and not using this liberty to licentiousness, nor to the civil injury or outward disturbance of others, as by the said concessions on record in the secretary's office of New Jersey, at Perth Amboy, in lib. 3, folio 66, &c., may appear. Wherefore and for that the said petitioners have also expressed their earnest desire that those of every religious denomination may have free and equal liberty and advantages of education in the said college, any different sentiments in religion notwithstanding We being willing to grant the reasonable requests and prayers of all our loving subjects, and to

promote a liberal and learned education among them—Know
ye therefore, that we, considering the premises, and being
willing for the future that the best means of education be established in our said province of New Jersey, for the benefit and
advantage of the inhabitants of our said province and others, do,
of our special grace, certain knowledge and mere motion, by
these presents, will, ordain, grant and constitute, that there be
a college erected in our said province of New Jersey, for the
education of youth in the learned languages and in the liberal
arts and sciences; and that the trustees of the said college and
their successors forever, may and shall be one body corporate
and politic, in deed, action and name, and shall be called, and
named and distinguished, by the name of the Trustees of the
College of New Jersey—and further, we have willed, given,
granted, constituted and appointed, and by this our present
charter, of our special grace, certain knowledge and mere
motion, we do, for us, our heirs and successors, will, give,
grant, constitute and ordain, that there shall, in the said college
from henceforth forever, be a body politic, consisting of trustees of the said College of New Jersey.   And for the more full
and perfect erection of the said corporation and body politic,
consisting of trustees of the College of New Jersey, we, of our
special grace, certain knowledge and mere motion, do, by these
presents, for us, our heirs and successors, create, make, ordain,
constitute, nominate and appoint, the Governor and Commander-in-Chief of our said Province of New Jersey, for the
time being, and also our trusty and well-beloved John Reading, James Hude, Andrew Johnston, Thomas Leonard, John
Kinsey, Edward Shippen and William Smith, Esquires, Peter
Van Brugh Livingston, William Peartree Smith and Samuel
Hazard, gentlemen, John Pierson, Ebenezer Pemberton, Joseph
Lamb, Gilbert Tennent, William Tennant, Richard Treat,
Samuel Blair, David Cowell, Aaron Burr, Timothy Johnes,
Thomas Arthur and Jacob Green, ministers of the gospel, to be
trustees of the said College of New Jersey.   That the said trus-

tees do, at their first meeting, after the receipt of these presents, and before they proceed to any business, take the oath appointed to be taken by an Act, passed in the first year of the reign of the late King George the First, entitled "An Act for the further security of his Majesty's person and government, and the succession of the crown in the heirs of the late Princess Sophia, being Protestants, and for extinguishing the hopes of the pretended Prince of Wales and his open and secret abbetors;" as also they make and subscribe the declarations mentioned in an act of parliment, made in the twenty-fifth year of the reign of King Charles the Second, entitled "An Act for preventing dangers which may happen from popish recusants;" and likewise take an oath for faithfully executing the office or trust reposed in them, the said oaths to be administered to them by three of his Majesty's justices of the peace, *quorum unus;* and when any new member or officer of this corporation is chosen, they are to take and subscribe the aforementioned oaths and declarations before their admission into their trusts or offices, the same as to be administered to them in the presence of the trustees, by such persons as they shall appoint for that service. That no meeting of the trustees shall be valid or legal for doing any buisness whatsoever, unless the clerk has duly and legally notified each and every member of the corporation of such meeting; and that before the entering on any business, the clerk shall certify such notification under his hand, to the board of trustees. That the said trustees have full power and authority or any thirteen or greater number of them, to elect, nominate and appoint, and associate unto them any number of persons as trustees upon any vacancy, so that the whole number of trustees exceed not twenty-three, whereof the president of said college for the time being, to be chosen as hereafter mentioned, to be one, and twelve of the said trustees to be always such persons as are inhabitants of our said province of New Jersey. And we do further, of our special grace, certain knowledge, and mere

motion, for us, our heirs and successors, will, give, grant and
appoint, that the said trustees and their successors shall, for
ever hereafter, be in deed, fact and name a body corporate and
politic; and that they, the said body corporate and politic, shall
be known and distinguished in all deeds, grants, bargains, sales,
writings, evidence, muniments or otherwise howsoever, and in
all courts forever hereafter, plead and be impleaded, by the name
of the Trustees of the College of New Jersey. And that they
the said corporation, by the name aforesaid, shall be able and
in law capable, for the use of the said college, to have, get, acquire, purchase, receive and possess lands, tenements, hereradita-
ments, jurisdictions and franchises, for themselves and their
successors, in fee simple or otherwise howsoever; and to purchase, receive or build, any house or houses, or any other
buildings as they shall think needful or convenient for the use
of the said college of New Jersey, and in such place or places
in New Jersey, as they the said trustees shall agree upon, and
also to receive and dispose of any goods, chattels, and other
things of what nature soever, for the use aforesaid; and also to
have, accept and receive any rents, profits, annuities, gifts, legacies, donations and bequests of any kind whatsoever, for the use
aforesaid, so, nevertheless, that the yearly clear value of the premises do not exceed the sum of two thousand pounds sterling:
And therewith or otherwise to support and pay, as the said trustees and their successors, or the major part of such of them as
(according to the provision herein afterwards) are regularly convened for that purpose, shall agree and see cause, the president,
tutors and other officers or ministers of the said college, their
respective annual salaries or allowances, and all such other
necessary and contingent charges as from time to time shall
arise and acrue, relating to the said college; and also to grant,
bargain, sell, let, set or assign, lands, tenements or hereditaments, goods or chattels, contract or do all other things whatsoever, by the name aforesaid, and for the use aforesaid, in as
full and ample manner, to all intent and purposes, as any nat-

ural persons, or other body politic or corporate is able to do, by the laws of our realm of Great Britain, or of our said province of New Jersey. And of our further grace, certain knowledge and mere motion, to the intent that our said corporation and body politic may answer the end of their erection and constitution, and may have perpetual succession and continue forever, we do for us, our heirs and successors, hereby will, give and grant, unto the said trustees of the College of New Jersey, and to their successors forever, that when any thirteen of the said trustees or of their successors are convened and met together as aforesaid, for the service of the said college, the Governor and Commander in chief of our said province of New Jersey, and in his absence, the president of the said college, and in the absence of the said Governor and president, the eldest trustee present at such meeting, from time to time, shall be president of the said trustees in all their meetings : and at any time or times such thirteen trustees convened and met as aforesaid, shall be capable to act as fully and amply, to all intents and purpose, as if all the trustees of the said college were personally present ; provided always, that a majority of the said thirteen trustees be of the said province of New Jersey, except after regular notice they fail of coming, in which case those that are present are hereby empowered to act, the different place of their abode notwithstanding ; and all affairs, and actions whatsoever, under the care of the said trustees, shall be determined by the majority or greater number of those thirteen, so convened and met together, the president whereof shall have no more than a single vote. And we do for us, our heirs and successors, hereby will, give and grant full power and authority, to any six or more of the said trustees, to call meetings of the said trustees, and to order notice to the said trustees of the times and places of meeting for the service aforesaid. And also we do hereby for us, and our heirs and successors, will, give and grant, to the said trustees of the College of New Jersey, and to their successors forever, that the said trustees do elect, nominate and appoint such a qualified person as they, or the major part of any thirteen of them convened for that purpose as above directed, shall think fit, to be the president of the said college, and to have the immediate care of the education and government of such students as shall be sent to, and admitted into the said college for instruction and education; and also that the said trustees do elect, nominate and appoint so many tutors and professors, to assist the president of the said college, in the education and government of the students belonging to it, as they, the said trustees, or their successors, or the major part of any thirteen of them, which shall convene for that purpose as above directed, shall, from time to time, and at any time hereafter, think needful and serviceable to the interests of the said college; and also, that the said trustees, and their successors, or the major part of any thirteen of them, which shall convene for that purpose, as above directed, shall at any time displace and discharge from the service of the said college such president, tutors and professors, and to elect others in their room and stead ; and also that the said trustees, or the successors, or the major part of any thirteen of them, which shall convene for that purpose, as above directed, do from time to time, as occasion shall require, elect, constitute and appoint a treasurer, a clerk, an usher, and a steward for the said college, and appoint to them, and each of them, their respective business and trusts, and displace and discharge from the service of the said college such treasurer, clerk, usher or steward, and to elect others in their room and stead; which president, tutors, professors, treasurer, clerk, usher and steward so elected and appointed, we do for us, our heirs and successors, by these presents, constitute and establish in their several offices, and do give them, and every of them, full power and authority to exercise the same in the said College of New Jersey, according to the direction, and during the pleasure of the said trustees, as fully and freely as any other, the like officers in our universities or any of our colleges, in our realm of Great Britain, lawfully may and ought to do.

And also that the said trustees, and their successors, or the
major part of any thirteen of them, which shall convene for that
purpose as above directed, as often as one or more of the said
trustees shall happen to die, or by removal or otherwise shall
become unfit or incapable, according to their judgment, to
serve the interest of the said college, do, as soon as conveniently may be, after the death, removal or such unfitness or incapacity of such trustee or trustees to serve the interest of the
said college, elect and appoint such other trustee or trustees
as shall supply the place of him or them so dying, or otherwise becoming unfit or incapable to serve the interest of the
said college; and every trustee so elected and appointed shall
by virtue of these presents, and of such election, and appointment, be vested with all the power and privileges which any of
the other trustees of the said college are hereby invested with.
And we do further, of our special grace, certain knowledge and
mere motion, will, give and grant, and by these presents do for
us, our heirs and successors, will, give and grant, unto the said
trustees of the College of New Jersey, that they and their successors, or the major part of any thirteen of them, which shall
convene for that purpose as above directed, may make, and
they are hereby fully empowered from time to time, freely
and lawfully to make and establish such ordinances, orders
and laws as may tend to the good and wholesome government
of the said college, and all the students and the several
officers and ministers thereof, and to the public benefit of the
same, not repugnant to the laws and statutes of our realm of
Great Britain, or of this our province of New Jersey, and
not excluding any person of any religious denomination
whatsoever from free and equal liberty and advantage of education, or from any of the liberties, privileges, or immunities
of the said college, on account of his or their being of a religious profession different from the said trustees of the said college; and such ordinances, orders and laws, which shall be so
as aforesaid made, we do, by these presents, for us, our heirs

and successors, ratify, allow of and confirm, as good and effec-
ual, to oblige and bind all the said students and the several
officers and ministers of the said college; and we do hereby
authorize and empower the said trustees of the college, and
the president, tutors and professors by them elected and appointed, to put such ordinances and laws in execution, to all
proper intents and purpose. And we do further, of our
especial grace, certain knowledge and mere motion, will, give
and grant, unto the said trustees of the College of New Jersey, that, for the encouragement of learning and animating the
students of the said college to diligence, industry and a laudable progress in literature, that they and their successors, or
the major part of any thirteen of them, convened for that purpose as above directed, do, by the president of the said college
for the time being, or by any other deputed by them, give and
grant any such degree and degrees to any of the students of
the said college, or to any others by them thought worthy
thereof, as are usually granted in either of our universities or
any other college in our realm of Great Britain; and that they
do sign and seal diplomas or certificates of such graduations,
to be kept by the graduates as perpetual memorials or testimonials thereof. And further, of our especial grace, certain
knowledge and mere motion, we do, by these presents, for us,
our heirs and successors, give and grant unto the said trustees
of the College of New Jersey and to their successors, that they
and their successors shall have a common seal, under which
they may pass all diplomas, certificates of degrees, and all
other the affairs and business of and concerning the said corporation, or of and concerning the said College of New Jersey,
which shall be engraven in such form and with such inscription as shall be devised by the said trustees of the said college,
or the major part of any thirteen of them, convened for the
service of the said college as above directed. And we do
further, for us, our heirs and successors, give and grant unto
the said trustees of the College of New Jersey and their suc-

cessors, or the major part of any thirteen of them, convened
for the service of the college as above directed, full power and
authority from time to time, to nominate and appoint all other
inferior officers and ministers, which they shall think to be
convenient and necessary for the use of the college, not herein
particularly named or mentioned, and which are accustomary
in our universities, or in any of our colleges in our realm of
Great Britain, which officers or ministers we do hereby empower
to execute their offices or trusts as fully and freely as any other
the like officers or ministers, in and of our universities or any
other college in our realm of Great Britain, lawfully may or
ought to do. And lastly, our express will and pleasure is,
and we do by these presents for us, our heirs and successors,
give and grant unto the said trustees of the College of
New Jersey and to their successors forever, that these our
letters patent, or the enrolment thereof, shall be good and
effectual in the law, to all intents and purposes, against us,
our heirs and successors, without any other license, grant or
confirmation from us, our heirs and successors, hereafter by
the said trustees to be had or obtained; notwithstanding the
not reciting or misrecital, or not naming or misnaming of the
aforesaid offices, franchises, privileges, immunities, or other the
premises, or any of them ; and notwithstanding a writ of *ad
quod damnum* hath not issued forth to inquire of the premises
or any of them, before the ensealing hereof; any statute, act,
ordinance or provision, or any other matter or thing to the contrary notwithstanding; to have, hold and enjoy, all and singular the privileges, advantages, liberties, immunities and all
other the premises herein and hereby granted and given, or
which are meant, mentioned or intended to be herein and
hereby given and granted, unto them the said trustees of the
said College of New Jersey, and to their successors forever.

" In testimony whereof we have caused these our letters to
be made patent, and the great seal of our said Province of
New Jersey to be hereunto affixed. Witness our trusty and

well-beloved Jonathan Belcher, Esquire, Governor and Commander in-Chief of our said Province of New Jersey, this fourteenth day of September, in the twenty-second year of our reign, and in the year of our Lord, one thousand seven hundred and forty-eight.

"I have perused and considered the written charter of incorporation, and find nothing contained therein inconsistent with his Majesty's interest or the honor of the Crown.

J. WARRELL, Att. Gen'l.

"September the 13th, 1748, this charter, having been read in Council, was consented to and approved of.

CHA. READ, Cl. Con.

"Let the great seal of the Province of New Jersey be affixed to this charter.

J. BELCHER.

"To the Secretary of the Province of New Jersey."[1]

The representation of the provincial government in the college corporation in the person of the Governor of New Jersey for the time being, seems to have met with opposition on the part of the founders of the College. In a letter to one of them, dated April 2, 1748, the Governor writes: "As to the matter of the president of the trustees, I think Mr. Burr was convinced with what I said, that it would be best to be always the King's Governor for the time being, which may be of service on many accounts. He is to be confined to a single vote, nor is he to call or adjourn a meeting but in conformity to the constitution. It is now 30 years since my first being one of the trustees of Harvard College[2] by virtue of my being a member of his Majesty's Council for the Massachusetts Bay, and I could never observe any inconveniency in that part of that charter. However I will consider and talk further with

---

[1] Given in the *History of the College of New Jersey*, I, 90–7. John Maclean, Philadelphia, 1877.

[2] Governor Belcher was graduated from Harvard College in 1699.

some of the Trustees on this article, and will give what dispatch I can to the charter."[1]

Four members of the Council of New Jersey were appointed by the charter to the Board of Trustees. They were nominated, however, as individuals, not as ex-officio members. According to Governor Belcher, the Assembly was ill disposed towards the College of New Jersey. He writes on June 27, 1748 :

" I am at present much discouraged about a college, not seeing where money will be found to build the house and to support the necessary officers; for the Assembly (many of them Quakers) will do nothing towards it, so that if carried into execution it must be by subscriptions—which I will encourage and do all in my power that so noble a design may not miscarry."[2]

He writes again in 1750: " When I consider the poverty of this little province where are very few people of fortunes, and great numbers of Quakers among us, who you know are enemies to what they call human learning and to orthodoxy in religion, and this sect has so much influence in the legislature that I almost despair of any help there towards the building and support of our college. We must therefore hope for and beg the benevolence and generosity of such well disposed Christians as may be induced to assist in this difficult under-taking, and may God speed the plough."[3]

Colonel Alford, of Boston, to whom the above plea was ad-

---

[1] *New Jersey Archives*, VII, 118. See also Maclean's *History of the College of New Jersey*, I, 87–89.

[2] *Ibid.*, VII, 146. In this same letter, which was addressed to a land company, known as the West New Jersey Society, the Governor remarks : " You very justly observe that the building of a college and putting forward inferior schools in the Province of New Jersey will promote trade, increase the inhabitants, make them see the advantage and beauty of government, and all these things must add considerable value to your estate in the rise of lands."

[3] *Ibid.*, VII, 579–80.

dressed, seems to have responded, for two years later Governor Belcher thanks him in the name of the trustees for his " kind and generous subscription for the encouragement and better establishment of this seminary put forward . . . for promoting the honor and interest of the kingdom of the blessed Jesus, as well as for giving an opportunity to the inhabitants of this and the neighboring provinces to improve themselves in religion and human literature." [1]

The Governor had already privately written to this gentleman : " I thank God and thank you for the generous and noble example you have set at the head of a subscription in favor of our poor college, which crawls along but very slowly. If we can by the favor of heaven get wherewith to build a proper house, and to support the president and two tutors, I am well satisfied this seminary would be a great blessing to these parts of America and in time would be more probable to furnish missionaries to the heathen nations than any other of our colleges." [2]

The Governor also proposed that an agent should be sent to England to solicit subscriptions, and on October 2, 1751, he suggested to President Burr to follow the example of Dr. Increase Mather on a similar occasion in behalf of Harvard College. The Governor adds : " Pillow this matter, and let me have your answer by the return of the post, and if you approve it, we must immediately send circular letters for a speedy meeting of the trustees, for there must not be a day lost. This great affair hangs heavy upon me." [3]

Funds for the College were eventually obtained, and in 1755 a building was erected at Princeton, which the trustees proposed to name " Belcher Hall " in honor of Governor Belcher.

---

[1] *Ibid.*, VIII, 109.　　　　　　　　[2] *Ibid.*, VIII, 10.

[3] *Ibid.*, VII, 618-9. President Burr was unable to go to England, but agents were sent over in 1753. They carried with them a petition for aid for the College from the Synod of New York to the General Assembly of the Church of Scotland. Their mission was highly successful. (Maclean's *History*, I, 149–152.)

But at the Governor's suggestion it was instead christened Nassau Hall in tribute to King William the Third.[1]

Governor Belcher died in 1757, and Francis Bernard succeeded him as royal governor. Among the royal instructions to Governor Bernard were the following : " Sect. 65. We do further direct that no schoolmaster be henceforth permitted to come from England and to keep school in the said province without the license of the said bishop of London, and that no other person now there or that shall come from other parts, shall be admitted to keep school in that our said province of New Jersey, without your license first obtained. . . .

"Sect. 67. . . . And it is our further will and pleasure that you recommend to the Assembly to enter upon proper methods for the erecting and maintaining of schools in order to the training up of youth to reading and to a necessary knowledge of the principles of religion."[2] . . .

The Assemblies of 1761 and '62, passed two lottery Acts in the interest of education, in 1761, " an Act to empower the church wardens and vestrymen of St. Peters Church, in the city of Perth Amboy, to raise by lottery a sum of money for repairing the church, parsonage, school house and ferry house in said city,"[3] and in 1762, " an Act to empower the trustees of the College of New Jersey to raise by a lottery,[4] a sum of money for the use of said college."[5] . . .

In 1763, William Franklin was appointed Governor and he

---

[1] *Ibid.*, I, 147.

[2] *N. J. Archives*, First Series, IX, 68, 69.

[3] *Acts of the General Assembly of the Province of New Jersey*, ch. 348, p. 245. Samuel Allinson, Burlington, 1776. This act was limited to one year.

[4] In 1749 the Board of Trustees had petitioned the Assembly for a lottery for the benefit of the College, and had been refused. Subsequently a lottery was set up for that purpose in Philadelphia, and in 1753-4 the General Court of Connecticut granted a license for a lottery to the trustees of the College of New Jersey. (See Maclean's *History*, I, 136-7.

[5] Allinson, ch. 364, p. 252.

continued in office until the Revolution. On February 21, 1769, he laid before his Council a draft of a charter for incorporating "The Trustees of the free schools of the Town of Woodbridge" which had been presented to him for his approbation.[1] It was referred for futher consideration and in the following May, "the Board resumed the consideration of the charter of "The Trustees of the free schools of the town of Woodbridge" which being again read paragraph by paragraph and some amendments made therein, the Council advised his Excellency to cause the great seal to be affixed thereto.[2]

Between 1730 and 1740 the Reformed Dutch Church in America became divided on a question of the ordination of clergymen. The party of the Coetus, in opposition to the party of the Conferentia, desired a separate ecclesiastical organization from that of the Classis of Amsterdam with an independent power of ordination. A provincial seminary of the Dutch Reformed persuasion was essential to this purpose; consequently after several vain petitions to the Governor of New Jersey for a charter for such an institution,[3] the ministers of the Coetus finally obtained a charter from the government and, in 1770, Queens College was founded.

CHARTER[4] OF QUEEN'S COLLEGE[5]

"George the third, by the grace of God, of Great Britain, France and Ireland, King, Defender of the Faith, &c. To all to whom these presents shall come greeting;

"Whereas our loving subjects being of the Protestant Re-

---

[1] *N. J. Archives*, First Series, XVIII. 1.   [2] *Ibid*, XVIII, 6.

[3] See the Historical Discourse delivered by the Hon. Joseph P. Bradley at the Centennial celebration of Rutgers' College, 1870, pp. 76–7.

[4] The original charter was granted on November 10, 1766, but it was found unsatisfactory, and the following charter was therefore obtained. See *The Charter of Queen's College in New Jersey, with Appendix*, printed for the Trustees at New Brunswick.

[5] Renamed Rutgers College in 1825.

formed religion, according to the constitution of the reformed churches in the United Provinces, and using the discipline of the said churches, as approved and instituted by the national Synod of Dort in the years one thousand six hundred and eighteen, and one thousand six hundred and nineteen, are in this and the neighbouring provinces very numerous, consisting of many churches and religious assemblies, the ministers and elders of which having taken into serious consideration the manner in which the said churches might be properly supplied with an able, learned and well-qualified ministry; and thinking it necessary, and being very desirous that a college might be erected for that purpose within this our Province of New Jersey, in which the learned languages and other branches of useful knowledge may be taught, and degrees conferred; and especially that young men of suitable abilities may be instructed in divinity, preparing them for the ministry, and supplying the necessity of the churches; for themselves and in behalf of their churches, presented a petition to our trusty and well-beloved WILLIAM FRANKLIN, ESQ., Governour and Commander-in-Chief, in and over our Province of New Jersey in America, setting forth that inconveniences are manifold and the expenses heavy, in either being supplied with ministers of the gospel from foreign parts, or sending young men abroad for education; that the present and increasing necessity for a considerable number to be employed in the ministry is great; that a preservation of a fund for the necessary uses of instruction very much depends upon a charter; and therefore humbly entreat, that some persons might be incorporated in a body politic, for the purposes aforesaid:

" And we being willing to grant the reasonable request and prayer of the said petitioners, and to promote learning for the benefit of the community and advancement of the Protestant religion of all denominations; and more especially to remove as much as possible the necessity our said loving subjects have hitherto been under, of sending their youth intended for the

ministry, to a foreign country for education, and of being sub-
ordinate to a foreign ecclesiastical jurisdiction:

"Know ye therefore, that considering the premises, we do of
our special grace, certain knowledge and mere motion, by these
presents, will, ordain, grant and constitute, that there be a
college, called *Queen's College*, erected in our said Province
of New Jersey, for the education of youth in the learned languages, liberal and useful arts and sciences, and especially in
divinity preparing them for the ministry and other good
offices: And that the trustees of the said college and their
successors for ever, may and shall be one body corporate and
politic, in deed, fact and name, and shall be called, known and
distinguished by the name of the *Trustees of Queen's College,
in New Jersey:* And we having further willed and constituted,
and by these presents of our special grace, certain knowledge
and mere motion, do for us, our heirs and successors, will, give,
grant, constitute and ordain, that there shall be from henceforth for ever a body politic consisting of the Trustees of the
said Queen's College, in New Jersey.

"And for the more full and more perfect erection of the said
corporation and body politic consisting of the Trustees of
Queen's College, in New Jersey; We do of our special grace,
certain knowledge and mere motion, by these presents, for us,
our heirs and successors, create, ordain, constitute, nominate
and appoint, the Governor or Commander in chief, the President of the Council, our Chief Justice, and our Attorney
General of said Colony, for the time being; Sir William Johnson, Baronet, and Johannes Henricus Goetschius, Johannes
Leydt, David Maurinus, Martinus Van Harlingen, Jacob R.
Hardenbergh, and William Jackson of our said Colony of
New-Jersey, Samuel Verbryk, Barent Vrooman, Maurice
Goetschius, Eilardus Westerlo, John Schuneman, of our Pro-
vince of New-York; and Philip Wyberg, and Jonathan Dubois
of the Province of Pennsylvania; Hendrick Fisher, Peter
Zabriskie, Peter Hasenclever, Peter Schenck, Tunis Dey,

Philip French, John Covenhoven, Henricus Kuyper, of our Colony of New-Jersey, Esqrs., and Simon Johnson, Philip Livingston, Johannes Hardenbergh, Abraham Hasbrouck, Theodorus Van Wyck, Abraham Lott, Robert Livingston, Levi Pauling, John Brinckerhoff, Nicholas Stillwill, Martinus Hoffman, Jacob H. Ten Eyck, John Haring, Isaac Vrooman, Barnardus Ryder, of our Province of New-York, Esqrs., Trustees of our said Queen's College, in New Jersey.

"And that the said trustees do at their first meeting, after the receipt of these presents and before they proceed to any business, take the oaths appointed to be taken by an act passed in the sixth year of our reign, entitled, " An Act for altering the " oaths of abjuration and assurance, and for amending so much " of an Act of the seventh year of her late majesty Queen Anne, " entitled, for the improvement of the union of the two king- " doms, as after the time therein limited, requires the delivery " of certain lists and copies therein mentioned to persons in- " dicted of high treason, or misprision of treason : as also that " they make and subscribe the declaration mentioned in an Act " of parliament, made in the twenty-fifth year of the reign of King Charles the second, entitled," An Act for preventing dangers which may happen from Popish recusants, and like- wise take an oath for faithfully executing the office or trust reposed in them, which said oaths shall be administered to them by any one of our justices of the supreme court, or judges of the inferior court of common pleas of this our Colony of New- Jersey ; and when, and as often as any new member or officer shall be elected or chosen hereafter pursuant to this our charter, he or they so elected or chosen shall take and subscribe the aforementioned oaths and declarations in the manner above directed, before his admission into his trust or office.

"And we do will and direct, that the first meeting of the said trustees shall be at or near the Court House in New Barba- does, in the County of Bergen, on the second Tuesday in May next, but all other meetings hereafter to be held, shall be at such times and places in our said colony, as the majority of the trustees from time to time shall think proper. And we do will and direct that no meeting of the trustees, succeeding the first already fixed, shall be valid, or legal, for doing any business whatsoever, unless public notice of such meeting shall have been given in the Gazette, or other public papers printed in New-York, at least three weeks before the day of meeting, signed by the president or person officiating as clerk to the trustees, for the time being; or unless the time and place shall be fixed by the majority of the trustees, at their last meeting, and notice thereof given as before directed.

" And we further will and grant that the said trustees, or any twelve, or greater number shall have full power and authority to elect by ballot, and not otherwise, any number of persons or trustees, at any, and upon any vacancy, so that the whole number of trustees do not exceed forty-one, and that not above one-third of the said number, at any time, be of those ordained ministers of the gospel; and that at their first and every meeting, the Governour of our Colony for the time being, shall be president of the trustees, and in his absence, the President of our Council, and in his absence, our Chief Justice, and in his absence, our Attorney General, each for the time being; and in case of their absence, we will, and order that the trustees present, shall elect and choose one from among themselves, who shall be president of the trustees at that meeting; which said president, hereinbefore appointed, or so chosen, is hereby authorised and empowered to be president of the trustees at the said meeting; to regulate their proceedings, take in suffrages, and have, over and above his vote as a trustee, a casting vote, when the votes of the trustees are equal.

" And we further of our special grace, certain knowledge, and mere motion, for us, our heirs and successors, will, give, grant, and appoint, that the said trustees and their successors shall forever hereafter, be in deed, fact, and name, a body corporate and politic, and that they the said body corporate and politic, shall be known and distinguished in all deeds, grants, bargains, sales, writings, evidences, moniments, or otherwise however, and in all courts for ever hereafter, shall and may sue, and be sued, plead and be empleaded, by the name of the *Trustees of Queen's College in New-Jersey;* and that the said corporation by the name aforesaid, shall be able, and in law capable, for the use of the said college, to have, get, acquire, purchase, receive and possess, lands, tenements, hereditaments, jurisdictions and franchises, for themselves and their successors, in fee simple or otherwise howsoever; and to purchase, receive, or build any house, or houses, or any other buildings as they shall think needful and convenient, for the use of the said Queen's College and in such place or places in this our Colony of New-Jersey, as they the said trustees, or the major part of them, met as aforesaid, shall agree upon; and also to receive any goods and chattels, lands or tenements, for the use aforesaid; and also to have, accept and receive, any rents, profits, annuities, gifts, legacies, donations and bequests of any kind whatsoever, for the use aforesaid: Nevertheless that the yearly clear value of the premises, do not exceed the sum of three thousand pounds sterling; and therewith or otherwise to support and pay (as the said trustees and their successors, or the major part of them which regularly convene for that purpose shall agree and see cause) the president, professors, tutors, and other officers or ministers of the said Queen's College, their respective annual salaries or allowances, and all such other necessary and contingent charges, as from time to time shall arise and accrue relating to the said Queen's College. And also to grant, bargain, sell, let or assign, lands, tenements, hereditaments, goods or chattels, and contract, or do all other things whatsoever by the name aforesaid, and for the use aforesaid, in as full and ample manner to all intents and purposes, as any natural person, or any other body politic or corporation, is able to do by the laws of our realm of Great Britain, or of our said Province of New-Jersey.

"And of our further grace, certain knowledge, and mere motion, to the intent that our said corporation and body politic, may answer the end of their erection and constitution, and may have perpetual succession, and continuance forever, We do for us, our heirs and successors, hereby will, give and grant, unto the said trustees of Queen's College in New-Jersey, and to their successors forever, that when any twelve of the said trustees for the time being, are convened and met together as aforesaid for the service of the said college, they shall be capable to act as fully and amply to all intents and purposes, as if all the trustees of the said college were personally present; and all matters whatsoever, under the care of the trustees, shall be determined by the majority of those twelve, or any greater number so convened and met together, as fully and effectually as if the same had been concluded by the plurality of votes of the whole number of trustees, met and assembled. And we do hereby give and grant full power and authority to any five or more of the said trustees, to call meetings of the said trustees from time to time, and to order notice to be given to the said trustees, of the time and places of meetings for the service aforesaid, as hereinbefore is directed.

"And also, we do hereby for us, our heirs and successors, will, give and grant unto the Trustees of Queen's College, in New-Jersey, and their successors forever, that the said trustees, from time to time, and forever hereafter, do elect, nominate and appoint such a qualified person, being a member of the Dutch Reformed Church aforesaid, as they or the major part of any twelve of them, convened for that purpose, as above directed, shall think fit, to be the president of the said college; and to have the immediate care of the education and government of such students as shall be sent and admitted into the said college for education and instruction; and shall and may, by and with the consent of the majority of the said trustees as aforesaid, confer all such honorary degrees as usually are granted and conferred in any of our colleges in any of our colonies in America; and also, that the said trustees do elect, nominate and appoint a professor in divinity, who shall and may read lectures in theology, instruct the students in the science of divine truths and the knowledge of the holy scriptures, who also may be president of the college, or not, as the trustees shall see meet and convenient; and also such a number of other professors and tutors, to assist the president of the said college, in the education and government of the students belonging to it, as they the said trustees, or their successors, or the major part of them, which shall convene for that purpose, as above directed, shall from time to time, and at any time hereafter, think necessary for the advantage and well being of the said college.

"Provided always, and it is hereby declared and expressly enjoined, that there shall always be, residing at or near said college, at least one professor, or teacher well versed in the English language, elected, nominated, maintained and supported by the said corporation, from time to time, and at all times hereafter, grammatically to instruct the students of the said college in the knowledge of the English language. Provided also, that all minutes of the meetings, and transactions of the trustees, and all rules, orders and regulations, relating to the government of the said college, and all accounts relating to the receipts, and payments of money, shall be in the English language, and no other.

"And we do hereby further give and grant to the said trustees, and their successors, or the major part of any twelve of them convened for that purpose, as above directed, full power and authority, at any time to displace and discharge from the service of the said Queen's College, such president, professor of divinity, professors and tutors, and to elect others in their room and stead; and also that the said trustees, or their successors as above directed, do, from time to time as occasion shall require, elect, constitute, and appoint a treasurer, (which treasurer shall give security to the trustees for the faithful performance of his office, for such sum and in such manner as

the said trustees shall see fit to require,) a clerk, and steward
for the said college, and shall likewise appoint to them, and
each of them, their respective business and trusts, and displace
and discharge from the service of said college, said treasurer,
clerk, or steward, and elect others in their room and stead ;
which president, professor of divinity, tutors, professors,
treasurer, clerk, and steward, so elected and appointed, We do
for us, our heirs, and successors, by these presents, constitute
and establish in their several offices, and do give them and
every of them, full power and authority, to exercise the same
in the said Queen's College, in New-Jersey, according to the
direction, and during the pleasure of the said trustees, as
fully and freely as any other the like officers in any of our
colleges in our realm of Great Britain, lawfully may or ought
to do.

"And also, that the said trustees, and their successors in the
manner above directed, as often as the place of any one or
more of the said trustees shall become vacant by the death,
removal or immoral conduct of any one of the members (which
conduct shall be determined by the trustees, or the majority of
them,) shall and may elect and appoint, in the manner before
directed, such other trustee, or trustees, to supply the place of
him or them so dying, or otherwise becoming unfit or incapable to serve the said college ; and every trustee so elected
and appointed, shall by virtue of these presents, and of such
election and appointment, be vested with all the powers and
privileges which any of the other trustees of the said college
are hereby invested with.

"And we do further of our special grace, certain knowledge,
and mere motion, will, give and grant, and by these presents,
for us, our heirs and successors, do give and grant unto the
said Trustees of the said Queen's College, in New-Jersey, that
they and their successors, convened for that purpose, as above
directed, may make, and they are hereby fully empowered
from time to time, freely and fully to make and establish such

ordinances, orders and laws as may tend to the good, whole-some government of the said college, and all the students, and the several officers and ministers thereof, and to the public benefit of the same, not repugnant to the laws and statutes o our realm of Great Britain, or of this our province of New^f Jersey; and such ordinances, orders and laws, which shall be so made as aforesaid, we do by these presents, for us, our heirs and successors, ratify, allow and confirm, as good and effectual to oblige and bind all the said students, and several officers and ministers of the said Queen's College; and we do hereby authorize and empower the said trustees of the said college, and the president, professor of divinity, professors and tutors, by them elected and appointed, to put such laws and ordinances in execution, to all proper intents and purposes.

"And we do further by these presents, for us, our heirs and successors, of our special grace, certain knowledge and mere motion, give and grant, unto the said Trustees of Queen's Col-lege, in New-Jersey, and to their successors, that they shall have a common seal, under which they may pass diplomas and certificates of advancement in literature, and the science of theology, as aforesaid; and that the said trustees of said col-lege, by deed or deeds of conveyance, leases, or other legal instruments, duly executed, under the hands of seven of the trustees, at any public meeting, convened as hereinbefore directed, and with the seal of the corporation affixed thereto, may pass the estate of the said corporation, in lands or tene-ments, in fee, or for years, to any person or persons; and the same deeds or leases shall pass the estate thereby intended to be granted or leased, to all intents and purposes; and to notify all the necessary affairs and business of and concerning the said corporation, or of and concerning the said Queen's College in New-Jersey; which common seal shall be engraved in such form, and with such inscription as shall be devised by the said Trustees of the said College, or the majority convened as above directed; and shall have a book or books of entry, for the use of the trustees to be in such custody, with all other writings as they shall appoint.

"And we do further for us, our heirs and successors, give and grant unto the said Trustees of Queen's College, in New Jersey, and their successors, or any twelve of them, as above said, full power and authority from time to time, to nominate and appoint all other inferior officers and ministers, which they shall judge necessary for the use of the College, not herein particularly named or mentioned ; which officers, or ministers, we do hereby empower to execute their offices or trusts, as fully and freely as any other the like officers and ministers in any of our colleges, in our realm of Great Britain, lawfully may or ought to do.

"And lastly, our express will and pleasure is, and we do by these presents, for us, our heirs and successors, give and grant unto the Trustees of Queen's College, in New-Jersey, and their successors forever, that these, our letters patent, or the enrolment thereof, shall be good and effectual in law to all intents and purposes, against us, our heirs and successors, without any other license, grant or confirmation from us, our heirs, and successors, hereafter by the said trustees to be had and obtained. Notwithstanding the not reciting or misreciting, or not naming or misnaming of the aforesaid officers, franchises, privileges, immunities, or other the premises, or any of them, and notwithstanding a writ of *Ad Quod Damnum* hath not issued forth to enquire of the premises, or any of them before the ensealing hereof, any statute, act, ordinance, provision, or any other matter or thing, to the contrary, notwithstanding : To have, hold and enjoy, all and singular, the privileges, advantages, liberties, immunities, and all other the premises herein or hereby granted and given, or which are meant, mentioned, or intended to be herein and hereby granted, unto them, the said Trustees of the said Queen's College, in New Jersey, and to their successors forever.

" In testimony whereof, we have caused these our letters to be made patent, and the great seal of our said province of New-Jeraey to be hereunto affixed. Witness, our trusty and well beloved, WILLIAM FRANKLIN, Esquire, Governour and Commander in Chief of our said province of New-Jersey, this twentieth day of March, in the tenth year of our reign, *Anno Domini*, one thousand seven hundred and seventy."

VIRGINIA

The colonization of Virginia was initiated in 1607 by the London branch of the Virginia Company, a trading corporation which came to consist of a large number of shareholders, and an executive council appointed by the shareholders and presided over by the treasurer of the Company. A colonial council and then a colonial governor was appointed by this council in England, and in 1619 provision for a colonial Assembly was made.

On November 18, 1618, the following instructions were given by the Council to the Colonial Governor: " Whereas by a special grant and license from his Majesty, a general contribution over this realm hath been made[1] for the building and

---

[1] About the year 1616 the King ordered the bishops of England to collect money for the erection of a college in Virginia. In 1619 Treasurer Sandys reported that about £1,500 had been raised by the bishops and that more subscriptions were expected. (*History of the Virginia Company of London*, p. 147, Edward D. Neill, Albany, 1869.) A few months later, Sir Edwin Sandys reported that the total receipts for the college for that year were £2,043 2s. 11½d., the disbursements amounting to £1,477 15s. 5d. In itemizing these figures the Treasurer states that "two persons unknown have given fair plate and other rich ornaments for two communion tables, whereof one for the college. . . . Another unknown person (together with a goodly letter) [*Ibid.*, pp. 168–170] hath lately sent to the Treasurer £550 in gold for the bringing up of children of the infidels: first, in the knowledge of God and true religion; and next in fit trades whereby honestly to live. Mr. Nicholas Ferrar, deceased, hath by his will given £300 for the college in Virginia, to be paid when there shall be ten of the infidels' children placed in it." . . . (*Ibid.*, pp. 181–2.) The donor of the £550 wrote again to the Company in 1621, complaining that his gift had not been applied according to his intent, and promising to increase it by £450 if eight or ten of the Virginians' children should be brought to England and placed in Christ's Hospital, or in a new foundation to be called the Virginian School and Hospital; otherwise, he wished his original gift to be expended upon the erection of a free school in Southhampton

planting of a college for the training up of the children of those infidels in true religion, moral virtue and civility, and for other godliness, we do, therefore, according to a former grant and order,[1] hereby ratify, confirm and ordain that a

Hundred, where both English and Virginians might be taught together. (*Ibid*, pp. 287-9.) After this letter was read in Court, Sir Edwin Sandys gave a summary of the whole transaction. He stated that the Company had finally resolved to settle the £550 upon Southhampton Hundred, "to undertake for a certain number of infidel children to be brought up by them in Christian religion and some good trade to live by;" but that Southhampton Hundred offered to pay one hundred pounds to be excused from the undertaking; that at length, however, after being earnestly pressed by the Court, that Society had agreed to use the money, "together with an addition out of the Society's purse of a far greater sum, towards the furnishing out of Captain Bluet and his company, being ten able, very sufficient workmen, with all manner of provisions for setting up of an ironwork in Virginia," the profits to be appropriated to the education of 30 Indian children in religion; that the Society had written to Governor Yeardly, Governor of Virginia and Captain of Southhampton Hundred, to employ his best care and industry therein, as a work whereon the eyes of God, angels and men were fixed; that the work had been checked by the death of Captain Bluet soon after his arrival in the colony and by the unwillingness of the Indians, but that a fresh supply had been sent over, and it was hoped that the donor " would receive good satisfaction of that faithful account which they should be able, and at all times ready, to give touching the employment of the said money." The Treasurer also observed that he thought it would be futile, judging from Sir Thomas Dale's experience, to bring over Indian children to England, and that the cost would be too great to build a free school for them in Virginia. He urged that the unknown donor should meet with the Southhampton Hundred Society and resolve upon some constant course for the "perfecting of this most pious work, for which he prayed the blessing of God to be upon the author thereof. And all the Company said, 'Amen.'" (*Abstract of the Proceedings of the Virginia Company of London*, prepared from the records in the Library of Congress by Conway Robinson, I, 163-5 in the *Collections of the Virginia Historical Society*, New Series, VII, Richmond, 1888.)

[1] I have been unable to find any specific record of this "former grant and order." In a letter of complaint addressed by the Company to Deputy-Governor Argall on August 22, 1618, a reference seems to be made to this grant. The Company write : "As for the debts and wages which you say you have paid for, we marvel you do not send us a note of the particulars, . . . if there be any such matter, or that you have provided any stuff for the college as you writ, yet you must not imagine that we are so insensible of reason as to suffer either of those to be a cloak for you to detain our hides or to convey away all our cattle and corn." (*History of the Virginia Company*, p. 117.)

convenient place be chosen and set out for the planting of a university at the said Henrico in time to come, and that in the mean time, preparation be there made for the building of the said college for the children of the infidels according to such instructions as we shall deliver. And we will and ordain that ten thousand acres, partly of the lands they impaled and partly of the land within the territory of the said Henrico, be allotted and set out for the endowing of the said university and college with convenient possessions." [1]

On May 26, 1619, Sir Edwin Sandys, the recently elected Treasurer of the Company, moved that 50 persons should be sent out to develop this college grant, and that they should retain one-half of their profits and give over the other half " to go in getting forward the work and for maintenance of the tutors and scholars." And in the following month it was agreed by the Court that a ship should be sent out for this purpose not later than the middle of the following July. [2]

On June 14, 1619, " it was moved by Mr. Treasurer that the Court would take into consideration to appoint a committee of choice gentlemen and others of his Majesty's Council for Virginia concerning the college, being a weighty business, and so great that an account of their proceedings therein must be given to the State." [3] And the same was done.

In the spring of 1619, one hundred children were supplied by the City of London to be sent out by the Company to Virginia, and as a contribution to this purpose £500 were subscribed by " divers well and godly disposed persons, charitably minded towards the plantation in Virginia." On February 2, 1620, the Company agreed that all these children should be educated and brought up in some good trade or profession, so that they might gain their livelihood by the time they were 21 years old, or by the time they had served

---

[1] Manuscript instructions to Yeardley. *Va. Records*, small folio, in Library of Congress. Quoted by Neill in *History of the Virginia Company*, p. 137.

[2] *Ibid.*, pp. 146–9.　　　　[3] *Ibid.*, p. 150.

their seven years apprenticeship.[1] These apprentices were very welcome to the colonists,[2] and so the following year the Company requested the City to supply some more children, and because people at home could bind out their children as apprentices for 5 marks, the Company agreed to send them to Virginia on the same terms.[3]

In 1621 Sir Francis Wyatt was commissioned Governor of Virginia by the Company. Besides the new charter which he carried with him providing for an elective Assembly, he was given certain personal instructions. Among others, he was bidden " to use means to convert the heathen, viz., to converse with some; each town to teach some children fit for the college intended to be built . . . . to put prentices to trades, and not let them forsake their trades for planting, or any such useless commodity." [4]

In 1622, the overseer and some of the tenants who had been sent over by the Company to settle the college land were killed in the Indian massacre which occurred in that year. And although the Company wrote to the Governor and Council in Virginia that the replanting of the college lands and the other places which had been deserted was " of absolute necessity lest the best fire that maintains the action here alive be put out," and urged them to take the college affairs into their consideration " not only as a public, but as a sacred matter," [5] there is no record of there settling of the " college plantation."

About this time an abortive attempt was also made by the Company for the provision of elementary education in Virginia. On October 24, 1621, the Court was informed that one Dr. Copeland [6] had collected £70 from his fellow passengers on

---

[1] *Proceedings of the Va. Co.*, I, 40. [2] *Ibid.*, I, 24. [3] *Ibid.*, I, 96.

[4] *The Statutes-at-Large,* being a collection of all the laws of Virginia, I, 114, 115. Compiled by William Waller Hening, New York, 1823.

[5] *History of the Va. Co.*, pp. 328, 329.

[6] Dr. Copeland was afterwards r 'mitted as a Free Brother of the Company, and

board one of the ships of the East India Company, for the building of a church or school in Virginia. A committee was consequently appointed to manage this affair and they reported that having taken " into consideration whether a church or school was most necessary, and might nearest agree to the intentions of the donors, it was conceived that for as much as each particular plantation, as well as the general, either had or ought to have a church appropriated unto them, there was therefore a greater want of a school than of churches. As also for that it was impossible, with so small a proportion, to compass so great a charge as the building of a church would require, they therefore conceived it most fit to resolve for the erecting of a public free school, which, being for the education of children and grounding of them in the principles of religion, civility of life and humane learning seemed to carry with it the greatest weight and highest consequence unto the plantation as that whereof both church and commonwealth take their original foundation and happy estate, this being also like to prove a work most acceptable unto the planters, through want thereof they have been hitherto constrained to their great costs to send their children from thence hither to be taught . . . . It was also thought fit that in honor of the East Indy benefactors, the same should be called the East Indy School, who shall have precedence before any other to prefer their children thither to be brought up in the rudiments of learning. It was also thought fit that this, as a collegiate or free school, should have dependence upon the college in Virginia, which

presented with 300 acres of land in Virginia in recognition of his zeal for the good of the colony. (*Ibid.*, pp. 252, 256.) Shortly before the news of the Indian massacre reached England, Copeland was appointed rector of the college at Henrico (*Ibid.*, p. 251, foot-note), and was allowed one-tenth of the profits of the labor of the college tenants. He was also to have pastoral charge of these tenants, with the benefit of a parsonage house, and he was appointed on the Council in Virginia. (*Va. Hist. Coll.*, VII, 218; *Virginia Carolorum*, pp. 196–7, foot-note, E. D. Neill, Albany, 1886. See, also, *Proceedings of the Virginia Company*, I, 146–7 and foot-note, 152, 165–6.)

should be made capable to receive scholars from the school into such scholarships and fellowships of said college, shall be endowed withal for the advancement of scholars as they arise by degrees and deserts in learning. That for the better maintenance of the schoolmaster and usher intended there to be placed, it was thought fit that it should be moved at the next Quarter Court that 1000 acres of land should be allotted unto the said school, and that five persons, besides an overseer of them, should be forthwith sent upon this charge, in the condition of apprentices, to manure and cultivate the said land, and that, over and above this allowance of land and tenants unto the schoolmaster, such as send their children to this school should give some benevolence unto the schoolmaster, for the better increase of his maintenance. That it should be specially recommended to the Governor to take care that the planters there be stirred up to put their helping hands towards the speedy building of the said school, in respect their children are like to receive the greatest benefit there by in their education; and to let them know that those that exceed others in their bounty and assistance hereunto shall be privileged with the preferment of their children to the said school before others that shall be found less worthy[1] . . . . " On November 19th, this report was approved by the Quarter Court, but the Court experienced difficulty in finding a schoolmaster, and so the colonial authorities were empowered to fill that place.[2] However in 1622, a carpenter and 5 apprentices were sent over to build a schoolhouse and, in 1623, the East India Company took up a collection for the school and handed over the proceeds to the Virginia Council.[3] One Caroloff was sent over to look after the school. In June, 1625, the Governor and Council of Virginia write to the home authorities: " We should be ready with our utmost endeavors to assist the pious work of the East India free school, but we must not dissemble that besides the

---

[1] *Hist. of the Va. Co.*, pp. 251-6.   [2] *Ibid.*, p. 256.

[3] *Va. Carolorum*, p. 196, foot-note.

unseasonable arrival, we thought the acts of Mr. Caroloff will overbalance all his other sufficiency, though exceeding good."[1] There is no further mention of the proposed foundation.

In 1624 the charter of the democratic Virginia Company was annulled and Virginia became a royal province. A royal Governor and Council were appointed by the King, and after an interval of five years a General Assembly was again convened.

At an Assembly held at James City, March 2, 1643, and consisting of Sir William Berkeley, Governor, 10 Councilmen and 27 Burgesses, representatives of ten counties, a general revisal of the laws of the province was undertaken. In it were included the following Acts:

ACT XVIII

" Be it also enacted and confirmed upon consideration had of the godly disposition and good intent of Benjamin Symms, deceased, in founding by his last will and testament a free school in Elizabeth County, for the encouragement of all others in the like pious performances, that the said will and testament with all donations therein contained concerning the free school and the situation thereof in the said county and the land appertaining to the same, shall be confirmed according to the true meaning and godly intent of the said testator, without any alienation or conversion thereof to any place or county."[2]

ACT XXXIV

" Whereas there hath been the general suffering of the colony that the orphans of divers deceased persons have been very much abused and prejudiced in their estates by the negligence of overseers and guardians of such orphans, Be it therefore enacted and confirmed, . . . And all overseers and guardians of such orphans are enjoined by the authority aforesaid to educate and instruct them according to their best

---

[1] *Hist. of Va. Co.*, pp. 256-7.   [2] *Hening*, I, 252.

endeavors in Christian religion and in rudiments of learning[1] and to provide for them necessaries according to the competence of their estates."[2] . . .

In 1646 an elaborate plan for industrial education was advanced by the Assembly. As the foregoing Act for the education of orphans was continued in the government's subsequent provisions for such children, so the following Act marks out the settled policy of the State in the matter of industrial training.

At a Grand Assembly begun at James City, the 5th of October, 1646.

ACT XXVII

" Whereas sundry laws and statutes by act of Parliament established, have with great wisdom ordained, for the better education of youth in honest and profitable trades and manufactures, as also to avoid sloth and idleness wherewith such young children are easily corrupted, as also for relief of such parents whose poverty extends not to give them breeding, that the justices of the peace should, at their discretion, bind out children to tradesmen or husbandmen to be brought up

---

[1] All subsequent legislation concerning orphans provided for their education in some sort. It was enacted in 1656 that they were " to be educated upon the interest of the estate, if it will bear it, according to the proportion of the estate; but if the estate be so mean and ir considerable that it will not reach to a free education, then that orphan be bound to some manual trade till one and twenty years of age, except some friends or relations be willing to keep them." . . (*Ibid.*, I, 416.) The courts were empowered to remove to other guardians orphans who were not maintained and educated according to their estates, or who, when apprenticed, were neglected in their industrial training. (*Ibid.*, II, 417.) See, also, *14th Charles II*, Chap. LXVI, and *4th Anne*, Chap. XXXIII. In this latter act it is ordered that orphans that are bound apprentices shall also be taught to read and write by their masters. (*Ibid.*, III, 375.) This is, likewise, provided for in *22d George II*, Chap. IV. In this Act male orphans may be bound apprentice to tradesmen, merchants and mariners, and female orphans " to some suitable trade or employment." (*Ibid.*, V, 452.)

[2] *Ibid.*, I, 260–1.

in some good and lawful calling.   And whereas God Almighty, among his many other blessings, hath vouchsafed increase of children to this colony, who now are multiplied to a considerable number, who if instructed in good and lawful trades, may much improve the honor and reputation of the country, and no less their own good and their parents comfort : But forasmuch as for the most part, the parents either through fond indulgence or perverse obstinacy, are most averse and unwilling to part with their children, Be it therefore enacted by authority of this Grand Assembly, according to the aforesaid laudable custom in the Kingdom of England, that the commissioners of the several counties respectively do, at their discretion, make choice of two children in each county at the age of eight or seven years at the least, either male or female, which are to be sent up to James City between this and June next to be employed in the public flax houses under such master and mistress as shall be there appointed in carding, knitting and spinning.   And that the said children be furnished from the said county with six barrels of corn, two coverlets, or one rug and one blanket, one bed, one wooden bowl or tray, two pewter spoons, a sow shote of six months old, two laying hens, with convenient apparel both linen and woolen, with hose and shoes.   And for the better provision of housing for the said children, it is enacted that there be two houses built by the first of April next of forty feet long apiece with good and substantial timber, the houses to be twenty foot broad apiece, eight foot high in the pitch and a stack of brick chimneys standing in the midst of each house, and that they be lofted with sawn boards and made with convenient partitions.   And it is further thought fit that the commissioners have caution not to take up any children but from such parents who by reason of their poverty are disabled to maintain and educate them.   Be it likewise agreed that the Governor hath agreed with the Assembly for the sum of 10,000 lbs. of tobacco to be paid him the next crop, to build and finish the said house in manner and form before expressed."[1]

During the session of Assembly in the spring of 1661, efforts were made for the provision of both elementary and secondary education.

By the Grand Assembly, held at James City, March 32d, 1660–1.

ACT XX

" Provision for a college

" Whereas the want of able and faithful ministers in this country deprives us of these great blessings and mercies that always attend upon the service of God, which want, by reason of our great distance from our native country, cannot in probability be always supplied from thence, Be it enacted, that for the advance of learning, education of youth, supply of the ministry and promotion of piety, there be land taken upon

---

[1] *Ibid.*, I, 336–7. In 1668 an Act was passed "empowering county courts to build work-houses, assisted by the vestry." "Whereas, the prudence of all states ought, as much as in them lies, to endeavor the propagation and increase of all manufactures conducing to the necessities of their subsistance, and God having blessed this country with a soil capable of producing most things necessary for the use of man, if industriously improved, It is enacted by this Grand Assembly and the authority thereof, that for the better converting of wool, flax, hemp, and other commodities into manufactures, and for the increase of artificers in the country, that the commissioners of each county court, with the assistance of the respective vestries, of the parishes of their counties, shall be and hereby are impowered to build houses for the educating and instructing poor children in the knowledge of spinning, weaving, and other useful occupations and trades, and power granted to take poor children from indigent parents to place them to work in those houses." (*Ibid.*, II, 266–7.) In 1727, in "an Act for . . . restraint of vagrants and idle people, . . and for making provision for the poor," it was ordered that church wardens should bind out as apprentices the children of all poor persons who were unable or who neglected to duly educate them or instruct them in the principles of Christianity. (*Ibid.*, IV, 212. See, also, 22 *George* II, Chap. XVIII.) In 1755 parish vestries were ordered to erect work houses in which to set the poor to work and to levy allowances in their parishes for the education of poor children in such houses until they were bound out according to law. (*Ibid.*, VI, 476–7.)

purchases for a college and free school, and that there be with
as much speed as may be convenient, housing erected thereon
for entertainment of students and scholars."[1]

ACT XXV

" A petition in behalf of the Church

"Be it enacted, that there be a petition drawn up by this
Grand Assembly to the King's most excellent Majesty for his
letters patent to collect and gather the charity of well disposed people in England for the erecting of colleges and
schools in this country, and also for his Majesty's letters to
both Universities of Oxford and Cambridge to furnish the
church here with ministers for the present, and this petition to
be recommended to the right honorable Governor, Sir William
Berkeley."[2]

The following order was also passed at this session :

"Whereas for the advancement of learning, promoting piety
and providing of an able and successive ministry in this country, it hath been thought that a college of students of the
liberal arts and sciences be erected and maintained, in pursuance thereof, the Right Honorable his Majesty's Governor,
Council of State, and Burgesses of the present Grand Assembly have severally subscribed several considerable sums of
money and quantities of tobacco (out of their charity and
devotion) to be paid to the honorable Grand Assembly, or
such treasurer or treasurers as they shall now, or their successors hereafter at any time appoint, upon demand, after a
place is provided and built upon for that intent and purpose.
It is ordered that the commissioners of the several county
courts do at the next following court in their several counties,
subscribe such sums of money and tobacco towards the furthering and promoting the said persons and necessary work,
to be paid by them, or their heirs, as they shall think fit, and

[1] *Ibid.*, II, 25.   [2] *Ibid.*, II, 30-31.

that they also take the subscriptions of such other persons at their said courts, who shall be willing to contribute towards the same. And that after such subscriptions taken, they send orders to the vestries of the several parishes in their several counties, for the subscription of such inhabitants and others who have not already subscribed, and that the same be returned to Francis Morrison, Esq."[1]

There is no evidence that the subscriptions provided for in the preceding order were forthcoming; for among the statements made by Governor Berkeley in 1671 to certain enquiries which had been submitted to him the previous year by the Commissioners of Foreign Plantations, he writes in answer to the question "What course is taken about the instructing the people within your government in the Christian religion?" "The same course that is taken in England out of towns; every man according to his ability instructing his children . . But, I thank God, there are no free schools nor printing, and I hope we shall not have these hundred years; for learning has brought disobedience and heresy and sects into the world, and printing has divulged them and libels against the best government. God keep us from both!"[2]

In 1685, Dr. James Blair was sent as missionary to Virginia by the Bishop of London, and four years later was appointed

[1] *Ibid.*, II, 37.

[2] *Ibid.*, II, 517. Hening states (II, 518) that the first evidence of printing in Virginia is an edition of the year 1733 of the revised laws of the province. There was no newspaper printed in Virginia until 1736. "February 21, 1682, John Buckner called before the Lord Culpepper and his council for printing the laws of 1680 without his Excellency's license, and he and the printer ordered to enter into bond in £100 not to print anything hereafter until his Majesty's pleasure should be known." Quoted by Hening (II, 518) from *Bland MS. pa.* 498. The above hot-tempered utterances of Governor Berkeley seem inconsistent with the views of the Assemblies of 1642, 1660 and 1661, of which he was no insignificant part. See, *The College of William and Mary*, pp. 13–14; Herbert B. Adams, Ph. D., *Circular of Information of the Bureau of Education*, No. I, 1887.

the Bishop's commissary or representative in the province. He seems to have agitated the suspended project for a college, and in 1691 he went to England as the agent of the legislature to solicit a royal charter.[1] The Bishop of London advised Commissary Blair to present the matter as a petition to the King in Council; but to this method of procedure Dr. Blair objected. In a letter to Governor Nicholson on December 3, 1691, he writes: "I told his Lordship that I never doubted the obtaining of the charter, but the great difficulty would be in obtaining a gift of such things from his Majesty as we had a mind to ask for the college; and that in order to this, the best way seemed to me to be to engage the bishops about Court zealously in the thing, and to get the King so prepared, that when the address was presented to him he should consult the bishops in it, it being an ecclesiastical affair, . . . and then at last, if it was necessary, that it might be brought before the Committee of Plantations to see what they had to say against it, but for the Council and the Committee of Plantations to be the first meddlers and contrivers of the business I did not like it, because, as his Lordship told me himself, the Church of England party was the weakest in the Council, and if there is any of the revenue to be spared, the courtiers are more apt to beg it for themselves than to advise the bestowing of it upon any public use."[2]

The Archbishop of Canterbury agreed with Dr. Blair about the method of managing the college interests in Court, and so through his influence, Dr. Blair obtained an audience with the King. He gives the following account of it to Governor Nicholson. "I kneeled down and said these words, 'Please your Majesty here is an humble supplication from the government of Virginia for your Majesty's charter to erect a free

---

[1] *Contributions to the Ecclesiastical History of the United States of America*, I, 74–76. Francis L. Hawks, New York, 1836.

[2] *Historical Collections of the American Colonial Church*, I, 3–5. Edited by William S. Perry, D. D., 1870.

school and college for the education of their youth ' . . .
He answered, ' Sir, I am glad that that colony is upon so good
a design, and I will promote it to the best of my power.' "[1]
The charter which Dr. Blair carried back with him in 1692
testifies to King William's good will.

" WILLIAM AND MARY, by the grace of God, of England,
Scotland, France and Ireland, King and Queen, defenders of
the faith, &c. To all whom these our present letters shall
come, greeting—

" Forasmuch as our well-beloved and faithful subjects, constituting the General Assembly of our Colony of Virginia,
have had it in their minds, and have proposed to themselves,
to the end that the Church of Virginia may be furnished with
a seminary of ministers of the gospel, and that the youth may
be piously educated in good letters and manners, and that the
Christian faith may be propagated amongst the Western Indians, to the glory of Almighty God ; to make, found and
establish a certain place of universal study, or perpetual college of divinity, philosophy, languages, and other good arts
and sciences, consisting of one president, six masters or professors, and an hundred scholars, more or less, according to
the ability of the said college, and the statutes of the same ; to
be made, increased, diminished, or changed there, by certain
trustees nominated and elected by the General Assembly
aforesaid, to wit, our faithful and well-beloved Francis Nicholson, our Lieutenant Governor in our Colonies of Virginia and
Maryland ; Wm. Cole, Ralph Wormley, William Byrd and
John Lear, Esquires ; James Blair, John Farnifold, Stephen
Fouace and Samuel Gray, clerks ; Thomas Milner, Christopher Robinson, Charles Scarborough, John Smith, Benjamin
Harrison ; Miles Cary, Henry Hartwell, William Randolph
and Matthew Page, gentlemen,[2] or the major part of them, or

---

[1] *Ibid.*, I, 5, 6.

[2] This original board of visitors and governors consisted, according to a contem-

of the longer livers of them, on the south side of a certain river, commonly called York river, or elsewhere, where the General Assembly itself shall think more convenient, within our Colony of Virginia, to be supported and maintained, in all time coming.

" I. And forasmuch as our well-beloved and trusty the General Assembly of our Colony of Virginia aforesaid, has humbly supplicated us, by our well-beloved in Christ, James Blair, clerk, their agent duly constituted, that we would be pleased, not only to grant our royal license to the said Francis Nicholson, William Cole, Ralph Wormly, William Byrd and John Lear, Esquires; James Blair, John Farnifold, Stephen Fouace and Samuel Gray, clerks ; Thomas Milner, Christopher Robinson, Charles Scarborough, John Smith, Benjamin Harrison, Miles Cary, Henry Hartwell, William Randolph, and Matthew Page, gentlemen, or the major part of them, or of the longer livers of them, to make, found, erect and establish the said college, but also to extend our royal bounty and munificence towards the erection and foundation of the said college, in such way and manner as to us shall seem most expedient : We, taking the premises seriously into our consideration, and earnestly desiring, that as far as in us lies, true philosophy, and other good and liberal arts and sciences may be promoted, and that the orthodox Christain faith may be propagated : And being desirous, that forever hereafter, there should be one such college, or place of universal study, and some certain and undoubted way within the said college, for the rule and government of the same, and of the masters or professors, and scholars, and all others inhabiting and residing therein, and that the said college should subsist and remain in all time coming ; of our special grace, certain knowledge, and mere motion, have granted and given leave, and by these presents do grant and

porary account, of the " Lieutenant Governor, four gentlemen of the Council, four of the clergy, and the rest named out of the House of Burgesses." (An Account of the Present State and Government of Virginia, *Mass. Hist. Coll.*, V, 164.)

give leave, for us, our heirs and successors, as much as in us lies, to the said Francis Nicholson, William Cole, Ralph Wormley, William Byrd and John Lear, Esquires; James Blair, John Farnifold, Stephen Fouace and Samuel Gray, clerks; Thomas Milner, Christopher Robinson, Charles Scarborough, John Smith, Benjamin Harrison, Miles Cary, Henry Hartwell, William Randolph and Matthew Page, gentlemen; that they or the major part of them or of the longest livers of them, for promoting the studies of true philosophy, languages, and other good arts and sciences, and for propagating the pure gospel of Christ, our only Mediator, to the praise and honor of Almighty God, may have power to erect, found and establish a certain place of universal study, or perpetual college, for divinity, philosophy, languages and other good arts and sciences, consisting of one President, six masters or professors, an hundred scholars, more or less, graduates and non-graduates, as abovesaid, according to the statutes and orders of the said college, to be made, appointed and established upon the place by the said Francis Nicholson, William Cole, &c., or the major part of them, upon the south side of York river, on the land late of Colonel — Townsend, deceased, now in possession of John Smith. near the port appointed or laid out for York county, by the said General Assembly, within our said Colony of Virginia; or if by reason of unwholesomeness, or any other cause, the said place shall not be approved of, wheresoever else the General Assembly of our Colony of Virginia, or the major part of them, shall think fit, within the bounds of the aforesaid colony, to continue for all times coming.

"II. And further, of our special grace, certain knowledge, and mere motion, we have granted, and given leave, and by these presents do grant, and give leave, for us, our heirs and successors, to the said Francis Nicholson, William Cole, etc., that they, or the major part of them, or of the longer livers of them, may be enabled to take, hold and enjoy, and that they may be persons apt and capable in law, for taking, holding and enjoying all man-

ors, lands, tenements, rents, services, rectories, portions, annuities, pensions and advowsons of churches, with all other inheritances, franchises and possessions whatsoever, as well spiritual
as temporal, to the value of two thousand pounds a year; and
all other goods, chattels, money and personal estate whatsoever
of the gift of any person whatsoever, that is willing to bestow
them for this use; or any other gifts, grants, assignments, legacies or appointments, of the same, or any of them, or of any
other goods whatsoever: But with this express intention, and
upon the special trust we put in them that they the said
Francis Nicholson, Wm. Cole, &c. or the major part of them,
or of the longer livers of them, shall take and hold the premises, and shall dispose of the same, and of the rents, revenues,
or profits thereof, or of any of them only for defraying the
charges that shall be laid in erecting and fitting the edifices of
the said intended college, and furnishing them with books, and
other utensils, and all other charges pertaining to the said college, as they, or the major part of them, shall think most expedient, until the said college shall be actually erected, founded
and established, and upon this trust and intention, that so soon
as the said college shall, according to our royal intent be erected and founded, the said Francis Nicholson, Wm. Cole &c. or
the longer livers or liver of them, and their or his heirs, executors, administrators or assigns, shall by good and sufficient
deeds and assurances in law, give, grant and transfer to the
said president and masters, or professors, or their successors,
the said lands, manors, tenements, rents, services, rectories,
portions, annuities, pensions and advowsons of churches, with
all other inheritances, franchises, possessions, goods, chattels
and personal estate aforesaid, or as much thereof as has not
been laid out and bestowed upon the building the said college,
or to the other uses above mentioned.

" III. And seeing the said General Assembly of our Colony
of Virginia, has named, elected or appointed, the said James
Blair, clerk, as a fit person to be president of the said college;

we of our special grace, certain knowledge, and mere motion, do approve, confirm and ratify the said nomination and election, and do by these presents make, create and establish the said James Blair first president of the said college, during his natural life.

"IV. And further we grant our special license to the said Francis Nicholson, Wm. Cole, &c., and their successors, or the major part of them, that they have power to elect and nominate other apt, fit and able persons, into the places of the masters or professors of the said college; and that, after the death, resignation or deprivation of the said president, or professors, or any of them, the said Francis Nicholson, Wm. Cole, &c., and their successors, or the major part of them, shall have power to put in, and substitute, a fit person, or persons, from time to time, into his or their place, or places, according to the orders and statutes of the said college, to be made, enacted and established, for the good and wholesome government of the said college, and of all that bear office, or reside therein, by the said Francis Nicholson, Wm. Cole, &c., or their successors, or the major part of them.

"V. And further, we will, and for us, our heirs and successors, by these presents, do grant, that when the said college shall be so erected, made, founded and established, it shall be called and denominated forever the College of William and Mary, in Virginia, and that the president and masters, or professors, of the said college, shall be a body politic and corporate, in deed and name; and that by the name of the President and Masters, or Professors, of the College of William and Mary, in Virginia, they shall have perpetual succession; and that the said president, and masters, or professors, shall forever be called and denominated the President, and Masters, or Professors, of William and Mary, in Virginia: And that the said president and masters, or professors, and their successors, by the name of the President and Masters, or Professors, of the College of William and Mary, in Virginia, shall be persons able and capable, apt and perpetual in law, to take and hold lordships, manors, lands, tenements, rents, reversions, rectories, portions, pensions, annuities, inheritances, possessions and services, as well spiritual as temporal, whatsoever, and all manner of goods and chattels both of our gift, and our heirs and successors, and of the gift of the said Francis Nicholson, Wm. Cole, Ralph Wormley, Wm. Byrd, and John Lear, Esquires; James Blair, John Farnifold, Stephen Fouace and Samuel Gray, clerks; Tho. Milner, Christopher Robinson, Charles Scarborough, John Smith, Benj. Harrison, Miles Carey, Henry Hartwell, Wm. Randolph and Matthew Page, gentlemen; or of the gift of any other person whatsoever, to the value of two thousand pounds, of lawful money of England, yearly, and no more, to be had and held by them and their successors forever.

"VI. And also, that the said president, and masters, or professors, by and under the name of the president, and masters, or professors, of the College of William and Mary, in Virginia, shall have power to plead and be impleaded, to sue and be sued, to defend and be defended, to answer and be answered, in all and every cause, complaint and action, real, personal and mixed, of what kind and nature soever they be, in whatsoever courts and places of judicature belonging to us, our heirs and successors, or to any person whatsoever, before all sorts of justices and judges, ecclesiastical and temporal, in whatsoever kingdoms, countries, colonies, dominions or plantations, belonging to us, or our heirs; and to do, act, and receive, these and all other things, in the same manner, as our other liege people, persons able and capable in law, within our said Colony of Virginia, or our Kingdom of England, do, or may act, in the said courts and places of judicature, and before the said justices and judges.

"VII. As also, that the said president, and masters or professors, and their successors shall have one common seal, which they may make use of in any whatsoever cause and business belonging to them and their successors; and that the president and masters or professors, of the said college, and their successors, shall have leave to break, change and renew, their said seal, from time to time, at their pleasure, as they shall see most expedient.

"VIII. And further of our more special grace, we have given and granted, and for us, our heirs and successors, we give and grant our special license, as far as in us lies, to the said Francis Nicholson, Wm. Cole, Ralph Wormley, Wm. Byrd and John Lear, Esquires; James Blair, John Farnifold, Stephen Fouace, Samuel Gray, clerks; Tho. Milner, Christopher Robinson, Charles Scarborough, John Smith, Benj. Harrison, Miles Cary, Hen. Hartwell, Wm. Randolph and Matthew Page, gentlemen; that they, or any other person or persons, whatsoever, after the said college is so founded, erected, made, created and established, may have power to give and grant, assign and bequeath, all manors, lands, tenements, rents, services, rectories, portions, annuities, pensions and advowsons of churches, and all manner of inheritance, franchises and possessions whatsoever, as well spiritual as temporal, to the value of two thousand pounds a year, over and above all burthens and reprisals, to the president, and masters or professors, of the said college, for the time being, and their successors, to be had, held and enjoyed, by the said president, and masters or professors, and their successors, forever; and that they, the said president and masters, or professors aforesaid, may take and hold, to themselves, and their successors, forever, as is aforesaid, manors, lands, tenements, rents, reversions, services, rectories, portions, pensions, annuities, and all manner of inheritances, and possessions whatsoever, as well spiritual as temporal, to the aforesaid value of two thousand pounds a year, over and above all burthens, reprisals and reparations: It not being our will, that the said president, and masters or professors of the said college, for the time being, or their successors, shall be troubled, disquieted, molested or aggrieved by reason, or occasion of the premises, or any of them, by us, our heirs and successors, or by any of our justices, escheators, sheriffs, or other bailiffs, or ministers, whatsoever, belonging to us, our heirs and successors.

"IX. And further, we will, and by these presents, do declare, nominate, ordain and appoint, the said Francis Nicholson, Wm. Cole, Ralph Wormley, Wm. Byrd and John Lear, Esquires; James Blair, John Farnifold, Stephen Fouace and Samuel Gray, clerks; Tho. Milner, Christopher Robinson, Charles Scarborough, John Smith, Benj. Harrison, Miles Cary, Henry Hartwell, Wm. Randolph and Matthew Page, gentlemen, and their successors, to be the true, sole and undoubted Visitors and Governors of the said college forever : And we give and grant to them, or the major part of them, by these our letters patents, a continual succession, to be continued in the way and manner hereafter specified; as also full and absolute liberty, power and authority of making, enacting, framing and establishing such and so many rules, laws, statutes, orders and injunctions, for the good and wholesome government of the said college, as to them the said Francis Nicholson, Wm. Cole, &c. and their successors, shall from time to time, according to their various occasions and circumstances, seem most fit and expedient: All which rules, laws, statutes and injunctions so to be made, as aforesaid, we will have to be observed, under the penalty therein contained: Provided not withstanding, that the said rules, laws, statutes, orders and injunctions, be no way contrary to our prerogative royal, nor to the laws and statutes of our Kingdom of England or our Colony of Virginia, aforesaid, or to the canons and constitutions of the Church of England, by law established.

"X. And further, we will and by these presents, for us our heirs and successors, do grant and confirm to the said visitors, and governors of the said college, and their successors, that they and their successors shall, forever, be eighteen men, or any other number not exceeding the number of twenty, in the whole, to be elected and constituted in the way and manner hereinafter specified; and that they shall have one discreet

and fit person that shall be elected and nominated, out of their
number, in the manner hereafter mentioned, that shall be, and
shall be called Rector of the said college: And we have appointed and confirmed, and by these presents, do appoint and
confirm the said James Blair, to be the present rector of the
said college, to be continued in the said office for one year next
ensuing the foundation of the said college, and thereafter till
some other of the visitors and governors of the said college
shall be duly elected, preferred and sworn into the said office;
and that from time to time, and in all time coming, after the
said year is expired, or after the death of the rector within the
year, the visitors and governors of the said college, or the
greater part of them, or of their successors, shall have power
to elect and nominate another discreet and fit person, from
amongst themselves to be rector of the said college, and that
he who is elected, preferred and nominated, as abovesaid, into
the place of rector of the said college, shall have power to
have, exercise and enjoy the said office of rector of the said
college, for one whole year, then next ensuing, and thereafter,
until some other rector of the said college shall be duly
elected, preferred and sworn into the said office: And to perpetuate the succession of the said rector, and of the said
visitors and governors of the said college, we will, ordain and
appoint, that as often as any one or more of the said visitors
and governors of the said college, shall die, or remove himself
and family out of our said colony, into any other country for
good and all, that then, and so often, the rector for the time
being, and the other visitors and governors of the said college,
then surviving and remaining within the colony, or the major
part of them, shall and may have leave to elect, nominate and
choose one or more of the principal and better sort of the inhabitants of our said Colony of Virginia, into the place or places
of visitor and governor, or visitors and governors, so dead or
removed, to fill up the aforesaid number of visitors and governors, for the said college; and that he or they so elected and

chosen, shall take his or their corporal oath, before the rector, and the other visitors and governors of the said college, or the major part of them, well and faithfully to execute the said office; which oath the said rector, and two or more of the visitors, shall have power to administer: And that after the taking of the said oath, he or they shall be of the number of the said visitors and governors of the said college.

"XI. And further, we will, and by these presents, for us, our heirs and successors, do grant and confirm, to the said president, and masters, or professors of the said college, and their successors, that they and their successors shall have one eminent and discreet person, to be elected and nominated, in the manner hereafter expressed, who shall be, and shall be called Chancellor of the said college: And we have appointed and confirmed, and by these presents, for us, our heirs, and successors, do appoint and confirm, our well beloved and right trusty the reverend father in God, Henry, by divine permission, Bishop of London, to be the first chancellor of the said college, to be continued in the said office for seven years next ensuing, and thereafter, until some other chancellor of the said college shall be duly elected and chosen into the said office: And that from time to time, and in all time coming, after these seven years have expired, or after the death of the said bishop, or of the chancellor, for the time being, the rector, and visitors, and governors of the said college for the time being, or the major part of them, shall and may have power to elect, choose and nominate, some other eminent and discreet person, from time to time, to be chancellor of the said college; and that he who is so nominated and elected to be chancellor of the said college, shall and may have, execute, and enjoy, the said office of chancellor of the said college, for the space of seven years then next ensuing, and thereafter until some other chancellor of the said college shall be duly elected and constituted.

"XII. Further, we will by these presents and for us, our heirs and successors, do grant and confirm to the said president, and masters, or professors, of the said college, and to their successors, that after the said college is erected, founded and established, they may retain and appoint some convenient place, or council chamber, within the said college; and that the rector and other visitors, and governors of the said college, or the major part of them, for the time being, as often as they shall think good, and see cause, may convocate and hold a certain court of convocation within the said chamber, consisting of the said rector, and visitors, and governors, of the said college, or the major part of them, in all time coming; and in the said convocation, may treat, confer, consult, advise and decree, concerning statutes, orders, and injunctions, for the said college.

"XIII. And further, we will, and by these presents, for us, our heirs and successors, do grant and confirm to the said president and masters, or professors of the said college, and their successors, or the major part of them, that from time to time, and in all time coming, the said rector and visitors, or governors of the said college, and their successors, or the major part of them, shall have power and authority yearly, and every year, on the first Monday which shall hapen next after the feast of the annunciation of the blessed Virgin Mary, to elect and nominate, and that they shall and may elect and nominate one of the said visitors or governors of the said college, to be rector of the said college, for one whole year then next ensuing: And that he, after he is so elected and chosen into the said office of rector of the said college, before he be admitted to execute the said office, shall, on the same day and in the same place, take his corporal oath before the last rector, and visitors, or governors of the said college, or any three of them, well and faithfully to execute the said office; and that after so taking the said oath, he shall and may execute the said office of rector of the said. college, for one whole year then next ensuing: And also, that every seventh year, on the same Monday, next after the feast of the annunciation of the blessed Virgin Mary, aforesaid, they shall, in like manner, have power and authority to elect and nominate another chancellor of the said college, to be continued for seven years then next ensuing: And that he who shall be elected, chosen, and nominated, into the office of chancellor of the said college, shall and may, immediately after such election and nomination, execute the office of chancellor of the said college for seven years then next ensuing.

"XIV. And that the charge and expense of erecting, building, founding and adorning, the said college at present, and also of supporting and maintaining the said president and masters or professors, for the future, may be sustained and defrayed, of our more ample and bounteous special grace, certain knowledge, and mere motion, we have given, granted, assigned, and made over, and by these presents for us, our heirs and successors, do give, grant, assign, and make over to the said Francis Nicholson, Wm. Cole, Ralph Wormley, Wm. Byrd and John Lear, Esqs.; James Blair, John Farnifold, Stephen Fouace and Samuel Gray, clerks; Tho. Milner, Christopher Robinson, Charles Scarborough, John Smith, Benj. Harrison, Miles Gray, Henry Hartwell, Wm. Randolph and Matthew Page, gentlemen, and their executors and assigns forever, the whole and entire sum of one thousand nine hundred and eighty five pounds, fourteen shillings and ten pence, of good and lawful money of England, that has been received and raised out of the quit-rents of the said colony, now remaining in the hands of William Byrd Esq. our auditor, or in whosesoever other hands the same now is, for our use, within the said colony: And, therefore, we command and firmly enjoin the said auditor, or any other person with whom the said money is deposited, or who is obliged to pay the same, immediately upon sight of these our letters patents, to pay, or cause to be paid, the said sum of one thousand nine hundred and eighty-five pounds, fourteen shillings and ten pence, to the said Francis Nicholson, Wm. Cole &c. or the major part of them, or of the longer livers of them, c. to their attorney, in that part lawfully constituted, with any other warrant, mandate, or precept to be obtained or expected from us, to be laid out and applied about and towards the building, erecting, and adorning, the said college, and to no other use, intent or purpose whatever.

" XV. Seeing also, by a certain act of parliament, made the twenty-fifth year of the reign of our royal uncle, Charles the Second, of blessed memory, entitled, An Act for the encouragement of the Greenland and Eastland trades, and for better securing the plantation trade, it was enacted, that after the first day of September, in the year of our Lord M. DC. LXXIII, if any ship, which by law, might trade in any of the plantations, should come to any of them to load, and take on board tobacco, or any other of the commodities there enumerated, and if bond were not first given, with one sufficient security, to carry the said tobacco to England, Wales or the town of Berwick upon Tweed, and to no other place, and there to unload and put the same on shore, (the dangers of the sea only excepted); in such case there should be paid to our said uncle, and his heirs and successors, one penny for every pound of tobacco so loaded and put on board, to be levied, collected, and paid in such places, and to such officers, and collectors, as should be appointed in the respective plantations, to collect, levy, and receive the same, and under such penalties, both to the officers and upon the goods as for non-payment of his Majesty's customs in England: And if it should happen, that any person or persons who are to pay the said duties, shall not have ready money to satisfy the same, that the officers who are appointed to collect the said duties, shall in lieu of the said ready money, take such a proportion of tobacco, that was to be shipped, as may amount to the value thereof, according to the usual rate of the said commodity, in such plantation respectively: All which things are to be ordered, and disposed, and these several duties are to be caused to be levied, by the commissioners of our customs in England, for the time being, under the authority and direction of the lord treasurer of England, or the commissioners of the treasury, for the time being, as by the said act of parliament, amongst other things therein contained, reference being thereto had, doth more fully appear; we, of our more bounteous grace, mere motion, and certain knowledge, have given and granted, and for us, and our successors do give, and grant, to the said Francis Nicholson, Wm. Cole, &c. and the other trustees above mentioned, and their heirs forever, the said revenue of one penny for every pound of tobacco in Virginia, or Maryland, in America, or either of them that shall be so loaded, and put on board, as is above said; and the nett produce which shall accrue in England, or elsewhere, by selling there the tobacco that shall be collected in our colonies of Virginia, and Maryland, in lieu of the penny that ought to be paid for every pound of tobacco so loaded and put on board, as is abovesaid: Provided always, that the commissioner of our customs in England, for the time being, shall name and appoint all the collectors and receivers of the said money and tobacco, and their inspectors and comptrollers, from time to time, as they have hitherto done: And that the salaries of the said collectors, receivers, and comptrollers, shall be deducted and paid out of the said revenue; and that the said Francis Nicholson, Wm. Cole, Ralph Wormley, Wm. Byrd and John Lear, Esq., James Blair, John Farnifold, Step. Fouace and Sam. Gray, clerks; Tho. Milner, Christopher Robinson, Charles Scarborough, John Smith, Benj. Harrison, Miles Gray, Henry Hartwell, Wm. Randolph and Matthew Page, gentlemen, and their successors, as also the president and masters, or professors, of the said college, and their successors, for the time being, shall be obliged to receive and observe such rules, orders, and instructions, as shall be transmitted to them, from time to time, by the said commissioners of our customs in England, for the time being, under the inspection and direction of the lord treasurer, or the commissioners of our treasury in England, for the time being, for the better and more exact collecting of the said duty, as by the said act of parliament, reference being thereto had, is more particularly directed and appointed: but with this express intention, and upon the special trust and confidence we place in the said Francis Nicholson, Wm. Cole, and the rest of the aforesaid trustees, that they, and the longest livers of them, and their heirs, shall take, hold, and possess the said revenue of a penny per pound, for every pound of tobacco aforesaid, with all its profits, advantages, and emoluments, to apply and lay out the same, for building and adorning the edifices and other necessaries for the said college, until the said college shall be actually erected, founded, and established, and with this express intention, and upon the special trust and confidence that so soon as the said college shall be erected and founded, according to our royal purpose, the said trustees, and the longest livers or liver of them, and his or their heirs, or assigns, shall, by good and sufficient deeds and assurances in law, give, grant, and transfer to the president, and masters, or professors, of the said college, this whole revenue, with all its profits, issues, and emoluments before mentioned, or so much thereof, as shall not have been expended and laid out for the aforesaid uses, to be held, possessed, and enjoyed, by the said president and masters, or professors, and their successors, forever.

" XVI. And also, of our special grace, mere motion, and certain knowledge, we have given and granted, and by these presents, for us, our heirs, and successors, do give and grant to Francis Nicholson, Wm. Cole, and the rest of the said trustees, and to the longest livers or liver of them, and to his or their heirs, the office of surveyor-general of our said Colony of Virginia, if the said office be now void, or whensoever and how often soever it shall hereafter fall void, to be had, held and executed, with all its issues, fees, profits, advantages, conveniences, liberties, places, privileges, and pre-eminence whatsoever, belonging to the said office, in as ample form and manner, as any other person, who has heretofore had, executed, or possessed the said office, ever had received or enjoyed, or ought to have, receive or enjoy, by the said trustees, and their heirs ; or by such officers and substitutes, as they or the major part of them, or of the longest livers of them, or of their heirs, shall from time to time nominate and appoint, until the said college shall be actually founded and erected : But with this express intention, and upon this special trust and confidence, which we place in the said Francis Nicholson, Wm. Cole, and the rest of the said trustees, that they and the longest livers of them, and their heirs, shall give back and restore to the president and masters, or professors, of the said college, for the time being, whatsoever money remains in their hands, that has risen from this office, during their administration, not yet laid out upon the building of the said college, and the other above-mentioned uses, as soon as the said college shall be actually erected and founded. And after the said college shall be actually erected and founded, we will, at the said office of surveyor-general, if it be then void, as often as it shall be void, for the time to come, shall be had, held, and executed, with all its profits and appurtenances above-mentioned, by the said president and masters, or professors, and their successors, forever : Provided always that the said Francis Nicholson, and the rest of the above-mentioned trustees, or the major part of them, or of the longest livers of them, and the president and masters, or professors, for the time being, shall from time to time, nominate and substitute such and so many particular surveyors for the particular counties of our Colony of Virginia, as our Governor-in-chief, and the Council of our said Colony of Virginia, for the time being, shall think fit and necessary.

"XVII. And also, of our more bounteous special grace, mere motion, and certain knowledge, we have given, granted, and confirmed, and by these presents, for us, and our heirs, and successors, do give, grant and confirm, to the said Francis Nicholson, Wm. Cole, and the rest of the trustees abovementioned, ten thousand acres of land, not yet legally occupied or possessed by any of our other subjects, lying, and being, on the South side of the Blackwater Swamp, and also other ten thousand acres of land, not legally occupied or possessed by any of our other subjects, lying and being in that neck of land, commonly called Pamunkey Neck, between the forks or branches of York River: which twenty thousand acres of land, we will have to be laid out and measured in the places above-mentioned, at the choice of the said Francis Nicholson, Wm. Cole, and the rest of the fore-mentioned trustees, or the major part of them, or of the longest livers of them, to be had and held by the said Francis Nicholson, Wm. Cole, and the rest of the above-mentioned trustees, and their heirs forever; but with this intention, and upon special trust and confidence, that the said Francis Nicholson, William Cole, and the rest of the said trustees, or the major part of them, or of the longest livers of them, so soon as the said college shall be actually founded and established, shall give, grant, let, and alienate the said twenty thousand acres of land to the said president and masters, or professors of the said colloge, to be had and held by them, and their successors, forever, fealty, in free and common soccage, paying to us, and our successors, two copies of Latin verses yearly, on every fifth day of November at the house of our Governor, or Lieutenant-Governor of Virginia, for the time being, forever, in full discharge, acquittance, and satisfaction of all quit-rents, services, customs, dues and burdens whatsoever, due, or to be due, to us, or our successors, for the said twenty thousand acres of land, by the laws and customs of England or Virginia.

"XVIII. And also, of our special grace, certain knowledge, and mere motion, we have given, and granted, and by these presents, for us and our successors, do give, and grant, to the said president, and masters, or professors of the said college, full and absolute power, liberty, and authority, to nominate, elect, and constitute one discreet and able person of their own number, or of the number of the said visitors, or governors, or lastly, of the better sort of inhabitants of our Colony of Virginia, to be present in the House of Burgesses, of the General Assembly of our Colony of Virginia, and there to act and consent to such things, as by the common advice of our said colony shall (God willing) happen to be enacted.

" XIX. And further, it is our pleasure, that such further confirmations and ratifications of the premises shall be granted, from time to time by us, our heirs and successors, to the said Francis Nicholson, and the rest of the trustees abovementioned, and to their successors, or to the president, and masters, or professors of the said college, or to their successors, for the time being, upon their humble petition under the great seal of England, or otherwise, as the attorney-general of us, our heirs, or successors, for the time being, shall think fit and expedient.

" In testimony whereof, we have caused these our letters to be made patent. Witness ourselves, at Westminster, the eighth day of February, in the fourth year of our reign.

By writ of the privy seal,   PIGOTT." [1]

Upon President Blair's return with this charter, the Assembly promptly decided upon a proper site for the building of the College, and upon an appropriation of a certain part of the state revenues for its support.

At a General Assembly begun at James City, the tenth day of October, 1693.

ACT III

"*An Act ascertaining the place for erecting the College of William and Mary in Virginia.*

" Whereas their Majesties have been most graciously pleased upon the humble supplication of the General Assembly of this country, by their charter bearing date the eighth day of February, in the fourth year of their reign, to grant their royal license to certain trustees to make, found,

---

[1] Given in *The History of the College of William and Mary*, pp. 3-16. Richmond, 1874.

erect and establish a college named the College of William
and Mary, in Virginia, at a certain place within this government known by the name of Townsends Land, and heretofore
appointed by the General Assembly, or if the same should be
found inconvenient, at such other place as the General
Assembly shall think fit, and whereas the said former designed place for divers causes is found to be very unsuitable
for such an use, and several other places have been nominated
in the room thereof, upon consideration of which, and a full
inquiry into the conveniences of each one of the said places,
the Middle Plantation, situated between York and James
rivers, appearing to be the most convenient and proper for
that design, Be it therefore enacted by the Governor, Council
and Burgesses of this present General Assembly and the
authority thereof, and it is hereby enacted that Middle Plantation be the place for erecting the said College of William and
Mary in Virginia, and that the said college be at that place
erected and built as near the church now standing in Middle
Plantation old fields as convenience will permit." [1]

ACT IV

"*An Act laying an imposition upon skins and furs for the
better support of the College of William and Mary in Virginia.*

" Be it enacted by the Governor, Council and Burgesses of
this present General Assembly and by the authority thereof,
and it is hereby enacted, that from and after the first day of
January next, there shall be satisfied and paid to their
Majesties, their heirs and successors, for and towards the
better support and maintenance of the College of William and
Mary in Virginia, speedily intended by God's grace to be
erected at Middle Plantation within this government, the
following duties, customs and impost for the following goods,
wares and merchandise which shall be exported, carried out
of their Majesties' dominion either by land or water, (that is

[1] *Hening*, III, 122.

to say) for every raw hide, three pence, for every tanned hide, **six pence,** for every dressed buckskin, one penny, three farthings, for every undressed buckskin, one penny, for every doe skin dressed, one penny, halfpenny, for every undressed doe skin, three farthings, for every pound of beaver, three pence, for every otter skin, two pence, for every wild-cat skin, one penny, halfpenny, for every mink skin, one penny, for every fox skin, one penny, halfpenny, for every dozen of racoon skins, three pence, and so proportionably for a greater or lesser quantity, for every dozen muskrat skins, two pence, and so proportionably for a greater or lesser quantity, and every elk skin, four pence, halfpenny.

" And be it enacted by the authority aforesaid, and it is hereby enacted, that the said duties, customs and impost shall be paid and satisfied by the person or persons exporting, or carrying out the same either by land or water, to the collector, or collectors which shall be appointed by the Governor, or Commander-in-Cheif for the time being, to receive the said duties, customs and impost, before the said goods, wares or merchandises shall be shipped off, exported or carried out of and from this dominion, either by land or water, and a certificate thereof obtained from the collector, or collectors of the district where such goods, wares and merchandises shall be so exported or carried away, signifying the payment and satisfaction of such duties, customs and impost as aforesaid, under the penalty of forfeiting such of the said goods, wares and merchandises which shall be shipped off, or loaden on board of any boat, sloop, ship or other vessel, in order to the exportation thereof by water, or endeavored to be carried out of this country by land, the one moiety thereof to their Majesties, their heirs and successors, to and for the better support of the government and the contingent charges thereof, the other moiety to him, or them that shall sue, or prosecute for the same in any court of record within this colony, by action of debt, bill, plaint or information wherein no essoin, protection, or wager of law shall be allowed.

" And be it further enacted, that the several collectors or officers appointed to collect and receive the said duties, customs and imposts, shall from time to time be accountable and pay the same to the Governors of the said College of William and Mary, or such other person or persons as shall be by them lawfully deputed, and that for the receiving and paying thereof, the said collector or collectors shall be allowed two per cent." [1]

By means of this appropriation and sundry private subscriptions [2] the college building was completed in 1700, and in it

[1] *Ibid.*, II, 123-4.

[2] In the Calendar of Virginia State Papers is included a bill for facilitating the payment of the donations to the College of William and Mary in Virginia. This Act is undated, but owing to its internal evidence, Francis Nicholson, Governor, the Queen dead, the King, William, still living, and the Trustees of the College active in establishing the school, the editor assigns it to the year 1698. He says, " the bill seems to have been suggested by the Council, but whether the House of Burgesses ever passed it cannot be determined."

" Whereas, for a continual supply of the ministry for the church of Virginia for the pious education of truth in morality and good learning, and for the propagation of the Christian faith in the West Indies, propositions have been made by certain persons piously inclined, for the founding and erecting a college or place of universal study within the dominion of Virginia pursuant to which said proposition, certain briefs were at several times issued for subscription to be made of free and voluntary donations toward the promoting and carrying on so good a work; to which said briefs or instruments of writing several persons did subscribe for divers sums of money, tobacco and other things, did by such subscription oblige themselves, their heirs, executors and administrators, to pay the said several sums of money, tobacco and other things in the said subscriptions mentioned at a time — —- to come to such person or persons as by law should be appointed to receive the same. Now, to the end, that the building and furnishing the said college may be carried on with the greater ease and expedition, and for the ——— about the persons to whom the said donations ——— Be it enacted by the Governor in Council and Burgesses Henry Harwell and Charles ———, Esq., James Blair, John ———, Benjamin Harrison and Miles Cary, Wm. Randolph Esqs., and Mathew Page, Gent., trustees and founders of the College of William and Mary, in Virginia, or the major part of them or of the longest livers or the longest liver of them, and his or their heirs shall be or are hereby declared to be persons apt and capable in law and sufficiently empowered by the charter granted by his present Majesty and the Queen of blessed memory to take and receive all such subscriptions or donations as before the date of this Act by any obligation or sub-

the House of Burgesses met until 1705 when the building was destroyed by fire.   In that year it was decided to locate the

scription have been made or given towards the building, erecting and founding a free school and college within the colony and dominion of Virginia, and that in case of refusal or non-payment of the said subscription or donation, or any part thereof by any person or persons whatsoever, the said Francis Nicholson and the rest of the trustees and founders aforementioned, or the major part of them, or of the longest livers or the longest liver of them, and his or their heirs shall be and are hereby declared and from henceeforward shall be taken and deemed to be apt and capable in law to sue, implead and prosecute all and every such person or persons whatsoever, and to use all other lawful ways and means for the recovery of all and every such subscription or subscriptions, donation or donations, and of every part and parcel thereof as fully and amply to all intents and purposes as if the said obligation had been expressly made payable to the said Francis Nicholson and the rest of the trustees and founders aforementioned, or to the major part of them, or the longest livers or the longest liver of them or their heir or heirs, to and for the uses, interest and purposes aforesaid, and after the receipt of any of the said subscriptions or donations, either by such legal process or by voluntary payment of any person or persons, the said trnstees and founders as aforesaid, are hereby fully empowered to acquit, exonerate and discharge all and every such person or persons whatsoever of and from the said payment or payments and every ——— ———— ——— ———— that all and every part and parcel of the said subscriptions or donations ——— ——— present Act or any part thereof.   Aud be it further enacted, &c., that the heirs, executors and administrators of any person or persons, deceased, who hath made any of the said subscriptions or donations, shall be and are hereby ——— and intended to be held and obliged to the payment thereof as ——— and firmly as any other person or persons whatsoever ———." (*Calendar of Virginia State Papers and other manuscripts*, 1652-1781.   Edited by William P. Palmer, M. D., Richmond, 1875.   I, 61-62.   Also foot-note, p. 61.)

There are some striking facts concerning the condition which the above bill implies, and the relation between the college and the government during the years 1693 to 1698, the interval between the two administrations of Governor Nicholson, which was marked by the coming of Sir Edmund Andros to Virginia, in the anonymous " *Account of the Present State and Government of Virginia*," which is supposed to have been written in England about 1697 by one who had been resident in Virginia.

" Towards the building he [the King] gave near two thousand pounds, in ready cash, out of the bank of quit-rents, in which Governor Nicholson left at that time about four thousand, five hundred pounds; and toward the endowment, the King gave the neat produce of the penny per pound in Virginia and Maryland, worth two hundred pounds per annum, and the surveyor general's place, worth fifty pounds per annum, and the choice of ten thousand acres of land in Pamunckey

new capitol at Middle Plantation.　A town to be known by the
name of Williamsburg was also to be settled there, and the

Neck, and ten thousand more on the south side of the Black-water swamp, which
were tracts of land till that time prohibited to be taken up.　The General Assembly also gave the college a duty on skins and furs, worth better than one hundred
pounds a year, and they got subscriptions in Virginia, in Governor Nicholson's
time, for about two thousand, five hundred pouuds towards the building.　With
these beginnings the trustees of the college went to work, but their good Governor,
who had been the greatest encourager in that country of this design (on which he
had laid out three hundred and fifty pounds of his own money) being at that time
removed from them, and another put in his place, that was of a quite different
spirit and temper, they found their business go on very heavily, and such difficulties in everything, that presently, upon change of the Governor, they had as many
enemies as ever they had friends; such an universal influence and sway has a
person of that character in all affairs of that country.　The gentlemen of the
Council, who had been the forwardest to subscribe, were the backwardest to pay;
then every one was for finding shifts to evade and elude their subscriptions, and the
meaner people were so influenced by their countenance and example (men being
easily persuaded to keep their money) that there was not one penny got of new
subscriptions, nor paid of the old two thousand, five hundred pounds but about five
hundred pounds.　Nor durst they put the matter to the hazard of a lawsuit, where
this new Governor and his favorites were to be their judges.　Thus it was with the
funds for building; and they fared little better with the funds for endowments; for
notwithstanding the first choice they are to have of the land by the charter, patents
were granted to others for vast tracts of land, and every one was ready to oppose
the college in taking up the land; their survey was violently stopped, their chain
broken, and to this day they can never get to the possession of the land.　But the
trustees of the college being encouraged with a gracious letter the King writ to the
Governor, to encourage the college, and to remove all the obstructions of it, went
to work, and carried up one-half of the designed quadrangle of the building, advancing money out of their own pockets where the donations fell short.　They founded
their grammar school, which is in a very thriving way, and having the clear right
and title to the land, would not be baffled in that point, but have struggled with
the greatest man in the government next the Governor, *i. e.*, Mr. Secretary
Wormley, who pretends to have a grant *in futuro* for no less than thirteen thousand acres of the best land in Paumunkey Neck.　The cause is not yet decided,
only Mr. Secretary has again stopped the chain, which it is not likely he would do,
if he did not know that he should be supported in it.

The collectors of the penny per pound likewise are very remiss in laying their
accounts before the governors of the college, according to the instructions of the
commissioners of the customs; so that illegal trade is carried on, and some of these
gentlemen refuse to give any account upon oath.—This is the present state of the
college.　(*Mass. Hist. Col.*, First Series, V, 164–166.)

Assembly opined that it would " prove highly advantageous and beneficial to his Majesty's royal College of William and Mary to have the conveniences of a town near the same."[1] The College, however, does not seem to have immediately enjoyed the promised advantages and benefits of this arrangement; for on October 23, 1710, Governor Spotswood writes to William Blathwayt, Surveyor and Auditor General of all the King's revenues in America, concerning the impoverished condition of the College : " I must, however, entreat you will be pleased to use your interest that no new draughts be made on the quit-rents of this colony till her Majesty's gracious instructions for re-building the College shall be accomplished, since you will observe by the accounts which Mr. Byrd tells me he sends by this conveyance, how much that revenue is sunk by the large drafts that have been lately made on it and the decrease of the price of tobacco. I have endeavored to make the Governors of the College sensible how much they already owe to your favor, and they all acknowledge it with the gratitude that becomes them . . . ."[2]

Alexander Spotswood, who was Governor of Virginia from 1710 to 1722, showed great devotion to the well being of the College. He was specially interested in its attempts at the education of Indian youths. In 1797 an Indian school had been annexed to the College by special endowment.[3] In 1711, Governor Spotswood remitted the tribute of skins required from the colony's tributary Indians on condition that two sons

---

[1] *Hening*, III, 422.

[2] *Spotswood Letters*, I, 17-18. Virginia Historical Society, Richmond, 1882.

[3] In 1691 the estate of the Hon. Robert Boyle was left in trust for such charitable and pious uses as the executors might think best. Consequently, 5,400 pounds sterling was invested in lands whose rents were appropriated to the education of Indian youths at the Colleges of William and Mary, and Harvard in Cambridge. For seven years Harvard's portion was £90, and then the Bishop of London arranged for the whole amount to go to the Virginian college. (*English Institutions and the American Indian*, p. 52. James A. James, Ph. D., in Johns Hopkins University Studies, Baltimore, 1894.)

of the chief men of each settlement should be sent to the Brasserton, the so-called Indian school in the College.[1] Referring to this remittance of one of the special gubernatorial perquisites, Spotswood writes to the Board of Trade on November 17, 1711 :

" I hope the example I have set with what I have recommended in my speech to the Assembly [on] the subject, will prompt them to settle some fund towards the education of the Indians,[2] since that already given to the College by Mr. Boyle [200 lbs.] is too small for the maintenance of so great a number as are like to be there in a short time." [3]

The Governor's hopes prove to have been ill-founded. On December 28, he writes to Lord Dartmouth: " I cannot but be much concerned to see this design [conversion of and friendship with the Indians] so much slighted, and such a violent disposition prevail among the Burgesses for extirpating all Indians without distinction of friends or enemies, that a project I laid before them for assisting the College to support the charge of these hostages, though proposed on such a foot as would not have cost the country one farthing, has been thrown aside without allowing it a debate in their House."[4] The Governor gives a different version of this episode to the Bishop of London on July 26, 1712.

" I could have wished our Assembly would have settled some fund for this service, but as they value themselves upon furnishing a handsome maintenance to a number of the orthodox clergy equal, if not exceeding all the other English plan-

---

[1] *Letters*, I, 122. Before this, the Indians in the College had been ransomed from other Indians who had held them as prisoners of war. (*English Institutions and the American Indian*, p. 52.)

[2] The Assemblies of 1655 and 1656 had offered to see to it that the Indian children who might be brought into the colony as hostages should be reared "in Christianity, civility, and the knowledge of necessary trades." The Assembly also agreed to recompense those persons in the colony who had such children in charge. (*Ibid.*, I, 396, 410.)

[3] *Ibid.*, I, 123.   [4] *Ibid.*, I, 134.

tations on the continent, there's very little expectations of bringing them either to augment the present salaries of the ministers or entering upon new expenses for evangelizing the heathen."[1]

In the same letter, the Governor appeals for aid in this work to the Society for Propagating the Gospel in Foreign Parts and to the nobility and gentry of England. He also suggests that the churches and schools thus established for the Indians might likewise profitably supply the needs of the more remote English in the colony.

Governor Spotswood was also solicitous of the other affairs of the College. July 28, 1711 he writes to Mr. Blathwayt: . . . "having seen the letter you writ to Colonel Diggs in behalf of Mr. Le Fevre, I very gladly embrace the opportunity of doing honor to your recommendation by getting the Governor of the College to receive him as mathematic professor with the salary of eighty pounds per annum."[2]   May 8, 1712, the Governor writes on the same business to the Bishop of London. . . . "I gave your Lordship an account of Mr. Le Fevre's admission into the College upon your Lordship's recommendation and am now to acquaint you that after a trial of three quarters of a year, he appeared so negligent in all the posts of duty and guilty of some other very great irregularities, that the Governors of the College could no longer bear with him, and were obliged to remove him from his office, though at the same time out of regard to the honorable recommendation he brought with him, they continued his salary for four months longer than he officiated. I'm apt to believe most of his irregularities were owing to an idle hussy he brought over with him, because since she left him, (for I got her a passage back to England last February) he has left off that scandalous custom of drinking, and appears quite another

---

[1] *Ibid.*, I, 175.   On this subject see also *Letters*, I, 156-7, 176-8; II, 63-4.
[2] *Ibid.*, I, 103.

man, being now settled at a gentleman's house for teaching
his son and some others of that neighborhood, and has a competent salary, enough to keep him from being any more bur-
densome to your Lordship or his other friends, especially if
the small exhibition which he says was promised him at his
leaving England is still continued, and I'm not without hopes,
from this extraordinary change in him, that he may yet recommend himself to his former place in the College."[1]

Even if the backslider was eventually reinstated in the College, he could not have continued long in the place, for in
June, 1716, the Governor writes to the Reverend Francis Fon-
taine in England that he had recommended him, Francis Fon-
taine, for the vacant chair of philosophy and mathematics and
that the Governors of the College had agreed to his appointment. The Governor furthermore assures the divine that if
he accepts the position he will be honored as being the first
professor of " university learning " in the colony ; for hitherto
owing to exigencies of building and destruction by fire, the
College had not "arrived to any greater perfection than a
grammar school." [2]

In 1718 a special appropriation was made by the Assembly
to the College.

At a General Assembly, begun at the Capitol the twenty-
third day of April, 1718.

CHAPTER III. " AN ACT FOR GRANTING ONE THOUSAND POUNDS
OUT OF THE PUBLIC FUND, FOR THE MAINTAINING AND
EDUCATING SCHOLARS OF THE COLLEGE OF
WILLIAM AND MARY

" One thousand pounds out of the fund in the hand of Colonel
Peter Beverley, Treasurer, is given to the Visitors and Governors, to be by them laid out for the maintaining and educating
such and so many of the ingenious scholars, natives of this
colony, as they shall think fit.

[1] *Ibid.*, I, 156–7.   [2] *Ibid.*, II, 166–7.

" Provided, that distinct accounts of this benefaction be kept and ready always for the inspection of the General Assembly, or their order."[1]

Of this Act Governor Spotswood in a report to the Board of Trade under date of August 14, 1718, writes as follows:

"The second is entitled An Act for granting one thousand pounds out of the public fund for the maintaining and educating scholars at the College of William and Mary. The title of this Act sufficiently expresses the intention. The money is to be laid out by the Visitors and Governors of the College, and the profit thereof applied towards the maintenance and education of such scholars as shall be chosen from time to time by the said Visitors. This being an act of charity, I readily give my assent, though there be some thing in it which I could have wished had been left out. I mean the partiality the Assembly has shown in confining the benefit of these scholarships solely to the natives of this colony, which, in my opinion, shows but little regard for the public interest in making such a distinction between the natives and others who remove hither; for seeing a person who brings in a family to dwell here contributes more to the increase of the country than he who by his birth and the fortune he receives from his ancestors, is necessarily determined to a residence, perhaps involuntary, the children of one have at least an equal right with those of the other to whatever advantages the country affords, and indeed as this case is rather more since the fund out of which this money is given hath arisen chiefly by the duties on foreign importation, to which the natives contributed very little; but there's no arguing against men of such selfish principles, and to have made the objection would have proved the loss of the charity. However, if your Lordships should for this cause disapprove the Act, it is in a manner suspended, for a time since the money can not be paid without my warrant, and the Governors of the College being yet unresolved

[1] *Hening,* IV, 74.

bout the manner of laying it out, I can easily delay the payment 'till your Lordships shall be pleased to signify your opinion thereon."[1]

During the next thirty years several orders and grants in aid of the College of William and Mary were made by the Assembly.

In 1723, the president, masters, professors and students, were exempted from all military service.[2] Schoolmasters had been exempted in 1705.[3]

In 1726, certain excise duties were granted to the College.

"AN ACT FOR LAYING A DUTY ON LIQUORS.

"XIX. And for as much as the present revenue of the College of William and Mary is not sufficient to maintain the full number of masters or professors required by the charter of the said College, and thereby the progress of learning hath been much obstructed, and the will of the royal founders in great measure frustrated,

"XX. Be it further enacted by the authority aforesaid, that the sum of two hundred pounds per annum, out of the said duty of one penny upon every gallon of wine, rum, brandy and other distilled spirits, by this Act imposed as aforesaid, is and shall be appropriated for the relief of the said College, for and during the said term of twenty-one years, shall be paid by the said Treasurer half yearly, in equal proportions, unto the surviving trustees of the said College, until the same shall be transferred to the president and masters and from and after such transfer then to the president and masters and their successors, for and towards the maintaining and supporting the full number of masters and professors, which are to reside in the said college.

"And if at any time there shall be no trustees of the said college residing in this country, before such transfer shall be

---

[1] *Letters*, II, 287–8.   [2] *Ibid.*, IV, 119.   [3] *Ibid.*, III, 336.

made, then the said sum of two hundred pounds shall be, in manner aforesaid, paid to the visitors and governors of the said college, or to such person as they shall appoint to receive the same."[1]

In 1734 was passed

"AN ACT FOR THE BETTER SUPPORT AND ENCOURAGEMENT OF THE COLLEGE OF WILLIAM AND MARY IN VIRGINIA.

"Whereas the College of William and Mary in Virginia, consisting of a president, six masters, or professors, and one hundred scholars, more or less, graduated or non-graduates, founded and endowed by William and Mary, of blessed memory late King and Queen of England, etc., by their royal charter, under the great seal of England, bearing date at Westminster, the eighth day of February, in the fourth year of their reign, and since encouraged and supported by several other gifts and donations, hath, of late, been much injured in its revenues by divers frauds and abuses, particularly in the exportation of tobacco from hence to other British plantations in America, without paying the duty of one penny per pound, imposed by a statute of the Parliament of England, made in the twenty-fifth year of the reign of King Charles the Second, which was granted by the said royal charter, among other things, to certain trustees therein appointed, for erecting, building and founding of said college, and since transferred by the survivors of them, pursuant to the charter, to the said president and masters, and in the exportation of skins and furs without paying the several duties imposed by an Act of the General Assembly, of the fourth year of the reign of the late Queen Anne, for the better support of the said college, so that by the deficiency of these revenues, which fall short of the annual expenses of the College about one hundred and fifty pounds per annum, it is fallen much in debt, and that must

[1] *Hening*, IV, 148-9.

increase when the edifices and buildings thereunto belonging shall require repairs, which must necessarily be expected.

"II. And, for as much as the supporting and encouraging so hopeful a work, is of the greatest importance to the people of this colony, for the advancement of learning, and the good education of youth, wherein we have already seen some good effects, Be it enacted, [here follow provisions for the swearing to of consignments of skins and tobacco.] . . .

"VII. And to the end the said duties upon skins and furs may not be defrauded by the carrying the same by land or water, into Maryland, Pennsylvania, or North Carolina, which is very easy and much practised by many people, not only to the impoverishing the College, but to the great diminution of the trade of this colony, Be it further enacted, that where any person, or persons shall hereafter be found travelling upon the frontiers with any skins or furs, it shall be lawful for any justice of the peace, sheriff or constable of the county where such person shall be found, to seize such skins or furs, unless the person, or persons carrying the same, shall produce a certificate under the hand of a justice of the peace in this colony, that he is an inhabitant of the colony; and, moreover, shall make oath that he will not carry the said skins or furs, or cause the same to be carried, into any other colony or province, without paying the said duties. And in case any skins or furs shall be hereafter seized by virtue of this act, one moiety thereof shall be forfeited to the person seizing the same, and the other moiety to the King, his heirs and successors, for the better support of the College of William and Mary in Virginia.

"VIII. And be it further enacted, that where any hides, skins or furs shall be exported, either by land or water, contrary to this or the said former Act, the owner shall forfeit the value thereof: And that one moiety of all the penalties herein inflicted and not otherwise disposed of, shall be to the King, his heirs and successors, for the better support of the College of William and Mary in Virginia, and the other moiety to the informer, to be recovered with costs by action of debt, or information, in any court of record within this dominion.[1]

"IX. And, to the end the said president and masters may not depend altogether upon the provisions herein made for the improvement of their revenues, which may be perhaps still precarious, but may receive a more certain relief, Be it further enacted, that after the twenty-fifth day of October, in the year of our Lord one thousand seven hundred and thirty-five, the whole duty of one penny for every gallon of rum, brandy, and other distilled spirits, and of wine imported, laid by one Act of the General Assembly, made at a session held in the twelfth year of the reign of the late King George the first, to continue for twenty-one years, out of which two hundred pounds per annum was appropriated for the relief of the said college, be given to the said president and masters and their successors for the residue of the said term; and shall be applied and disposed of to such good uses, for the better support of the College, as by the visitors and governors of the College, or the greater part of them, shall from time to time be directed and appointed; so as some part thereby shall be laid out and applied for buying such books for the use of the scholars and students in the College, as the said visitors and governors, or the greater part of them, shall think most necessary; and such books so to be bought, shall be marked thus, 'The Gift of the General Assembly of Virginia, in the year 1734,' and shall forever be preserved and kept in the public library of the said College.

"And be it further enacted, That the president, masters, scholars and students of the College of William and Mary in Virginia, and all the domestic servants belonging to the College, be from henceforth exempted from being listed as tith-

---

[1] Similar provisions were made in 1748 to prevent the fraudulent exportation of tobacco. (*Ibid.*, VI, 92–94.)

ables in the county of James-City, and from paying any public, county or parish levies, forever."[1]

In 1744 the duty on hides was raised to 2s. 6d. for every raw hide and 5s. for every tanned hide exported out of the province. This increase of revenue was planned for the benefit of the College, the former revenue having been found " by experience . . . insufficient to answer the purposes for which the same was laid."[2]

In 1745, the whole of the excise tax—one penny upon every gallon of wine, rum, brandy and other distilled spirits—was appropriated "to the relief" of the College of William and Mary for a term of eleven years. It was to "be applied and disposed of for the founding scholarships, and such other good uses, for the better support of the College, as by the Visitors and Governors of the said College, or the greater part of them, shall, from time to time, be directed and appointed, and not otherwise ; and shall be accounted for to the Assembly."[3]

This Act was continued in 1759, 1764, 1766 and 1769. In this last year the duty was taken off beer and ale. And at this time the founding of professorships, as well as scholarships, is urged upon the Visitors and Governors of the College.

In 1752, Lord Dinwiddie came to Virginia as royal Governor. In reply to the welcoming address made to him by the President and Masters of the College, he said :

" I have always looked on seminaries of learning with an awful respect and true regard. The College of William and Mary is undoubtedly a very great blessing to Virginia. The education of the young gentlemen in the different sciences, the examination into their several genuises, the cultivating their minds with morality, virtue, religion and honor, so far as to qualify them for the services of their country, is a very great

[1] *Ibid.*, IV, 429–433.

[2] *Ibid.*, V. 236–7. Four years later a return was made to the former customs (*Ibid.*, VI, 91–2.)

[3] *Ibid.*, V, 317–318.   [4] *Ibid.*, VIII, 335–6.

and important charge which is reposed in you . . . I shall watch every opportunity wherein I can be of use or service to the College."[1]

Governor Dinwiddie did prove to be anxious for the prosperity of the College. On September 12, 1757, he writes to the Lord Bishop of London :

" . . . The Visitors of the College, and indeed the country in general, have for many years been greatly dissatisfied with the behaviour of the Professor of Philosophy [Rev. Wm. Preston] and the Master of the Grammar School, [Rev. Wm. Robinson] notoriously on account of intemperance and irregularity laid to their charge, but also because they had married, and contrary to all rules of seats of learning, kept their wives children and servants in college, which must occasion much confusion and disturbance. And the Visitors having frequently expressed their disapprobation of their families remaining in college, about a year ago they removed them into town, and since that time, as if they had a mind to show their contempt of the Visitors, they have lived much at home, and negligently attended their duty in college. In a meeting, therefore, on the twentieth of May last, there was a complaint laid before them of their neglect of duty and immoral conduct, being often very drunk and very bad examples to the students, on which it was ordered that the President should write to your Lordship to be so kind as to recommend and send over two proper persons in their room. The Professor of Philosophy declared his intention of going home, which prevented a strict enquiry into his conduct. He goes home in the fleet, which is happy for the College and the country, for he is a warm, turbulent man, and I fear has been the chief promoter of all the disturbances lately here."[2]

During the next ten years several special Acts for elementary

---

[1] *The Official Records of Robert Dinwiddie, in the Collections of the Virginia Historical Society*, I, 5. Edited by R. A. Brock, Richmond, 1883.

[2] *Ibid.*, II, 696–7.

education and an additional appropriation to the College were passed by the legislature. In 1752 the legislature passed an additional Act for incorporating the borough of Norfolk—Section 9 reads as follows : " IX And whereas at the time of laying out the aforesaid town of Norfolk, a lot, or parcel of land, was laid off and set apart, for the use of a school, for the benefit of the inhabitants of the said Borough and County of Norfolk, which said lot, or parcel of ground, is capable of being improved and built upon, Be it enacted by the authority aforesaid, that the Court of the said County of Norfolk, and the mayor, recorder and aldermen of the said borough, or the major part of them, shall have full power and authority to build on, or let the said lot, or parcel of land, for any term of years, for the use and benefit of the said school, and to provide and agree with an able master for the said school, capable to teach the Greek and Latin tongues, which said master, before he be received or admitted to keep school, shall undergo an examination before the masters of the College of William and Mary, and the minister of Elizabeth parish, for the time being, and produce a certificate of his capacity, and also a license from the Governor, or Commander in Chief of this dominion, for the time being, agreeable to his Majesty's instructions ; which said master, qualified as aforesaid, shall continue in such office during his good behavior, and no longer."[1] Ten years later the attention of the government was again turned to the administration of the Norfolk town school. It appeared that " by reason of the variety of opinions frequently happening " between the county justices and the mayor, recorder and aldermen of the borough in the choice of a schoolmaster and in the government of the school, the school had been greatly neglected and the good intentions of the Assembly's Act of 1752 in great measure frustrated. Accordingly the Assembly proceeded to vest the right of nominating a schoolmaster wholly in the mayor, recorder and aldermen of the borough.[2]

[1] *Ibid.*, VI, 265.   [2] *Ibid.*, VII, 510–511.

In 1753 and Act was passed " for enabling the justices of the peace of the county of Elizabeth City, and the minister and church wardens of the parish of Elizabeth City, in that county, to take and hold certain lands devised by the will of Benjamin Sym, for a free school, and other charitable uses."

"Whereas Benjamin Sym, late of the county of Elizabeth City, deceased, was in his life time seized in fee-simple, of a tract or parcel of land, containing two hundred acres, or thereabouts, with a marsh contiguous thereto; situate, lying, and being in the county of Elizabeth City, and being so seized, by his last will and testament bearing date the twelfth day of February, in the year of our Lord, one thousand six hundred and thirty-four, devised the use of the said land (by the description of two hundred acres of land being in the Poquoson River), with the milk, and increase of eight milch cows, for the maintenance of a learned, honest man, to keep upon the said ground a free school for the education and instruction of the children of the adjoining parishes of Elizabeth City, and Kiquotan, viz., from Mary's-Mount downwards, to the Poquoson River, and declared his will and desire to be, that the justices of the peace of the said county, (by the name and title of the worshipful the commanders, and the rest of the commissioners of this liberty) with the minister and church wardens of the said parish of Elizabeth City, should see his said will, from time to time justly and truly performed, and further declared his will and desire to be, that when there should be a sufficient increase of the said cattle, part of them should be sold and the money raised by such sale, laid out in building a school-house; and that the residue of the said increase, after the schoolmaster should have a sufficient stock, should be applied towards repairing the school-house, and maintaining poor children, or decayed or maimed persons, according to the directions of the said justices, minister and church wardens.

" II. And whereas the charitable intentions of the said Benjamin Sym, the donor, hath not been effectually fulfilled, to the end that the said charity may be more beneficial for the future.

" III. Be it enacted by the Lieutenant-Governor, Council, Burgesses of this present General Assembly, and it is hereby enacted by the authority of the same, that the present justices of the peace of the said county of Elizabeth City, and such as after them shall succeed to be justices of the peace for the said county, during the time they shall so continue justices; the present minister of the said parish of Elizabeth City, and such as after him shall succeed to be minister thereof, during the time they shall so continue or be in the same office, and the present church-wardens of the said parish of Elizabeth City, and such as after them shall succeed to be church-wardens thereof, during the time they shall so continue in the same office; shall and may be trustees and governors of the said free school, and of the said tract or parcel of land and marsh, with the appurtenances at all times hereafter forever. And that the said trustees and directors shall forever hereafter stand and be incorporated, established and founded, in name and deed, a body politic and corporate, to have continuance forever, by the name of the Trustees and Governors of Sym's free school in the County of Elizabeth City, and that they, the said trustees and governors, may have perpetual succession, and that by that name they and their successors may forever after have, hold, and enjoy the above mentioned tract or parcel of land, containing by estimation two hundred acres, according to the known and reputed bounds thereof, and the marsh aforesaid, with the appurtenances; and that the said trustees and governors, and their successors, or the greater part of them, by the same name shall and may have power, ability and capacity, to demise, lease and grant the said tract or parcel of land and marsh, with the appurtenances, and the present stock of cattle being thereon, and belonging thereto, for any term of years not exceeding twentyone years, or for any term of years determinable upon one, two, or three lives or for one, two, or three lives, reserving the best and most improved rent that can be got for the same; and to take, acquire, and purchase, and to

sue and be sued, and to do, perform, and execute all other lawful acts and things, good, necessary, and profitable, for the said
corporation, in as full and ample a manner and form, to all intents, constructions and purposes, as any other incorporation,
or body politic or corporate, fully and perfectly founded and
incorporated, may do. And that the said trustees and governors, and their successors for the time being, may have and
use a common seal for the making such their demises, leases,
and grants, and for the doing all and every other thing and
things touching, or in any wise concerning, the said incorporation; and that the said trustees and governors, and their successors for the time being, or the greater part of them, shali
and may have full power and authority, by writing under their
common seal, to nominate and appoint when, and as often as
they shall think good, such person as they shall approve of, to
be master of the said free school; which said master, before
he be received or admitted to keep school, shall undergo an
examination before the minister of the said parish, for the time
being, and produce a certificate of his capacity, and also a
license from the Governor or Commander-in-chief of this
dominion, for the time being, agreeable to his Majesty's instructions. And the said trustees and governors, and their
successors for the time being, shall and may have full power
and authority to visit the said free school, and to order, reform
and redress all disorders and abuses in and touching the government and disposing of the same, and to remove the said
master, as to them, or the greater part of them, shall seem just,
fit, and convenient. And that the said trustees and governors,
and their successors, or the greater part of them for the time
being, shall apply the rents to be paid for the said tract or
parcel of land, with the appurtenances, and stock of cattle,
aforesaid, to the maintenance of the said school-master, and
erecting and keeping in repair a sufficient school-house for his
dwelling, and teaching the children of the adjoining parishes of
Elizabeth City and Kiquotan, viz. from Mary's-Mount down-

wards, to the Poquoson river; and the surplus, in case there shall be any, to the maintenance of such poor children, or decayed or maimed persons, as the said trustees and governors, and their successors, or the major part of them, shall think fit.

"IV. And be it further enacted by the authority aforesaid, that the said trustees and governors, and their successors, or the greater part of them for the time being, shall have full power, ability and capacity, by the name aforesaid, to sue for, and recover all rents, and arrears of rents, and all and every sum and sums of money, due for the occupation of the said tract or parcel of land, by virtue of any agreement or contract, heretofore made with the present justices of the peace of the said county, and minister and church-wardens of the said parish, or their predecessors, or the greater part of them, against the person and persons from whom the same are due, his and their executors and administrators; and also all damages sustained by occasion of not repairing the houses on the said tract of land, or by the occasion of the breach of any other part of such contract or agreement, any law, or custom to the contrary, notwithstanding.

"V. Saving to the King's most excellent Majesty, his heirs and successors, and to all and every other person and persons, bodies politic and corporate, their heirs and successors, other than the person and persons claiming as heir or heirs of the said Benjamin Sym, all such estate, right, title, claim and demand, which they, or any of them, should or might have, of, in, to, or out of the premises, or any of them, or any part thereof."[1]

In 1756 an Act was passed "for appointing trustees to lease out certain lands and slaves, and for other purposes therein mentioned."

"I. Whereas Henry Peasley, formerly of the County of Glocester, deceased, was in his life time, and at the time of his death, seized in fee-simple of a tract or parcel of land, con-

[1] *Ibid.*, VI, 389–392.

taining six hundred acres, or thereabouts, lying and being in the Parish of Abingdon, in the said county, and being so seized by his will and testament in writing, bearing date the seventeenth day of March, in the year of our Lord, one thousand six hundred and seventy-five, devised the same by the description of the land he then lived on, together with ten cows and one breeding mare, for the maintenance of a free school forever, to be kept with a schoolmaster for the education of the children of the Parishes of Abingdon and Ware, forever.

"II. And whereas several slaves have been by different persons, since the above devise, given for the same purposes, but, by reason of the inconvenient situation of the said land, few children frequent the free school kept there, so that the charitable intention of the said Henry Peasley, and the other donors, is of little benefit to the said two parishes.

"III. And whereas it is represented to this present General Assembly, by the ministers, church wardens, and vestrymen of the said two parishes of Abingdon and Ware, that if proper persons were impowered to lease out the said land and slaves, the annual rents thereof would be sufficient to support and maintain a free school in each of the said parishes for the education of the children residing there. Be it therefore enacted, by the Lieutenant-Governor, Council and Burgesses, of this present General Assembly, and it is hereby enacted by the authority of the same, that the present ministers, church wardens, and vestrymen of the said two parishes of Abingdon and Ware, and the ministers, church wardens and vestrymen of the same parishes, for the time being, shall and may be, and they are hereby nominated and appointed trustees and governors of the said lands, slaves and other premisses forever; and that the said trustees and governors shall forever hereafter, stand, and be incorporated, established, and founded, in name and deed, a body politic and corporate to have continuance forever, by the name of the Trustees and Governors of Peasley's Free School, and that they the said trustees and gov-

ernors may have perpetual succession, and that by that name
they and their successors may forever hereafter have, hold and
enjoy the above-mentioned tract or parcel of land, slaves and
other premises, with their increase, and that the said trustees
and governors and their successors, or the greater part of
them, by the same name, shall and may have power, ability,
and capacity to demise, lease and grant the said tract or parcel
of land, slaves and other premises, for any term of years, not
exceeding twenty-one years, or for any term of years determinable upon one, two, or three lives, or for one, two, or three
lives, reserving the best and most improved rents that can be
got for the same, and to take, acquire and purchase, and to sue
and be sued, and to do, perform and execute all other lawful
acts and things, good, necessary and profitable for the said incorporation, in as full and ample a manner and form, to all intents, constructions and purposes, as any other incorporation
or body politic and corporate, fully and perfectly founded and
incorporated, may do; and that the said trustees and governors, and their successors, for the time being, may have and
use a common seal for making such their demises, leases and
grants, and for the doing all and every other thing and things
touching, or in any wise concerning, the said incorporation.

"IV. And be it further enacted, by the authority aforesaid,
that they, the said trustees and governors, and their successors,
or the greater part of them, shall and may, and they are hereby
impowered and required, to erect and found a free school in
some convenient part of each of the said parishes of Abingdon
and Ware, and by writing under their common seal, to nominate and appoint when, and as often as they shall think necessary, such person, or persons, as they shall approve of to be
masters of the said free school, respectively, which masters,
before they be admitted to keep school, shall undergo an examination before the minister of the parish in which the school
he shall be appointed master of shall be situated, and produce
a certificate of his capacity, and also a license from the Gover-

nor or Commander-in-chief of this dominion, for the time being, agreeable to his Majesty's instructions. And the said trustees and governors shall issue and apply the rents of the said tract or parcel of land, slaves and other premises for the erecting, maintaining and supporting a free-school and schoolmaster, in each of the said parishes forever, for the education of the children of the said parishes respectively, and the said trustees and governors, and their successors, for the time being, shall and may have full power and authority to visit the said free-schools, and to order, reform and redress all disorders and abuses in, and touching, the government and disposing of the same, and to remove the masters, as to them, or the greater part of them, shall seem just, fit, and convenient.

"V. And be it further enacted, by the authority aforesaid, that the said trustees and governors, and their successors, or the greater part of them, for the time being, shall have full power, ability and capacity, by the name aforesaid, to sue for and recover all rents and arrears of rent, and all and every sum and sums of money due for the use and occupation of the said tract or parcel of land, slaves and other premises, by virtue of any agreement or contract heretofore made by any person or persons whatsoever.

"VI. Saving to the King's most excellent Majesty, his heirs and successors, and to all and every other person and persons, bodies politic and corporate, their heirs and successors, other than the person or persons claiming as heir, or under the will of the said Henry Peasley, all such estate, right, title, claim and demand, which they, or any of them, should or might have, of, in, to, or out of the premises, or any of them, or any part thereof." [1]

In 1759 three pounds of the tax upon pedlars' licenses was appropriated to the College of William and Mary. At the same time it was provided that one-half the fine of £20

---

[1] *Ibid.*, VII, 41–43.

incurred by tax collectors through failure to enforce the law, was to go to the College.[1]

Chapter 30 of the laws passed at this same legislative session was,

"AN ACT FOR THE BETTER REGULATING EATON'S CHARITY-SCHOOL.

"I. Whereas notwithstanding the act of General Assembly, made in the third and fourth years of the reign of his present Majesty, intitled, An Act to enable the justices of the peace of the County of Elizabeth City and the minister and church-wardens of the Parish of Elizabeth City, in the said county, for the time being, to take and hold certain lands, given by Thomas Eaton, and to let leases thereof,[2] part of the said lands hath been unprofitable, the trustees having neglected to let the same; and it is doubted whether the said trustees have power to recover damages for any waste committed on the said land by the tenants, or for breach of contract in not building and planting thereon according to the terms of the leases, or for any arrearages of rent, the said trustees not being incorporated by the said act, and some of the said leases being either lost, or in the custody of the tenants who will not produce them: Be it therefore enacted, by the Lieutenant-Governor, Council, and Burgesses, of this present General Assembly, and it is hereby enacted, by the authority of the same, that the present justices of the peace of the said County of Elizabeth City, and ministers and churchwardens of the said Parish of Elizabeth City and their successors, during the time they shall so continue in their respective offices, shall and may be trustees and governors of the charity-school on the said land, with the appurtenances, and shall forever hereafter stand and be incorporated, established and founded, in name and deed, a body politic and corporate, to have continuance forever by the name of Trustees and Governors of Eaton's Charity-school, in

---

[1] *Ibid.*, VII, 284-5.

[2] *Ibid.*, IV, 306. Title only given by Hening.

the County of Elizabeth City, and shall and may have perpetual succession, and by that name forever. hereafter have,
hold and enjoy the said land with the appurtenances; and
that the said trustees and governors, and their successors, or
the greater part of them, by the same name, shall and may
have power, ability and capacity to demise, lease and grant
any part of the said tract of land, with the appurtenances, not
already letten, for any term of years not exceeding twenty-one,
or for any term of years determinable upon one, two or three
lives, reserving the best and most improved rent that can be
got for the same; and to take, acquire and purchase, sue and
be sued, and to do, perform and execute all other acts and
things good, necessary and profitable for the said incorporation, in as full and ample manner and form, to all intents,
constructions and purposes, as any other incorporation or
body politic or corporate may do; and may have and use a
common seal for making such their demises, leases and grants,
and for doing all and every other thing and things touching
or concerning the said incorporation; and that the said
trustees and governors, and their successors, for the time
being, or the greater part of them, shall and may have full
power and authority, by writing, under their common seal, to
nominate and appoint, when, and as often as they shall think
good, such person as they shall approve of to be master of the
said charity-school, such master having been first examined
by the minister of the said parish for the time being, and
producing from him a certificate of his capacity, and a license
from the Governor or Commander-in-chief of this dominion,
for the time being, agreeable to his Majesty's instructions.
And the said trustees and governors, and their successors, for
the time being, shall and may have full power and authority
to visit the said charity-school, and to order and reform the
government thereof and to remove the said master as to them,
or the greater part of them, shall seem just and convenient;
and that the said trustees and governors, and their successors,

or the greater part of them, for the time being, shall apply the rents of the said land, with the appurtenances, to the maintenance of the said master and erecting and keeping in repair sufficient houses for his dwelling and teaching the children entitled to the said charity, and the surplus, in case there shall be any, to the other purposes mentioned in the will of the said Thomas Eaton, recited in the said Act.

" II. And be it further enacted, by the authority aforesaid, that the said trustees and governors, and their successors, or the greater part of them, for the time being, shall have full power, ability, and capacity, by the name aforesaid, to sue for and recover damages for any waste or trespass committed on the said land, and for not building, planting on and improving the same according to the terms of any leases heretofore made, and all rents and arrears of rents against the person or persons from whom the same are due, his and their executors and administrators ; and, in case any person or persons, holding any part of the said land by virtue of any lease or leases, will not produce such lease or leases, or accept of a new lease or leases, and cause the same to be recorded in the court of the said County of Elizabeth City, within six months after the passing of this Act, such lease or leases shall be void, and the said trustees and governors, and their successors, or the greater part of them, shall and may demise and let such tenements in the same manner as if such lease or leases had never been made.

" III. And whereas it will be for the benefit of the said charity if part of the timber and woods on the said land are sold : Be it therefore enacted, that the said trustees and governors, and their successors, shall have full power to sell the said timber and woods off the said land, reserving as much as will be sufficient for building on, repairing and fencing the same, in such manner as shall appear to them to be most beneficial for the said charity, and shall apply the interest thereof, and of the money to be recovered for the damages, rents and arrearages aforesaid, to the purposes hereinbefore mentioned.

" IV. And whereas the said foundation hath been abused by admitting a great number of children into the said school, whose parents are well able to pay for their education, for remedy whereof, Be it enacted by the authority aforesaid, that no person shall enjoy the benefit of the said charity school without consent of the master for the time being, except such poor children as the said trustees and governors, and their successors, or the greater part of them, shall from time to time declare to be the proper objects of the pious founder's charity.

" V. Saving to the King's most excellent Majesty, his heirs and successors, and to all and every other person and persons, bodies politic and corporate, their heirs and successors, other than the person and persons claiming as heir or heirs of the said Thomas Eaton, all such estate, right, title, claim and demand which they, or any of them, should or might have of, in, to or out of the premises, or any of them, or any part thereof.

" VI. Provided always, that no lease shall hereafter be made of the said land, or any part thereof, to the said trustees or their successors, or to any other person or persons to their use or benefit."[1]

[1] *Ibid.*, VII, 317–320.

MARYLAND

In 1632 Charles I. granted the territory which was bounded on the north by the 40th parallel and on the south west by the Potomac River, to Cecelius, Lord Baltimore, to whom palatine rights of government were also given. In 1633 a company of about 300 persons was sent over by the Proprietor, and within the next ten years the colony was increased by Puritan exiles from Virginia. From this time until 1664 constant strife and dissension existed in the province between the appointees of the Catholic proprietor and the representatives of the Puritan colonists. The first regular legislative body was convened in January, 1638, by Lieutenant-governor Calvert. It consisted of the Lieutenant-governor and three Councillors appointed by the Proprietary and 47 of the freemen and proxies of freemen in the province. In 1649 the Assembly was divided into two houses.[1]

The first indication of the attitude of these bodies towards education is to be found in the laws which they enacted for the protection of orphans and orphans' estates. At a session held at St. Mary's, on September 27, 1663, an additional Act for the Advancement of Children's Estates was returned to the Council from the Lower House, " wherein they desired the words ' handicraft, trade ' might be struck out." The Upper House " ordered that answer be returned that to strike out those words, ' handicraft, trade,' was to destroy the very thing intended by the act, which was to breed up all the indigent youth of this province to handicraft trade and no other."[2]

[1] *The History of Maryland*, II, 49, 55, 349. John Leeds Bozman. Balti. more, 1837.

[2] *Proceedings and Acts of the General Assembly of Maryland*, January, 1637– September, 1664, p. 470. *Archives of Maryland.* Edited by William Hand Browne. Baltimore, 1883.

This bill was passed in accordance with the desire of the Upper House. It provided " First that no account be allowed for diet, clothes, physic or else against any orphans' estates, but they be educated and provided for by the interest of the estate and increase of their stock according to the proportion of their estates, if it will bear it. But if the estate be so mean and inconsiderable that it will not extend to a free education, that it is enacted that such orphans shall be bound apprentices to some handicraft, trade or other person at the discretion of the court, until one and twenty years of age, except some kinsman or relation will maintain them for the interest of the sole estate they have without diminution of the principal, ... That the court take able and sufficient security for orphans' estates and enquire yearly of the security, and if the court see cause, to have it changed and called in and placed as the court shall think fit. The said court to enquire also whether the orphans be kept maintained and educated according to their estates, and if they find any notorious defect, to remove the orphans to their other guardians, and also for those that are bound apprentices to change their masters if they use them rigorously or neglect to teach them their trades."[1] This Act was disapproved by the Proprietary in 1669 and a new Act for the preservation of orphans' estates was passed in 1671.[2] The new Act originated in the Lower House. It was read on October 16 in the Upper House. Four amendments were made, the first of which maintaining that " care must be taken to have the children educated in the religion of their deceased parents."[3] In a general Act that was passed in 1715 for testamentary administration, the liberality of this proviso was restricted. " X. Provided always, That where any person, being a Protestant, shall die, and leave a widow and children, and

---

[1] *Ibid.*, p. 495.

[2] *Laws of Maryland*, 1663, ch. 16 and note. Thomas Bacon. Annapolis, 1765.

[3] *Maryland Archives. Proceedings and Acts*, 1666–1676, p. 317.

such widow shall intermarry any person of the Romish communion, or be herself of that opinion and profession, it shall and may be lawful for his Majesty's Governor and Council, within this province, upon application to them made, to remove such child or children out of the custody of such parents, and place them where they may be securely educated in the Protestant religion."

In this Act the same reference was made to the free education of orphans as in previous Acts, and it was left to the discretion of the county courts to bind out poor children to "mariners or some handicraft trade." The justices of the county courts were also directed to annually summon a jury of twelve "good and lawful" men to enquire upon oath "whether the orphans be kept, maintained and educated, according to their estates? And whether apprentices are taught their trade, or rigorously used, and turned to common labor at the ax or hoe, instead of learning their trades? And if they find that orphans are not maintained and educated according to their estates, or apprentices neglected to be taught their trades, upon pretence that the last year is enough to learn their trade, that they remove them to other guardians and masters. And in case the jury find that any apprentice is not taught his trade, but put to other labor as aforesaid, the county court shall condemn the master of such apprentice to make the apprentice such satisfaction, as in justice his years of labor, or other work, shall deserve."[2]

[1] *Bacon's Laws*, 1715, ch. XXXIX.

[2] *Ibid.*, section XXI.

An interesting case of the application of these orphan and apprenticeship laws is entered on the legislative journals of May 13, 1682. On that day the Lower House sent the following message in writing to the Upper House: "This House have read a certificate from the Commissioners of St. Mary's County Court concerning Wadden Hanse, the daughter of one Hanse, a Swede, who was killed at the Susquehanna fort; and thereupon voted that £4000 be raised this year out of the public and ordered to be paid in St. Mary's county, that £1000 thereof be paid to William Wherritt for his keeping the child hitherto, that the other

On April 13, 1671, at a session held at East St. Mary's, a bill was introduced in the Upper House "for the Founding and Erecting of a School or College within this Province for the Education of Youth in Learning and Virtue."[1]

Two days later the Lower House took this bill into consideration, and "resolved that this House is willing to assent to this Act with these amendments, viz: That the place where the said college shall be erected shall be appointed by the Assembly most convenient for the country.[2]

"2. That the tutors or school masters of the said school or college may be qualified according to the reformed Church of England or that there may be two school masters, the one for the Catholic, and the other for the Protestant children, and that the Protestants may have liberty to choose their school master.

"3. That a time be appointed when the work shall begin and be set on foot.

"4. That the Lord Proprietor be pleased to set out his declaration of what privileges and immunity shall be enjoyed by the scholars that shall be brought up or taught at such school or college."

These amendments killed the bill, much to the regret of the Proprietaries, as may be inferred from the tenor of the correspondence between Governor Calvert and his father,

---

£3000 be paid to the commissioners of St. Mary's County to be by them paid to such person as shall take the child as an apprentice or orphan child, till she shall come to 18 years of age, the person that takes her to oblige to teach the girl to read and sew. Also voted that the girl be further considered when she comes to marry, or at the expiration of her time." The Upper House concurred with these votes on the same day. (*Archives of Maryland. Proceedings and Acts of the Assembly*, 1678–1683, p. 312.)

[1] *Ibid., Proceedings and Acts*, etc. April, 1666–June, 1676, p. 262.

[2] St. Mary's, the seat of the proprietary government, was not thought to be "most convenient for the country." After the Puritan revolution the capitol was removed to Annapolis.

[3] *Ibid.*, pp. 263–4.

Lord Baltimore. On June 2, 1673, the Governor writes: "Your Lordship's of the 21 of November, on the behalf of Mr. Robert Douglas, I received by his own hand, whom at present I entertain at my own house and employ him to teach my children, and shall give him all the encouragement that lies in my power. Shall endeavor the promoting of a school house and make him the master. In the mean time, till he can more advantageously dispose of himself, he shall be where he is; but doubt he will not find the people here so desirous of that benefit of educating their children in that nature as he might probably expect, for the remoteness of the habitation of one person from another will be a great obstacle to a school in that way that I perceive your lordship arrives at, and that would much conduce to the profit and advantage of the youth of this province."[1]

In spite of Lord Baltimore's evident zeal for education, nothing was accomplished by the government in that direction during the remainder of the 60 years of proprietary rule.

In 1692 a rebellion against proprietary authority was successful in the province and Maryland became a crown colony. The Protestant Episcopal church was established and a poll tax of 40 pounds of tobacco was levied for its support. The step from a government church to government schools was short, and to Governor Nicholson, ex-governor of Virginia and governor to Maryland in 1694, it seemed highly necessary.

At the opening of the Assembly in September, 1694, Governor Nicholson sent a message proposing "that a way be found out for building of a free school, and the maintenance for a schoolmaster and usher and writing master that can cast accounts."[2] The Governor also proposed to give £50 towards the building and £25 sterling a year during his

---

[1] Quoted in *History of Maryland*, p. 15. Bernard C. Steiner, Ph. D. *United States Bureau of Education, Circular of Information*, No. 2, 1894.

[2] *History of Education in Maryland*, p. 19. Bernard C. Steiner, Ph. D. *United States Bureau of Education, Circular of Information*, No. 2, 1894.

continuance in office towards the maintenance of the master. Sir Thomas Lawrence, secretary of the province, subscribed 5000 pounds of tobacco for the building and 2000 pounds per annum while in office towards the support of the masters. Four members of the Council subscribed 2000 lbs. of tobacco, 2 members, 1200 pounds, 3 members, 1000 pounds, and Councillor Brooke and Auditor General Randolph promised the respective yearly subscriptions of £5 3s. and £10 sterling.[1] On October 3 the Lower House replied to the Governor's message: "We have endeavored as far as able to follow your Excellency's example and in order thereunto have contributed towards the building such a free school as your Excellency hath proposed the sum of 45,400 pounds of tobacco and some absent members as yet have not subscribed; and doubt not that every well minded person within this province will contribute towards the same. And upon consideration thereof have had some debate concerning the building of one free school on the western and another on the eastern shore, and have nominated Severn and Oxford for the two places, which debate we leave to your Excellency's consideration and appointment. And to that end and purpose humbly desire a conference with your Excellency and council to consider of the best ways and methods to establish the same."[2] At this session the legislature enacted four laws bearing directly and indirectly upon education.

Chapter I was "An Act for the encouragement of learning and advancement of the natives of this province."[3]

Chapter XIX was "An Act for the imposition of 4 pence per gallon on liquors imported into this province." Its purpose was to raise money "for building and repairing court houses,

[1] *History of Maryland*, I, 350. J. Thomas Scharf, Baltimore, 1879.
[2] *Ibid.*

[3] *Bacon's Laws*, 1694, ch. I. Only the titles of this and the three following laws are given by Bacon. Nor are the texts of the laws to be found in any of the earlier compilations.

free schools, bridewells, or such public services."[1] The Act
was continued in 1695 for three years.[2]

Chapter XXIII was "an Act for laying an imposition on
several commodities exported out of this province." The
"imposition" was laid upon furs, beef, bacon, etc., for the
maintenance of free schools.[3]

Chapter XXXI was "a supplicatory Act to their sacred
Majesties, for erecting of free schools."[4]

Upon the signing of these session laws by the Governor, the
Assembly addressed a vote of thanks to him for his support of
religion and education.[5] The Assembly also wrote to the
Bishops of London and Canterbury in reference to their school
legislation. To the Bishop of London they write, on October
18, 1694:

"May it please your Lordship, under so glorious a reign,
wherein by God's providence, his true religion has been so
miraculously preserved, should we not endeavor to promote it,
we should hardly deserve the name of good Protestants or
good subjects ; especially considering how noble an example
is set before us by their Majesties' royal foundation now vigor-
ously carried on in Virginia. We have therefore in Assembly
attempted to make learning an handmaid to devotion, and
founded free schools in Maryland, to attend on their college in
that country. We only beg their Majesties' confirmation of an
act we have proposed for their establishment and of your Lordship a share of that assistance and care you have taken in promoting so great and so good a design as that of the College.
So charitable a founder of a school in opposition to that shop
of poisoning principles set open in the Savoy, we are confident
will favor our like pious designs in this province, wherein in-

[1] *Ibid.*   [2] *Ibid.*, chapter 20.

[3] *Ibid.*   [4] *Ibid.*

[5] *Council Proceedings, Liber F F.*, 791, 927, 1029. Cited in *An Historical
View of the Government of Maryland*, I, 263. John V. L. McMahon,
Baltimore, 1831.

structing our youth in the orthodox, preserving them from the infection of heterodox tenets and fitting them for the service of church and state in this uncultivated part of the world, are our chiefest aim and end." [1]

The assistance of the Archbishop of Canterbury was also requested by the Assembly, and Secretary Lawrence and Mr. Frisby of the House of Burgesses were commissioned to wait upon the Archbishop in person and entreat his grace to take upon himself the patronage of the free school. [2] The acceptance of the Archbishop was laid before the Assembly on October 13, 1695, and two days later the Upper House instructed the Lower House to send his lordship a letter of thanks. [3]

Governor Nicholson writes to the Archbishop, on May 26, 1698: " I . . . hope in God that before this by your Grace's interest, the laws are passed, especially that for free schools." [4]

In October, 1695, and in May, 1696, the Upper House made two unsuccessful proposals to the Lower House that the revenue that had been already raised by the tax on furs, etc., should be laid out on the building of a small schoolhouse and the maintenance of a schoolmaster. [5]

On September 18, 1695, the Upper House also proposed that the sheriffs should proceed to collect the school subscriptions. To this proposition the Lower House answers: " The tobacco that is subscribed is thought to be in good and secure hands, and when the work is begun and the workmen are agreed with by the trustees of the said free school, then the subscribers will be ready to pay their several subscriptions." [5]

On September 25, the Upper House informs the Lower that the Bishop of London has sent over a schoolmaster and that the school building must therefore go forward, and a collection of the subscriptions be made. [1] Consequently on September

[1] *Historical Collections relating to the American Colonial Church*, IV, 1–2.

[2] *Ibid.*, IV, 3.   [3] *Scharf's History*, I, 352.

[4] *American Col. Church Coll.*, IV, 26.

[5] *Steiner's History*, p. 20.

29, the Lower House resolves that the school trustees should speedily meet together and begin the building of a schoolhouse and to that end get in the school subscriptions as they were needed. "As to the schoolmaster, the House desire his Excellency will make him reader of some parish, and that he have half the 40 lbs. per poll,[1] if the same exceed not 10,000 lbs. of tobacco."[1]

On October 1, the Upper House renewed its request that some part of the fur revenue should be granted to the schoolmaster. On October 2, the Lower House replied that sufficient encouragement had already been granted to him by their recent resolves. On October 7, Schoolmaster Geddes was appointed reader of All Saints parish by the Governor at a salary of 10,000 lbs. of tobacco per annum "until further order." On June 3, 1697, Mr. Geddes was "placed out as undermaster to the college school in Virginia to save a present charge and to gain himself the more experience against the school here is built."[2]

In 1696 the Supplicatory Act for free schools which had been passed in 1694 was revised and amended in accordance with the King's instructions,[3] and then re enacted by legislature as

"A PETITIONARY ACT FOR FREE SCHOOLS.

"To His Most Excellent Majesty, &c.

"Dread Sovereign, From the sincerity of our humble and loyal hearts, we offer to your sacred person, our most dutiful and sincere thanks, for your royal care and protection to us, for your Majesty's princely zeal and pious care of our mother, the Church of England, and extending your royal benediction to our neighboring colony, your Majesty's subjects and territory of Virginia, in your gracious grant and charter[4] for the

[1]*Steiner's History*, 20–21.   [2]*Ibid.*, 21.
[3]*American Col. Church Coll.*, IV, 28.
[4]This charter granted the revenue from the impost on tobacco exported from Maryland as well as from Virginia to the College of William and Mary. See p. 374.

propagation of the college, or place of universal study, in that your Majesty's said Colony. In humble contemplation whereof, and being excited by his present Excellency Francis Nicholson, Esq., your Majesty's Governor of this your province, his zeal for your Majesty's service, pious endeavors and generous offers for the propagation of Christianity and good learning, herein we become humble suitors to your most sacred Majesty, to extend your royal grace and favor to us your Majesty's subjects of this province, represented in this your Majesty's General Assembly thereof, that it may be enacted.

"II. And may it be enacted, by the King's most excellent Majesty, by and with the advice, prayer and consent of this present General Assembly, and the authority of the same, that for the propagation of the gospel, and the education of the youth of this province in good letters and manners, that a certain place or places, for a free school or schools, or place of study of Latin, Greek, writing, and the like, consisting of one master, one usher, and one writing master or scribe, to a school, and one hundred scholars, more or less, according to the ability of the said free school, may be made, erected, founded, propagated and established under your royal patronage. And that the most reverend father in God Thomas, by Divine Providence Lord Archbishop of Canterbury, Primate and Metropolitan of all England, may be chancellor of the said schools; and that, to perpetuate the memory of your Majesty, it may be called King William's School, and managed by certain trustees, to be chosen and appointed by your sacred Majesty, to wit.,—as also by the following trustees, nominated and appointed by this present General Assembly, that is to say, by your Majesty's said Governor, Francis Nicholson, Esq.; the Honorable Sir Thomas Lawrence, Baronet, Col. George Robotham, Col. Charles Hutchins, Col. John Addison, of your Majesty's honorable Council of this province; the reverend divine, Mr. Peregrine Cony, and Mr. John Hewett, together with Robert Smith, Kenelm Cheseldyne, Henry Coursey, Edward Dorsey, Thomas Ennals, Thomas Tasker, Francis Jenkins, William Dent, Thomas Smith, Edward Boothby, John Thompson, and John Bigger, gentlemen, or the greatest part, or the successors of them, upon and in a certain place of this province, called Ann-Arundel Town, upon Severn River, and at such other place or places, as by the General Assembly of this province shall be thought convenient and fitting, to be supported and maintained in all time coming. And that your Majesty will, for your heirs and successors, grant and give leave to the said Francis Nicholson, Esq., and trustees abovesaid, or the major part or longest livers of them, that they may be enabled to take, hold and enjoy, and that they may be apt and capable in law, for taking, holding and enjoying, all manors, lands, tenements, rents, services, rectories, portions, annuities, pensions, with all other inheritances, franchises and possessions whatsoever, spiritual or temporal, to the value of fifteen hundred pounds sterling, and all other goods, chattels, money and personal estate whatsoever, of the gift of any person whatsoever, that is willing to bestow them, for the said use, or any other gifts, grants, assignments, legacies, or appointment of the same, or any of them, or of any other goods whatsoever, with this express intention and trust put in them, that the said Francis Nicholson, and other the trustees aforesaid, or the major part or the longest livers of them, shall take and hold the premises, and shall dispose of the same, and of the rents, revenues and profits thereof, or of any of them, only for the defraying the charges that shall be laid out in erecting and fitting the edifices of the said free school or schools, as they, or the major part of them, shall think most expedient, until the said free school or schools shall be actually erected, founded and established; and upon the trust and intention, that as soon as the said free school or schools shall be erected and founded, the said Francis Nicholson, and other the trustees above named, shall, from time to time, and at all times hereafter, apply all lands, tenements, rents, annuities, goods, chattels, profits, incomes, or advantages whatsoever, real or personal, or as much as shall not be laid out and bestowed upon building the said free school or schools as aforesaid, as shall be hereafter expressed.

" III. And, that when the said free school or schools, shall be so erected and established, the said Francis Nicholson, and other the trustees above named, or the major part of the longest livers of them, shall apply and appropriate to the use, benefit and maintenance, out of the revenues or incomes to the said trustees for the use aforesaid, the sum of one hundred and twenty pounds sterling per annum, for the salary, support and maintenance of the said first mentioned free school, master, usher and scribe, and the necessary repairs and improvements of the same, as to the said Francis Nicholson, and trustees aforesaid, the major part or survivors of them, shall seem expedient from time to time to ordain in the premises.

" IV. And that for the uses and purposes aforesaid, they, the said Francis Nicholson, and the trustees aforesaid, the survivors, or the major part of them, shall, and may be incorporated into a body politic, by the name of the Rectors, Governors, Trustees and Visitors of the Free Schools of Maryland; with full power to plead and be impleaded, to sue and be sued, to defend and be defended, to answer and be answered, in all and every cause, complaint and action, real, personal or mixed, of whatsoever kind or nature it shall be, whatsoever courts and places of judicature belonging to your Majesty, your heirs and successors, or by, from, or under your royal grant or authority.

" V. And, that your Majesty will be graciously pleased to give and grant your special license, as far as your Majesty see expedient, to the said Francis Nicholson, Esq.; and the other trustees aforesaid, that they, or any of them, or that any person or persons whatsoever, after the said free school or schools is, or are so erected, founded and established, or before, may have power to give and grant, assign and bequeath all or any manor, lands, tenements, rents, services, portions, annuities, pensions, inheritances, franchises, and possessions whatsoever, spiritual or temporal, to the value of fifteen hundred pounds sterling per year, besides all burthens, reprisals, and reparation, to them the said Francis Nicholson, and others the governors, trustees and visitors of the said free school of Maryland, the major part or survivors of them incorporate, for the uses aforesaid, to them and their successors forever.

"VI. And further, that the said Francis Nicholson, and other the governors, trustees and visitors aforesaid, the longest livers and successors of them, be the true, sole and undoubted visitors, trustees and governors of the said free school or schools, in perpetual succession forever, to be continued in the way and manner hereafter specified, with full and absolute power, liberty and authority in making and ordaining such laws, orders and rules, for the good government of the said free school, or schools, as to them the said trustees and governors and visitors aforesaid, and their successors, shall from time to time, according to the various occasions and circumstances, seem most fit and requisite. All which shall be observed by the master, usher, tutors and scholars of the said school, upon the penalties therein contained.

" VII. Provided notwithstanding, that the said rules, laws and orders, be no ways contrary to your Majesty's prerogative royal, nor to the laws and statutes of your Majesty's Kingdom of England, or Province of Maryland aforesaid, or to the canons and constitutions of the Church of England by law established.

" VIII. And that they, the said governors and visitors and trustees aforesaid, and their successors, shall forever be eighteen men, and not exceeding twenty in the whole, to be elected and constituted in the way and manner hereafter specified; of which one discreet and fit person, that shall be called Rector of the said tree school and schools. And that, from time to time, and in all times coming, the said rector shall exercise the said office during one year (death and legal disability excepted) and after, until some others of the said visitors and governors of the said school and schools shall be duly elected, preferred and sworn to the said office. And that, from time to time, and at all times coming, after the said year is expired, or after the death of the said rector, the visitors or governors of the said school or schools, or the greatest part of them, or their successors, should have power to elect and nominate another discreet and fit person from amongst themselves, to be rector of the said free school or schools ; and that he, who is so elected, preferred and nominated into the place of rector as aforesaid, shall have power to have, exercise, and enjoy the said office of rector for one whole year, except before excepted, then next ensuing ; and thereafter until some other rector of the said school or schools shall be duly elected, preferred to, and sworn in the said office.

" IX. And to perpetuate the succession of the said governors, rectors and visitors, that as often as one or more of the governors or visitors of the said school or schools shall die or remove himself and family out of this province into any other country for good and all, that then, and so often, the rector for the time being, and the other visitors and governors of the said free school and schools, then surviving and remaining within the province, or the major part of them, shall and may have leave to elect, nominate and choose, one or more of the principal and better sort of the inhabitants of the said province, into the place or places of the said visitors and governors so dead or removed ; and so to fill up the number of the visitors and governors of the said school and schools : And that he and they, so elected and chosen, shall take his and their corporal oath before the rector and other visitors and governors as aforesaid, or the major part of them, well and faithfully to execute the said office : Which oath the rector and two or more of the said visitors shall have power to administer. And that, after taking the said oath, he or they shall be of the number of the said visitors and governors of the said school or schools.

" X. And further, that the said rector, for the time being, by and with the advice and consent of three or more of the said governors and visitors shall and may, from time to time, and as often as need shall require, and they see convenient, call and convocate the said governors and visitors together, to do, consult and consent to such things, as for the propagation, good and benefit of the said free school or schools, shall be ordained and established. And that the said governors and visitors shall, and may hold such their court or convocation in such free school, or such part thereof, as to them shall seem convenient. And shall and may, from time to time, punish any disorder, breaches, misdemeanors or offences, of any master, usher, or scribe, or scholars, of any such free school or schools, against any orders, laws or decrees of the said governors and visitors aforesaid. And if they find cause, to alter, displace and turn out, any master, usher or scribe, of any such school or schools, and put others in their steads and places, as to the said rector, governors and visitors of the said school or schools, or the major part of them, shall seem convenient and fitting.

" XI. And also, that the said rectors, governors and visitors of the said free school or schools, and their successors, shall have one common seal, which they may make use of in whatsoever cause and business belonging to them and their successors, relating to the said office of rector, governors and visitors of the said free school or schools. And that the said governors and visitors may have leave to break, change and renew their said seal, from time to time at their pleasure, as they shall see most expedient.

" XII. And further, that it may please your Majesty to grant to the said rector, governors and visitors aforesaid, of the said free school or schools aforesaid, that as soon as they shall be enabled by any gifts, grants, pensions, donations, or incomes, of any manors, lands, tenements, or other estate whatsoever, real or personal exceeding the sum of one hundred and twenty pounds per year, allotted and allowed for support and reparations of the first free school at Severn, as aforesaid; that then, as they shall be enabled as aforesaid, the said rector, governors and visitors, shall proceed to erect, found and build, one other free school at the town of Oxford, on the eastern shore of this province, in Talbot county, or in such other place of the same county, as to the said rectors, governors and visitors as aforesaid, shall seem most expedient. And, after the same shall be built, founded and established, to appropriate and apply to the said second free school (out of the treasure accruing to them for the benefit and advantage of free schools aforesaid, over and above the one hundred and twenty pounds per year, allowed as aforesaid, to the first free school) the like sum of one hundred and twenty pounds per year, for the benefit, advantage and support of such second free school, and shall and may place a master, usher and scribe therein, as in the other first free school as aforesaid, and shall in all respects be under the same benefits, privileges, injunctions and restrictions, as the said first free school.

" XIII. And also, after the said second free school is built, erected, founded and furnished, the said rectors, governors and visitors, shall as fast as they shall be enabled as aforesaid, proceed to the erecting other and more free schools in this province, that is to say, in every county of this province at present, one free school. And shall and may be impowered to establish, constitute, enjoin and restrain, to and under the same benefits, advantages, instructions and restrictions as aforesaid, and appropriate and apply such and so much of the said revenue, not before disposed or ordained to each free school, as to them shall seem most convenient and expedient, not exceeding one hundred and twenty pounds per annum, as aforesaid." [1]

[1] *Bacon's Laws*, 1696, ch. XVII.

After the passage of this Act, Governor Nicholson, "excited by a laudable zeal and pious inclination of promoting a free school within the town and port of Annapolis," contributed three lots which he owned in that town together with £10 sterling to the building of a school house. At the same time he "prevailed" upon one Anthony Workman, inn keeper, to advance £150 sterling for the building of a house on the aforesaid lots, which house was to remain in the possession of Anthony Workman during his natural life and "afterwards to remain over to the use of the free schools." This arrangement was successfully carried out, for in 1715, in view of the fact that the records of the transaction which had been ordered to be entered upon the legislative journals could not be found, (the journals being "defaced and torn") the legislature formally vested the title to the house and land in the Rector, Governors and Visitors of the Free School at Annapolis.[1]

Upon the establishment of the Church of England in Maryland, the Bishop of London sent out Dr. Bray as his commissary to that colony. Dr. Bray is reported to have been able "to do many public services in Maryland, to settle and procure a support for several new ministers, to fix and furnish some parochial libraries and to provide schoolmasters, very much to the advancement of religion in those parts."[2] In 1704 the legislature passed an Act for securing these parochial libraries. According to this Act the libraries were to be cared for by the parish ministers who were accountable for them to the Governor, Council and vestry. The vestries were required to inspect the libraries twice during the year on pain of forfeiture of 1,400 pounds of tobacco. Moreover, the Governor was empowered to appoint one or more visitors for the general supervision of all the libraries.[3]

[1] *Bacon's Laws*, 1715, ch. IV. See also sec. XVI of ch. XXIV, 1696.

[2] Humphrey's *Account of the Society for the Propagation of the Gospel*, p. 12.

[3] *Bacon's Laws*, 1704, ch. LVI.

In 1704, upon a representation that the one school which had been erected under the Act of 1696, King William's, at Annapolis, was in need of funds,[1] the legislature passed an Act laying an export duty upon several kinds of skins and furs for the maintenance of a free school or schools within the province. The duty was "for every bear-skin, nine pence sterling; for beaver, four pence per skin; for otter, three pence per skin; for wild-cats', foxes', minks', fishers' and wolfs' skins, one penny, halfpenny per skin; for musk-rat, four pence per dozen; for raccoons, three farthings per skin; for elk skins, twelve pence per skin; for deer skins dressed or undressed, four pence per skin; for young bear and cub skins, two pence per skin."

Non-residents not trading directly with England were required to pay double these amounts. In case of fraudulent shipment, the property was to be confiscated, one-half to go to the informer, and one-half to the school fund. Shipmasters who were party to such fraud were to be fined 5000 lbs. of tobacco, one-half of which was likewise to be paid over to the school fund. This Act also imposed an export tax upon non-resident exporters of beef, bacon and pork: for dried beef and bacon, 12 pence the hundred weight; for pork and undried beef, 12 pence the barrel.[2]

In 1723, the above export duties on skins and furs were repealed by the legislature, and in their stead the following imposts were laid upon non-resident importers of pork, pitch and tar: "For every barrel of pork, the sum of one shilling per barrel, or for every hundred weight thereof, six pence; for pitch, one shilling per barrel; for tar, six pence per barrel." These duties were appropriated to the Free School Society, whereas one-half of the property confiscated in the case of fraudulent importation, was appropriated " towards the use of public schools in the several counties."[3]

[1] *Steiner's History*, p. 23.

[2] *Bacon's Laws*, 1704, ch. XXVII.   [3] *Ibid.*, 1723, ch. XI.

Governor Hart called a convention of the Episcopal clergy at Annapolis in June, 1714, and put certain enquiries to them concerning the demoralization of the established colonial church.[1] Question 5 was, "Are there any schoolmasters within your respective parishes that came from England and do preach without the Lord Bishop of London's license? or that come from other parts, and teach without a license from the Governor?"[2] The answers to these enquiries were drawn up by 21 clergymen. In reference to the question concerning schools, they state that "the case of schools is very bad; good schoolmasters are very much wanting, what we have very insufficient, and of their being qualified by the Bishop of London's or Governor's license, it has been entirely neglected."[3]

In 1715,[4] it having been represented to the legislature that the trustees of the free schools lay "under great difficulties in procuring a meeting of a competent number" at their meetings according to their act of incorporation, it was enacted that the rector and five of the governors and visitors should be deemed to constitute a quorum for the Free School Society.[5]

In 1717 an Act was passed "for laying an additional duty of 20 s. current money per poll on all Irish servants, being Papists, to prevent the growth of Popery by the importation of too great number of them into this province; and also the additional duty of 20 s. current money per poll on all negroes, for raising a fund for the use of public schools within the several counties of this province." Sections 3 and 4 of this Act refer to this latter provision.

"III. And be it further enacted [etc.,] that from and after the time aforesaid [12 months after the close of this General As-

---

[1] *Contributions to the Ecclesiastical History of the United States*, II, 137.
[2] *American Col. Church Coll.*, IV, 74.   [3] *Ibid.*, IV, 76.   See also IV, 98.
[4] In this year the proprietary authority was re-established in the colony.
[5] *Bacon's Laws*, 1715, ch. IV, sec. III.

sembly], for every negro imported into this province, either by land or water, the importer or importers of such negroes, shall pay unto the naval officer aforesaid, the sum of twenty shillings current money per poll, over and above the twenty shillings sterling per poll, imposed by a former Act of Assembly of this province, on penalty and forfeiture of five pounds current money per poll, for every negro kept back or unaccounted for; . . .

" IV. Which said duties of twenty shillings current money per poll, shall, for the advancement of learning, be applied towards the encouragement of one public school in every county within this province (that is to say) one equal share thereof towards the support of each school, according to the directions of such Act or Acts of Assembly, as shall hereafter direct therein."[1]

This Act appears to have been open to misconstruction, and so, in 1728, an explanatory Act was passed, in which it was definitely stated that resident as well as non-resident owners of trading vessels were liable to these poll taxes on Papists and negroes[2]

In 1763, an additional poll tax of two pounds was imposed on every imported negro, and the penalty for fraudulent importation was raised from 5 to 10 pounds. The revenue from this additional tax, as well as one-half of the forfeiture money was appropriated to the county schools. The Act was limited to three years.[3]

In 1719, under an Act for the application of such intestate estates as have no legal representatives, etc., it was provided that after the satisfaction of creditors, the balance of such estates was to be paid over to one of the public treasurers " to be applied to the use of schools" within the several counties

[1]*Bacon's Laws*, 1717, ch. X.

[2]*Bacon's Laws*, 1728, ch. VIII, sections 4 and 5.

[3]*Ibid.*, 1763, ch. XXVIII.

of the province. In case legal representatives eventually appeared, the money was to be refunded out of the school stock.[1]

In 1720, an Act was passed " for raising a duty of three pence per hogshead on all tobacco exported out of this province." Of this sum three half pence were appropriated to "the use of public schools." This Act was continued in 1721, in 1723 and in 1726, expiring in 1727.[2]

On October 26, 1723, the legislature passed

" AN ACT FOR THE ENCOURAGEMENT OF LEARNING AND ERECTING SCHOOLS IN THE SEVERAL COUNTIES WITHIN THIS PROVINCE.

" Whereas, the preceding Assemblies for some years past have had much at heart the absolute necessity they have lain under in regard both to duty and interest; to make the best provision in their power for the liberal and pious education of the youth of this province, and improving their natural abilities and acuteness (which seems not to be inferior to any) so as to be fitted for the discharge of their duties in the several stations and employments they may be called to, and employed in either in regard to Church or State; and for that end laid an imposition on sundry commodities exported out of, and others imported into this province, and other fines, for the raising a fund for the erecting and supporting a good school in each county within this province, which has succeeded with such desired effect, that it is now thought necessary, and is prayed that it may be enacted, and Be it enacted, by the right honorable the Lord Proprietor, by and with the advice and consent of his Lordship's Governor, and the Upper and Lower Houses of Assembly, and the authority of the same, that in some convenient time after the end of this present session of Assembly, there shall (for the ends before mentioned) be erected one school in each county within this province, at the most convenient place as near the center of the county as may be, and as may be most convenient for the boarding of chil-

[1]*Bacon's Laws*, 1719, ch. XIV.   [2]*Bacon's Laws*, 1720, ch. XV.

dren, at the discretion of the visitors or the major part of them, that are hereafter nominated, appointed and empowered by this Act, in each county. And be it therefore enacted, by the authority, advice and consent aforesaid, that for the time being, the seven several persons hereafter named for each county, be, and are hereby nominated, appointed and named visitors and are empowered with full and sufficient authority for discharging the several offices, duties and trusts, reposed in and required of them by this Act, within the several and respective counties within which they reside (that is to say) for St. Mary's County, the Rev. Leigh Massey, James Bowles Esq., Nicholas Lowe Esq., Mr. Samuel Williamson, Col. Thomas Trueman Greenfield, Mr. Thomas Waughop, and Cap. Justinian Jordan ; for Kent County, the Rev. Richard Sewall, the Rev. Alexander Williamson, James Harris Esq., Col. Edward Scott, Mr. Simon Wilmer, Mr. Gideon Pearce, Mr. Lambert Wilmer ; for Ann-Arundel County, the Rev. Mr. Joseph Colebatch, Col. Samuel Young, William Lock Esq., Capt. Daniel Mariartee, Mr. Charles Hammond, Mr. Richard Warfield, and John Beale Esq.; for Calvert County, the Rev. Mr. Jonathan Cay, John Rousby Esq., Col. John Mackall, Col. John Smith, Mr. James Heigh, Mr. Walter Smith of Leonard's Creek, Mr. Benjamin Mackall; for Baltimore County, the Rev. Mr. William Tibbs, Col. John Dorsey, Mr. John Israel, Mr. William Hamilton, Mr. Thomas Tolley, Mr. John Stokes, and Mr. Thomas Sheredine ; for Charles County, the Rev. Mr. William Machonchie, Mr. Gustavus Brown, Mr. George Dent, Capt. Joseph Harrison, Mr. Robert Hanson, Mr. Samuel Hanson and Mr. Randal Morris ; for Talbot County, the Rev. Mr. Henry Nicholls, Col. Matthew Tilghman Ward, Robert Ungle Esq., Mr. Robert Goldsborough, Mr. William Clayton, Mr. John Oldham, and Mr. Thomas Bozman; for Somerset County, the Rev. Mr. Alexander Adams, the Rev. Mr. James Robertson, Mr. Joseph Gray, Mr. Robert Martin, William Stoughton Esq., Mr. Robert King, and Mr. Levin

Gale; for Dorchester County, the Rev. Mr. Thomas Howell, Col. Roger Woolford, Maj. Henry Ennalls, Capt. John Rider, Capt. Henry Hooper, Capt. John Hudson, and Mr. Govert Lockerman; for Caecil county, Col. John Ward, Maj. John Dowdall, Col. Benjamin Pearce, Mr. Stephen Knight, Mr. Edward Jackson, Mr. Richard Thompson, and Mr. Thomas Johnson, junior; for Prince George's County, the honorable Charles Calvert Esq., Governor, the Rev. Mr. Jacob Henderson, Mr. Robert Tyler, Col. Joseph Belt, Mr. Thomas Grant, Mr. George Noble, and Col. John Bradford; for Queen Ann's County, the Rev. Mr. Christopher Wilkinson, Philemon Lloyd Esq.; Richard Tilghman Esq., Mr. James Earl, senior, Mr. William Turbutt, Mr. Augustine Thompson, and Mr. Edward Wright.

"The which persons, so nominated, appointed, authorized and named, for the several and respective counties as aforesaid or the major part of them, in case of death, or absence of any are hereby required with all convenient speed, to meet at such place within their county as to them shall seem meet, to qualify themselves for the office of visitors of their county schools, which they are to do, by taking the several oaths appointed by Act of Assembly, and signing the oath of abjuration, and the test, according to the directions thereof; and also taking an oath for the discharge of the several duties and trusts reposed in them, in the words following: 'I, A. B., do swear that I will dully and faithfully discharge the duties and trusts committed to me, as a visitor of   county school, according to the best of my skill and cunning. So help me God.' The which oaths are to be administered by any of the four persons last named for the county, to the person first named, or in his absence, to any one of three persons first named that shall be present, the which person being sworn as aforesaid, shall administer the oaths aforementioned to all the rest; and so successively, the persons first named that shall be present, shall always administer the said oaths to any that have been absent, or that shall hereafter be elected and chosen, pursuant to the direction of this Act, to supply the place of any that shall be dead, or removed out of the county. And the aforesaid persons, or the major part of them, being sworn as aforesaid, shall be constituted and qualified as visitors of the school of their said county, and as such, are hereby invested with full power and authority, as a body politic, to plead and be impleaded, to sue and be sued, to defend and be defended, to answer and be answered, in all and every cause, complaint and action, real, personal or mixed, of whatsoever kind or nature it shall be, in any of the courts and places of judicature within this province; and that they, or any of them, or any other person or persons whatsoever, either before or after such school shall be erected, founded and established, in any county as aforesaid, have full power to give and grant, assign and bequeath, all or any manors, lands, tenements, rents, services, portions, annuities, pensions, inheritances, franchises and possessions whatsoever, spiritual or temporal, to the value of one hundred pounds sterling, per annum (besides all burthens, reprisals and reparations) to them the said visitors, or the major part, or survivors of them incorporate, for such county school, to them and their successors forever. And further, that the said persons so incorporate, the longest livers and successors of them, shall be the true, sole and undoubted visitors of such schools in perpetual succession forever; to be continued in the way and manner hereafter specified; with full and absolute power, liberty and authority, in making and ordaining such laws, orders and rules for the good government of the said schools, as to them the said visitors, and their successors shall, from time to time, according to their various occasions and circumstances, seem to them most fit and requisite; all which shall be observed by the master, usher, tutor, and scholars of the said school, upon the penalties therein contained. Provided always, that the said rules, laws and orders, be no wise contrary to the royal prerogative, nor to the laws and statutes of England, and Acts of Assembly of this province, or to the canons and constitutions of the Church of England by law established. And for the perpetuating the succession of the aforementioned number of seven visitors to each school as aforesaid; Be it enacted, by the authoriy, advice and con- sent aforesaid, that as often as any one or more of the visitors of any of the aforesaid schools shall die, or remove himself and family out of the province, or into any other county to reside, that then and so often, the visitors for the time being, then surviving and remaining within the county, or the major part of them, be, and are hereby author- ized and required to elect, nominate and choose, one or more of the principal and better sort of the inhabitants of the county, into the place and room of the said visitors of such school, so dead or removed, and so to fill up the full number of visitors for each school; the which persons so elected and chosen from time to time, are always to be qualified in the same manner as is before mentioned. And be it further enacted, that the visi- tors (for the time being) of such school, being qualified as aforesaid, be, and are hereby authorized and directed with all convenient speed, to purchase one hundred acres or more of land, for the use of such school, having a special regard as to its conveniency, that it be as near as possible in such place in the county, as is before directed for the erecting of schools, by this Act; the which land, when so purchased, the visitors are to assign such part of it as they shall see meet, not to exceed one moiety thereof, to be built upon, and cleared (if not before built on and cleared) for the conveniency of making corn and grain, and for pasturage, for the encouragement, use and bene- fit of the master of such school, for the time being; the other moiety whereof is to be preserved in woodland ground, and no other use made thereof by such master, without the license and direction of the said visitors, than what may be absolutely necessary for fire-wood, and the repairing of the houses and fencing already built and made, or to be built and made, on

such other moiety thereof, and that no master be permitted
either by himself or by any other person, on any pretense whatsoever, to plant any tobacco on such land or plantation; and
the visitors of the several schools as aforesaid, are further empowered and directed, in case there shall not be sufficient
building upon any such land at the time of making a purchase
thereof for a dwelling house and necessary conveniences for
the master, and for keeping a school therein, and ground
cleared sufficient for the use aforesaid, that then they shall
with all possible speed, agree with such workmen and laborers
or other person, in the best manner they can, that will undertake the necessary buildings and improvements upon such
lands, for the uses aforementioned; and the visitors aforesaid
are likewise hereby directed to take all proper methods for the
encouraging good school masters, that shall be members of
the Church of England, and of a pious and exemplary lives and
conversations, and capable of teaching well the grammar, good
writing, and the mathematics, if such can conveniently be got;
and that they allow every such master for his encouragement
for the present (besides the benefit and use of his plantation)
the sum of twenty pounds per annum, and to take such other
measures, or make such other agreements, from time to time,
for the future, as the circumstances will admit of, as may give
due encouragement to one or more masters, and be necessary
and useful for the improving and perpetuating such school.
And further, the visitors of every school, after it shall be
erected, are hereby required to meet thereat, at least four times
a year, to inspect into and consider thereof, and direct the
necessary affairs thereof. And for the enabling the visitors of
the schools as aforesaid, for the purchasing of lands, and erecting of schools, and encouraging of masters in manner as aforesaid, Be it enacted, that the money already raised for the use
of county schools, and that is now in the public treasurer's
hands, being divided into twelve equal parts, answering to the
number of county schools now to be erected, the treasurers in

whose hands such money lies, are hereby required to make due payment of one of those twelve parts or dividends of money in their hands, to the visitors of the schools for each county or the major part of them, or their orders, whensoever they shall have occasion to draw on such treasurers for the same; and the like payment shall, from time to time, be made to the visitors as aforesaid, by the treasurers, of the like dividends that shall hereafter arise, due to such schools, and some to their hands; and the visitors of the schools as aforesaid, are hereby empowered to dispose of all such money as they shall receive from time to time, in such manner as may be most for the encouragement and advancement of such schools. And be it likewise enacted, that the visitors of each school, to be constituted, qualified and incorporated in manner aforesaid, or the major part of them and their successors, be, and hereby are enabled to take, hold and enjoy, and be apt and capable in law, for taking, holding and enjoying, all manors, lands, tenements, inheritances, franchises and possessions whatsoever, spiritual or temporal, to the value of fifteen hundred pounds sterling, and all other goods, chattels, money and personal estate whatsoever, of the gift of any person whatsoever, that already hath or hereafter shall be willing to bestow them for the use of the said school, or any other gifts, grants, assignments, legacies or appointments of the same or any of them, or any other goods whatsoever; to be applied by the visitors for the uses and in manner as afore mentioned: And the said visitors are likewise hereby authorized to receive all and every such fines and forfeitures as have already arisen due or that shall hereafter arise due to their several county schools, in whose hands soever the same are lodged, and upon refusal or delay of payment thereof, that then they may, at their discretion exercise the powers and authorities, (given them as a body politic by this Act) for the recovery of the same; the which fines and forfeitures are likewise to be applied to the uses and in manner aforesaid. Provided always, that the visitors to be appointed for every such school as aforesaid, and their successors, from time to time, are hereby empowered to appoint a register, and allow him a reasonable salary, who is hereby obliged to keep a fair account of all their proceedings, and of the applications by them to be made of all moneys, tobaccoes, or other commodities or matters or things whatsoever, that shall come to their hands by virtue of the authorities given them by this Act, which shall at all times hereafter be subject to the examination and correction of the General Assembly of this province. And be it further enacted, that every person by this Act appointed as a visitor of the county schools, or that shall hereafter be nominated and appointed as such, pursuant to the direction hereof, that shall willfully refuse or delay to take upon him the said office, shall forfeit and pay for every such refusal or delay, the sum of five hundred pounds of tobacco for the use of the school of that county where such offense shall be committed ; to be recovered in his Lordship's name, or at the visitors suit, before the justices of that county court by bill, plaint or information, wherein no essoin protection or wager of law shall be allowed." [1] Five years after the passage of this Act, it was found expedient to pass an Act to supply some of its defects. " Several inconveniences and much damage " had been caused by the negligence of school visitors, and consequently it was enacted " that in case any of the visitors of the said schools, shall hereafter willfully and obstinately refuse or neglect to meet, and be present at any of the times appointed for the meeting of the said visitors, so that the necessary affairs of the said school or schools cannot be transacted and directed, that then it shall and may be lawful for the visitors of each school, or the major part of such visitors, who shall so meet, are hereby directed and empowered to nominate and choose one or more of the principal and better sort of the inhabitants of the county, into the place and room of the said visitor so refusing or neglecting " . . . . It is further enacted " that the

---

[1] *Bacon's Laws*, 1723, ch. XIX.

master of every public school within this province, shall, and is hereby required to teach as many poor children gratis, as the visitors or the major part of them, of the respective schools shall order, or be immediately discharged and removed from his trust in the said school, and a new master put in."[1]

From 1741 to 1776 several Acts were passed concerning the administration of the different county schools.

In 1741, the visitors of the Kent County school were empowered to divide part of the school lands into lots and lease them out for the use of the master. In case of vacancy in the post of master, the rents were to be applied to the use of the school.[2]

In 1765, the majority of the visitors of Kent County school were empowered to lease out upon ten days' notice part of the school land in lots not exceeding three acres[3] to the highest bidder for a term not exceeding 21 years. They were likewise authorized to renew expiring leases, and to apply all the rents that were taken in to the greatest advantage of the school.[4]

In 1746, an Act was passed for establishing a county school in Worcester County, a new division that had been made through the division of Somerset County.[5] Seventeen years later the visitors of the Somerset County school were ordered to pay over to the Worcester school one-half of the school fund which was in their hands at the time of the division of the two counties. At the same time the visitors of the Worcester school were directed " with all convenient speed " to purchase four lots in Snow Hill town—the funds of the school being insufficient to purchase the 100 acres pursuant to the

---

[1] *Ibid.*, 1728, ch. VIII.   [2] *Ibid.*, 1741, ch. I.

[3] Three years later this limitation was removed by a supplementary Act. At this time, the visitors were also empowered "to lay out 10 acres of the school land, including the school house and free school spring, for the use of the master." *Laws of Maryland*, 1768, ch. XX. Annapolis, 1787.

[4] *Ibid.*, 1765, ch. XXX.

[5] *Bacon's Laws*, 1746, ch. VII.

school law of 1723—and to cause the erection of a public school for the use of the county.[1]

In 1753, the visitors of St. Mary's County school were empowered to add to their number.[2] Five years later, the school house was destroyed by fire, and an Act was passed enabling the visitors to sell the school land—the site having been found very inconvenient for a school—and to purchase another piece of ground with the proceeds and erect a school house.[3]

In 1763, an Act was passed "for erecting a public school in Frederick County" on the ground that "it is reasonable that education should be extended equally to the several parts of the province." Seven visitors were appointed, and a share of the county school fund was paid to them with which they were to purchase one acre in Frederick Town and erect a school house.[4]

In 1768, seven new visitors were appointed for the public school in Frederick County. They were empowered to buy half an acre of ground in Frederick Town and to build a school house, and the colony treasurer was directed to pay over to them a dividend of the county school duties.[5]

In 1770, the free schools of Somerset and Worcester Counties were united by act of legislature. Ten visitors were appointed from each county and empowered to dispose of the old school lands and to devote the proceeds, together with all the moneys in the hands of the former visitors and all moneys which had been subscribed to the respective schools, to the erection of a new school at a place most convenient for each county. The public treasurers were also directed to pay over two dividends of the county school revenue [6] to this new board.[7]

[1] *Ibid.*, 1763, ch. XVI.   [2] *Ibid.*, 1753, ch. XIX.

[3] *Ibid.*, 1758, ch. XIII.   [4] *Ibid.*, 1763, XXXII.

[5] *Laws of Maryland*, 1787. 1768, ch. VI.

[6] *Ibid.*, 1770, ch. XII.

[7] In 1774 this board was reduced from 20 to 7 members. *Ibid.*, 1774, ch. XII.

In 1774, the free schools of Saint Mary's, Charles and Prince George's Counties were also united by act of legislature. The consolidated school was to be erected at the Cool Springs, and to be called Charlotte Hall. It was to be governed by a president and 21 trustees or visitors, of which 15 were to constitute a quorum. The other conditions of consolidation were similar to those of the consolidation act of 1770.[1] In this same year, an Act was passed relative to the administration of King William's School in Annapolis. The governing board was empowered "to receive any gift, devise or conveyance of goods, chattels or lands, according to the estate given, and not exceeding an annual income of £200 sterling. In the absence of the rector, seven members of the board could act in all matters relating to the school. The register was directed to give personal notice to every member resident in Annapolis, or to leave a written notice at his house, of any intended meeting of the corporation. He was also to give similar notice to any non-resident member whom he knew to be in town. Failure to notify members involved a fine of 20 s. which was to be applied to the use of the school.[2]

The establishment of a collegiate institution was several times brought to the attention of the legislature during the 18th century. In 1732 an extremely liberal and comprehensive plan for founding a college at Annapolis was presented to the Upper House of Assembly. It was read and recommended to the Lower House.[3] In 1754, Governor Sharpe, in his opening address to the legislature, observed: "Shall I also take the liberty of intimating what considerable benefit must accrue to the inhabitants and what honor must redound to yourselves from the foundation of a more perfect and more public seminary of learning in this province; a scheme this, long since put in execution among our neighbors, to whom our youth are still obliged, much to the disadvantage and discredit of this

---

[1] *Ibid.*, 1774, ch. XIV.   [2] *Ibid.*, 1774, ch. XV.

[3] *Steiner's History of Education in Maryland*, pp. 26–29.

province, to recur for a liberal education. Of such an establishment your descendants and late posterity will reap the advantage and remember the present age with gratitude. From my knowledge of what vast pleasure and satisfaction his Lordship receives from being able to contribute to and promote the reputation, honor and prosperity of his province,[1] I will presume to encourage you to expect something more than his bare approbation of such a proposal." [2]

Accordingly, on May 6, the question was put in the Lower House whether the fund that had been appropriated to the county schools and the money which would arise on the sale of the lands and houses belonging to them, should be applied towards the erection of one public seminary of learning within the province. It was carried in the affirmative, 38 to 13. On May 28, the question whether the establishment of this seminary should be referred to the next Assembly or not, was decided by the casting vote of the Speaker in the negative. But here the matter came to a standstill.[3]

In 1761 a bill was introduced "for the appropriation of ordinary licenses towards the support of a college in Annapolis." This bill was warmly supported by the people's delegates; but it was opposed by the Proprietary and his representatives. Governor Sharpe, in writing to Lord Baltimore on June 23, 1761, tried to justify the apparent disloyalty of one Dr. Stuart, in voting for this bill. The Governor states that Dr. Stuart was "obliged to vote against his inclination for appropriating the ordinary licenses as a fund for its [the projected college] support, or run a great risk of being rejected at the next elec-

---

[1] On May 2, 1754, Governor Sharpe writes to Lord Baltimore: "The trustees of the Charity School about to be established in Talbot county [for poor children and negroes] gratefully accept your Lordship's proposals and are preparing a thankful address for the most kind testimony of your Lordship's approbation." (*Archives of Maryland. Correspondence of Governor Horatio Sharpe*, II, 55.) This address was forwarded to Lord Baltimore by the Governor on August 8. (*Ibid.*, II, 79. See also *Steiner's History*, pp. 34–6.)

[2] Given in *Steiner's History*, p. 29.   [3] *Ibid.*, p. 30.

tion by the inhabitants of this city [Annapolis], many of whom expecting to receive vast advantages from such an institution were apt to think every one an enemy to the town who would not vote for a college at all events." [1]

On October 19, Cecilius Calvert writes to Governor Sharpe in reference to this matter, that Lord Baltimore " will not allow such a strip of his right or from his secretary office, and thereof he depends you will follow his instructions." [2]

In 1763, the Lower House passed, by a vote of 21 to 19, the report of a committee which recommended that the house in Annapolis, which was intended for a Governor's residence, should be completed and appropriated for a college building. The 3000 pounds necessary for this end were to be appropriated from funds in the hands of the commissioners of the loan office. The running expenses were estimated at £1380, distributed as follows : president, or first master, £300 ; second, third and fourth masters, each £200 ; mathematical master, £200 ; two English and writing masters, £100 each, and five servants and a boy, £60. This amount was to be raised by a tax on ordinary licenses, estimated at £600 ; from a tax from 5 to 10 shillings on bachelors, estimated at £420 ; from the Hon. Benedict Calvert's donation to King William's School of £40, and from the profits arising on 80 boys at £4 per annum. [3]

On November 19, the Upper House sent a message to the Lower House on this bill, which states that : " Satisfied that the establishment of a college or seminary of learning in this province on a good foundation would be productive of many great advantages to the inhabitants, we are much pleased to find that you are also convinced of the expediency of such an establishment." The Upper House, however, objected to the bill as it had been drawn up by the Lower House, and as the end of the session was at hand, it was decided to postpone the discussion of the subject. [4]

---

[1] *Correspondence of Governor Horatio Sharpe*, II, 525. See also, 523.

[2] *Ibid.*, II, 545.   [3] *Steiner's History*, p. 30.   [4] *Ibid.*, pp. 30–31.

In October, 1773, Governor Eden recalled the subject of a collegiate foundation to the attention of the legislature. He said in his message : " Permit me to recommend to your reflections the extensive utility which can not fail to flow from an establishment in this province of a regular seminary for our youth, liberally instituted and supported, and to express my warmest wishes that it may engage your peculiar attention." [1]

[1] *Ibid.*, p. 31.

SOUTH CAROLINA

In 1663 and 1665 Charles II. granted to eight persons that region in America which was bounded on the north by latitude 36° 30', on the south by the 29th parallel, on the east by the Atlantic and on the west by the Pacific Ocean. Proprietary rights of government and trade were given together with the land, and a feudal system of government was drawn up for this territory in 1669 under the name of "the fundamental constitutions;"[1] but this plan of government was never actualized among the Virginian and New England dissenters and Quakers who began to come into the northern part of the country in 1653, nor among the immigrants from Barbadoes and England, the Scotch-Irish, the Dutch New Yorkers, and the French Huguenots who settled the southern part of the colony between 1665 and 1686. In both these divisions a governor and council came to be appointed by the proprietaries and an assembly to be elected by the people. In 1700, the Assembly of South Carolina made provision for the library of 225 volumes which had been donated to the colony two years previous through the influence of Dr. Thomas Bray, commissary of the Bishop of London in Maryland.[2]

---

[1] It is remarkable that in this instrument of government, which was drawn up by the ablest philosopher and the ablest statesman of the time, there is no provision of any kind for education. This omission was probably deliberate. Locke was an outspoken advocate of private instruction. (See *The History of South Carolina under the Proprietary Government*, p. 108. Edward McCrady, New York, 1897.)

[2] *Education in South Carolina*, p. 41. Edward McCrady, Jr. In the collections of the Historical Society of South Carolina. Charleston, 1883.

" AN ACT FOR SECURING THE PROVINCIAL LIBRARY AT
CHARLESTOWN IN CAROLINA.

" Whereas, at the promotion of the Rev. Mr. Thomas Bray,
and the encouragement and bounty of the right Honorable
the true and absolute Lords and Proprietors of this Province,
and the aforesaid Dr. Bray, and the inhabitants of this Province, a library hath been sent over to Charlestown, for the use
of this province, and it is justly feared that the books belonging to the same will quickly be embezzeled, damaged or lost,
excepting a law be passed for the effectual preservation of the
same.

" I. Be it therefore enacted by his Excellency John Earl of
Bath, Palatine, and the rest of the true and absolute Lords and
Proprietors of this Province, by and with the advice and consent of the rest of the members of the General Assembly, now
met at Charlestown, for the south-west part of this province,
and by the authority of the same, that the Provincial Library
of Carolina shall be, continue and remain in the hands, custody
and possession and safe-keeping of the incumbent or minister
of the Church of England, in Charlestown, in this province, for
the time being; which said incumbent is and shall be hereby
bound and obliged to keep and preserve the several and respective books therein, from waste, damage, embezzlement,
and all other distruction (fire and all other unavoidable acci-
dents only excepted), and is and shall be hereby accountable
for the same, and every book thereof, to the commissioners
hereafter nominated; And to that end and purpose, the incumbent of Charlestown, and his successors, shall pass two
receipts for the books belonging to the library aforesaid, one
to the commissioners hereafter named, and the other to the
church-wardens of Charlestown for the time being, in which
receipts the titles of each book shall be inserted; and in case
all or any of the books is or shall be found to be wasted, endamaged or embezzled, or any otherwise destroyed, except as

before excepted, the respective incumbent, his executors or administractors, are and shall be hereby bound and obliged to answer double the value of the same; and the said commissioners are hereby empowered to sue for the same, in any court of record in this province, by bill, plaint, or information, or other action, wherein no essoign, protection, injunction or wager of law shall be allowed; and what thereby shall be recovered, reasonable charge and expences deducted, to employ and dispose towards the completing and perfecting the aforesaid library, so wasted, endamaged, embezzled or otherwise destroyed, within the space of twelve months after such recovery.

" II. And be it further enacted by the authority aforesaid, that in case of the death or removal of the incumbent of Charlestown, in this province, that then the respective churchwardens of Charlestown shall immediately take into their respective hands, custody, possession and safe-keeping, all the books belonging to the said library, and shall be answerable for the same to the commissioners hereafter nominated.

" III. And be it further enacted by the authority aforesaid, that the church-wardens of Charlestown, upon their receiving of the books belonging to the said Provincial Library into their custody, shall compare the same with the catalogue and receipt for the same, in their custody, and if any of the books are wanting or damaged, they shall give an account thereof in twenty days time at farthest, to the commissioners hereafter mentioned, who are hereby impowered to sue the said incumbent, or, in case of his death, his executors or administractors, for the same, as aforesaid; And in case the said church-wardens refuse to give such account, then they, their executors and administractors, are hereby made accountable to the commissioners hereafter named, for all the books belonging to the said library, and contained in the catalogue thereof.

" IV. And be it further enacted by the authority aforesaid, that the inhabitants of this province shall have liberty to borrow any book out of the said Provincial Library, giving a receipt for the same to the incumbent of Charlestown, for the time being, with a promise to return the said book or books; if a folio, in four months time; if a quarto, in two months time; if an octavo, or under, in one month, upon penalty of paying three times the full value of the said book or books so borrowed, in case of failure of returning or damnifying the same: And the said incumbent is hereby obliged to enter such receipt in a book, to be fairly kept for that purpose, and upon the same being returned, shall note it returned, on the other side or column of the said book, and not cross or blot the same: And in case the persons that borrowed any book or books out of the said library, doth refuse to return the same, or doth damnify the said book, upon complaint thereof given by the said incumbent, his executors or administractors, to two or more of the commissioners, and by them, or any five of them, to the chief justice of this province for the time being, or any two justices of the peace, it shall be lawful, and the said chief justice, or any two justices of the peace, are hereby empowered and required, by warrant of distress, directed to any of the constables of this province, to levy three times the value of such book or books, on the goods and chattels of the person so refusing to deliver, or damnifying the same; and for want of such distress, to commit the person to prison, till satisfaction be made to the incumbent.

" V. And be it further enacted by the authority aforesaid, that the commissioners hereafter named shall make, or cause to be made, seven catalogues of all and singular the books in the said library, and the same being fairly written, one of which shall be sent to England to the right honorable the Lords Proprietors of this Province; one to the right reverend father in God, the Lord Bishop of London; one to the aforesaid Rev. Dr. Bray; one to be entered on record in the Secretary's office of this province; one to be in the custody and for the use of the commissioners hereafter named, under which the incumbent shall sign a receipt for the respective books; one to be in the custody of the church-wardens of Charlestown, for the time being, under which the incumbent shall also sign a receipt for the respective books ; and one to be fairly entered in a book for that purpose to be kept by the incumbent in the said library, that so any person may know what books are contained in the said library.

"VI. And be it further enacted by the authority aforesaid, that the commissioners hereafter named, after making an exact catalogue of all and singular the respective books in the said library, shall, and are hereby empowered to, appraise and rate each book, at a price certain, in the current money of this province ; which appraisement shall be an established rule to judge and determine the value of the said books, in case any suit is brought by the said commissioners against any person that shall detain or damnify any of the said books, or against the incumbent of Charlestown, or his executors or administractors.

"VII. And be it further enacted by the anthority aforesaid, that the commissioners hereafter named, or any five of them, shall, every year, on the fifth day of November, resort to the house built for the incumbent of Charlestown, where the said library shall be kept, and there examine the books thereof by the catalogue, and see that there be the full number, and that they are not damnified nor spoiled: And therefore the incumbent is hereby required, in lending any of the several books out of the said library, notwithstanding the time usually allowed by this Act, to oblige the said persons to return all such books as they borrow, to the said incumbent, ten days before the said fifth day of November, that so all and singular the books belonging to the library aforesaid, may be exposed to the view of the said commissioners, the better to enable them to judge if they are any way damnified or spoiled, and to give their order accordingly.

"VIII. And be it further enacted by the authority aforesaid, that James Moore, Esq., now Governor of Carolina, Joseph

Morton, Nicholas Trott, Ralph Izard, Esqs., Capt. Job Howes, Capt. Thomas Smith, Mr. Robert Stevens, Mr. Joseph Croskeys and Mr. Robert Fenwicke, or any five of them, be, and are hereby nominated to be, commissioners and trustees, for the due inspection and preservation of the library aforesaid, and all and singular the respective books to the same belonging: And they, or any five of them, shall have power to commence or bring any suit or action given by this Act: And in case by death or absence, there be not five of the said commissioners in this province, that the Governor for the time being shall nominate such person or persons as shall make the number of the commissioners five, which shall have all the power given the said commissioners in this Act, and shall so continue until the next meeting of the General Assembly of this province, who shall then choose so many persons as shall make up the full number of nine; which persons so chosen by an ordinance of a General Assembly, shall, and are hereby declared to, be the commissioners and trustees required by this Act; and they or any five of them, to have and execute all and singular the powers given the commissioners above named by this Act.

"IX. And be it further enacted by the authority aforesaid, that the commissioners above named, after having examined the respective books belonging to the library aforesaid, if they find any books wanting, shall summons such persons as have the said books in their custody, to deliver the same in twenty days after such notice in writing left with the persons, or their places of abode; and in case any persons shall fail or refuse to deliver the said respective books to the said commissioners, or any five of them, that upon complaint being made by the said commissioners, or any five of them, to the chief justices of this province, for the time being, or any two justices of the peace, against such persons refusing to deliver the said books, that the said chief justices, or any two justices of the peace, are hereby authorized, empowered and required, by warrant of distress, directed to any of the constables of this province, to levy to the treble value of such respective book or books, on the goods and chattels of the person or persons so refusing the same, and to make sale of the same, rendering the overplus to the owner; and for want of such distress, to commit the persons to prison till satisfaction be made.

" X. And be it further enacted by the authority aforesaid, that all persons that have borrowed or have in their custody any of the books belonging to the Provincial Library aforesaid, shall, on or before the first day of January next, return the same to the present incumbent of Charlestown, upon the penalty of the forfeiture of treble the value of each book not returned as aforesaid, the better to enable the commissioners before named to make a perfect catalogue of the books belonging to the library aforesaid.

" Read three times, and ratified in open Assembly, November 16, 1700.

> JAMES MOORE (L. S.),
> JOHN WICH (L. S.),
> EDMD. BELLINGER (L. S.),
> ROBERT GIBBES (L. S.),
> HENRY NOBLE (L. S.)."[1]

Three years after the passage of this Act, Chief Justice Trott informed the Lower House that Dr. Bray had sent sundry books as a further addition to the public library, together with additional books for a layman's library. The chief justice was accordingly instructed to write and thank Dr. Bray for his gift.[2] In May following the Receiver was instructed to pay £5 15 s. for transcribing the catalogue of the library books.[3]

In the Church Acts of 1704 and 1706, a room was reserved in the house of the rector of the Parish of St. Philips, Charleston, for the use of the Provincial Library.[4]

---

[1] *The Statutes at large of South Carolina*, VII, 13-16. Edited by Thomas Cooper, M. D., LL. D. Columbia, 1837.

[2] *McCrady's History*, p. 353.   [3] *Ibid.*   [4] *Statutes*, II, 237, 286.

In 1710, the legislature passed

"AN ACT FOR THE FOUNDING AND ERECTING OF A FREE SCHOOL,
FOR THE USE OF THE INHABITANTS OF SOUTH CAROLINA

"Whereas, it is necessary that a free school be erected for the instruction of the youth of this province in grammar and other arts and sciences and useful learning, and also in the principles of the Christian religion; and whereas several charitable and well disposed Christians, by their last wills and testaments, have given several sums of money for the founding of a free school, but no person as yet is authorized to take the charge and care of erecting a free school, according to the intent of the donors, and to receive the said legacies, if tendered, nor to demand the same, in case of refusal to pay the same; so that for want of some person or persons, or body politic and corporate, proper for the lodging the said legacies therein, the same are not applied according to the pious and charitable intention of the testators or donors;

"I. Be it therefore enacted by his Excellency William Lord Craven, Palatine, and the rest of the true and absolute Lords and Proprietors of this province, by and with the advice and consent of the rest of the members of the General Assembly, now met at Charleston for the south west part of the province, and by the authority of the same, That the Honorable Colonel Edward Tynte, Esq., Governor, Colonel Thomas Broughton, Esq., Landgrave Joseph Morton, Mr. William Gibbon, Colonel George Logan, Richard Beresford, Esq., Arthur Middleton, Esq., Capt. John Abraham Motte, Colonel Hugh Grange, Ralph Izard, Esq., Lieut. Colonel Alexander Parris, Esq., Capt. Lewis Pasquereau, Dr. Gideon Johnston, Dr. Francis Lejau, Mr. Alexander Wood, and Nicholas Trott, Esq., or any nine of them, and their successors, to be elected in manner as hereafter is directed, be, and shall forever hereafter be one body politic and corporate, in deed and in name, by the name of the Commissioners for Founding, Erecting, Governing, Ordering and Visiting a School for the Use of the Inhabitants of

South Carolina ; and that they and their successors, by the same name, by the authority aforesaid, be fully made, ordained, constituted and declared one body politic and corporate, in deed and in name, and that by the same name they and their successors by that name shall and may perpetual succession, and that they and their successors by that name shall and may forever hereafter be persons able and capable in law to purchase, have, take, receive and enjoy to them and their successors, land, messuages, tenements, rents, liberties, privileges, jurisdictions, franchises, and other hereditaments, whatsoever, of whatsoever nature, kind, quality or value they be, in fee and in perpetuity; and also estates for lives and for years, and all manner of goods, chattels and things whatsoever, of what name, nature, quality and value soever they be, for the better support and maintenance of masters or teachers for the said school, and also for the erecting of school houses and convenient dwelling houses for the accommodation of the said several masters and teachers. And that by the name aforesaid, they shall and may be able to plead and be impleaded, answer and be answered unto, defend and be defended in all courts and places whatsoever, and before whatsoever judge or judges, justice or justices, or other officer or officers belonging to this province, in all and singular actions, plaints, pleas, matters and demands of what kind, nature and quality soever they be. And to act and to do all other matters and things in as ample manner and form as any other the inhabitants of this province, being persons capable in law, or any other body corporate or politic, by the laws of England can or may have, purchase, receive, possess, take, enjoy, grant, set, let, demise, plead and be impleaded, answer and be answered unto, defend and be defended, do, permit and execute. And that the said commissioners, and their successors forever hereafter, shall and may have a common seal to serve for the causes and business of them and their successors, to change, break, alter and make new the said seal, from time to time, and at their pleasure, as they shall think best.

" II. And for the better execution of the purpose aforesaid, Be it further enacted by the authority aforesaid, that the said commissioners and their successors forever, shall and may on the second Tuesday in July, yearly meet at some convenient place to be appointed by the president of the said Commissioners, between the hours of eight in the morning and five in the afternoon, and that they, or the major part of them that shall then be present, shall choose one president and vice-president, and such other officers, ministers and servants as shall be thought convenient to serve in the said offices for the year ensuing; and that the said president and all officers then elected shall, before they act in their respective offices, take an oath, to be to them administered by the president, or in his absence, by one of the vice-presidents of the year preceding, who are hereby authorized to administer the same, for the faithful and due execution of their respective offices and places during the said year.

"III. And be it further enacted by the authority aforesaid, that the first president of the said commissioners shall be the Honorable Colonel Edward Tynte, Esq., Governor, and that the said president shall within three days after the ratification of this Act, cause summons to be issued to the several commissioners herein particularly mentioned, to meet on the second Tuesday of June next ensuing, at such place as he shall appoint, and that they, or the major part of such of them as shall then be present, shall proceed to the election of such other officers, ministers and servants as to them shall seem meet; which said officers, from the time of their election into their respective offices, shall continue therein until the second Tuesday in July which will be in the year of our Lord one thousand seven hundred and eleven, and from thenceforward until others shall be chosen in their places in manner aforesaid.

"IV. And be it enacted by the authority aforesaid, that if it shall happen that any of the persons at any time chosen into any of the said offices shall die, or on any account be removed from such office at any time between the said yearly days of election, that, in such case. it shall be lawful for the surviving and continuing president, or any of the vice-presidents, to issue summons to the several members of the body corporate to meet at the usual place of the annual meeting of the said commissioners, at such time as shall be specified in the said summons, and such members as shall meet upon such summons, or the major part of them, shall and may choose an officer or officers in the room of such person or persons so dead or removed, as to them shall seem meet.

" V. And be it further enacted by the authority aforesaid, that in case of death or removal from this province of any of the said commissioners, that then it shall be lawful for the president, or any one of the vice-presidents, to issue summons to the several surviving commissioners to meet at the usual place of the annual meeting of the said commissioners, at such time as shall be specified in the said summons, and that such members as shall meet upon such summons, or the major part of them, shall or may choose a commissioner or commissioners in the room or place of such person or persons, so dead or removed, as to them shall seem meet.

" VI. And be it further enacted by the authority aforesaid, that it shall and may be lawful for the said commissioners and their successors to meet at some convenient place to be appointed for that purpose, on the second Tuesday in February and July and oftener if occasion requires, upon public summons given five days before, then and there to transact the business of the said commissioners, and to put in force and execute the several powers given them by this Act; and no act done in any assembly of the said commissioners shall be effectual and valid unless the president or one of the vice-presidents and eight members of the said commissioners, at least, be present, and the major part consenting thereunto.

" VII. And be it further enacted by the authority aforesaid, that all gifts or legacies formerly given, for the use of a free school for this province, by any person or persons whatsoever, are hereby appropriated for the use of the school intended to be founded and erected, pursuant to the several powers granted to the said comissioners by this Act; and the said commissioners and their lawful successors are hereby authorized and impowered to demand and sue for the same, either by action of debt, suit, bill, plaint or information, in any court of record in this province, wherein no essoign, protection, privilege, injunction, or wager of law, or stay of prosecution by *non vult ulterius prosequi*, or otherwise, shall be admitted or allowed.

"VIII. And be it further enacted by the authority aforesaid, that if any action, claim, suit or information shall be commenced or prosecuted against any person or persons, for what he or they shall do in pursuance or execution of this Act, such person or persons so sued may plead the general issue not guilty, and upon issue joined, give this Act and the special matter in evidence; and if the plaintiff or prosecutor shall become non-suit, or suffer discontinuance, or if a verdict pass against him, the defendant or defendants shall recover his or their treble costs, for which he or they shall have the like remedy as in any case by law is given to the defendants. And a receipt signed by such person or persons as shall be lawfully chosen and appointed treasurer to the said commissioners, shall be a sufficient discharge to such executor or executors as shall pay such legacies. And the moneys so received by such treasurer, shall be disposed by order of the said commissioners and their successors, towards the purchasing of lands and the erecting of a school house and dwelling houses, for the use of the several masters and professors.

"IX. And be it further enacted by the authority aforesaid, that the said commissioners and their successors shall have power, and they are hereby authorized and empowered, to take up by grant from the Lords Proprietors, or purchase, have, take and receive from any other person or persons soever, so much land as they shall think necessary for the use and conveniency of the several masters and teachers; and also direct the building of a school house upon the same, and such dwelling houses and convenient out-houses and buildings for the accommodation of the several masters and teachers; and shall also nominate and appoint one or more persons to be supervisor or supervisors for the said buildings. The said several buildings to be on such places on the said land, so taken up or purchased or received as aforesaid, and of such dimensions and of such materials as the said commissioners shall order and direct.

" X. And be it further enacted by the authority aforesaid, that the said commissioners and their successors shall have power, and lawful authority to nominate and appoint a fit person to be master of the said school, by name and style of Preceptor and Teacher of grammar and other arts and sciences to be taught in the School for the Province of South Carolina; and so from time to time, when and as often as the said place of master of the said school, by death, resignation, deprivation, or otherwise, shall become void, shall nominate and appoint a fit person to succeed to be master of the said school.

" XI. And be it further enacted by the authority aforesaid, that the person to be master of the said school, shall be of the religion of the Church of England, and conform to the same, and shall be capable to teach the learned languages, that is to say, the Latin and Greek tongues, and also the useful parts of the mathematics.

" XII. And be it further enacted by the authority aforesaid, that these commissioners and their successors, shall have power and authority, under their common seal, to set down and prescribe such orders, rules, statutes, and ordinances for the order, rule and good government of the said school, and of the masters, teachers, ushers and scholars thereof, as to them and their successors shall seem meet and convenient; and that the same orders, rules, statutes and ordinances, so by them made and set down, shall be and stand in full force and strength in law, so always that the same be reasonable, and not repugnant nor contrary to the established laws of this province. And the said commissioners for the time being shall have full power and authority to visit the said school, and to order, reform, and redress all disorders and abuses in and touching the government of the same; and further, to censure, suspend and deprive any of the masters, teachers or professors of the said school, or the usher or ushers thereof for the time being, as to them shall seem just, fit and convenient.

"XIII. And be it further enacted by the authority aforesaid, that the said master or teacher of the said school shall have, hold, occupy, possess and enjoy, to him and his lawful successors, all such land as shall, pursuant to this Act, be taken up, purchased, had or received for the use of the master of the said school, and the school house, and dwelling house, and the out-houses, and other buildings upon the same.

"XIV. And be it further enacted by the authority aforesaid, that in case the commissioners shall think it necessary that there be an usher appointed for the said school, that then the usher of the said school shall be chosen by the master, but approved of by the said commissioners and their successors.

"XV. And because it is necessary that a fit person to teach the youth of this province to write, and also the principles of vulgar arithmetic and merchants' accounts, Be it therefore enacted by the authority aforesaid, that a fitting person shall be nominated and appointed by the said commissioners, to teach writing, arithmetic, and merchants' accounts.

"Read three times, and ratified in open Assembly this eighth day of April, Anno Dom. 1710.

EDW. TYNTE,
F. TURBERVILLE,
ROBERT GIBBES,
ROBERT DANIELL,
THO. BROUGHTON."[1]

[1] *Ibid.*, II, 342–346.

Two years later, further provision was made by the legislature for the colonial library under an Act entitled "An additional Act to the several Acts relating to the establishment of religious worship in this province and now in force in the same, and also to the Act for securing the Provincial Library at Charlestown in Carolina." Governor Charles Craven, Arthur Middleton, Charles Hart, Colonel George Logan and Colonel Hugh Grange were nominated to fill the vacancies which had occurred in the Library Commission through the decease of its members, and the commission was empowered to fill its own vacancies thenceforward. The commission was directed to meet yearly on the third Wednesday of March and the third Wednesday of October, at the same place where the church commissioners were appointed to meet, and to choose a day to inspect the library in accordance with law. Failure on the part of a commissioner to meet at these appointed times involved a forfeiture of 20 s., unless an excuse was submitted to and accepted by the major part of the commissioners at a subsequent meeting. Sections 25 and 26 of this Act provide for a restriction upon the circulation of the Provincial Library and for the extension of the commissioners' control over certain recently established parochial libraries.

"XXV. And whereas, by the said Act all the inhabitants of this province, without any exception, may have liberty to borrow any book out of the Provincial Library, giving a receipt for the same, which unrestrained liberty hath already proved very prejudicial to the said library, several of the books being lost and others damnified, and therefore, for the preservation of the said library, it will be necessary to lodge a discretional power in the person that keeps the same, to deny any person the loan of any book that he shall think will not take care of the same; Be it therefore enacted by the authority aforesaid, that in case any person shall desire to borrow any book out of the said Provincial Library, which the keeper of the said library hath just reason to think will not take care of the said book and return the same in time, that in such case the said library keeper may refuse such person the loan of any book; anything in the said Act for securing the library, to the contrary hereof in any wise notwithstanding.

"XXVI. And whereas, there are several parochial libraries belonging to the rectors or ministers of the several parishes in this province, given for the use of them and their lawful successors by the honorable Society for the Propagation of the Gospel in Foreign Parts, and by the honorable Francis Nicholson, Esq., and other charitable persons; for the better preservation of the said libraries, Be it enacted by the authority aforesaid, that the Commissioners for the Provincial Library shall have power to authorize and empower any one or more persons, as to them shall seem convenient, to make catalogues of the books belonging to each of the said parochial libraries, and to dispose of the said catalogues as before directed by the said Library Act, and also to impower any of the said persons to visit the said libraries and to compare the books with the catalogues and see that they are in good order, and further to exercise all the powers and authorities given by the said Library Act to the Commissioners of the Provincial Library."[1]

On the same day of the passage of this Act, an Act was also passed entitled

"AN ACT FOR THE ENCOURAGEMENT OF LEARNING.

(One-half of a leaf of the original Act is torn off. What remains is here copied.)

"Whereas, several sums of money have been given by well disposed persons for building a free school, which cannot at this time be done conveniently; to supply which defect for the present,

"I. Be it enacted, by his Excellency the Palatine, and the rest of the true and absolute Lords Proprietors of Carolina, by and with the advice and consent of the rest of the members of

[1] *Ibid.*, II, 374-6.

the General Assembly, now met at Charlestown for the south-
west part of the said province, and by the authority of the
same, that from and after the ratification of this Act, John
Douglas shall be and is hereby declared to be Master of a
Grammar School in Charlestown, for teaching the Greek and
Latin languages, and shall choose one usher to the said school,
who is empowered and required to assist the master aforesaid
in teaching the languages, reading, English, writing, arithmetic or such other parts of the mathematics as he is capable
to teach.

*   *   *   *   *   *

"III. And Whereas, Mr. Benjamin Dennis is sent over by
the recommendation of the honorable Society for the Propagation of the Gospel in Foreign Parts,[1] to be a school-master
for the parish of St. James, Goose Creek, in which parish he
having been a considerable time to great satisfaction and approbation of their inhabitants thereof, therefore worthy our
consideration, and whereas there cannot be sufficient provision

---

[1] The Society for the Propagation of the Gospel in Foreign Parts was incorporated in 1701 through the efforts of Dr. Bray, Dr. Stanley, Bishop Compton,
Archbishop Tenison, etc. It was the natural outcome of the practice of the Established Church of sending out ministers for the " charge and cure of souls " in
his Majesty's fleets and in the lands to which those fleets were bound. This
missionary work was supported by endowments and donations from the sover
eigns, nobility, gentry and clergy of England. The undertaking of the Society
was threefold—the care and instruction of the English settled in the colonies,
the conversion of the Indians and the conversion of the negroes. (*An Historical Account of the Incorporated Society for the Propagation of the Gospel in
Foreign Parts*, pp. 22-23. David Humphreys, D. D., London, 1733.) The
missionaries sent by this Society to South Carolina " represented frequently
. . . . the great want of schools in this Province, for the instruction of the
children in the principles of religion, and teaching convenient learning." (*Ibid.*,
p. 124.) Dr. Le Jeau had been sent as missionary by the Society for the Propagation of the Gospel to the parish of Goosecreek in 1706, and while there he " did
very earnestly press the Society to allow a salary for a schoolmaster in his parish."
Mr. Dennis was consequently appointed schoolmaster there in 1710. We are
told that " he had a good number of scholars for several years, till the Indian war
broke out, which dispersed the people and all his scholars." (*Ibid.*, p. 124.)

made for the maintenance of the said Dennis in the parish, by reason of the neglect of many of the said parishioners, which for the future (if not prevented) will be a discouragement to the honorable societies sending over such school-masters as will be wanting in this province; to prevent which, and that some encouragement may be given to the the said Dennis out of the public treasury, Be it enacted by the authority aforesaid, that from and after the ratification of this Act the public receiver for the time being shall pay unto the aforesaid Mr. Benjamin Dennis a salary of sixteen pounds a year, which salary shall be paid at four equal quarterly payments, and shall continue to be paid during the space and term of three years after the ratification of this Act.

" IV. Be it further enacted by the authority aforesaid, that the aforementioned John Douglas, school master aforesaid, shall take and receive for each scholar to whom is taught in the school aforesaid the Greek and Latin tongues, the sum of three pounds a year, and so a proportional sum for a longer or shorter time ; and for every scholar to whom is taught English, writing, arithmetic or any other parts of the mathematics, such a sum as shall be agreed upon betwixt the master aforesaid and the learner himself or any other in his behalf; and that two-thirds of all money received from the scholars taught in the school aforesaid, by the master and usher above mentioned, shall be for the proper use of the master, John Douglas, aforesaid, and the other third part for the use of the usher.

" V. Be it likewise enacted by the authority aforesaid, that if any person refuse or neglect to pay what he agreed to pay to the school master above mentioned, either for being taught or for having any other taught by his agreement or order, such sum so neglected or refused to be paid shall be recovered by the master aforesaid, after such manner as is directed by one Act, entitled an Act for the trial of small and mean causes.

" VI. Be it further enacted by the authority aforesaid, that in case of the death or surrender of the school master aforesaid, another shall be appointed in his place by order of the General Assembly, and shall enjoy the salary and other benefits allowed by this Act, as if he were therein expressly mentioned.

" VII. Be it further enacted by the authority aforesaid, that the school master above mentioned, shall not be superseded or divested of the place, salary and perquisites given unto him by this Act, by any other authority whatsoever, unless by ordinance of the General Assembly.

" VIII. Whereas, by an Act entitled an Act for erecting and founding a free school, etc., there is no provision made for choosing a president on the death, absence or resignation of the president nominated in the said Act, and whereas, Colonel Edward Tynte, the president nominated by the Act aforesaid, is since deceased, by which means the surviving commissioners cannot proceed to transact the business of the said Act; Be it therefore enacted, that the honorable Charles Craven Esq., Governor, be and is hereby nominated and appointed president to the said commissioners, and hereby declared to have all the powers and authorities which by the said Act were vested in Colonel Edward Tynte, aforesaid, as fully and to all intents and purposes whatsoever, as if the said Charles Craven was nominated president in the body of the said Act.

" IX. And be it further enacted, that if any of the said commissioners shall neglect to attend, being duly summoned as in the said Act is directed, such commissioner or commissioners shall forfeit ten shillings for every day that the commissioners shall meet to transact the business of that Act, unless he or they so neglecting to attend shall give the commissioners, or the major part of them, such reasons as to them shall be satisfactory ; and the forfeitures arising by the neglect of the said commissioners to attend, shall be disposed of as the majority of the commissioners then met shall order and appoint.

" Read three times and ratified in open Assembly, the seventh day of June, 1712.

> CHARLES CRAVEN,
> CHARLES HART,
> ARTHUR MIDDLETON,
> THO. BROUGHTON,
> RICH. BERESFORD,
> SAM. EVELEIGH."[1]

In the following December the School Act of 1710 and the foregoing Act for the encouragement of learning, were repealed, and an Act for the founding and erecting of a free school in Charleston, etc., was passed. With the exception of certain administrative details this Act embodied all the provisions of the Act of 1710.

Governor Craven, Charles Hart, Thomas Broughton, Nicholas Trott, Arthur Middleton, Richard Beresford, William Rhett, the Reverend Mr. Gideon Johnston, the Rev. Dr. Francis Legau, Robert Maul, Ralph Izard, Landgrave Joseph Morton, Col. George Logan, Col. Alexander Parris, Col. Hugh Grange and William Gibbon, " or any seven of them," were nominated school commissioners, and were directed to meet together every March and October. At the first meeting of the commission, the president, who, as in the former Act, was the governor of the province was to be sworn in to the faithful and due discharge of his trust, and this oath was to be administered to him by the chief justice, or, in his absence, by any two of the commissioners; the president was then to administer a similar oath to the other officers that might be elected by the commissioners. The president or one of the vice-presidents, and six commissioners instead of eight, as provided in the previous Act, were to constitute a quorum. A fine of 10 s. was imposed for every day's absence from a meeting of the commission, unless reasons for such absence were found satisfactory by a majority of the commissioners. The Act appointed

---

[1] *Ibid.*, II, 376–378.

Mr. John Douglass the first master of the school, and directed that all future school masters should not only conform to the Church of England, as was provided in the Act of 1710, but should also " catechise and instruct the youth in the principles of the Christian religion," as professed by that church. Sections 14 to 32 of this Act contain additional educational provisions.

" XIV. And for an encouragement to all charitable and well disposed persons to contribute liberally towards the erecting and founding of the said school or academy, Be it further enacted by the authority aforesaid, that any person or persons that within seven years after the ratification of this Act, will contribute twenty pounds, current money of this province, towards the erecting and founding of the said school, and will pay the same to the treasurer appointed by the said commissioners, that he or they shall have power to nominate any one person to be taught free in the said school for the space of five years after such gift, provided the person nominated by him or them shall so long live, but in case of the death of the person so nominated to be taught free, then that privilege to cease, and not another person to be nominated in his room or place; and so proportionably for so many twenty pounds as any person will give, so many persons to be taught free for five years, as aforesaid, provided the number of scholars so in the whole to be taught free, do not exceed the number of twenty.

" XV. And be it further enacted by the authority aforesaid, that the school master shall have, hold, occupy, possess and enjoy to him and his lawful successors, all such land as shall, pursuant to this Act, be taken up, purchased, had or received for the use of a school master of the said school, and the school house, and dwelling houses, and the out houses and other buildings upon the same; and also, as a further encouragement unto him, shall have and receive out of the public treasury of this province, the full sum of one hundred pounds per annum, to be paid him half yearly, and the public receiver for the time being is hereby authorized, required and commanded punctually to pay the same out of the public treasury.

"XVI. And be it further enacted by the authority aforesaid, that in consideration of the said school master being allowed the use of the lands, dwelling house and other buildings upon the same land, and also the yearly salary of one hundred pounds per annum, he shall teach freely, and without any manner of fee or reward whatsoever, over and above the number of free scholars to be appointed by each person contributing twenty pounds as aforesaid, any number of scholars not exceeding twelve, the same scholars to be taught free, to be nominated and appointed by the above named commissioners and their lawful successors.

"XVII. And be it further enacted by the authority aforesaid, that for every scholar the said master shall teach, besides those who by this Act are appointed to be taught free, he shall be allowed at the rate of four pounds per annum, current money of this province, to be paid him by the parent or guardian of such scholar.

"XVIII. And be it further enacted by the authority aforesaid, that in case the said school master shall have more scholars in his said school than any one man can well manage, then and in such case, the said commissioners, or the major part of them that shall meet, shall order and appoint a fit person to be usher of the said school, and for his encouragement shall be allowed by order of the said commissioners and their successors, not exceeding fifty pounds per annum, to be paid him half yearly out of the public treasury of this province, . . . and over and above that, shall be allowed for every scholar that is under his charge (excepting those that by this Act are appointed to be taught free) at the rate of thirty shillings per annum, which sum of thirty shillings shall be allowed out of the four pounds per annum before directed to be paid for each scholar that is not taught free ; and in case any dispute or difference shall arise between the master and the usher, what scholars shall belong to the more immediate charge of the master and which to the usher, that the same shall be decided by the commissioners and their successors.

" XIX. And because it is necessary to give encouragement to a fit person that will undertake to teach the youth of this province to write, and also the principles of vulgar arithmetic and merchants' accounts; Be it further enacted by the authority aforesaid, that a fit person shall be nominated and appointed by the said commissioners, to teach writing, arithmetic, and merchants' accounts, and also the art of navigation and surveying, and other useful and practical parts of mathematics, and for his encouragement shall be allowed by order of the said commissioners and their successors, not exceeding fifty pounds per annum, to be paid him half yearly, out of the public treasury of this province, . . . and in consideration of the said yearly salary to be paid him, he shall be obliged to teach free all such persons as by this Act are appointed to have their learning free, and for other scholars that are not to be taught free, he shall be allowed for teaching them writing, at the rate of thirty shillings per annum, if writing and arithmetic, forty shillings, if merchants' accounts, fifty shillings per annum, and if the mathematics, at such rate as he shall agree with the several parents and guardians of the said children, not exceeding six pounds per annum.

" XX. And be it further enacted by the authority aforesaid, that as to the public salaries appointed by this Act to be paid out of the public treasury of this province, the public receiver for the time being is hereby authorized, required and commanded to pay the same out of the remaing part of the moneys received for the duties upon skins and furs, after payment of the ministers' salaries appointed by the Act of Assembly of this province commonly called the Church Act, and also of the parochial charges, and all other charges and sums of money that are appointed to be paid by one Act of Assembly of this province, entitled a further Additional Act to an Act entitled an Act for the establishment of religious worship in this province, according to the Church of England, and for erecting of churches for the public worship of God, and also for the maintenance of ministers, and the building convenient houses for them, ratified in open Assembly the eighth day of April, one thousand, seven hundred and ten; and also all the moneys appointed to be paid by one other Act of Assembly of this province, entitled an Additional Act to the several Acts relating to the establishment of religious worship in the province, and now in force in the same, and also to the Act for securing the Provincial Library at Charlestown, in Carolina, ratified in open Assembly the seventh day of June, one thousand, seven hundred and twelve; and the remaining part of the moneys received upon the duties on skins and furs, after the payments above mentioned being deducted, is hereby appropriated to the payments of the several salaries appointed by this Act to be paid . . . . And in case the remaining part of the moneys received out of the said duties upon skins and furs, after the deduction aforesaid, shall not be sufficient to discharge the several salaries appointed to be paid by this Act, that in such case, what is wanting to discharge the same, the said public receiver for the time being is hereby strictly charged and required to pay what is wanting to discharge the same, out of the public treasury.

" XXI. And as a further and more general encouragement for the instructing of the youth of this province in useful and necessary learning; Be it enacted by the authority aforesaid, that as soon as a school master is settled in any other, or all the rest of the parishes of this province, and approved by the vestry of such parish or parishes, such school master so approved, from time to time, shall receive the sum of ten pounds per annum, out of the public treasury, by quarterly payments, and the public receiver is hereby required to pay the same.

" XXII. And be it further enacted, that the vestry of each

parish in this province shall have power, and they are hereby empowered, to appoint a place where the parish school shall be built, and shall draw upon the public receiver towards building the same, the sum of twelve pounds current money, and the public receiver is hereby required to pay the same accordingly."[1]

In 1719 the people of South Carolina rebelled against the proprietary rule, the proprietary charter was forfeited to the Crown and Carolina became a royal province. During the administration of Francis Nicholson, royal Governor from 1721 to 1724, two educational Acts were passed by the legislature.

In 1722, under an Act additional to an Act entitled "An Act for Establishing County and Precinct Courts" the justices of these courts were authorized to purchase lands, erect a free school in each county and precinct, and to assess the expense upon the lands and slaves within their respective jurisdictions. They were to appoint masters who were to be "well skilled in the Latin tongue," and who were to be allowed £25 proclamation money per annum. Ten poor children were to be taught gratis yearly, if sent by the justices.[2]

In 1724 an Act was passed " for founding and erecting, governing, ordering and visiting a free school at the town of Dorchester, in the parish of St. George, in Berkeley County, for

---

[1] *Ibid.*, II, 389–396.

[2] The title only of this Act is given in Cooper's *Statutes*. The above abstract is given by McCrady in his *Education in South Carolina*, p. 10, from the text of the Act in Trott's *Laws of South Carolina* (p. 898), a work inaccessible to the writer.

Ten days prior to the passage of this Act an Act was passed giving certain powers to the general court at Charles City which were allowed to the county and precinct courts. Section IV gave "full power to this general court to sue for all legacies, gifts and donations given to free schools and other public uses within the jurisdiction." *The Public Laws of the State of South Carolina*, p. 120. John F. Grimké, Philadelphia, 1790.

the use of the inhabitants of the province of South Carolina."[1] The text of this Act is lost and its content can only be inferred from the following Act which bears the same title and which was passed ten years later by the legislature.

"Whereas, by the blessing of almighty God, the youth of this province are become very numerous, and their parents so well inclined to have them instructed in grammar, and other liberal arts and sciences, and other useful learning, and also in the principles of the Christian religion, that the free school erected, authorized and established in Charlestown for this purpose, is not sufficient fully to answer the good intent of such an undertaking: And whereas, several of the inhabitants of this province who have a numerous issue, and live at such a distance from the said free school now established in Charlestown, that their circumstances may not be sufficient to permit them to send their children thither to be educated, whereby they may be deprived of so great a benefit; and it therefore appearing necessary that one or more schools be founded and erected in other part or parts of this province as shall be most convenient for the carrying on so laudable a design, we therefore most humbly pray your most sacred Majesty that it may be enacted,

"I. And be it enacted, by his Excellency Robert Johnson, Esq. Governor of this his Majesty's Province of South Carolina, by and with the consent and advice of his Majesty's Honorable Council and Assembly of this Province, and by the authority of the same, that the Honorable Alexander Skene, Thomas Waring, Joseph Blake, Arthur Middleton, Ralph Izard, Robert Wright, Paul Jenys, Walter Izard, Benjamin Waring, Esqrs. the Rev. Francis Vernod, Walter Cattell and

[1] *Statutes*, III, 236. A Congregational Church from Dorchester, Massachusetts, settled in 1696 on the Ashley River about 20 miles from Charlestown and remained at this place which they called Dorchester, as a distinct settlement, until 1752 when they removed to Medway, Georgia. See McGrady's *History of South Carolina under the Proprietary Government*, pp. 326–7.

John Williams, Esqrs. and their successors to be elected as hereinafter directed, be and shall forever hereafter be one body politic and corporate in deed and in name, by the name of the Commissioners for the founding, erecting, governing, ordering and visiting a Free School at the town of Dorchester, in the Parish of St. George, in Berkley County, for the use of the inhabitants of South Carolina; and that they and their successors by the same name, by the authority aforesaid, be fully made, ordained, constituted and declared one body politic and corporate in deed and in name; and that by the same name, they and their successors shall and may have perpetual succession; and that they and their successors by that name, shall and may forever hereafter be persons able and capable in law to purchase, have, take, receive and enjoy to them and their successors, lands, messuages, tenements, rents, liberties, privileges, jurisdictions, franchises, and other hereditaments of whatsoever nature, kind, quality or value they be, in fee, and in perpetuity, and also estates for lives and for years, and all other manner of goods, chattels and things whatsoever, of what name, nature, value or quality soever they be, for the better maintenance and support of masters or teachers for the said school; and also for the erecting of school houses and convenient dwelling houses for the accommodation of the said school masters and teachers; and that by the name aforesaid they shall and may be able to plead and be impleaded, answer and be answered unto, and to defend and be defended in all courts and places whatsoever, and before whatsoever judge or judges, justice or justices, or other officer or officers belonging to this province, in all and singular actions, plaints, pleas, matters and demands, of what nature, kind, or quality soever may be, and to act and do all other matters and things in as ample manner and form as any other the inhabitants of this province being persons able and capable in law, as any other body politic or corporate, by the laws of England can or may have, purchase, receive, possess, take, enjoy, set, let, demise,

plead and be impleaded, answer and be answered unto, defend
and be defended, do, permit and execute; and that the said
commissioners and their successors forever hereafter, shall and
may have a common seal to serve for the causes and business
of them and their successors, and to change, break, alter and
make new the said seal from time to time, and at their pleasure
as they shall think best; and the said commissioners shall
take the State oaths, and an oath for the faithful execution of
their offices.

" II. And for the better execution of the purposes aforesaid,
Be it further enacted by the authority aforesaid, that the said
commissioners and their successors forever, shall and may
yearly on St. George's Day, being the three and twentieth day
of April (unless it shall be on Sunday, and then on the Monday following) meet at some convenient place to be appointed
by the president of the said commissioners, for the time being,
between the hours of nine and twelve in the morning of the
same day, and that they, or any three of them that shall be
then present, shall choose a president for the year ensuing,
and that such president shall (before he acts in his said office)
take the State oaths, to be administered to him by any one
justice of the peace, who is hereby authorized and empowered
to administer the same, as also an oath for the faithful and due
execution of his office and place during the said year, and
until discharged of the same.

" III. And be it further enacted by the authority aforesaid,
that the president of the said commissioners shall be the Hon.
Alexander Skene, Esq., and that the said president shall,
within forty days after the ratification of this Act, cause summons to be issued to the several commissioners hereinbefore
particularly mentioned, to meet on such a day, and at such a
place as he shall appoint; and the said president is hereby empowered, then and there to administer to the said commissioners the State oaths, as also an oath for the due execution
of their offices; and that they, or the major part of them as

shall be then present, shall proceed to the election of such officers, ministers and servants as shall be thought convenient, to serve for the year ensuing ; and that each of such officers, ministers and servants as shall be then elected, shall take the State oaths, and an oath to be to them administered by the president of the said commissioners, for the faithful and due execution of their respective offices and places until duly discharged of the same.

"IV. And be it further enacted by the authority aforesaid, that if any of the persons at any time chosen into any of the said offices shall die, resign, or any account be removed from such offices, at any time between such yearly days of election, that in such case it shall and may be lawful for the president for the time being, to issue summons to the other commissioners to meet at the usual place of annual meeting, at such time as shall be specified in the said summons, and such commissioners as shall meet upon such summons (provided not less than five in the whole), or the major part of them, shall and may choose an officer or officers, in the room or place of such person or persons so dead or removed, as to them shall seem meet.

"V. And be it further enacted by the authority aforesaid, that in case of the death, resignation or removal from this province of any of the said commissioners, that then it shall be lawful for the president, for the time being, to issue out his summons to the several surviving and remaining commissioners, to meet at the usual place of the annual meeting of the said commissioners, at such time as shall be specified in the said summons ; and that such members as shall meet upon any summons, (provided not less than five in the whole) or the major part of them, shall or may choose a new commissioner or commissioners, in the room or place of such person or persons so dead or removed, as to them shall seem meet.

"VI. And be it further enacted by the authority aforesaid, that in case of the death, resignation or removal from this province of the president, any five or more of the commissioners shall meet and choose another president for the remaining part of the year, who shall have and enjoy all the powers and authorities given and granted to the president by this Act appointed.

"VII. And be it further enacted by the authority aforesaid, that it shall and may be lawful for the said commissioners and their successors, to meet at some convenient place in the said parish, to be appointed for that purpose, on the twenty-third day of April, being St. George's day, or oftener if occasion require, upon public summons given ten days before, then and there to transact the business of the said commissioners, and to put in force and execute the several powers given them by this Act; and no Act done in any assembly of the said commissioners, shall be effectual and valid, unless the president and four members of the said commissioners at least be present, and the major part consenting thereunto.

"VIII. And be it further enacted by the authority aforesaid, that if any of the said commissioners shall neglect to attend, being duly summoned, as in this Act is directed, such commissioner or commissioners shall forfeit ten shillings for every day that the commissioners shall meet to transact the business of this Act, unless he or they so neglecting to attend, shall give the commissioners, or the major part of them, such reasons as to them shall be satisfactory; and the forfeitures arising by the neglect of the said commissioners to attend, shall be disposed of as the majority of the commissioners then met shall order and appoint.

"IX. And be it further enacted by the authority aforesaid, that all gifts, legacies and voluntary subscriptions that shall or may hereafter be given or subscribed to or for the use of the free school by this present Act established, by any person or persons, are hereby appropriated to and for the sole use and benefit of the said school; and the several commissioners appointed by this Act, and their lawful successors, are hereby authorized and empowered to demand and sue for the same in the courts of this province or elsewhere, by all such lawful ways and means for the recovery and obtaining of the same, as they might or could do if the said gifts, legacies and subscriptions had been given to them expressly by name, and a receipt signed by such person or persons as shall be appointed treasurer to the said commissioners, shall be a sufficient discharge to such executor or executors as shall pay such legacies and subscriptions; and the money so received by such treasurer, shall be disposed of by order of the said commissioners and their successors, for the use and benefit of the school by this Act intended to be established, in such manner as the majority of them shall think most proper and convenient.

" X. And be it further enacted by the authority aforesaid, that the said commissioners and their successors, shall have power, and they are hereby authorized and empowered, to take up by grant from his Majesty, or purchase, have, take and receive from any other person or persons whatsoever, so much land as they shall think necessary and convenient for the masters and teachers of the school hereby intended to be established, and shall direct the building of such honses as may be necessary to be erected thereon for their accommodation; the said buildings to be in such places on the said lands so taken up or purchased as aforesaid, and of such dimensions and material as the said commissioners shall order and appoint.

" XI. And be it further enacted by the authority aforesaid, that the master of the said school shall be capable to teach the learned languages, Latin and Greek tongues, and to catechise and instruct the youth in the principles of the Christian religion.

" XII. And be it further enacted by the authority aforesaid, that the said commissioners and their successors, shall have power and authority under their common seal, to set down and prescribe such orders, rules, statutes and ordinances for the order, rule, good government and management of the said school, and for the master or teacher and scholars thereof, as to them and their successors, from time to time shall seem meet and convenient; and that the same orders, rules, statutes and ordinances so by them made and set down, shall be and stand in full force and virtue in law; Provided always that the same be reasonable and fit, and not repugnant or contrary to the established laws of this province; and the said commissioners for the time being, shall have full power and authority to visit the said school, and to order, reform and redress all disorders and abuses in and touching the government of the same; and further to censure, suspend and deprive any of the masters, ushers or teachers of the said school, as to them shall seem just, fitting and convenient.

"XIII. And be it further enacted by the authority aforesaid, that if any action, claim, suit or information, shall be commenced or prosecuted against any person or persons, for what he or they shall do in pursuance or execution of this Act, such person or persons so sued, may plead the general issue, not guilty, and upon issue joined, give this Act and the special matter in evidence; and if the plaintiff or prosecutor shall become nonsuit or suffer discontinuance, or if a verdict pass against him, the defendant or defendants shall recover his or their treble costs, for which he or they shall have the like remedy as in any case where costs by law are given to the defendant.

 "Paul Jenys, Speaker.

"In the Council Chamber, 9th April, 1734.

"Assented to: Robt. Johnson."[1]

Later on in the century the attention of the legislature was again directed to this school. An Act in 1756 recites that all the original commissioners were dead and that no successors had been appointed. Accordingly, the rector of St. George's Parish for the time being and Henry

[1] *Ibid.*, III, 378–383.

Middleton, Walter Izard, Ralph Izard, Daniel Blake, John Ainslie, Benjamin Waring, Richard Waring, and Joseph Waring are appointed commissioners. Oaths of office are to be administered by any two of the commissioners. If the commissioners refuse to fill vacancies in their body within six months after such vacancy occurs, the vestry and church wardens of the parish are directed to choose a new commissioner or commissioners. In addition to the use of the school house, dwelling house, out-houses and other buildings, the schoolmaster is to be paid half yearly £25 proclamation money out of the church fund in the colony treasury and in return the schoolmaster, ushers and teachers are to instruct gratis ten poor scholars, "and as many more as the president and any four of the . . . commissioners shall from time to time, according as the public or school salaries may or shall be hereafter increased, approve of and judge fit to nominate and appoint."[1] On May 21, 1757, an Act was passed for "supplying the defects in the execution" of the Act of the preceding year. This Act states that "through sickness and other unavoidable accident" the commissioners named in the Act of 1756 did not meet at the appointed time and place and that, consequently, doubts had arisen concerning the lawfulness of any other meeting. It was accordingly enacted that if the requisite number of commissioners did not meet at the regularly appointed time, that the meeting might be adjourned from day to day until a quorum was finally obtained.[2]

In 1733 the legislature passed

"AN ACT FOR ERECTING A FREE SCHOOL AT CHILDSBURY.

"Whereas, nothing conduces more to the private advantage of every man, or the public benefit of a country in general than a liberal education, and the same cannot be had without due encouragement to persons qualified to instruct youth; and Mr. James Child, late of this province, deceased, desiring as far as

[1] *Ibid.*, IV, 23-24.   [2] *Ibid.*, IV, 41-42.

lay in his power to promote the same, did in and by his last will and testament, give and bequeath the sum of five hundred pounds current money of Carolina, towards the encouragement of a grammar school and other learning at Childsbury in St. John's Parish, in Berkley County; and also did further give, devise and bequeath the sum of one hundred pounds like money, and a lot to build a convenient house for the said school, and left the same to certain trustees in his said will named, to manage the same according to the directions of his will; and the said sums being far too short for the said purposes, several gentlemen, well weighing the great want of necessary learning in this province, and being desirous to encourage so good an undertaking, (according to their several abilities,) have by voluntary subscription raised the sum of two thousand, two hundred pounds like current money, to be added to the legacy of the said James Child, and have also chosen trustees to be joined with those named in the said Mr. James Child's will, to manage the said sums for the use of the said school, and as visitors to order, direct and govern the said school; we therefore humbly pray your most sacred Majesty that it may be enacted.

" I. And be it enacted, by his Excellency, Robert Johnson, Esq., Governor, by and with the advice and consent of his Majesty's honorable Council and the Commons House of Assembly of this province, and by the authority of the same, that the said several sums given and bequeathed in and by the last will and testament of the said James Child, for the use of the said school, and the several sums raised by subscription for the same use, be for the future united and declared to be one individual fund for the purpose aforesaid, and that the same shall not be applied or diverted to any other use or uses whatsoever.

" II. And be it further enacted by the authority aforesaid, that the Hon. Thomas Broughton, Esq., Lieut. Governor, the Rev. Mr. Thomas Hassell, Anthony Bonneau, John Harleston,

Nathaniel Broughton, Thomas Cordes and Francis Lejau, Esquires, shall be trustees for the said school, and that they shall have full power and authority to manage the several legacies and subscriptions already given and made, and which shall from time to time hereafter be made, devised or given for the use of the said school, according to their discretion.

" III. And be it enacted by the authority aforesaid, that they or the majority of them, shall have full power and authority to elect a master or masters, usher or ushers, and appropriate such a sum or sums for a salary or salaries out of the income of the said fund, as they shall think proper; and also the said master or masters, usher or ushers, to turn out and others to elect; and to make such rules for the better ordering and governing the said school, as they or a majority of them shall in their discretion think necessary.

" IV. And be it further enacted by the authority aforesaid, that the trustees are hereby empowered to receive from time to time, such sum or sums of money, houses, lands, tenements, or any other gifts or legacies, as any well disposed persons shall think fit to give or bequeath unto them for the use of the said school, and to build such house or houses as they shall think necessary and convenient.

" V. And be it further enacted by the authority aforesaid, that no person shall be a trustee, except he hath subscribed an hundred pounds, and no person shall have a vote in electing trustees, except he hath subscribed fifty pounds for the use of the said school; and that after the death of any of the subscribers, their heirs or assigns by them appointed, shall have the same privileges as the subscribers themselves had, or of right ought to have.

" VI. And be it further enacted by the authority aforesaid, that upon the death or resignation of any of the trustees, the survivors of them shall give notice to the subscribers, or to the heirs or assigns of such of the subscribers as shall be dead, within three months to meet at Childsbury, at a certain day, to elect another trustee in the place of the person deceased.

"VII. And be it further enacted by the authority aforesaid, that the trustees or the majority of them, be obliged to meet at Childsbury once in three months at least, to consider of all things for the benefit of the said school, and that if any of them omit meeting for the space of one whole year without a reasonable excuse, to be approved of by the rest of the trustees or the majority of them, that then it shall be lawful for them to declare his place to be vacant; and in such case, they shall give notice to the subscribers to meet and elect another trustee in his room, as in case of death or resignation; and if the trustees shall neglect or refuse to summon the subscribers to meet within the time aforesaid to elect a trustee or trustees, that then the subscribers may meet and elect a trustee or trustees, of their own accord, and the said person or persons so elected, shall be deemed to be a trustee or trustees, and have the same power and authority to act jointly with the others as those named in this Act.

"VIII. And whereas, Francis Williams, late of Berkley County, deceased, did in and by his last will and testament empower his executors to dispose of such sums as were remaining of his estate, to such charitable uses as they thought fit; his said executors have given the sum of two hundred pounds to the said school, Be it enacted by the authority aforesaid, that the interest of the said sum be appropriated to the teaching so many poor scholars as the trustees shall think proper.

"IX. And be it further enacted by the authority aforesaid, that if any charitable person or persons, shall hereafter subscribe any sum or sums of money to the said school, or give the same by will, he or they so subscribing or giving (or their assigns by them appointed) shall have the same privileges as those who have already subscribed, subject, nevertheless, to the exceptions in this Act mentioned.

" X. And be it further enacted by the authority aforesaid, that the trustees above mentioned and their successors, are hereby empowered to lend the said moneys out at interest, and to take bonds or notes, or any other instruments of writing, and to purchase lands and let them out by the year or lease them for a term of years; and the said bonds, notes and other instruments of writing, shall be in the name of themselves and their successors, for the use of the said school; and they are hereby empowered to demand and sue for any rents, legacies, notes, bonds or any other moneys that are or shall hereafter become due unto them, and to take possession of any houses, lands or tenements which shall be given or bequeathed to them for the use of the said school.

" PAUL JENYS, Speaker.

" In the Council Chamber, 9th June, 1733.

" Assented to: ROBT. JOHNSON."[1]

In 1740, the legislature passed two Acts " to encourage the better settling and improvement of Beaufort Town, on Port Royal Island, in Granville County." Both Acts provided that every person who obtained grants for lots in this town and who failed to build houses on them according to certain specifications within three years should pay an annual fine of two pounds proclamation money until the conditions were fulfilled. These forfeitures were to be paid to seven or less commissioners who were to be discreet and fit persons nominated by the governor of the province for the time being, under the name of Commissioners of the Free School at Beaufort. And this school was to be established by the commissioners for the education of poor children.[2]

During the last three decades of the colonial period, the Assembly of South Carolina passed several private Acts incorporating various educational agencies. The Charlestown Library Society was incorporated in 1754.[3] The Winyan

---

[1] *Ibid.*, III, 364–366.   [2] *Ibid.*, III, 574–6.

[3] *The History of South Carolina*, II, 378. David Ramsay, M. D., Charleston, 1809.

Indigo Society was incorporated in 1756 for the improvement of the culture and manufacture of indigo and the endowment of a free school.[1] The Fellowship Society, which appropriated one-half of its funds to the care of the insane and the other half to the education of poor children, was incorporated in 1769.[2]

During the colonial period no provision was made in South Carolina for collegiate education, although certain attempts were made to interest the government in its behalf. In 1723 the Rev. Thomas Morrit, who had been "fixed" as school-master at Charlestown by the Society for the Propagation of the Gospel, presented a plan to the Lower House for the founding of a college.[3] Again in 1769, an elaborate bill was drawn up providing for public schools and for a college of South Carolina, but no action was taken by the legislature in this direction.[4]

[1] *Ibid.*, II, 363.   [2] *Ibid.*, II, 363.

[3] *History of Higher Education in South Carolina*, p. 52. Colyer Mereweather. *Bureau of Education, Circular of Information*, No. 3, 1888.

[4] *Ibid.*

NORTH CAROLINA

THE first General Assembly of North Carolina was held between 1664 and 1665. It consisted of 20 Representatives from the four precincts of the colony, of a Governor[1] commissioned by the Proprietaries and of a Council appointed by the Governor with the consent of the Proprietaries.

In North Carolina as in South Carolina, the first legislative[2] action for the educational betterment of the colony was an Act to secure the library which Commissary Bray had sent to North Carolina in the year 1700. This collection was valued at £100; but after its establishment at Bath, it seems to have fallen into careless hands and its value was much impaired. The Act for its preservation is given in the revisal of the laws in 1715. The provisions of the Act are similar to those of the Library Act of South Carolina. The Governor, Councillors, Chief Justice, Secretary, Speaker of Assembly, Attorney General and the members of the precinct court and ten others are named library commissioners. They are directed to appoint a library keeper to be responsible for the books until the settle-

---

[1] Until 1689 the Governor was commissioned as the Governor of Albemarle, from 1689 to 1712 as Deputy Governor of the Governor of South Carolina.

[2] The highest judiciary body in the colony was a general court composed of a chief justice and seven assistants appointed by the Proprietaries. At a general court met on Feb. 25, 1695, at which Deputy Governor Thomas Harvey was present, a certain orphan boy who had been left destitute was "bound unto the said Thomas Harvey and Sarah his wife until he be at the age of 21 years, and the said Thomas Harvey to teach him to read." (*The Colonial Records of North Carolina*, I, 448, edited by William L. Saunders, Raleigh, 1886. See also *Beginnings of the Common School System in the South*. Stephen B. Weeks, Ph. D. Published in the *Report of the Com. of Educ.*, 1896-97, p. 1381).

ment of a minister in the parish, the minister to be ex-officio library keeper.[1]

In this same revisal of the laws is "an Act concerning orphans." By this Act, precinct courts are directed to grant "letters of tuition or guardianship" to proper persons "for the care of bringing up and education of all orphans." Section 3 enacts "that all orphans shall be educated and provided for according to their rank and degree, out of the income or interest of their estates or stocks, if the same will be sufficient; otherwise such orphan shall be bound apprentice to some handicraft trade, (the master or mistress of such orphans not being of the profession of the people called Quakers) until they shall come of age"[2]

In 1728, North Carolina became a royal province. In 1734 Gabriel Johnston[3] was commissioned the second royal governor of the province. He continued in office for 18 years. In an address which he made to the Assembly on September 21, 1736, embodying recommendations of much needed reforms he arraigned the colony for its lack of religion and education in these terms:

"I shall begin with observing the deplorable and almost total want of divine worship throughout the province. . . . After observing this, nobody will be surprised at the many disorders which have always prevailed among us, especially when it is considered how little care is taken of the education of youth. In all civilized societies of men, it has always been looked upon as a matter of the greatest consequence to their peace and happiness, to polish the minds of young persons with some degree of learning, and early to instil into them the principles of virtue and religion, and that the Legislature has never yet taken the least care to erect one school, which

---

[1] *A Collection of all the Public Acts of Assembly of the Province of North Carolina*, pp. 34–37, Newbern, 1752.   [2] *Ibid.*, p. 30.

[3] Governor Johnson had been a student in the University of St. Andrews, Scotland.

deserves the name in this wide extended country, must in the judgment of all thinking men, be reckoned one of our greatest misfortunes. To what purpose, gentlemen, is all your toil and labor, all your pains and endeavors for the advantage and enriching your families and posterity, if within yourselves you cannot afford such an education as may qualify them to be useful to their country and to enjoy what you leave them with decency."[1]

To this the Upper House made answer on September 25 : "We lament very much the want of divine public worship (a crying scandal in any, but more especially in a Christian community); as well as the general neglect in point of education, the main source of all disorders and corruptions, which we should rejoice to see removed and remedied, and are ready to do our parts towards the reformation of such flagrant and prolific evils."[2]

On October 7, the Lower House presented to the Governor a list of grievances drawn up by a committee of that House, concerning the collection of quit rents, the violation of an Indian treaty, the removal of magistrates from office, etc. In his response, the Governor discussed these several points in order and then observed in conclusion: "I am sorry they [the committee on grievances] have been so remiss in their duty as to present so few grievances and those, so little material. In any other country besides this, I am satisfied they would have taken notice of the want of divine worship, the neglect of the education of youth, the bad state of your laws and the impossibility to execute them. Such as they are grievances which will deserve redress, but these, it seems, are not reckoned grievances in this part of the world. The more unhappy for the people you represent; for all the world must now see who is to be blamed for neglecting matters so essential to the peace, quiet and good government of the province."[3] The

---

[1] *Col. Rec.*, IV, 227. See also *Ibid.*, IV, 228.

[2] *Ibid.*, IV, 231.   [3] *Ibid.*, IV, 239.

following year, March 4, 1737, the Governor again referred to the subject in his opening speech to the Assembly: It is so short a time since I laid the miserable state of your public affairs before you that I flatter myself I have no occasion to remind you of them at present. I shall only therefore once more assure you that if you are disposed to take any measures for maintaining and establishing the public worship of Almighty God, making any provision for the education of youth or the reformation and better execution of your laws, I am come with a most sincere intention of concurring with you in promoting such valuable ends."[1]

In spite of Governor Johnston's appeal, nothing was done for education by the legislature until April, 1745, when in the Lower House "Mr. Craven brought in a bill for an Act to empower the Commissioners for the Town of Edenton to keep in repair the town fences and to erect and build a pound, bridges, public wharf and market house as also to erect and build a school house in the said town and other purposes therein mentioned."[2]

This bill was passed by both Houses and assented to by the Governor on April 20, 1745. The Act empowered the town commissioners to appropriate the money arising from the sale of town lots to defray the expense of erecting the school house, market house, etc. The commissioners were furthermore empowered to "receive donations and subscriptions towards defraying the expenses of building the school house in the said town, and apply the same accordingly;" . . . and also to "commence suits or actions for the recovery of any sums given or subscribed to be paid, for the purpose aforesaid, by any person or persons whosoever."[3]

On April 5, 1749, "a bill for an Act for founding, erecting, ordering and visiting a free school at   for the use of the inhabitants of this province," was introduced in the Upper

[1] *Ibid.*, IV, 271-2.   [2] *Ibid.*, IV, 786, 787, 788, 790.
[3] *Laws*, 1752, pp. 203-4.

House,[1] and on April 8 it was read for the first time and passed by that House.[2] It was then sent down to the Lower House.[3] On April 10, it was read for the second time in the Lower House and "passed with amendments."[4] There is no further record of this bill, and as no reference is made to it in the revisals of the laws in 1751 and 1752, it probably never became a law.

In Governor Johnston's opening address to the Assembly in April, 1752, after recommending the past behaviour of the legislators in reforming prevalent abuses and enormities, he recommends to their diligence and assiduity to take in particular "the most effectual measures for promoting religion and virtue and suppressing vices and immorality, which are come to such a dreadful height in the province."[5]

In answer to this speech the Lower House promised to take measures "whereby the public worship of Almighty God may be effectually supported" and "the virtuous education of our youth promoted." Accordingly, on April 7, a bill was brought up from the Lower House and passed in the Upper House "for the better establishing the church, for erecting of schools, and for granting to his Majesty certain rates and duties for the support of the same."[6] There is no further record of this bill.

In 1754, the legislature passed an Act granting an aid to the King of £40,000 in bills of public credit. Section 12 of this Act appropriated £6,000 "for the founding and endowing a public school, in such manner and under such regulations as the Governor, or Commander in Chief, for the time being, the Council and General Assembly, shall order, direct and appoint."[7]

---

[1] *Col. Rec.*, IV, 990. [2] *Ibid.*, IV, 979.

[3] *Ibid.*, IV, 993. [4] *Ibid.*, IV, 994.

[5] *Ibid.*, IV, 1318. [6] *Ibid.*, IV, 1335, 1332.

[7] *A Complete Revisal of all the Acts of Assembly of the Province of North Carolina*, p. 158, Newbern, 1773.

Governor Johnston died in 1752. In October, 1754, Governor Dobbs arrived in the province and held office for a period of ten years. He was continually solicitous for the promotion of colonial education. On December 24, 1754, he laid before the Assembly a plan for an endowed school, of which one George Vaughan, an Irish merchant, had written to him.

"'Twas the dependence I had on your goodness and public spirit which I had observed from my earliest acquaintance with you, that under God induced the donation of one thousand pounds yearly forever for the propagation of the Gospel among the Indian natives in and near your government, and that you and your successors as Governors, the Council and the Assembly of North Carolina be perpetual trustees for this donation to commence after the death of my said nephew. . . . My said nephew . . . having informed me that he shew my letters to some of the members of your Council and Assembly for said province and that they assured him that provided my donation was not confined to the Indians only, but made to extend as an academy or seminary for religion and learning to all his Majesty's subjects in North Carolina, they in that case would enlarge my donation by a reasonable tax on each negro in that province. Whereupon my lawyer . . . . . . in conference with my Lord Bishop of Derry . . . both concurred in advising me to suspend the execution of said deeds [of endowment] . . . until by some Act of Assembly a perpetual tax was fixed to induce me to alter my original scheme, and until said Bishop in conference with the Society in London for the Propagation of the Gospel and on their recommendation to the King and Council, a charter and further encouragement may be obtained. . . . So as this public good may be put on as rational and lasting a foundation as human wisdom can advise, I make no doubt of your zeal and expedition in laying the purpose of this my letter in proper form before the states of said province."[1] Influenced by this

[1] *Col. Rec.*, V, 144b–144c.

offer of Mr. Vaughan, on January 9, 1755, a Committee of the Lower House on Propositions and Grievances reported among other particulars "That under a sense of the many advantages that will arise to the province from giving our youth a liberal education (whether considered in a moral, religious or political light) a public school or seminary of learning be erected and properly endowed. And that for effecting the same, the sum of £6,000 already appropriated for that purpose be properly applied."[1] This committee also urged "that vagrants be restrained from strolling and wandering about, and that children whose parents are unable or neglect to educate and teach them some useful business may be bound out to proper trades."[2] Three days previous to this report, on January 6, the Lower House had agreed to a motion of the Upper House to devote the £6,000 in question to war purposes.[3] Two days before this decision, Governor Dobbs had written to the Board of Trade: "What I have chiefly observed since I came here as to the wants and defects of this province, is first the want of a sufficient number of clergymen to instil good principles and morality into the inhabitants and proper schoolmasters to instruct their youth . . . But as all the chief planters now are sensible of their wants and difficulties, the Assembly is determined to give a proper encouragement to learned and pious clergymen and to encourage schools."[4] A tax was levied to pay back this borrowed school fund,[5] but in 1757 the returns of this tax upon the approval of the Board of Trade[6] were appropriated to war purposes instead of to its original object. Governor Dobbs, however, continued to push the question of an educational provision. In his opening speech to the Assembly on November 23, 1758, he says, "I must also recommend to you the erecting proper schools in the province, for the education of youth in the reformed Protestant religion, and in

---

[1] *Ibid.*, V, 298–9. [2] *Ibid.*, V, 299.
[3] *Ibid.*, V, 267, 268. [4] *Ibid.*, V, 315, 316.
[5] *Ibid.*, V, 573. [6] *Ibid.*, V, 749, also 640.

moral religious principles, otherwise in the next age we shall have a succession of infidels, deists, enthusiasts and sectaries to the disgrace of our holy religion and destruction of the society."[1] On November 24, the Lower House made answer: "The regard your Excellency discovers for the rising generation and future ages in recommending the establishing schools for the education of youth, is a fresh instance of that public spirit and benevolent disposition which has ever been discernable in all your conduct; and we beg leave to assure your Excellency that nothing shall be wanting to promote a work of such interesting consequences, though at present we are somewhat at a loss in what manner to accomplish it; the sum of £6000 having been heretofore granted for that purpose, by an Act under a suspending clause, which has not yet had the Royal assent."[2] On November 25, the Upper House said in response to the Governor's speech: "We have at heart nothing more than the defences of the country, the promoting true religion, the education of our youth in the reformed Protestant religion and moral virtues, the support of our credit and the encouragement of our commerce."[3] The following month, the Lower House drafted a petition to the King for aid in the support of churches and schools. In a letter to the Board of Trade, dated January 22, 1759, Governor Dobbs takes exception to the sending of this petition and opines that "one public provincial school for the languages, etc., would be enough to be endowed, and the county schools be only for English scholars to learn to read, write and account with some other branches of the mathematics."[4]

In his opening speech on November 23, 1759, the Governor reiterates his injunction concerning the founding of the schools.[5] But the next month, in view of the fact that he has been forbidden by the King to pass any paper bills of credit as legal tender and that payment of the troops is in arrears

[1] *Ibid.*, V, 1014.   [2] *Ibid.*, V, 1041.   [3] *Ibid.*, V, 1016.
[4] *Ibid.*, VI, 5.   [5] *Ibid.*, VI, 134.

and that the only money in the Treasury is that which has been returned on the borrowed school fund, the Governor suggests that this ready money be again devoted to war expenses.[1] The Governor's suggestion was accepted by the legislature and the school fund was again paid out.[2] In a letter to the Board of Trade on January 19, 1760, the Governor proposes that the Board advise the King to allow the borrowed money, after its return to the provincial treasury through taxation, to be at length appropriated to the building of schools.[3] In his speech on November 11, 1760, he again urges the legislature to " seriously consider of giving encouragement for schools to be paid for the education of your youth in Christian principles and in other branches of learning that may make them valuable members of society;"[4] In 1761, the Lower House resolved that as there was not sufficient money in the treasury to pay the salaries of the judges of Superior Court or the allowances to the General Assembly or the claims of the frontier scouting parties, etc., the glebe and school fund should be drawn upon for those purposes and should be afterwards replaced by a tax for the contingent fund. The Upper House concurred in this resolve.[5] In 1762, the Lower House voted the school fund as a supply to the Governor for the garrisoning of forts Johnston and Granville. The borrowed sum was to be returned by special tax.[6] This year, in response to the Governor's annual recommendation about the building of schools the Upper House promised its co-operation in the following terms : " Your Excellency's warm recommendation of laws for the proper encouragement of schools for the education of the rising generation in the principles of religion and virtue . . . merits our most grateful acknowledgement, as the necessity of our having such laws are but too obvious and will be highly conducive of the happiness and interest of this

[1] *Ibid.*, VI, 150–1.   [2] *Ibid.*, VI, 151, 153, 207, 219.

[3] *Ibid.*, VI, 219.   [4] *Ibid.*, VI, 450.

[5] *Ibid.*, VI, 657, 658, 661, 686, 691.   [6] *Ibid.*, VI, 831.

province, and your Excellency may be assured we shall heartily concur with the other House in passing such bills as may secure to us those desirable ends."[1] On December 9, it was ordered by the Lower House that " thanks . . . be given to the Reverend James Reed for his sermon preached at the beginning of this session of Assembly, recommending the establishing public schools for the education of youth, and that he be desired to furnish the printer[2] with a copy thereof, in order that the same may be printed and dispersed in the several counties within this province.[3] On December 13, 1763, on a petition presented to the Board of Trade by an agent of the Lower House of the Assembly, " their lordships took into consideration the Act passed in North Carolina in 1754 by which a sum of money is appropriated for erecting schools and endowment of parishes, and it appearing that this Act had been found upon a former examination to be liable to great objection and that an instruction had been given to the Governor to recommend to the Assembly to amend it in those points in which it was objected to, which recommendation the Assembly had refused to comply with, their lordships were of opinion that it was not fit to grant what the Assembly now desired until they thought proper to comply with his Majesty's reasonable expectation in what had been recommended to them."[4] In spite of this decision of the Board of Trade, a few months later, March 29, 1764, Governor Dobbs in writing to the Board says that the Assembly had applied to him to recommend to the King through the Board of Trade a re-issuance of the bills of credit originally issued for religious and educational ends.[5] On February 3 of this year, the Governor recommended to the Assembly " as a wise measure, to raise a fund to encourage schools in each parish that at least the appearance

---

[1] *Ibid.*, VI, 841.

[2] Dr. Weeks draws attention to the fact that this was probably the first actual appropriation for education. p. 1384.　　　　　　　　[3] *Ibid.*, VI, 955.

[4] *Ibid.*, VI, 1006.　　　　　　[5] *Ibid.*, VI, 1036–37.

of religion may be kept up in this province."[1] On February 8, the Upper House assured his Excellency " that whatever may tend to support, not only the appearance but the real existence and practice of true religion in this province and contribute in any shape to the prosperity and happiness of the people and to the honor of your Excellency's administration, shall always meet with our hearty and zealous occurrence.."[2] On February 20, a " bill for the building of a house for a school and the residence of a school master in the town of New Bern"[3] was introduced in the Lower House and sent to the Upper House for concurrence.[4] On February 28, the bill was read for a second time, amended and passed by the Upper House.[5] On March 2, the bill was read for a third time in the Upper House and passed by that body.[6]

In 1766 the above Act was repealed and the four lots which had been appropriated to the school in Newbern,—three lots having been appropriated by the Act of 1764 and one lot having been purchased since then by the school subscribers—were

---

[1] *Ibid.*, VI, 1091.   [2] *Ibid.*, VI, 1093-4.

[3] On January 1, 1764, Mr. Thomas Tomlinson had opened a private school in Newbern. A subscription was started for the building of a school house, and on June 21, 1764, Missionary James Reed of Craven County writes to the Secretary of the Society for the Propagation of the Gospel that he has received for this purpose about £110 sterling in notes drawn to his order. (*Rec.*, VI, 1048.)

On May 16, 1765, Missionary Reed and 39 residents of Newbern petitioned Governor Tryon to use his influence with the Society to settle a salary upon Schoolmaster Tomlinson, since part of the money that had been subscribed was "already expended in purchasing materials for a large and commodious school house." (*Ibid.*, VII, 35-36.)

On July 31, Governor Tryon enclosed this petition to the Society with the following remarks : " I had a long conversation with Mr. Tomlinson, and from the sense and decency of his behaviour and the general good character he maintains, obliges me to warmly solicit the Society in his behalf. He is the only person of repute of that profession in the country." (*Ibid.*, VII, 104.)

[4] *Ibid.*, VI, 1174.   [5] *Ibid.*, VI, 1113.

[6] *Ibid.*, VI, 1120. The title only of this Act is given in the revisal of 1773, p. 326.

vested in a body of eleven school trustees or directors who were to be elected by and form the subscribers to the school. These trustees were incorporated under the name of the "Incorporated Society for promoting and establishing the public school in Newbern," and they were given all the rights of a body politic and corporate. The trustees were required to swear to the oaths of government and to a special oath of office before a magistrate. They were also directed to elect a treasurer from among themselves who was to give bond for £2,000 and to report annually to the board of trustees. This board was also empowered to fill its own vacancies. Section 3 of the Act provides "that no person shall be admitted to be master of the said school, but who is of the established Church of England; and who, at the recommendation of the trustees or directors, or the majority of them, shall be duly licensed by the Governor or Commander in Chief for the time being."

The preamble and the ninth section of this Act set forth its purpose and general character: "Whereas a number of well-disposed persons, taking into consideration the great necessity of having a proper school or public seminary of learning established, whereby the rising generation may be brought up and instructed in the principles of the Christian religion, and fitted for the several offices and purposes of life, have at a great expense erected and built, in the town of Newbern, a convenient house for the purposes aforesaid; and being desirous that the same may be established by law on a permanent footing, so as to answer the good purposes by the said persons intended: Be it enacted, etc."

"IX. And whereas the aforesaid contributors being desirous that the benefits arising from the said school may be as extensive as possible, and that the poor, who may be unable to educate their children there, may enjoy the benefits thereof: Be it enacted, etc., that a duty of one penny per gallon on all rum or other spirituous liquors imported into the river Neuse, be paid, for and during the space of seven years, from and after the passing of this Act, by the importers thereof, for and towards raising a fund for the education of ten poor children in the said school (to be chosen by the trustees) whose parents may be unable to pay for the same. And that the said duty be part of the common stock of the said school, and to be appropriated as aforesaid, and towards giving a salary of £20 per year to the master of the said school towards enabling him to keep an assistant."[1] . . .

In 1768 an Act was passed reaffirming the school title to the land in Newbern and empowering the school trustees to collect the subscriptions due to the school.[2]

The above legislation was very strongly objected to by the King's Counsel as violating the statute of limitations,[3] the Board of Trade recommended its disallowance,[4] and consequently it was repealed by the King in Council in June 1771.[5] Two years later, however, in view of the facts that the School Society of Newbern had erected "a large and convenient building for the use and accommodation of the master and scholars" of the school, and that it was inconvenient to erect any other buildings on the school lots, an Act was again passed appropriating the aforesaid lots to the use of the school for ever.[6]

On December 28, 1767, a bill was introduced into the Lower House for establishing a school house in the town of Edenton.

On January 4, the Assembly received the following message from the Council in reference to this bill: "On reading a third time the bill for establishing a school house in the town of Edenton, we observe you have deled the following clause, viz.: Provided also that no person shall be admitted to be

---

[1] *Revisal*, 1774, pp. 359–361.   [2] *Ibid.*, p. 450. Title only given.
[3] *Rec.*, VIII, 266.   [4] *Ibid.*, VIII, 276–7.   [5] *Ibid.*, VIII, 616.
[6] *Revisal*, 1773, p. 552.   [7] *Col. Rec.*, VII, 586.

master of the said school, but who is of the established Church of England and who at the recommendation of the trustees or directors, or the majority of them, shall be duly licensed by the Governor or Commander in Chief for the time being, which clause we propose steting.   If you agree thereto, please send some of your members to see the same done, otherwise we cannot agree to pass the bill."[1]   The Lower House answered on the same day that they could not agree to the proposed clause.   Whereupon the Upper House rejected the bill.[2]   The following year Mr. Hewes, the promoter of the preceding measure, introduced another bill into the Lower House under the title of a bill for vesting the school house in Edenton in trustees.[3]   This time the bill was passed by both Houses;[4] but it was rejected by the Governor[5] on the ground that the words " with the approbation of his Excellency the Governor or Commander in Chief for the time being" in the commissioners' appointment of the school master were not as full and comprehensive·as the qualifications for a school master in the Newbern school bill of 1766.[6]   In the same letter in which Governor Tryon thus states his objection to the repealed school bill, he continues, "should your Lordship [Lord Hillsborough] judge the above objection immaterial, I imagine there will be no difficulty in getting the bill re-enacted next session, if your Lordship will honor me with your sentiments and the return of the bill.   Though these institutions are extremely wanted in this colony, yet the foundations of them cannot be too securely laid by the legislature."[7]

The next year the Edenton school was finally chartered under an Act for vesting the school house in Edenton in trustees.   The preamble of this Act reads : " Whereas the inhabitants of the town of Edenton, for the promoting the education of youth, and encouragement of learning, have by voluntary subscription purchased two lots, and erected a convenient

---

[1] *Ibid.*, VII, 598.   [2] *Ibid.*, VII, 600.   [3] *Ibid.*, VII, 943.
[4] *Ibid.*, VII, 954, 970.   [5] *Ibid.*, VII, 978.   [6] *Ibid.*, VIII, 6.   [7] *Ibid.*, VIII, 6–7

school house thereon, in an agreeable and healthy situation in the said town, therefore for the rendering more useful and effectual so laudable an undertaking ; Be it enacted, etc. The trustees were empowered to receive subscriptions and donations, to " employ one or more person or persons, of approved morals, and well instructed in the languages, to preside in, and keep the said school," and to have the general management of the institution. The school master was required to belong to the established Church and to be duly licensed by the Governor.[1]

At the opening of the session of 1770–1, Governor Tryon announced that but for the troubled state of the colony he would have recommended the establishment of " a public seminary in some part of the back country . . . for the education of youth," and suggested that possibly at a more favorable opportunity the legislature might not lose sight of this beneficial object."[2] The Upper House responded : " The idea of a public seminary in this province for the education of youth, as suggested by your Excellency is a fresh proof of your tender concern for its prosperity. The object is important, morals and good government depend greatly upon early instruction and virtuous example, and we hope in this, or some future session, a foundation may be laid for so desirable a purpose."[3] The Lower House responded: " We entirely agree with you, sir, in the measure you propose of establishing a public school in the frontier part of this province. We are convinced that the peace and happiness of society much depends on a pious and liberal education of its members. To neglect an object so interesting and important, is to withhold from this country a blessing that will necessarily accrue to it, from a rising and instructed generation."[4]

On December 27, the Lower House appointed a committee of its own members " to prepare and bring in a bill to estab-

[1] *Revisal*, 1773, pp. 478–9.　　[2] *Col. Rec.*, VIII, 285–6.
[3] *Ibid.*, VIII, 289–90.　　[4] *Ibid.*, VIII, 312.

lish a public seminary in the western part" of the province.[1]
As an outcome of this action the Queen's College was incorporated by the government.[2]

"AN ACT FOR FOUNDING, ESTABLISHING AND ENDOWING QUEEN'S COLLEGE IN THE TOWN OF CHARLOTTE IN MECKLENBERG COUNTY.

" Whereas the proper education of youth has always been
considered the most certain source of tranquility, happiness
and improvement both of private families and of states and
empires and there being no institution or seminary of learning
established in this province, whither the rising generation may
repair, after having acquired at a grammar school a competent
knowledge of the Greek, Hebrew and Latin languages to imbibe
the principles of science and virtue and to obtain under learned,
pious and exemplary teachers in a collegiate or academic
mode of instruction, a regular and finished education in order
to qualify them for the service of their friends and country,
and whereas several grammar schools have been long taught
in the western part of this government, in which many students
have made very considerable progress in the languages and
other literary attainments, and it being thought by many pious,
learned and public-spirited persons that great and singular
benefits and advantages would be derived to the public, could
some one of them receive the encouragement and sanction of
a law, for the establishment thereof on a lasting and permanent
basis, wherefore be it enacted by the Governor, Council and
Assembly, and by the authority of the same, that Messrs.
Edmund Fanning, Thomas Polk, Robert Harris, Jr., Abraham

[1] *Ibid.*, VIII, 338.

[2] During the decade 1760–1770 several schools and academies were opened in
the province by the Presbyterians, a sect that had been rapidly increasing in the
western part of North Carolina since the ingress of the Scotch and Scotch Irish in
1735. It was one of these small classical schools that was chartered by the government as Queen's College. (*The Church and Private Schools of North Carolina*, pp. 31, 44–5. Charles Lee Raper, Greensboro, 1898.)

Alexander, Hezekiah Alexander, John McNitt Alexander,
Ezekiel Polk, Thomas Neal, Wm. Richardson, Hezekiah T.
Balch, Joseph Alexander, Waitstell Avery, Henry Patillo and
Abner Nash, be and they are hereby formed and incorporated
into a body politic and corporate, by the name of the Fellows and
Trustees of the Incorporated Society for Founding Establishing and Endowing Queens College in Charlotte Town by that
name to have perpetual succession and a common seal, and
that they and their successors by the name aforesaid shall be
able and capable in law to purchase, have receive enjoy possess
and retain to them and their successors forever, in special
trust and confidence to and for the uses and purposes of founding establishing and endowing the said college, and supporting a president of the same and the number of three or less
tutors, any lands, rents, tenements and hereditaments of what
kind nature or quality whatsoever and also to sell, grant,
demise, alien or dispose of the same, and also receive and take
any charity, gift or donation, whatsoever to the said college
and by the same name to sue implead be sued and impleaded,
answer and be answered in all courts of record whatsoever.
And be it further enacted by the authority aforesaid that
Edmund Fanning, Thomas Polk, Robert Harris, Jr., Abraham
Alexander, Hezekiah Alexander, John McNitt Alexander,
Ezekiel Polk, Thomas Neal, Wm. Richardson, Hezekiah
Balch, Joseph Alexander, Waitsell Avery, Henry Patillo and
Abner Nash, trustees and fellows or a majority of them are
hereby authorized, required and directed to meet at the grammar school in the county of Mecklenberg aforesaid on the first
day of March next after the passing of this Act then and
there to elect, nominate, constitute and appoint by commission
in writing under their hands sealed with the common seal of
the said college, some learned, pious, exemplary and discreet
person to be president of the said college and in like manner
three or a less number of tutors duly qualified for instructing
and educating of the students of the said college and from

time to time thereafter at the said school until the College shall be erected in the town of Charlotte aforesaid and then in the hall of the said college to convene and meet together and under their common seal to make such rules, regulations and ordinances for the admission or dismission of the president and tutors of the said college and for ascertaining the time of the admission of students or members and also the time of their continuance at college before they shall be entitled to receive the degree of Batchelor and Master of Arts, which said degrees the president of the said college for the time being is hereby authorised and empowered to confer at the public commencement on such as may be thought deserving of receiving the honors of the said seminary of learning and in testimony thereof to give and deliver to the said student so graduated a diploma under the seal of the said college and signed by the president and a majority of the said fellows and trustees. Also for directing the mode of instruction and the course of studies to be pursued by the several classes, and for the better regulating and well ordering the morals, studies and collegiate exercises of the students and members of the said college as to them shall seem requisite and necessary and best calculated to answer the good purposes hereby intended, provided always that the said rules and ordinances correspond and be as near as may be agreeable the laws and customs of the Universities of Oxford and Cambridge or those of the colleges in America. And provided further that no person shall be admitted to be president of the said college but who is of the Established Church and who upon being nominated and appointed by the fellows and trustees as aforesaid or the majority of them shall be duly licensed by the Governor or Commander-in-chief for the time being. And be it further enacted by the authority aforesaid that the said fellows and trustees before they be deemed qualified to enter on the execution of the trust reposed in them by this Act do before some magistrate, take the several oaths of government, subscribe the test, and also take the following oath to wit, I, A. B. do swear that I will duly and faithfully to the best of my skill and ability execute and discharge the several trust, power and authorities wherewith I am invested by an Act of Assembly, for founding, establishing and endowing of a College in Charlotte and that in all things for the well ordering and government thereof I will do equal and impartial justice to the best of my knowledge, so help me God. And be it further enacted by the authority aforesaid, that the said fellows and trustees or a majority of them after their qualification as aforesaid shall meet at the school house the first day of March next after the passing hereof, to nominate and elect out of their number a fit and proper person to be treasurer to the said society, which treasurer shall be annually elected on the first Tuesday in March, into whose hands shall be paid all moneys or belonging to the said school, he first giving bond and security in the sum of three thousand pounds proclamation money to the first in nomination of his brother fellows and trustees for the faithful discharge of his office and the trust reposed in him, and that the said treasurer shall annually on the said first Tuesday in March settle his accounts with the fellows and trustees of all disbursements, donations, gifts, bequests or other charities that may belong or accrue to the said college the preceding year, and upon the said treasurer's neglect or refusal to settle and pay over to the succeeding treasurer what money may be in his hands belonging to the said society the same method of recovery may be had against him as is provided for the recovery of moneys from sheriffs or other persons chargeable with public moneys. And whereas it will be necessary that a successor of the fellows and trustees should be kept up, be it enacted by the authority aforesaid, that on the death, refusal to qualify or removal out of the province of the said fellows and trustees the remaining fellows and trustees, or a majority of them, elect other fellows and trustees in the room and stead of those dead, removed out of the province or refusing to act, which fellows and trustees so elected, nominated and appointed shall be vested with the same trusts, powers and authorities as other fellows and trustees, he or they first taking the several oaths by this Act directed for his or their qualification,   And the said fellows and trustees being desirous that some certain revenue be raised for founding, establishing and endowing the said college, Be it enacted by the authority aforesaid, that a duty of six pence per gallon on all rum or other spirituous liquors brought into and disposed of in Mecklenberg County be paid for and during the space of ten years from and after the passing of this Act, by the owners and carriers thereof, for and towards raising a fund for the purposes aforesaid, which said duty shall be collected, accounted for and paid to the treasurer of the said college in the same manner and under the same penalties and restrictions as other duties on spirituous liquors are now paid and collected by law.

WILLIAM TRYON,

JAMES HASELL, President,

RICHARD CASWELL, Speaker.

Read three times and ratified in open Assembly the 15th day of January, 1771."[1]

This Act was repealed by the King. The legislature then passed a new Act of incorporation in the form of an amendment to the original Act.[2]   This second Act was also negatived by the King in 1773 on the following representations of the Board of Trade: 1. That if this college were incorporated it would operate as a "seminary for the education and instruction of youth in the principles of the Presbyterian Church." 2. That "a foundation professedly for general uses ought not in regularity to be supported by a tax partially imposed upon any one county in particular." 3. That the Act was unaccompanied by a clause of suspension.[3]

---

[1] *Col. Rec.*, VIII, 486–490.

[2] *Laws*, 1773, p. 501.   [3] *Col. Rec.*, IX, 250, also 811.

In support of the first of these enumerated objections, the Lords of Trade quote the following passage from Governor Tryon's communication to them of March 12, 1771 : "It [the law in question] is but the outline of a foundation for the education of youth that the necessity for such an institution in that country is obvious and the propriety of the mode therein adopted must be submitted to your Majesty; that although the President is to be of the established Church and licensed by the Governor, yet the fellows, trustees and tutors, he apprehends, will be generally Presbyterians, the College being promoted by a respectable settlement of that persuasion from which a considerable body marched to Hillsborough in September 1768 in support of government."[1]

[1] *Ibia.*, IX, 249-50.

APPENDIX A.

TABLE OF GRANTS AND APPROPRIATIONS OF THE COLONIAL GOVERNMENTS TO COLLEGES AND SCHOOLS.[1]

	Colleges.			Schools.		
	Land.	Money.	Revenues.	Land.	Money.	Revenues.
Massachusetts ..	18,900 acres	£23,403	From Charlestown Ferry.	3,500 acres	....	One-half of fine (£4) for breaking excise law (1700–1710); one-half of fine (40s.) upon negligent tax assessors (1703).
Connecticut	1,500 acres	£25,403	From New Haven Long Wharf.	2,425 acres	£1,078 and 40s. upon every £1,000 of taxes (1700–1754), 10s. (1754–1766), 20s. (1766–1767), 40s. (1767–).	Arrears of excise tax (1766) and interest on excise fund in colony treasury.
New Hampshire.	......	£100	....	....	....	....
Rhode Island.	......	....	....	....	....	....
New Netherlands and New York.	.....	£3,500	....	....	5,445 guilders, £790.	....
Pennsylvania ...	2,500 acres	£4,500	....	....	....	....
Delaware.......	....	....	....	....	1,068 florins.	....
New Jersey	......	....	....	Matininuck Island.	....	....
Virginia........	30,000 acres	£2,985	From office of Surveyor-General; from duties on tobacco, skins, furs, liquors; from license tax; from fines upon negligent tax collectors.	1,000 acres	....	....
Maryland	....	....	From duties on tobacco.	....	45,000 lbs. tobacco.	From duties on skins, furs, beef, pork, pitch, tar, tobacco, papist servants, negroes; intestate estates without legal representatives.
South Carolina..	....	....	....	....	£48 and £300 annually (1712–). £22 to every parish school established, £25 annually (1756–).	From fines upon negligent land contractors in Beaufort.
North Carolina .	....	....	From liquor duties (10 years).	3 lots in Newbern.	£6,000.	From liquor duties (9 years).
Georgia	......	....	....	....	....	....

[1] This table presents, necessarily, only an approximate calculation. In many cases the grants were made in the fluctuating values of paper currency or "proclamation money;" moreover, no attempt has been made to estimate the returns from the grants of specific sources of revenue; and, finally, many of the grants, both of land and money, were never realized.

APPENDIX B. AUTHORITIES QUOTED

MASSACHUSETTS

Records of the Governor and Company of the Massachusetts Bay in New England. Edited by Nathaniel B. Shurtleff, M. D. Boston, 1853–54.

The Acts and Resolves, public and private, of the Province of the Massachusetts Bay. Edited by Ellis Ames and Abner Cheney Goodell. Boston, 1869–95.

State Papers of the United States of America. Edited by Ebenezer Hazard, A. M. Philadelphia, 1794.

Court Records of Massachusetts (MSS. in Massachusetts State Library).

Temporary Acts and Laws of his Majesty's Province of the Massachusetts Bay in New England. Boston, 1742.

Records of the Colony of New Plymouth in New England. Edited by N. B. Shurtleff, David Pulsifer and others. Boston, 1855–61.

Report of the Record Commissioners of the City of Boston, 1881.

Dedham Records: Town and Selectmen. Edited by Don Gleason Hill. Dedham, 1892–94.

History of New England. John G. Palfrey. Boston, 1892.

Collections of the Massachusetts Historical Society: Third Series. Boston, 1825–46.

The Evolution of the Massachusetts Public School System. George H. Martin, A. M. New York, 1894.

A History of the Grammar School of Roxbury. C. K. Dillaway. Boston, 1860.

A History of Harvard University. Benjamin Pierce, A. M. Cambridge, 1833.

The History of Harvard University. Josiah Quincy, LL. D. Boston, 1860.

English Institutions and the American Indian. James A. James, Ph. D. (Johns Hopkins University Studies in Historical and Political Science.) Baltimore, 1894.

CONNECTICUT

The Public Records of the Colony of Connecticut. Edited by James Hammond Trumbull and Charles J. Hoadly. Hartford, 1850–90.

Records of the Colony and Plantation of New Haven from 1638 to 1649. Edited by Charles J. Hoadly, M. A. Hartford, 1857.

Records of the Colony or Jurisdiction of New Haven from May, 1653, to the Union. Edited by Charles J. Hoadly, M. A. Hartford, 1858.

The General Laws and Liberties of Connecticut Colonie. Cambridge, 1673: Reprinted at Hartford, 1865.

Acts and Charters of Connecticut. New London, 1718.

A Complete History of Connecticut, civil and ecclesiastical, from the emigration of its first planters from England in 1630 to 1713. Benjamin Trumbull, D. D. Hartford, 1797.

The River Towns of Connecticut. Charles M. Andrews. (Johns Hopkins University Studies in Historical and Political Science.) Baltimore, 1889.

The History and Genealogies of Ancient Windsor. Henry R. Stiles, A. M., M. D. Hartford, 1891.

A History of the Old Town of Stratford and the City of Bridgeport, Connecticut. Rev. Samuel Orcutt. Published under the auspices of the Fairfield County Historical Society, 1886.

History of New Britain, with Sketches of Farmington and Berlin, Connecticut. David N. Camp, A. M. New Britain, 1889.

The Republic of New Haven. Charles H. Levermore, Ph. D. Baltimore, 1886.

Papers of the New Haven Colony Historical Society. New Haven, 1865-94.

Collections of the Massachusetts Historical Society: First Series.

The History of Education in Connecticut. Bernard C. Steiner, A. M. Bureau of Education. Circular of Information No. 2. 1893.

An Historical Discourse, pronounced before the graduates of Yale College, August 14, 1850. By Theodore D. Woolsey.

Yale College: A Sketch of its History. William L. Kingsley. New York, 1879.

Biographical Sketches of the Graduates of Yale College, with Annals of the College History. Franklin B. Dexter, A. M. New York, 1885.

The Founding of Yale College. Franklin B. Dexter. (New Haven Historical Society Papers, vol. iii.) New Haven, 1882.

NEW HAMPSHIRE

Acts and Laws of his Majesty's Province of New Hampshire. Portsmouth, 1761.

Acts and Laws of his Majesty's Province of New Hampshire. Portsmouth, 1771.

Records of New Hampshire: Provincial Papers: Edited by Nathaniel Bouton, D. D. Concord, 1867—Nashua, 1873.

The History of New Hampshire. Jeremy Belknap, A. M. Philadelphia, 1784.

Annals of Portsmouth. Nathaniel Adams. Portsmouth, 1825.

An Historical Address, delivered at Hampton, New Hampshire, December 25, 1838. By Joseph Dow, A. M. Concord, 1839.

Collections of the New Hampshire Historical Society. Concord, 1827-66.

The History of Education in New Hampshire. Nathaniel Bouton.

The History of Dartmouth College. Baxter Perry Smith. Boston, 1878.

RHODE ISLAND

Records of the Colony of Rhode Island and Providence Plantations in New England. Edited by John Russell Bartlett. Providence, 1856-65.

Acts and Laws of his Majesty's Colony of Rhode Island and Providence Plantations in America. Boston, 1719.

The Charter and Laws of the Colony of Rhode Island and Providence Plantations in America. Newport, 1730.

Rhode Island Schedules.

History of the State of Rhode Island and Providence Plantations. Samuel G. Arnold. New York, 1859.

History of Brown University with illustrative documents. Reuben A. Guild. Providence, 1867.

History of Higher Education in Rhode Island. William H. Tolman, Ph. D. United States Bureau of Education. Circular of Informotion No. I, 1894.

NEW YORK

The Colonial Laws of New York. Albany, 1894.

The Documentary History of the State of New York. Edited by Edmund B. O'Callaghan, M. D. Albany, 1850–51.

Documents relative to the Colonial History of the State of New York. Edited by Edmund B. O'Callaghan, M. D., LL. D., and others. Albany, 1856–83.

Journal of the General Assembly of the Colony of New York. New York, 1764–66.

Journal of the Legislative Council of the Colony of New York. Albany, 1861.

The Records of New Amsterdam from 1653 to 1674. Edited by Berthold Fernow. New York, 1897.

Laws and Ordinances of New Netherland, 1638–1674. Edited by Edmund B. O'Callaghan. Albany, 1868.

The Annals of Albany. Joel Munsell. Albany, 1850–59.

The History of New Netherland. Edmund B. O'Callaghan. New York, 1846.

History of the State of New York. John R. Brodhead. New York, 1874.

The History of the Late Province of New York, from its Discovery to 1762. By the Hon. William Smith. (Collections of the New York Historical Society.) New York, 1829.

History of the New Netherlands, Province of New York and State of New York. William Dunlap. New York, 1839.

Annals of Public Education in the State of New York from 1626 to 1746. Daniel J. Pratt, A. M. Albany, 1872.

History of the School of the Reformed Protestant Dutch Church in the City of New York. Henry W. Dunshee. New York, 1853.

Charters, Acts and Official Documents of Columbia College in the City of New York. Compiled by John B. Pine. New York, 1895.

The Origin and Early History of Columbia College. George H. Moore, LL. D. New York, 1890.

PENNSYLVANIA

Statutes at large of Pennsylvania. Compiled by James T. Mitchell and Henry Flanders. Published, 1896.

Charters and Laws of the Province of Pennsylvania (1682–1700.) Compiled by Geo. Staughton, B. M. Nead, Tho. McCamant. Harrisburg, 1879.

Colonial Records: Minutes of the Provincial Council of Pennsylvania. Philadelphia, 1852–60.

Laws of the Commonwealth of Pennsylvania. Philadelphia, 1803.

Votes and Proceedings of the House of Representatives of the Province of Pennsylvania. Philadelphia, 1752–76.

The History of Pennsylvania. Robert Proud. Philadelphia, 1797.

History of Education in Pennsylvania. James P. Wickersham, LL. D. Lancaster, 1886.

Benjamin Franklin and the University of Pennsylvania. Edited by F. N. Thorpe, Ph. D. Bureau of Education. Circular of Information No. 2. 1892.

A Catalogue of the books belonging to the Library Company of Philadelphia, to which is prefixed a short account of the institution with the charter, laws and regulations. Philadelphia, 1835.

DELAWARE

Pennsylvania Archives: Second Series. Edited by John B. Linn and William H. Egle. Harrisburg, 1874–90.

Laws of the State of Delaware. New Castle, 1797.

NEW JERSEY

The Grants, Concessions and Original Constitutions of the Province of New Jersey. Compiled by Aaron Leaming and Jacob Spicer. Philadelphia. [1758].

Record of the Governor and Council of East Jersey. Jersey City, 1872.

Acts of the General Assembly of the Province of New Jersey, 1702–1776. Compiled by Samuel Allinson. Burlington, 1776.

Archives of the State of New Jersey. Edited by W. A. Whitehead and others. Newark, 1880–97.

The History of the College of New Jersey. John Maclean. Philadelphia, 1877.

The Planting of Princeton College. John De Witt. (Presbyterian and Reformed Review.) April, 1897.

Princeton College Bulletin for February, 1891.

An Historical Discourse delivered by the Hon. Joseph P. Bradley at the Centennial Celebration of Rutgers College in 1870.

VIRGINIA

The Statutes-at-Large, being a Collection of all the Laws of Virginia. Compiled by William Waller Hening. New York, 1823.

Calendar of Virginia State Papers and other manuscripts (1652–1781). Edited by Wm. P. Palmer, M. D. Richmond, 1875.

History of the Virginia Company of London. Edward D. Neill. Albany, 1869.

Virginia Carolorum. Edward D. Neill. Albany, 1886.

Collections of the Virginia Historical Society. Richmond, 1882–92.

The College of William and Mary. Herbert B. Adams, Ph. D. Bureau of Education. Circular of Information No. I. 1887.

The History of the College of William and Mary. Richmond, 1874.

Historical Collections relating to the American Colonial Church. Edited by William S. Perry, D. D., 1878.

Contributions to the Ecclesiastical History of the United States. Francis L. Hawks, D. D. New York, 1839.

MARYLAND

Archives of Maryland. Edited by William Hand Browne. Baltimore, 1883–94.
Laws of Maryland at Large. Compiled by Thomas Bacon. Annapolis, 1765.
Laws of Maryland. Annapolis, 1787.
History of Maryland. J. Thomas Scharf. Baltimore, 1879.
An Historical View of the Government of Maryland. John V. L. McMahon. Baltimore, 1831.
The History of Maryland. John Leeds Bozman. Baltimore, 1837.
History of Education in Maryland. Bernard C. Steiner, Ph. D. United States Bureau of Education. Circular of Information No. 2. 1894.
An Historical Account of the Incorporated Society for the Propagation of the Gospel in Foreign Parts. David Humphrey, D. D. London, 1730.

SOUTH CAROLINA

The Statutes at Large of South Carolina. Compiled by Thomas Cooper, M. D., LL. D., and David J. McCord. Columbia, 1836–41.
The Public Laws of the State of South Carolina. John F. Grimké, LL. D. Philadelphia, 1790.
The History of South Carolina under the Proprietary Government. Edward McCrady. New York, 1897.
The History of South Carolina, from its first Settlement in 1670, to the year 1808. David Ramsay, M. D. Charleston, 1809.
History of Higher Education in South Carolina. Colyer Meriwether. Bureau of Education. Circular of Information No. 3. 1888.
Education in South Carolina. Edward McCrady, Jr. Collections of the Historical Society of South Carolina.) Charleston, 1883.

NORTH CAROLINA

The Colonial Records of North Carolina. Edited by William L. Saunders. Raleigh, 1886–90.
A Collection of all the Public Acts of Assembly of the Province of North Carolina. (Davis' Revisal.) Newbern, 1752.
A Complete Revisal of all the Acts of Assembly of the Province of North Carolina. (Davis' Revisal.) Newbern, 1773.
Beginnings of the Common School System in the South. Stephen B. Weeks, Ph. D. Published in the Report of the Commissioner of Education. 1896–97.
The Church and Private Schools of North Carolina. Charles Lee Raper. Greensboro, 1898.

GEORGIA (See Preface)

Education in Georgia. Charles Edgeworth Jones. Bureau of Education. Circular of Information No. IV. 1888.

GENERAL INDEX

Academical degrees: Corporation of Harvard College empowered to confer, 33; Trustees of Yale College, 123; Corporation of Yale College, 152; Trustees of Dartmouth College, 182; Fellows of College of Rhode Island, 190, 194; Governors of the College of the Province of New York, 269–70; Trustees of the Academy and Charitable School of Philadelphia petition for power to confer, 304; petition granted, 307; Trustees of the College of New Jersey empowered to confer, 322, 330; Trustees of Queen's College, N. J., 342; President of Queen's College, N. C., 496.

Academy and Charitable School in the Province of Pennsylvania: see College, Academy and Charitable School in the Province of Pennsylvania.

Albany: scholars at Latin School in New Amsterdam, 213; schoolmasters licensed, 223, 224; municipality grants teacher's license, 227 footnote 4; Governor Bellamont proposes educational scheme to Indians at, 231.

Amsterdam Chamber: see Dutch West India Company.

Amsterdam, City of: to provide schoolhouse and schoolmaster for colonists on the Delaware, 314, 315.

Amsterdam, Classis of: in charge of colonial education, 198; correspondence with Governor Stuyvesant about schoolmaster, 202; party in Reformed Dutch Church desirous of independence from, 336.

Analyzing: to be forwarded in Harvard College, 42.

Anatomy: recommended by the General Court as a study in Harvard College, 12.

Andros, Governor: appoints William Hubbard rector of Harvard College, 32.

Annapolis: free school at, 423; Episcopal convention at, 425; plan for a college at, 437, 438, 439.

Antipœdo baptism: see Baptists.

Apprenticed: ignorant children to be, 59, 68, 75, 80, 357 footnote 1; indigent orphans to be, 355 footnote 1, 408, 409, 480.

Apprentices: education of, 74–5, 78–80, 95, 112–13, 223, 355 footnote 1, 408, 409, 479 footnote 2; provision against false indenture of, 107; sent from London to Virginia planters, 350–1; Governor of Virginia charged with oversight of, 351.

Appropriations: Cape Fishery to Plymouth school, 7 footnote 1; £400 for a college from General Court of Massachusetts, 7–8; Charlestown Ferry to Harvard College, 9; Cambridge rate to Harvard College, 18; £100 annually to Harvard College, 22; gratuity to President Chauncy, 26; to afflicted son of President Chauncy, 26 footnote 1; for salary of President of Harvard College, 26, 31, 33, 34, 37, 39, 42, 44, 49 footnote 7, 51, 52, 54; to Governor Bellamont in behalf of Harvard College, 39; for President's house, 44, 52; for buildings at Harvard College, 45, 56, 57, 58; to Marblehead as compensation for the call of its minister to Harvard College, 54; to faculty of Harvard College, 54; for indemnity of Harvard students, 57; to Mr. Elliott for missionary work, 71 footnote 1; from Hartford to town school, 76 footnote 1; from Windsor, Wethersfield and Stratford to town schoolmasters, 76 footnote 1; for fellowship in Harvard College from General Court of Connecticut, 77; for colony school at New Haven, 84, 86, 88; of surplus in Connecticut treasury to county schools; to schools at Hartford and New Haven, 96; at New London and Fairfield, 97; of 40 s. upon every £1,000 of taxable property to Connecticut schools, 98, 108–9; for Indians' education in Connecticut, 113, 114, 115, 116, 117, 118; to Yale College, 122, 125, 128, 138, 139, 144, 145, 146, 147–8, 153, 155, 156, 157, 161, 162, 163; to Saybrook school, 130; to Wethersfield and Windham as compensations for the call of their ministers to Yale College, 143, 145; to Indian school from New Hampshire Legislature, 170; to Dutch schoolmasters, 204, 205, 206 footnote 2, 218, 219, 221; from New York Legislature to New York grammar school, 234–5, 243–5, 247; to college, 253; to College, Academy and Charitable School of the Province of Pennsylvania from Proprietary Thomas Penn, 310–11; to College of William and Mary from William and Mary, 372, 374, 375; from Virginia Legislature, 379–80, 381 footnote 2, 387, 389, 392, 393, 402; from Maryland Legislature to Swedish orphan, 409 footnote 2; to schools, 412, 413, 424, 425–6, 427; from South Carolina Legislature to Provincial Library, 447; to school teachers, 458, 461, 462, 463, 464; for building parish schools, 465; from North Carolina Legislature for a public school, 483, 485; for school at Newbern, 490–1; to Queen's College, 498. See Land Grants.

Baltimore, Lord: desirous of a school in Maryland, 411.
Baptists: President Dunster a Baptist, 20; of Rhode Island plan for a college, 185; 22 trustees, 8 fellows and president of College of Rhode Island to be, 189, 190; Baptist Society of Providence incorporated, 197; of Philadelphia protest against Episcopal Church, 297 footnote; professor in College, Academy and Charitable School of Pennsylvania, 311.
Bath: library in, 479.
Beaufort: commissioners for school in, 477.
Belcher, Governor: promotes College of New Jersey, 322, 332, 333, 334; trustee of Harvard College, 332.
Bellamont, Governor: addresses Massa-

chusetts Assembly in support of Harvard College, 37, 38; instructions about teachers' licenses to, 228; proposes to educate New York Indians, 231; vacates lease of Kings Farm to Trinity Church, 248.
Bequests: Rev. John Harvard to the college at Cambridge, 8; Mr. Stoughton to Harvard College, 12; to Harvard College, schools, etc., provided for by Massachusetts Legislature, 14 footnote 1; of Ezekiel Rogers to Harvard College, 55 footnote 2; Edward Hopkins to education in Connecticut, 84, 87; to Hartford school, 96 footnote 1; to help maintain schools in Connecticut, 98; Robert Bartlet to New London School, 99; Nicholas Farrar to college in Virginia, 348 footnote 1; of Benjamin Symms to school in Elizabeth County, Va., 354, 396; Robert Boyle to Harvard College and College of William and Mary, 384 footnote 3; Henry Peasley to school in Virginia, 399; Thomas Eaton to school in Virginia, 403; in South Carolina for a free school, 448; for school at Childsbury, S. C., 474, 476.
Bergen: controversy between town government and schoolmaster, 219–21; sheriffs and schepens empowered to provide school-house, 226; ordered to support schoolmaster, 226–7.
Berkeley, Sir William: a petition for erection of schools, etc., in Virginia recommended to, 358; objects to free schools and printing, 359.
Bernard, Governor: approves of a college in western Massachusetts, 55; names Hollis Hall, 56; sends message to Legislature on the rebuilding of Harvard Hall, 57.
Blair, James: missionary to Virginia, 359; commissary of Bishop of London, 360; presents petition for a college charter to the King, 360–1; named president of College of William and Mary by Virginia Assembly, 364.
Books: bequeathed by John Harvard to the college at Cambridge, 8 footnote 5; Corporation of Harvard College to provide, 14, 57; to be procured for New Haven colony school, 84; schoolmaster Peck empowered to

use, 89, 90; donated to the Collegiate School (Yale College), 129 footnote 4, 130 footnote 1; controversy about removal of Yale College books to New Haven, 130, 131–4; Dutch West India Company provide public school-master with, 208 footnote 3, 211, 213; Governors of College of New York to appoint college text-books, 268; laws of Pennsylvania to be among text-books of colony schools, 280; to be introduced by law into Pennsylvania, 282; to be provided in College, Academy and Charitable School of the Province of Pennsylvania, 301; to be supplied in College of William and Mary, 392.

Boston: Elder, appointed an overseer of Harvard College, 10; maintenance of school in, 61 footnote 1; 1,000 acres granted for school, 62; overseers of the poor empowered to apprentice neglected children, 68.

Bowen, Governor: plans school system for Providence, 196 footnote 3.

Brattle, Thomas: tutor at Harvard College, 32.

Bray, Dr. Thomas: provides schoolmasters and parochial libraries for Maryland, 423; provides library for South Carolina, 441, 442, 447; catalogue of Charleston Library to be sent to, 444; a founder of the Society for Propagating the Gospel, 457 footnote 1; sends library to North Carolina, 479.

Brief: from Connecticut Assembly for a collection for the conversion of the colony Indians, 118, 119; for Rector's house in Yale College, 139; for divinity chair in Yale College, 157–8; from George III. for a collection for College of New York and College, Academy and Charitable School of Pennsylvania, 275, 310, 311; from James I. for a college in Virginia, 348–9.

Brooklyn: support of schoolmaster in, 217–18.

Broughton, Lieutenant Governor: trustee for Childsbury School, S. C., 474.

Brown University: see College of Rhode Island.

Burlington: grant of Matininuck Island for school at, 317.

Calvert, Governor: employs private teacher, 411; desirous of promoting school in Maryland, 411.

Cambridge: named by General Court of Massachusetts, 8; Elder, appointed an overseer of Harvard College, 10; rate appropriated to Harvard College, 18; expelled students forbidden to remain in, 27; Massachusetts Legislature meets in, 56; support of school in, 61 footnote 1; 1,000 acres granted for school, 62; grants land to Harvard College, 85 footnote 3.

Catechising: to be performed weekly by parents and masters in Connecticut, 74; inquiry in Connecticut regarding, 100; for Connecticut Indians, 113; weekly at Hampton, N. H., 164 footnote 1; of Governor Stuyvesant's children, 213; desired at New Harlem, 221; of Dutch School children, 222; Elias Neau licensed for, 237; for youth in South Carolina, 471.

Catechism: Massachusetts Elders instructed to draw up a, 58 footnote 4.

Charitable: work of Roxbury grammar school so-called, 63; donations in Connecticut exempt from taxation, 95; contributions to conversion of Lebanon Indians, 118, 119, 171; donations to College of the Province of New York in trust, 251; subscriptions to the Academy and Charitable School of Pennsylvania, 301; exportation of children to Virginia, 350; intention of Henry Peasley in founding free school in Virginia, 400; bequests in South Carolina for a free school, 448; donors of libraries to South Carolina, 456; Dorchester School, 476.

Charity: of people in England desired for a college in Virginia, 358; of members of Virginia Assembly directed to a college, 358; scholarship endowment in College of William and Mary an act of, 388. See Schools.

Charleston: library at, 442, 447; grammar school in, 457, 460, 466; schoolmaster at, 478.

Charlestown: ferry revenue granted to to Harvard College, 9, 22; advanced to President Chauncy, 23; Elder, appointed an overseer of Harvard College, 10; roads repaired by Harvard College, 53; support of school

breaking Massachusetts school laws, 62, 63, 64, 65, 67–8; for breaking excise law in Massachusetts appropriated to town schools, 65; for neglecting to assess taxes in Massachusetts appropriated to town schools, 66; for teaching without license in Massachusetts, 67; exacted at the Massachusetts Court for Indians, appropriated to Indian education, 71 footnote 1; for breaking school laws in Connecticut, 74, 76, 79, 80, 93–4, 96, 98; for teaching without license in Connecticut, 107; for failure to instruct Indian apprentices in Connecticut, 113; for breaking school laws in New Hampshire, 165, 167, 168; in Pennsylvania, 281, 283; for breaking customs laws, appropriated to College of William and Mary, 391; upon negligent tax collectors, appropriated to College of William and Mary, 402–3; for breaking customs laws in Maryland, appropriated to schools, 424, 426; for refusing to serve as visitor in Maryland county schools, appropriated to school fund, 434; negligence of register of King William's School punishable by, 437; failure to attend meetings of Provincial Library Commissioners of South Carolina punishable by, 455; also of Charleston School Commision, 459, 460; also of Dorchester School Commission, 470; incurred by settlers at Beaufort, appropriated to school, 477.

Franklin, Benjamin: promotes library in Philadelphia, 299; trustee of Academy and Charitable School of Pennsylvania, 301.

Frederick County: Act for schools in, 436.

Free Education: provided for 20 youths in New York grammar schools, 241–2; ordered for orphans in Virginia, 355, footnote 1; in Maryland, 408, 409; free schooling for poor children in Maryland, 435. See Schools.

Girls' education: in industry, 59, 355 footnote 1, 356; poor girls in Massachusetts to be taught reading, 59 footnote 1; in Connecticut, 75, 80; in Hampton, N. H., 164, footnote 1; not provided for by New York grammar school, 234; provided for in William

Penn Charter School, 284, 287, 289; in College, Academy and Charitable School of Pennsylvania, 309; education of the orphan Wadden Hanse in Maryland, 409 footnote 2.

Guilford: willing to co-operate in establishing a college in Connecticut, 80 footnote 2; appropriates school house to colony school, 84; a possible site for colony school, 86.

Hampshire county: inhabitants petition Massachusetts Assembly for college charter, 55.

Hampton: schoolmaster at, 164 footnote 1.

Hart, Covernor: convention of Episcopal clergy called at Annapolis by, 425.

Hartford: town school in, 76 footnote 1; 600 acres granted to grammar school, 92; annual grant to colony school at, 96; grammar school to be constantly maintained at, 97; establishment of the Collegiate School (Yale College) desired at, 125, 126; compensated for loss of college, 130.

Harvard College: established at Cambridge, 8; *Overseers* appointed by the General Court, 10, 21; powers, 10, 14, 20, 22, 23–4, 47; advised by General Court to write to church elders for voluntary contribution to College, 16; empowered to dismiss President Dunster, 20–1; charged by General Court with superintendency of orthodoxy and morality of college teachers, 21; provision for a president's house referred by General Court to, 23, 25; advised by General Court to end disagreements in College, 27–9; petition Massachusetts legislature for enlargement of corporation, 47; oppose ecclesiastical liberality in corporation, 47–8; petition General Court for President Colman's salary, 50, 51; Episcopalian clergymen petition to be made, 53–4; remonstrate against establishment of a western college, 55; petition General Court for a new building, 56–7; poor scholars at, 11; Massachusetts colony in debt to, 11; *Corporation* established by General Court, 13; powers and privileges, 13–15; petition General Court, 15, 17, 20 footnote 3, 36, 42, 45, 48, 52 foot-

423; donor of parochial libraries to South Carolina, 456.

Non-sectarianism : provided for in College of Rhode Island, 193-4 : College, Academy and Charitable School of Pennsylvania, 311.

Norfolk : officials empowered by Virginia Legislature to provide for school in, 395.

Oratory : taught in the colony school of New Haven, 89.

Orphans : to be taught reading, writing and some trade or skill in Pennsylvania, 281, 283; to be educated in Christianity and in the rudiments of learning in Virginia, 354-5; to be given a free education or trained to some trade in Maryland, 408-9; likewise in North Carolina, 480.

Parents : of Harvard scholars to keep them in the colony, 17 footnote 1; responsible for children's education, 59, 66, 74, 78-9, 95-6, 223, 281, 283; to pay schoolmasters in Massachusetts, 61; also in Connecticut, 76; neglectful of children's education, 68; authority of, 93 footnote 4, 223; to be informed of punishment of their sons at Yale College, 160; to direct instruction of schoolmaster at Dover, 164 footnote 1; to reward schoolmaster at New Amsterdam, 212; instruct their children in Virginia, 359; orphans in Maryland to be educated in religion of their, 408-9.

Patroons : of New Netherlands, to support schoolmasters, 198-9; of Delaware, to support schoolmasters, 313.

Penn, William : views on relation of government to education, 279 footnote 1.

Petitions : President Dunster to the General Court of Massachusetts, 9 footnote 7, 11, 12, 20 footnote 3; to Commissioners of the United Colonies, 11, 15 footnote 3; Corporation of Harvard College to General Court, 15, 17, 20 footnote 3, 36, 45, 48, 52 footnote 1, 55 footnote 2; President Chauncy to General Court, 24-5; Elnathan Chauncy to General Court, 26 footnote 1; President Rogers to General Court, 31 footnote 6; Massachusetts Legislature to the King, 38; to

Massachusetts Legislature from President Leverett, 44; from Overseers of Harvard College, 47, 50, 51, 55; from daughters of President Leverett, 49 footnote 7; from Episcopalians, 53-4; from Hampshire County, 55; from Charlestown, Cambridge and Boston, 62; from West Wing of Rutland, 68; schoolmaster Peck to Jurisdiction Court of New Haven, 88-90; to General Court of Connecticut from inhabitants of Poquanock, 94; from Deputies of New London, 104; from Middletown, 104; from inhabitants of New London, 105, 108; from New London school committee, 108; in behalf of Mohegan Indians, 114, 115; from Eleazar Wheelock, 118; from founders of Collegiate School, 120; from Hartford trustees of the Collegiate School, 125-6; from the Trustees of Yale College, 140, 142, 154, 156, 159; from Yale students, 154, 159; from President Clap, 157; Congregational ministers to Governor Wentworth, 169; Dr. Wheelock to New Hampshire Legislature, 170; residents of Rhode Island to Legislature, 185, 196; corporation of College of Rhode Island to Legislature, 196; residents of East Greenwich to Legislature, 197; to provincial government of New York from Dutch schoolmasters, 205, 206 footnote 2, 207, 212 footnote 2, 213-14, 215; from burgomasters and schepens of New Amsterdam, 206-7, 215, 219; from Midwout, 216; from Middleburgh, 216-17; from Breuckelen, 217-18; from Bushwick, 218-19; from Bergen, 219-21, 226, 227; from New Harlem, 221; from Flatbush, 228 29; from New Utrecht, 230-1; Common Council of New York City to Governor Montgomery, 235; to New York Legislature from inhabitants of New York, 239, 240; from schoolmaster Malcolm, 247; trustees of college lottery fund to Governor De Lancey, 254; Governors of the College of New York to Governor De Lancey, 272; to Lower House of New York Legislature, 274, 275; to George III., 276; Quakers of Philadelphia to Pennsylvania Legislature, 284-6; trustees of Academy and Charitable

located at, 196; school at, 196 footnote 3.

Public Service: scholars for, 17, 22, 106, 120, 121; children to be trained for, 58, 60, 61 footnote 1, 75, 80.footnote 2, 83 footnote 1, 84, 86, 88, 97, 222; Roxbury grammar school for, 62; New ,Haven colony exempts from poll taxes students for, 88; Yale students trained for, 148, 158; learning for, 186, 240, 306; youth to be qualified for, 287, 393, 414, 427, 481, 487, 494.

Public welfare: learning necessary to, 16, 36, 162, 480; dependent upon Harvard College, 36; education of, 21, 74, 80, 83, 473, 487; public schools of importance to, 99, 106, 186, 201, 232, 287, 485–6; Collegiate School (Yale College) conducive to, 124; a New Hampshire college conducive to, 169; a New York college conducive to, 249; seminary of Church of England needed for the, 277; dependent upon education of youth, 287, 300, 352, 493; learning promotes, 318, 337; industrial education of, 356, 357 footnote 1; support of College of William and Mary of great importance to, 391; a college at Annapolis would conduce to, 437, 438, 439, 440.

Punishment: of Harvard students by fine and whipping, 23, 27; in Yale College referred to Connecticut Legisislature, 159; of Yale students to be put on record, 160; of children and servants according to law in New York, 223; in College of New York, 268–9.

Quakers: 5 trustees of College of Rhode Island to be, 189; petition Pennsylvania Legislature for incorporation of Philadelphia charity school, 284; hostile to College, Academy and Charitable School of Pennsylvania, 308; unwilling to support College of New Jersey, 333; reputed to be enemies of human learning, 333; orphans in North Carolina not to be apprenticed to, 480.

Queen's College, N. J.: charter of, 336–47.

Queen's College, N. C.: incorporation of, 494–98; opposed by King, 498; a Presbyterian institution, 499.

Reformed Dutch Church: empowerd by William III. to appoint a schoolmaster, 228; senior minister named a Governor of College of New York, 259; directed to fill divinity chair in College, 272–4; schoolhouse built in Pennsylvania by, 312; Queen's College incorporated through the Coetus party in the, 336; president of College to be a member of, 342.

Religion: good literature necessary to, 45, 61 footnote 1; dependent upon education, 66, 69, 169, 337, 300, 485–6; dependent upon reading, 70; Connecticut schools aim to increase, 100, 106; decay in Connecticut, of 100; Collegiate School (Yale College) conducive to, 124; schoolmaster necessary to, 199, 200; contention in College, Academy and Charitable School of Pennsylvania hurtful to, 311; College of New Jersey provides opportunity for improvement in, 334; education of children in Maryland in religion of parents, 408; in Protestant, 408–9; advanced in Maryland by parochial libraries and schoolmasters, 423.

Religious instruction: an object of Harvard College, 10; to be given by Vice-President Willard in Harvard College, 42; in charge of Elders in Massachusetts, 58 footnote 4; to be enforced by selectmen in Massachusetts, 59; likewise in Connecticut, 74, 79; Indian apprentices in Connecticut to receive, 113; desired for Indians in Connecticut, 116–7; in College of Rhode Island, 194; prescribed for children and servants in New York, 223; for the youth in Swedish Delaware, 314; in New Jersey, 335; for Indian children in Virginia, 349, 350; object of a public free school in Virginia, 352; prescribed for orphans in Virginia, 355; given by parents to children in Virginia, 359; for orphans in Maryland, 408–9; aim of Maryland free schools, 414, 416; school in South Carolina necessary for, 448; lack of schools in South Carolina for, 457 footnote 1; according to Church of England, prescribed for Charleston grammar school, 461; desired by parents in South Carolina, 466; of social conse-

AMERICAN EDUCATION:
ITS MEN, IDEAS, AND INSTITUTIONS
An Arno Press/New York Times Collection

Series I

Culver, Raymond B. **Horace Mann and Religion in the Massachusetts Public Schools.** 1929.

Curoe, Philip R. V. **Educational Attitudes and Policies of Organized Labor in the United States.** 1926.

Dabney, Charles William. **Universal Education in the South.** 1936.

Dearborn, Ned Harland. **The Oswego Movement in American Education.** 1925.

De Lima, Agnes. **Our Enemy the Child.** 1926.

Dewey, John. **The Educational Situation.** 1902.

Dexter, Franklin B., editor. **Documentary History of Yale University.** 1916.

Eliot, Charles William. **Educational Reform: Essays and Addresses.** 1898.

Ensign, Forest Chester. **Compulsory School Attendance and Child Labor.** 1921.

Fitzpatrick, Edward Augustus. **The Educational Views and Influence of De Witt Clinton.** 1911.

Fleming, Sanford. **Children & Puritanism.** 1933.

Flexner, Abraham. **The American College: A Criticism.** 1908.

Foerster, Norman. **The Future of the Liberal College.** 1938.

Gilman, Daniel Coit. **University Problems in the United States.** 1898.

Hall, Samuel R. **Lectures on School-Keeping.** 1829.

Hall, Stanley G. **Adolescence: Its Psychology and Its Relations to Physiology, Anthropology, Sociology, Sex, Crime, Religion, and Education.** 1905. 2 vols.

Hansen, Allen Oscar. **Early Educational Leadership in the Ohio Valley.** 1923.

Harris, William T. **Psychologic Foundations of Education.** 1899.

Harris, William T. **Report of the Committee of Fifteen on the Elementary School.** 1895.

Harveson, Mae Elizabeth. **Catharine Esther Beecher: Pioneer Educator.** 1932.

Jackson, George Leroy. **The Development of School Support in Colonial Massachusetts.** 1909.

Kandel, I. L., editor. **Twenty-five Years of American Education.** 1924.

Kemp, William Webb. **The Support of Schools in Colonial New York by the Society for the Propagation of the Gospel in Foreign Parts.** 1913.

Kilpatrick, William Heard. **The Dutch Schools of New Netherland and Colonial New York.** 1912.

Kilpatrick, William Heard. **The Educational Frontier.** 1933.

Knight, Edgar Wallace. **The Influence of Reconstruction on Education in the South.** 1913.

Le Duc, Thomas. **Piety and Intellect at Amherst College, 1865-1912.** 1946.

Maclean, John. **History of the College of New Jersey from Its Origin in 1746 to the Commencement of 1854.** 1877.

Maddox, William Arthur. **The Free School Idea in Virginia before the Civil War.** 1918.

Mann, Horace. **Lectures on Education.** 1855.

McCadden, Joseph J. **Education in Pennsylvania, 1801-1835, and Its Debt to Roberts Vaux.** 1855.

McCallum, James Dow. **Eleazar Wheelock.** 1939.

McCuskey, Dorothy. **Bronson Alcott, Teacher.** 1940.

Meiklejohn, Alexander. **The Liberal College.** 1920.

Miller, Edward Alanson. **The History of Educational Legislation in Ohio from 1803 to 1850.** 1918.

Miller, George Frederick. **The Academy System of the State of New York.** 1922.

Monroe, Will S. **History of the Pestalozzian Movement in the United States.** 1907.

Mosely Education Commission. **Reports of the Mosely Education Commission to the United States of America October-December, 1903.** 1904.

Mowry, William A. **Recollections of a New England Educator.** 1908.

Mulhern, James. **A History of Secondary Education in Pennsylvania.** 1933.

National Herbart Society. **National Herbart Society Yearbooks 1-5, 1895-1899.** 1895-1899.

Nearing, Scott. **The New Education: A Review of Progressive Educational Movements of the Day.** 1915.

Neef, Joseph. **Sketches of a Plan and Method of Education.** 1808.

Nock, Albert Jay. **The Theory of Education in the United States.** 1932.

Norton, A. O., editor. **The First State Normal School in America: The Journals of Cyrus Pierce and Mary Swift.** 1926.

Oviatt, Edwin. **The Beginnings of Yale, 1701-1726.** 1916.

Packard, Frederic Adolphus. **The Daily Public School in the United States.** 1866.

Page, David P. **Theory and Practice of Teaching.** 1848.

Parker, Francis W. **Talks on Pedagogics: An Outline of the Theory of Concentration.** 1894.

Peabody, Elizabeth Palmer. **Record of a School.** 1835.

Porter, Noah. **The American Colleges and the American Public.** 1870.

Reigart, John Franklin. **The Lancasterian System of Instruction in the Schools of New York City.** 1916.

Reilly, Daniel F. **The School Controversy (1891-1893).** 1943.

Rice, Dr. J. M. **The Public-School System of the United States.** 1893.

Rice, Dr. J. M. **Scientific Management in Education.** 1912.

Ross, Early D. **Democracy's College: The Land-Grant Movement in the Formative Stage.** 1942.

Rugg, Harold, et al. **Curriculum-Making: Past and Present.** 1926.

Rugg, Harold, et al. **The Foundations of Curriculum-Making.** 1926.

Rugg, Harold and Shumaker, Ann. **The Child-Centered School.** 1928.

Seybolt, Robert Francis. **Apprenticeship and Apprenticeship Education in Colonial New England and New York.** 1917.

Seybolt, Robert Francis. **The Private Schools of Colonial Boston.** 1935.

Seybolt, Robert Francis. **The Public Schools of Colonial Boston.** 1935.

Sheldon, Henry D. **Student Life and Customs.** 1901.

Sherrill, Lewis Joseph. **Presbyterian Parochial Schools, 1846-1870.** 1932 .

Siljestrom, P. A. **Educational Institutions of the United States.** 1853.

Small, Walter Herbert. **Early New England Schools.** 1914.

Soltes, Mordecai. **The Yiddish Press: An Americanizing Agency.** 1925.

Stewart, George, Jr. **A History of Religious Education in Connecticut to the Middle of the Nineteenth Century.** 1924.

Storr, Richard J. **The Beginnings of Graduate Education in America.** 1953.

Stout, John Elbert. **The Development of High-School Curricula in the North Central States from 1860 to 1918.** 1921.

Suzzallo, Henry. **The Rise of Local School Supervision in Massachusetts.** 1906.

Swett, John. **Public Education in California.** 1911.

Tappan, Henry P. **University Education.** 1851.

Taylor, Howard Cromwell. **The Educational Significance of the Early Federal Land Ordinances.** 1921.

Taylor, J. Orville. **The District School.** 1834.

Tewksbury, Donald G. **The Founding of American Colleges and Universities before the Civil War.** 1932.

Thorndike, Edward L. **Educational Psychology.** 1913-1914.

True, Alfred Charles. **A History of Agricultural Education in the United States, 1785-1925.** 1929.

True, Alfred Charles. **A History of Agricultural Extension Work in the United States, 1785-1923.** 1928.

Updegraff, Harlan. **The Origin of the Moving School in Massachusetts.** 1908.

Wayland, Francis. **Thoughts on the Present Collegiate System in the United States.** 1842.

Weber, Samuel Edwin. **The Charity School Movement in Colonial Pennsylvania.** 1905.

Wells, Guy Fred. **Parish Education in Colonial Virginia.** 1923.

Wickersham, J. P. **The History of Education in Pennsylvania.** 1885.

Woodward, Calvin M. **The Manual Training School.** 1887.

Woody, Thomas. **Early Quaker Education in Pennsylvania.** 1920.

Woody, Thomas. **Quaker Education in the Colony and State of New Jersey.** 1923.

Wroth, Lawrence C. **An American Bookshelf, 1755.** 1934.

Series II

Adams, Evelyn C. **American Indian Education.** 1946.

Bailey, Joseph Cannon. **Seaman A. Knapp: Schoolmaster of American Agriculture.** 1945.

Beecher, Catharine and Harriet Beecher Stowe. **The American Woman's Home.** 1869.

Benezet, Louis T. **General Education in the Progressive College.** 1943.

Boas, Louise Schutz. **Woman's Education Begins.** 1935.

Bobbitt, Franklin. **The Curriculum.** 1918.

Bode, Boyd H. **Progressive Education at the Crossroads.** 1938.

Bourne, William Oland. **History of the Public School Society of the City of New York.** 1870.

Bronson, Walter C. **The History of Brown University, 1764-1914.** 1914.

Burstall, Sara A. **The Education of Girls in the United States.** 1894.

Butts, R. Freeman. **The College Charts Its Course.** 1939.

Caldwell, Otis W. and Stuart A. Courtis. **Then & Now in Education, 1845-1923.** 1923.

Calverton, V. F. & Samuel D. Schmalhausen, editors. **The New Generation: The Intimate Problems of Modern Parents and Children.** 1930.

Charters, W. W. **Curriculum Construction.** 1923.

Childs, John L. **Education and Morals.** 1950.

Childs, John L. Education and the Philosophy of Experimentalism. 1931.

Clapp, Elsie Ripley. Community Schools in Action. 1939.

Counts, George S. The American Road to Culture: A Social Interpretation of Education in the United States. 1930.

Counts, George S. School and Society in Chicago. 1928.

Finegan, Thomas E. Free Schools. 1921.

Fletcher, Robert Samuel. A History of Oberlin College. 1943.

Grattan, C. Hartley. In Quest of Knowledge: A Historical Perspective on Adult Education. 1955.

Hartman, Gertrude & Ann Shumaker, editors. Creative Expression. 1932.

Kandel, I. L. The Cult of Uncertainty. 1943.

Kandel, I. L. Examinations and Their Substitutes in the United States. 1936.

Kilpatrick, William Heard. Education for a Changing Civilization. 1926.

Kilpatrick, William Heard. Foundations of Method. 1925.

Kilpatrick, William Heard. The Montessori System Examined. 1914.

Lang, Ossian H., editor. Educational Creeds of the Nineteenth Century. 1898.

Learned, William S. The Quality of the Educational Process in the United States and in Europe. 1927.

Meiklejohn, Alexander. The Experimental College. 1932.

Middlekauff, Robert. Ancients and Axioms: Secondary Education in Eighteenth-Century New England. 1963.

Norwood, William Frederick. Medical Education in the United States Before the Civil War. 1944.

Parsons, Elsie W. Clews. Educational Legislation and Administration of the Colonial Governments. 1899.

Perry, Charles M. Henry Philip Tappan: Philosopher and University President. 1933.

Pierce, Bessie Louise. Civic Attitudes in American School Textbooks. 1930.

Rice, Edwin Wilbur. The Sunday-School Movement (1780-1917) and the American Sunday-School Union (1817-1917). 1917.

Robinson, James Harvey. The Humanizing of Knowledge. 1924.

Ryan, W. Carson. Studies in Early Graduate Education. 1939.

Seybolt, Robert Francis. The Evening School in Colonial America. 1925.

Seybolt, Robert Francis. Source Studies in American Colonial Education. 1925.

Todd, Lewis Paul. Wartime Relations of the Federal Government and the Public Schools, 1917-1918. 1945.

Vandewalker, Nina C. The Kindergarten in American Education. 1908.

Ward, Florence Elizabeth. The Montessori Method and the American School. 1913.

West, Andrew Fleming. Short Papers on American Liberal Education. 1907.

Wright, Marion M. Thompson. The Education of Negroes in New Jersey. 1941.

Supplement

The Social Frontier (Frontiers of Democracy). Vols. 1-10, 1934-1943.